palgrave law masters

land law

Company Law   Janet Dine and Marios Koutsias
Constitutional and Administrative Law   John Alder
Contract Law   Ewan McKendrick
Criminal Law   Jonathan Herring
Employment Law   Deborah J Lockton
Evidence   Raymond Emson
Family Law   Kate Standley and Paula Davies
Intellectual Property Law   Tina Hart, Simon Clark and Linda Fazzani
Land Law   Mark Davys
Landlord and Tenant Law   Margaret Wilkie, Peter Luxton, Jill Morgan and Godfrey Cole
Legal Method   Ian McLeod
Legal Theory   Ian McLeod
Medical Law   Jo Samanta and Ash Samanta
Sports Law   Mark James
Torts   Alastair Mullis and Ken Oliphant
Trusts Law   Charlie Webb and Tim Akkouh

If you would like to comment on this book, or on the series generally, please write to lawfeedback@palgrave.com.

palgrave law masters

land law

mark davys

Senior Teaching Fellow, Keele University

Ninth edition

This edition first published 2015 by PALGRAVE

Palgrave in the UK is an imprint of Macmillan Publishers Limited, registered in England, company number 785998, of 4 Crinan Street, London N1 9XW.

Palgrave Macmillan in the US is a division of St Martin's Press LLC, 175 Fifth Avenue, New York, NY 10010.

Palgrave is a global imprint of the above companies and is represented throughout the world.

Palgrave® and Macmillan® are registered trademarks in the United States, the United Kingdom, Europe and other countries.

ISBN 978–1–137–47568–8

This book is printed on paper suitable for recycling and made from fully managed and sustained forest sources. Logging, pulping and manufacturing processes are expected to conform to the environmental regulations of the country of origin.

A catalogue record for this book is available from the British Library.

Typeset by MPS Limited, Chennai, India.

Printed and bound by CPI Group (UK) Ltd, Croydon, CR0 4YY

For Annabelle

Contents

Part I Introduction

Part II The estates and interests

Part III Sharing interests in land

Preface

> This book is intended to be a clear and straightforward explanation of basic land law rules, a text which both introduces the subject and will be referred to during a land law course.

The world has moved on since Kate Green wrote these words in the preface to the first edition of this book, published in 1989. However, although the law and the teaching of law have changed, land law's reputation as a difficult subject seems to remain undented. So, this new edition of *Land Law* is offered, like its predecessors, as an introduction to the subject and as a companion to be referred to along the way. Sometimes this book gives directions. Sometimes it invites the reader to stop, stare and (hopefully) consider. Sometimes, as with the maps of old, the territory will be marked, figuratively at least, '*Hic sunt dracones*' ('Here be dragons').

Land law continues to develop: section 71 of the Tribunals, Courts and Enforcement Act 2007 has finally been brought into force and the Supreme Court's decision in *Scott v Southern Pacific Mortgages Ltd* [2014] 3 WLR 1163 was published just in time to be incorporated into Chapter 15. Commonhold continues in its obscurity (which may, or may not, explain why it is now found in Chapter 4 rather than Chapter 6).

Like its recent predecessors, this edition of *Land Law* is supported by resources on a companion website. Hopefully, the tools found there will nurture engagement with the primary sources of law – the cases and the statutes – in ways that a mere textbook cannot. Many of these resources are signposted in the text by the symbol ⭐.

I wish to express my gratitude to Kate Green and Joe Cursley for entrusting me with the ongoing realisation of their vision for this text. My thanks are also due to those who have shared with me their enthusiasm for the study and practice of land law – and most of all to Ian Lennox, alongside whom, in the closing years of the twentieth century, at least one articled clerk and assistant solicitor discovered a love of land law and its practice. My students continue (sometimes despite themselves) to nurture my excitement for the subject. So far as this edition is concerned, I particularly wish to thank Rob Gibson and Nicola Cattini at Palgrave and my colleagues Ray Cocks, Michael Haley, Lara McMurtry and Mark Shelton, who have each contributed to this edition in their own way; any errors remain, of course, my own. I remain grateful to Andrew Meggy for helping convert my sketches into meaningful diagrams.

The law is stated as at the end of October 2014.

Mark Davys
All Saints, 2014

Table of cases

Table of legislation

UK secondary legislation

Resources

The companion website to accompany this book can be found at:
www.palgrave.com/davys9e

Resources posted on this site include:

- updates on the law – revised half-yearly or otherwise as appropriate;
- quizzes – covering all the chapters except for Chapter 1;
- suggested answers to the end of chapter exercises found in this book;
- advice on how to approach problem questions and essay questions

The symbol 🐦 occurring in the text indicates where particularly relevant material can be found on the companion website.

References

For convenience, only one citation is usually given for each case referred to in the text. Neutral citations are given only when the case did not appear in one of the major series of law reports by the end of October 2014.

The following major textbooks are referred to in this book:

Burn and Cartwright, *Cheshire and Burn's Modern Law of Real Property* (18th edn, Oxford University Press 2011): referred to as 'Cheshire'

Gray and Gray, *Elements of Land Law* (5th edn, Oxford University Press 2009): referred to as 'Gray and Gray'

Harpum, Bridge and Dixon, *Megarry & Wade: The Law of Real Property* (8th edn, Sweet & Maxwell 2012): referred to as 'Megarry and Wade'

For an accessible introduction to the 'story' of land law, see Gardner, *An Introduction to Land Law* (3rd edn, Hart Publishing 2012). To begin exploring land law in its wider, socio-economic context, see Cowan, Fox O'Mahony and Cobb, *Great Debates in Property Law* (Palgrave Macmillan 2012).

Glossary

*Numbers in brackets, such as (8.6) refer to the section in this book where the term is introduced or explained. References to terms explained elsewhere in the Glossary appear in **bold**.*

A

abatement:	A self-help remedy allowing a **dominant tenement** owner to enforce an easement (8.6).
absolute interest:	An interest that is neither **conditional** nor **determinable** (4.2). Note that this is not the same as '**absolute title**' (see later).
absolute title:	The best class of **title** available to a registered proprietor of an **estate** in land (15.6.1).
adverse possession:	The acquisition of title by dispossessing the original owner for the requisite period (see Chapter 13).
alienation:	The act of transferring property to another.
animus possidendi:	'Intention to possess'; a requirement for title to be acquired by **adverse possession** (13.3.2).
assignment:	The transfer of an interest in land, usually the interest of a **landlord** or **tenant** (5.3).
'authorised guarantee agreement' (AGA):	A form of guarantee falling within section 16 of the Landlord and Tenant (Covenants) Act 1995 (6.4.2).

B

beneficial interest:	The interest of a **beneficiary**; the **equitable** right to the benefits of the land (for example, occupation or **rent**) as distinct from the legal ownership vested in a **trustee** (2.4).
beneficiary:	The person entitled in equity to land or other property held on **trust** (2.4); also used to describe persons entitled to benefit under a will.

C

charge:	An interest securing the payment of money. Although often used synonymously with **mortgage**, a charge does not automatically give the lender an estate in the land. Charges by way of legal mortgage do transfer an estate by virtue of section 87 of the LPA 1925. (Chapter 7)
chattel:	Property other than land (2.2.1). For historical reasons, leasehold estates are *chattels real* not real property (see 1.3.2), but this is rarely significant today.
chattels real:	**Leases**.
commonhold:	A form of registered **freehold** that can be used to divide the ownership of a building or **estate** with shared common parts (4.5).

common intention constructive trust:	A **trust** arising out of an express or implied agreement to share the ownership of property (14.3).
conditional interest:	An interest that gives the grantor the right to re-enter the property (and terminate the interest) if a specified event occurs or fails to occur; compare **absolute interest**, and **determinable interest** (4.2).
constructive trust:	One of a number of types of **trust** that arise by operation of law rather than express words (14.3; see also, **resulting trust**).
conveyance:	A formal legal document (other than a will) transferring property or **title**.
co-ownership:	A form of ownership where **title** is shared between two or more people (concurrent co-ownership is considered in Chapter 10).
covenant:	A promise made in a **deed**.
covenantee:	The person to whom the promise in a **covenant** is made.
covenantor:	The person making the promise in a **covenant**.

D

deed:	A formal legal document satisfying the requirements of section 1 of the Law of Property (Miscellaneous Provisions) Act 1989 (12.5.1).
demesne **land:**	Land which the Crown owns for itself as feudal overlord (15.11)
demise:	A **lease**; the land is 'demised' to the tenant (5.3).
determinable interest:	An interest that lasts only until a specified event occurs or does not occur; compare **absolute interest,** and **conditional interest** (4.2).
disposition:	The creation or transfer of an interest (12.4.2(b)).
distress, also **distraint:**	An ancient remedy for the non-payment of **rent**, entitling the landlord to seize goods belonging to the tenant, replaced by the provisions of Part 3 of the Tribunals, Courts and Enforcement Act 2007 from 6th April 2014 (6.5.1(b)).
dominant tenement:	The land to which the benefit of a right, such as an **easement** is attached.

E

easement:	A right enjoyed over a **servient tenement** for the benefit of a **dominant tenement** (Chapter 8).
entail, also **fee tail:**	An interest in land that can only be inherited by the issue of the original grantor (4.2).
equitable:	A right or remedy operating only in equity (2.3.2(b) and 2.3.3).
equity of redemption:	The rights of the mortgagor in the land subject to the **mortgage**, in particular, the right to recover the mortgaged land upon payment of the moneys due (7.2.2 and 7.4.1).

Equity's Darling:	A *bona fide* purchaser of a legal **estate** for value without notice (16.2.2).
estate:	An interest in land that allows its owner **exclusive possession** of the land for a prescribed period (2.3.1 and 2.3.2). Alternatively, (i) the property of a deceased person, or (ii) an area of land.
estate contract:	A contract for the creation or sale of an interest in land (12.3 and 12.4.2(b)).
estoppel:	An equitable doctrine preventing a person from denying facts stated by her or which she has led or allowed another to believe are true. There are various forms of estoppel, each with its own rules. **Proprietary estoppel** is the most common type of estoppel encountered when studying land law (see later and 14.4).
exclusive possession:	The rights of an owner of land, in particular the right to exclude other people, including a landlord, from the land (5.5.3).

F

fee simple absolute in possession:	The larger of the two legal **estates** and the basic unit of ownership in English land law (Chapter 4).
fee tail:	An interest in land that can only be inherited by the issue of the original grantor (4.2).
fixture:	An object that is part of the land (that is, not a **chattel**). There are rules as to who may remove different types of fixtures (2.2.1).
foreclosure:	The transfer of legal and equitable title in mortgaged land to the **mortgagee** (lender), free from all the rights of the **mortgagor** (7.5.4).
forfeiture, also **right of entry:**	The right of a **landlord** to re-enter the land subject to a **lease** following a breach of **covenant** by the tenant (6.5.1(c) and 6.5.2(a)).
freehold:	An **estate** of uncertain duration; now usually used to refer to the only such estate capable of existing at law, the **fee simple absolute in possession** (Chapter 4).

H

headlease:	The **lease** out of which a lesser leasehold **estate** has been granted (5.3).
hereditaments:	Rights in property that survive the death of the owner; they can be inherited.
human rights:	Rights that protect an individual from unfair treatment or discrimination by the State (1.4).

I

implied trust:	A **trust** that is created by operation of law rather than by express words or statutory provision (11.2).
in gross:	A right that exists without benefiting a **dominant tenement**.

injunction:	A court order requiring a person to do or refrain from doing a specified act.
interests capable of overriding, also overriding interests:	Interests in a **registered title** capable of binding third parties even though they do not appear in the **Register of Title** (15.8).
inter vivos:	'Among the living'; taking effect during the lifetime of the transferor (compare a gift in a will, which will only take effect upon the death of the person making the gift).
ius accrescendi:	The right of survivorship (10.3.1).

J

joint tenancy:	A form of concurrent **co-ownership** in which all the co-owners own the whole **title** to the whole land; compare **tenancy in common** (10.3.1).

L

land charge:	an interest in **unregistered land** capable of protection through registration in the Land Charges Register under the Land Charges Act 1972.
lease:	A **term of years absolute** in possession, the lesser of the two legal **estates** in land (Chapter 5).
lessee:	The tenant.
lessor:	The immediate landlord.
licence:	Permission to enter on land (Chapter 3).

M

mesne:	'Middle' (as in *mesne* landlord at 5.3).
minor:	A person under 18 years of age.
minor interest:	An interest in **registered land** requiring protection by registration pursuant to the LRA 1925. The term is not used in the LRA 2002.
mortgage:	The transfer of property as security for a loan or other obligation; see also, **charge** (Chapter 7).
mortgagee:	The person to whom the interest in mortgaged land is granted, the lender (7.2.1).
mortgagor:	The person creating a **mortgage**, the borrower (7.2.1).

N

new tenancy:	A **lease** granted on or after 1 January 1996 (see section 1(3) of the Landlord and Tenant (Covenants) Act 1995).
notice, doctrine of:	The rule, now of limited application, which governed whether a purchaser of an unregistered legal **estate** for value took the **title** subject to any equitable interests in the land. There are three types of notice: actual, constructive and imputed (see 16.2.2). Proper registration of a **land charge** in the Land Charges Register is deemed to be notice of the charge (16.3).

notice on the Register:	An entry in the **Register of Title** protecting the priority of the interest to which it refers (15.7).
notice to quit:	The method by which a landlord or a tenant terminates a **periodic tenancy**.

O

overreaching:	A statutory procedure whereby a **beneficial interest** is detached from the land and transferred to the proceeds of sale (11.6.1).
overriding interests, also interests capable of overriding:	Interests in a **registered title** that are capable of binding third parties even though they do not appear in the **Register of Title** (15.8).
overriding lease:	A **lease** granted under section 19 of the Landlord and Tenant (Covenants) Act 1995 (6.3.3).

P

periodic tenancy:	A **tenancy** for a specific period (monthly, yearly, etc.), which continues to run until one of the parties serves **notice to quit** (5.5.2(b)).
personal rights:	Rights that regulate a particular relationship and which are usually only binding upon the parties to that relationship (1.3). These rights are also referred to as 'obligations' and typically arise out of contracts and the commission of a tort.
prescription:	Acquisition of an **easement** by long user (8.5.3).
privity of contract:	The relationship between the original landlord and the original tenant; this contractual relationship continues even if one or both of them has assigned the **lease**.
privity of estate:	The relationship between the landlord for the time being and the tenant for the time being.
profit à prendre:	The right to take something from somebody else's land (8.8).
property rights:	Rights that are capable of binding third parties (1.3).
proprietary estoppel:	An **equitable** doctrine enabling a claimant to enforce an informal representation or assurance relating to land that the claimant has relied upon to her detriment because it would be unconscionable for the person who made the representation or assurance to be allowed to enforce his strict legal rights (14.4).
puisne **mortgages:**	A legal **mortgage** of unregistered land not protected by the deposit of title deeds and which must be protected by registering a Class C(i) land charge under the Land Charges Act 1927 (16.3.2(a)).

Q

quasi-easement:	An interest in land that would amount to an **easement**, but for the fact that the **dominant** and **servient tenements** are owned by the same person (8.4.3).

R

real property:	Usually used to refer to land, although **leases** are actually *chattels real.*
rectification of the Register of Title:	The correction of a mistake in the **Register of Title** that prejudicially affects the title of the registered proprietor (15.9.1). Not to be confused with the **equitable** remedy of rectification (12.4.3(d)).
Register of Title, also **Title register**:	The record of the extent and ownership of an **estate** in land that has been registered at the Land Registry, together with the registered interests to which it is subject (Chapter 15).
registered title, or registered land:	a system in which **title** to land is based on or proved by entries in a State controlled register of title; in England and Wales, a reference to land that falls within the scheme contained in the LRA 2002 (2.5.1, Chapter 15).
remainder:	An interest in land that will not take effect until a prior interest has expired (for example, to A for life, remainder to B in fee simple).
rent, also **rent service**:	Usually shorthand for 'rent service', the payments made to a landlord by the tenant under the terms of a **lease**.
rentcharge:	A periodic sum charged on **freehold** land (see LPA 1925, s 1(2)(b)). Not to be confused with **rent service**, payable under the terms of a **lease**.
resulting trust:	A trust arising by operation of law in which the **beneficial interest** is vested in the person who financed the acquisition of that property or in the person who transferred the property to the legal owner without also transferring the entire beneficial interest (14.2).
reversion:	The right remaining to the grantor of an interest after that interest has been granted. For example, a landlord's right to repossess the land at the end of the lease is the 'landlord's reversion'.
reversionary leases:	A **lease** with a term that will begin at a date in the future (5.5.2(a)).
right of entry, also forfeiture:	The right of a landlord to re-enter the land subject to a lease following a breach of **covenant** by the tenant (6.5.1(c) and 6.5.2(a)). A right of re-entry may also be attached to a **rentcharge**.

S

seisin:	Historically, the right to possess a particular piece of land. Unity of seisin of the **dominant tenement** and **servient tenement** extinguishes an **easement** (8.4.3).
servient tenement:	The land which is subject to a right, such as an **easement**.
settlement, also **settled land**:	A disposition of property granting a series of successive interests in land. Previously used to keep land 'in the family' and regulated under the Settled Land Act 1925, this method of land ownership is now almost obsolete.

severance:	The conversion of a **joint tenancy** into a **tenancy in common** (10.5).
subject to contract:	An express arrangement that the parties do not wish to have legally binding consequences until further steps, usually the completion of certain formalities, have been taken (12.1).
Sublease, also **subtenancy:**	A **lease** granted out of a leasehold estate (the **headlease**). The sublease must be for a term that is shorter than that of the **headlease** (5.3).

T

tacking:	The use of an existing **mortgage** or **charge** to secure a further loan from the same lender (7.7.1).
tenancy:	Another word for **lease**. The two words can be used interchangeably, although tenancy tends to be used for shorter or informal leases.
tenancy in common:	A form of concurrent **co-ownership** in which the beneficial title is divided between the co-owners in separate interests; compare **tenancy in common** (10.3.2).
tenure:	Almost all land in England is ultimately held from a lord, usually the Crown. *Tenure* describes the conditions upon which the land is held. The doctrine of tenure is almost obsolete, although its terminology is used to describe the relationship between landlords and tenants (historically not tenure at all) and co-owners.
term of years absolute:	A **lease** (2.3.1).
title:	The right to hold an **estate** in land; proof of such a right.
trust:	An equitable doctrine allowing ownership to be divided between the legal owner (the **trustees**) and beneficiaries who have an **equitable** right to enjoy the land (2.4).
trustee:	The owner of the legal **title** to land that is subject to a trust.
trustee in bankruptcy:	The person appointed to manage the estate of a person who is bankrupt.
trust for sale:	A **trust** where the property is held subject to an immediate and binding duty to sell it (although the sale may be postponed). The LPA 1925 provided that almost all land held concurrently by co-owners was held on a statutory trust for sale, but this was repealed by the Trusts of Land and Appointment of Trustees Act 1996 with effect from 1 January 1997 (11.1).
trust of land:	See Section 1(1)(a) of the Trusts of Land and Appointment of Trustees Act 1996 (11.1).

U

unregistered title, or **unregistered land:**	in England and Wales, land that does not yet fall within the scheme of **registered title** contained in the LRA 2002 (2.5.2, Chapter 16).

W

words of severance: The words in the grant or transfer of land indicating that it is to be held by the new owners as **tenants in common** (10.4.2).

waiver: The abandonment of a legal right.

Part I

Introduction

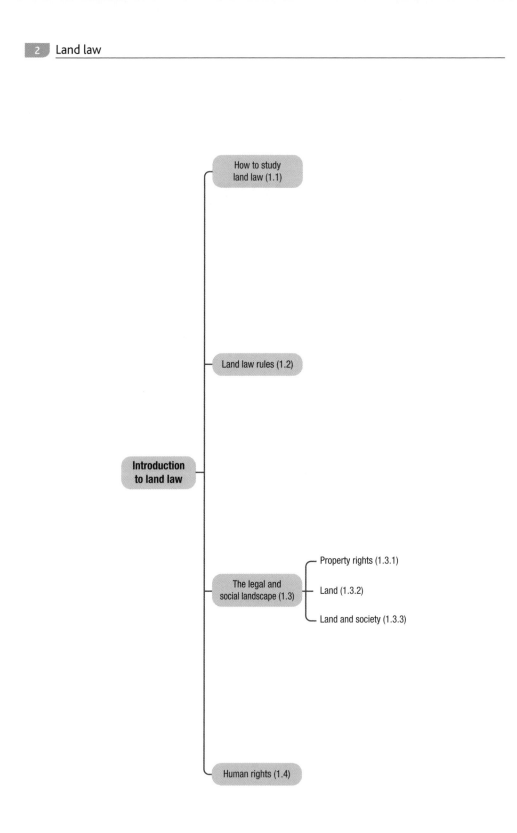

Chapter 1

Introduction to land law

Key concepts

- **Human rights** – rights that protect an individual from unfair treatment or discrimination by the State.
- **Personal rights** – rights that regulate a particular relationship and which are usually only binding upon the parties to that relationship.
- **Property rights** – rights that are capable of binding third parties.

1.1 How to study land law

Land law is an interesting and challenging subject, involving profound questions about the way we choose to live our lives, for land is vital to human life. In any society – even our technological, high-speed one – the use of land is of the utmost importance. Where the supply of land is limited, as in England and Wales, the problems can be acute. The dry and legalistic façade created by the artificial language and technical concepts of land law tends to conceal the fundamental issue: land law is really just about the sharing out of our limited island.

Land law has been developing ever since people got ideas about having rights over certain places, probably beginning with the cultivation of crops. Through the long process of development, there have been periods of gradual change, and also more dramatic times, such as the Norman conquest of 1066, the property legislation of 1925 and, most recently, the Land Registration Act 2002. By and large, lawyers have continued to use and adapt the words and ideas of their predecessors. Although land law has kept its feudal roots and language, it is a thoroughly contemporary subject concerned with realities of daily life and existence. However, the law and its terminology can seem obscure (sometimes as though cloaked in the fog, rather than the mists, of time), so it is perhaps best at the start to treat it like a foreign language. The vocabulary soon becomes natural, especially through reading the reports of cases. Reading about the same topic in different books will also help. When encountering a technical term, especially for the first time, the most important thing that a law student can do is to pause and be sure that she knows what it means in context (by consulting the Glossary at pages [xxvii] to [xxxiv] of this book, for example). Only then is it safe to continue.

As explained further below, land lawyers tend to be principally, but not exclusively, concerned with various rights to land, called 'interests in land'. They might talk about someone 'owning land' or 'owning property', but really they mean someone owning *an interest in* the land, or, more technically, *having property in* the land. These interests (the 'property') are not the land itself (the earth and the buildings), but abstract concepts, such as the freehold and the lease. When ownership of a building is transferred from one person to another:

> The building has not moved. What is transferred by a transfer of property is the bundle of rights and obligations relating to that building (*R (on the application of the Lord Chancellor) v Chief Land Registrar* [2006] QB 795 (QB) per Stanley Burnton J at [25]).

The different types of abstract interest in land recognised by English law are introduced in Chapter 2, and the most important are considered in more detail in Part II of this book.

The first thing to do when studying any aspect of land law is to grasp the definition thoroughly. That means asking:

- what does it mean; and
- how do I recognise it?

This helps to avoid two of the most depressing things that can happen to land law students. The first is staring at a problem without having any idea of what it is about. The second (possibly worse) is recognising what the problem is about, but feeling incapable of writing anything down. If in doubt, start by identifying the interests in the land.

Some authors compare land law to playing chess: there are various 'pieces' (which correspond to interests in land), and they can be moved about according to strict rules. Others liken the rules which constitute land law to a complicated machine: moving one lever, or adjusting one valve, will have a significant effect on the end product. The owner of an interest in land has limited freedom of action, and one small change in her position can affect the relative value of other interests in the land. In practical terms, the complicated connections within the machine mean that one part of the subject cannot be fully grasped until all the others have been understood. There is no single starting place: it is necessary to watch the machine, piece by piece, until the connections become clear. It is useful, from the beginning, to ask, 'What would happen if …?'; if one lever is moved, what interests will be affected, and why?

As a consequence of the complex definitions and the interdependent rules, land law may only make sense when the course is nearly complete. However, in the meantime, it is necessary to make mistakes in order to grasp the way the rules relate to one another. It *will* eventually come together, with hard work and faith and hope; the charity, with any luck, will be provided by the teacher.

The language used by land lawyers expresses the way in which they think they see the world. This is a world in which people's relationships to land can only occur within the legal structure of interests in land, so lawyers squeeze the facts of ordinary life into the pre-existing moulds of 'the interests'. A land law student's job is to learn the shapes of the moulds and imitate the squeeze; then she will be able to operate the whole machine. Finally, armed with this knowledge and skill, she may begin to question whether land law really does operate like this in practice.

1.2   Land law rules

Land law is made up of rules in statutes and cases; case law rules are further divided into legal and equitable rules. That is, the rules were created:

- by an Act of Parliament; or
- by either
  - a court of 'common law'; or
  - a court of 'equity'.

The development of these two sets of rules is well described by others (for example, Part II of Cheshire, 2011, and Simpson, 1986). It is merely outlined here.

The customs which became known as the 'common law' were enforced with extraordinary rigidity by judges who followed the strict letter of the law. Aggrieved citizens (in the absence of crusading television journalists and social media campaigns) wrote begging letters to the King. These received replies from his 'secretary', the Chancellor, who employed the King's power to override the decisions of the King's judges. Appealing to the Chancellor's conscience (or to 'equity') grew in popularity, and from about 1535 the Chancellor's court (Chancery) was regularly making decisions overriding the law in the King's court.

However, this new system of justice did not set out to replace the rules of law, but merely to intervene when conscience required it. To quote from the judgment in *Dudley and Ward v Dudley* [1705] 24 ER 118, 120, equity

> qualifies, moderates, and reforms the rigour, hardness, and edge of the law, and is an universal truth ... this is the office of equity, to support and protect the common law from shifts and crafty contrivances against the justice of the law. Equity therefore does not destroy the law, nor create it, but assist it.

The courts of common law and the Court of Chancery existed separately, each with distinct procedures and remedies, to the great profit of the legal profession. Eventually, things became intolerably inefficient (see, for example, the seemingly perpetual case of *Jarndyce v Jarndyce* in Charles Dickens' *Bleak House*), and the two courts were merged by the Judicature Acts 1873 and 1875. Despite this merger, lawyers continued to keep the legal and equitable rules and remedies separate. (There is an account of legal and equitable interests today in Section 2.3.2.)

The year 1925 is an emotive date for land lawyers because it saw a major revision of the rules of property law in England and Wales. The law was actually changed by a very large Law of Property Act in 1922, but that Act was not brought into force; instead it was divided into a number of shorter statutes all dated 1925.

The 1925 statutes contained many radical reforms. They also contained 'wordsaving' provisions, some of which had appeared in earlier statutes. At one time, lawyers were 'paid by the yard', so the more words they used, the better for their bank balances. In the 1925 Acts, Parliament ensured that many common promises in land transactions no longer needed to be spelled out in full because they would be implied by statute. In effect, the customs of conveyancers (lawyers who manage the transfer of land) became enshrined in statute. Significant examples of such provisions that will be encountered when studying land law are set out in Table 1.1.

One of the aims of the 1925 legislation was to make conveyancing (the buying, selling, mortgaging and other transfers of land) simpler in order to revive the depressed market in land and to make it easier to deal with commercially. It is impossible to say whether it had this effect. Certainly, the reasons for the great increase in home ownership in the twentieth century were not connected to the reforms, some of which were inappropriate to the modern world of owner-occupation. More recent statutes have introduced further reforms to better reflect modern attitudes to land ownership and to equip land law for the electronic age (including, for example, the Trusts of Land and Appointment of Trustees Act 1996 and the Land Registration Act 2002, respectively).

Table 1.1 Significant examples of 'wordsaving' in the Law of Property Act 1925

	Provision	**Referred to in this book**
Section 62	Buildings, fixtures (see Section 2.2.1) and other interests automatically included in a conveyance of land	Section 8.5.2(c) (easements and profits) and 12.5.1(d) (the effect of a deed of transfer)
Sections 78 and 79	The benefit and burden of covenants (promises about the use of the land) automatically run with the land	Sections 9.4.2(b), 9.5.1(c) and 9.5.2(a) (freehold covenants)
Sections 101 and 103	The power of a mortgagee (the lender) to sell the mortgaged land under certain circumstances	Section 7.5.2 (mortgages)

Most of the statutory rules used by today's land lawyers are found in the following statutes:

- **Law of Property Act 1925** (usually abbreviated to 'LPA 1925') expressly referred to in all but one chapter of this book;
- **Land Registration Act 2002** (usually 'LRA 2002') which replaced the LRA 1925: see, especially, Chapter 15;
- **Trusts of Land and Appointment of Trustees Act 1996** ('TOLATA' in this book) which replaced the Settled Land Act 1925 and amended the LPA 1925: see, especially, Chapter 11;
- **Land Charges Act 1972** (usually 'LCA 1972') which replaced the LCA 1925: see Section 16.3.

Care should be taken when citing or referring to a particular statute, as there are often Acts of Parliament with similar (or even identical) names from different years.

1.3   The legal and social landscape

Land law is one branch of the wider discipline of property law. Traditionally, property law was divided into the rules that applied to land (the law of 'real property') and the rules that applied to every other type of property (the law of 'personal property'). Over time, further branches have been added, including the law of 'intellectual property', which is concerned with the ownership of ideas (including patents, trade marks and copyright).

Before studying the rules of land law, it is important to take time to consider the following questions:

- what do we mean by 'property'?
- why are there special rules for land?
- what is land law about, or, to put it another way, what are all these rules for?

1.3.1   Property rights

English law recognises a distinction between rights that are 'personal' and rights that are 'property' rights. Most other legal systems recognise a similar distinction, although the terminology differs. Personal rights are rights that regulate a particular relationship between a limited number of people, usually because they have each entered the relationship voluntarily (the law of contract) or because one person has acted in breach of her legal obligations to the others (the law of torts). Property rights are much more powerful: they are rights that are capable of binding third parties. When the law recognises a person as having 'property' in an object, it is recognising that she has a significant degree of control over that object – a degree of control that necessarily limits the rights exercisable by others in respect of the same object.

This description of property rights is all very well, but it only takes us so far. It enables us to identify which interests are given proprietary character by English law, but it does not provide us with a tool for deciding when and whether new rights should be added to the list – or, indeed, whether some rights should be removed. Not all the interests now recognised as proprietary have always been so. Both leases and freehold covenants are relatively late additions, and the twentieth century saw a determined effort by some judges to raise certain types of licence to proprietary status (see Chapter 3):

> Few concepts are quite so fragile, so elusive and so frequently missed as the notion of property … Our daily references to property therefore tend to comprise a mutual conspiracy of unsophisticated semantic allusions and confusions which we tolerate – frequently, indeed, do not notice (Gray and Gray, 2009, para 1.5.1).

In the case of *National Provincial Bank Ltd v Ainsworth* [1965] AC 1175 (HL), Mr Ainsworth left his wife, who continued to live in the former matrimonial home. The matrimonial home was originally owned by Mr Ainsworth, but when he incorporated his business he transferred the house to his new company and used the house to secure the company's debts. When the company failed to repay its debts, the bank sought possession of the house from Mrs Ainsworth. The House of Lords had to decide whether Mrs Ainsworth's occupation of the house amounted to a property interest in it; in other words, was her right to occupy the house as Mr Ainsworth's wife binding on the bank? This kind of problem, where a transaction between buyer and seller (or a borrower and a lender) involves a third person's interest in land, appears in various forms throughout this book. It is a kind of eternal triangle, as in Figure 1.1. In this case, Mr Ainsworth is the seller (granting a mortgage is equivalent to a sale for these purposes), and the bank is the buyer.

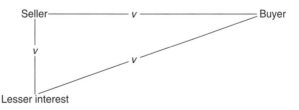

Figure 1.1   The eternal triangle

Although their Lordships were sympathetic to Mrs Ainsworth's plight, they felt unable to give her interest proprietary status. Lord Wilberforce said:

> Before a right or an interest can be admitted into the category of property, or of a right affecting property, it must be definable, identifiable by third parties, capable in its nature of assumption by third parties, and have some degree of permanence or stability (at 1247–48).

There is, as Kevin and Susan Gray, in particular, have observed, a certain circularity in this approach. What rights bind third parties? Proprietary ones. What rights are proprietary? Those capable of binding third parties. In fact, the question 'What rights should be recognised as having the power of property?' is one that must be answered by the society of which the law is part. Different societies will answer the question in different ways, and the same society may answer the question differently at different times. These issues are explored in more detail in Part 1.5 of Gray and Gray (2009).

1.3.2 Land

Almost all legal systems have special rules about the ownership of land which do not apply to other types of property. This reflects the significance of land to human beings and its distinctive characteristics when compared with other types of resources.

At the most basic level, human beings are land animals; they need somewhere to put their bodies, a piece of land on which to 'be'. On the emotional plane, humans must have contact with land, their roots in the earth. Physically, they need air to breathe and space in which to move about, eat and shelter. All these are provided by land.

As a resource, land has other special characteristics. Except in the rare cases of land falling into, or being thrown up from, the sea, it is geographically fixed and immovable; it is also ultimately indestructible. Its nature means that the boundaries between one piece of land and another are normally touching, so neighbouring owners are aware of one another's business. Further, to its occupant one piece is never exactly the same as another: each is unique. Even in apparently uniform tower blocks, each floor, each flat, has its own particular characteristics.

The permanence and durability of land are matched by its flexibility. It has an infinite number of layers, and is really 'three-dimensional space'. A plot of land can be used by a number of people in different ways simultaneously: one person can invest her money in it, while two or more live there, a fourth tunnels beneath to extract minerals and half a dozen more use a path over it as a short-cut, or graze their cattle on a part of it.

Land can be shared consecutively as well as simultaneously; that is to say, people can enjoy the land one after another. The great landowning families traditionally created complicated 'settlements' of their estates, whereby the land would pass through the succeeding generations as the first owner desired. Each 'owner' only had it for a lifetime and could not leave it by will because, at death, it had to pass according to the directions in the settlement. In this way, the aristocratic dynasties preserved their land, and consequently their wealth and their political power.

These characteristics of land mean that the law has developed special rules relating to property in land. It is important, therefore, to know whether a particular object or resource is real property (land) or personal property. The rules for determining this are considered in Section 2.1.

By now, it should be clear that in English law, the word 'personal' is used to describe both a type of right and a type of property. It is possible to have personal rights over land (for example, many of the licences discussed in Chapter 3) and property rights (ownership) over personal property.

1.3.3 Land and society

It has already been observed that each society develops its own cultural attitudes to its land. These attitudes are coloured by the kind of land (for example, desert or jungle), because this determines the uses to which it can be put. The view taken of land is also influenced by its scarcity or otherwise, and by the economic system. In places where land was plentiful, it was not normally 'owned'. When European colonists arrived in America, the indigenous people believed that:

> the earth was created by the assistance of the sun, and it should be left as it was ... The country was made without lines of demarcation, and it is no man's business to divide it ... The earth and myself are of one mind. The measure of the land and the measure of our bodies are the same ... Do not misunderstand me, but understand me fully with reference to my affection for the land. I never said the land was mine to do with as I chose. The one who has the right to dispose of it is the one who created it (McLuhan, *Touch the Earth* (Abacus 1972) 54).

Similarly, native Australians regarded the land with special awe. As concluded in one of the cases about Aboriginal land claims, it was not so much that they owned the land, but that the land owned them (*Milirrpum v Nabalco Pty Ltd* (1971) 17 FLR 141). Native title was recognised as part of Australian land law in the landmark case of *Mabo v Queensland (No 2)* [1992] HCA 23; (1992) 175 CLR 1. A traditional African view was that the land was not capable of being owned by one person but belonged to the whole tribe:

> land belongs to a vast family of which many are dead, a few are living and countless numbers still unborn (West African Lands Committee Cd 1048, 183).

In early English land law, the fundamental concept was 'seisin'. The person who was seised of land was entitled to recover it in the courts if she was disseised. Originally, 'the person seised of land was simply the person in obvious occupation, the person "sitting" on the land' (Simpson, 1986, 40). Seisin thus described the close relationship between a person and the land she worked and lived on. This simplicity was refined and developed over centuries, and the concepts of ownership and possession took over. Nevertheless, actual possession can still be of great importance in land law, for example, in claims of adverse possession (see Chapter 13).

Over the past three or four hundred years, the land law of England and Wales has been developing alongside the growth of capitalism and city living. There has been a huge population increase. In 1603, there were about four million people; by 2011, there were some 56 million in England and Wales, about 151,000 square kilometres (that is, about 2,700 square metres of surface area per person, although, of course, most people are confined to a comparatively tiny urban space). During the second part of the twentieth century, there was also an enormous increase in the number of ordinary people who owned land. The percentage of households living in owner-occupied accommodation (a house or a flat) more than doubled between 1971 and 2001 to nearly 70 per cent (Census 2001). However, this trend reversed in the early years of the twenty-first century as more and more people were unable or unwilling to take on the responsibilities of owner occupation. By the time of the 2011 Census, the percentage of households living in owner-occupied accommodation had fallen to 64 per cent, with a corresponding increase in the percentage of households renting accommodation from private and social sector landlords.

For the majority of owner-occupiers, the land they own is subject to a huge debt in the form of a mortgage. Despite this, the land will probably be regarded as both a home and an investment. It is an expression of the landowner's personality and a retreat from the world; at the same time, it represents a status symbol and, they hope, an inflation-proofed savings bank and something to leave to their children (or to be used to finance health care at the end of their lives). For other people (for example, those who rent their home on a weekly tenancy), home ownership, with its apparent psychological and financial advantages, may be only a hope for the future. In the meantime, their relationship with their land may be less secure, subject to the authority of a landlord. However, in a lawyer's view, tenants are also 'landowners', albeit for a limited period of time and subject to certain restrictions (see Section 2.3.1 and Chapters 5 and 6).

It can be seen from this brief survey of land use in England and Wales that the same piece of land may be subject to a number of levels of ownership (for example, by a landlord and by a tenant, both of whom may have also granted mortgages to financial institutions). What is more, there are different motivations for owning land. Different people will have different expectations of their property, and one of the tasks of the land lawyer is to try to reconcile these various demands when they come into conflict. The main three motives for owning land are set out in Table 1.2, with examples of how they influence land law. (For more detail, see Gray and Gray, 2009, paras 1.5.40–57.)

In order to maximise the value of land, ownership must be capable of being freely and safely traded, while people who have lesser interests in the land must also feel secure. The market certainly seems to have an influence on the development of the law. When there was a slump at the end of the nineteenth century, judges tried to ensure that liabilities attached to land (that is, the lesser, third-party interests) were minimised so that the land would be attractive to buyers. Conversely, periods of booming prices, such as the 1970s, 1980s and the early 2000s, tend to stimulate a greater interest in the

Table 1.2   Three underlying motives for land ownership

Motive	Consequence	Examples
Land as the location of human existence (for example, shelter and work)	The law must reflect the reality of land use and give value to the interests of those in actual occupation. Parliament may need to intervene to protect the vulnerable from the unscrupulous. However, land must also be freely and conveniently transferable to enable its enjoyment.	Seisin (see Section 1.3.3). Protecting the interest of people in occupation: paragraph 2 of Schedule 3 to the LRA 2002 (see Section 15.8.2). Parliamentary protection for residential tenants and residential mortgagees (see Chapters 5, 6 and 7).
Land as an investment	Interests in land are treated as investment assets: they need to be freely marketable and realisable, free from the risk of undisclosed interests. It is more convenient to think of interests in land as abstract concepts than as physical land.	*National Provincial Bank Ltd v Ainsworth* [1965] AC 1175 (HL) (see Section 1.3.1). The doctrine of overreaching (which transfers beneficial interests from the land to the proceeds of sale of the land; see Section 11.6.1).
Land as a community resource	Land needs to be managed and protected for the wider good of society rather than the profit of the individual owner.	Private rights, such as covenants (see Chapter 9). State intervention, such as planning regulations (planning law lies beyond the scope of this book). The conservation of nature and natural resources (see Rodgers, 2009).

security of such lesser, third-party interests. A falling market, such as that of the early 1990s and that of the end of the first decade of the twenty-first century, produces its own response, significantly influenced by the interests of lenders, such as building societies and banks (see Chapter 7).

1.4 Human rights

The Human Rights Act 1998, which came into force on 2 October 2000, means that the rules and practices of land law are now open to challenge if they offend against rights contained in the European Convention on Human Rights. The Act requires the courts to interpret legislation 'in a way which is compatible with the Convention rights' (s 3). It is directly applicable against public authorities (s 6), which include courts and tribunals, central and local government and any body exercising functions of a public nature. In *R (on the application of Weaver) v London & Quadrant Housing Trust* [2010] 1 WLR 363 (CA) the Court of Appeal had to decide whether evicting a social tenant for non-payment of rent was a public act or a private act within section 6(5). The majority concluded that the housing association was acting publicly: the status of an act depends upon the context in which it occurs (in this case, the provision of social housing) not the nature of the right being exercised (in this case, contractual).

The extent to which the Act is applicable in a dispute between two private individuals (what is known as its 'horizontal' effect) is uncertain. It may be that it has wider horizontal effect than originally intended, since the section 3 requirement applies even if the parties are private individuals, and section 6 prevents the courts (as public bodies) from interpreting common law as well as statute in a way which is incompatible with Convention rights. This does not mean that the Convention rights must be referred to explicitly in every judgment; what matters is that the rules that the court is applying are themselves Convention compliant. For example, giving due consideration to the factors set out in section 15 of TOLATA 1996 (see Section 11.5.2) will ordinarily be sufficient to discharge the duty to balance the Convention rights of the parties without further reference to the Human Rights Act (*National Westminster Bank plc v Rushmer* [2010] 2 FLR 362 (Ch)).

In the context of land law, the most important Convention rights are:

- ▶ Article 1, Protocol 1 – the right to peaceful enjoyment and protection of possessions;
- ▶ Article 8 – the right to respect for a person's private and family life and home;
- ▶ Article 6 – the right to a fair and public hearing; and
- ▶ Article 14 – the right to enjoy Convention rights without discrimination.

Article 1, Protocol 1 guarantees a person's right to enjoy her property free from interference from the State except where such interference is in the public interest and in accordance with the law. This might well allow the compulsory purchase of a person's land by a local authority, for example. It certainly permits long leaseholders to buy the freehold of their land under the Leasehold Reform Act 1967 because it is in the interests of social justice that they should be able to do so (see *James v UK* (1986) 8 EHRR 123 and Section 5.6).

Under Article 8, no public authority may interfere with the exercise of the right to respect for a person's private and family life and home, except in accordance with the law and to the extent that it is necessary in a democratic society. In *Harrow LBC v Qazi*

[2004] 1 AC 983, the House of Lords held that the Article concerned rights of privacy rather than property. Consequently, it could not be used to defeat contractual and proprietary rights to possession, including the powers of a local authority to recover possession from a former tenant. However, in *Connors v UK* (66746/01) (2005) 40 EHRR 9, the European Court of Human Rights at Strasbourg decided that there were circumstances in which the exercise by a public authority of an unqualified proprietary right under domestic law to repossess its land would constitute an interference with the occupier's right to respect for his home. For repossession in these circumstances to be lawful, it must be shown that the authority had sufficient procedural safeguards in place to ensure that so serious an interference with the occupier's rights was justified and proportionate in the circumstances of the case.

For a number of years after *Connors*, the House of Lords continued to hold that the relevant question in Article 8 cases was not whether repossession was a proportionate remedy in the particular case, but whether the statutory scheme under which possession was being sought was Article 8 compliant (see, for example, *Kay v Lambeth BC* [2006] 2 AC 465 (HL) and *Doherty v Birmingham City Council* [2009] 1 AC 367 (HL)). However, in *Manchester City Council v Pinnock* [2011] 2 AC 104 (SC) the Supreme Court accepted that English courts must consider the question of the proportionality of a local authority's action within the circumstances of the individual case, provided that the issue was raised by the claimant (see, also, *Hounslow LBC v Powell* [2011] 2 AC 186 (SC)). This is unlikely to give rise to a flood of successful challenges to eviction. First, the reasoning in *Pinnock* is expressly confined to cases concerning local authorities (at [50]): it does not apply to private landlords. Second, the proportionality of a local authority's action is only one of a number of factors that the court must take into account. In most cases, it is likely to be outweighed by others, including the local authority's proprietary interest in the land and its duty to properly manage and allocate its housing stock.

The effect of the Human Rights Act and the Convention rights it incorporates will be further discussed where relevant during the course of this book.

Summary

1.1 In your approach to land law, it is essential to grasp the language and definitions of interests in land as well as the rules about them.

1.2 The rules of land law are based on those found in case law. However, many of the rules have been significantly modified by Parliament, and land law is increasingly concerned with statutory interpretation. The most important statutes are:

- Law of Property Act (LPA) 1925;
- Land Registration Act (LRA) 2002;
- Trusts of Land and Appointment of Trustees Act (TOLATA) 1996; and
- Land Charges Act (LCA) 1972.

1.3 Land law is primarily concerned with rights of property (ownership) in land. The status of particular rights in land will depend upon the values and priorities of individual societies. There are a number of different reasons why a person might wish to enjoy 'ownership' of land. Where land is shared, these different motivations can give rise to conflict, which the law must resolve.

1.4 The provisions of the Human Rights Act 1998 must be considered when considering land law issues.

Further reading

Burn and Cartwright, *Cheshire and Burn's Modern Law of Real Property* (18th edn, Oxford University Press 2011) ch 1

Gray and Gray, *Elements of Land Law* (5th edn, Oxford University Press 2009) Part 1.5

Rodgers, 'Nature's Place? Property Rights, Property Rules and Environmental Stewardship' (2009) 68 CLJ 550

Simpson, *History of the Land Law* (2nd edn, Clarendon Press 1986)

Thompson, 'Possession Actions and Human Rights' [2011] 75 Conv 421

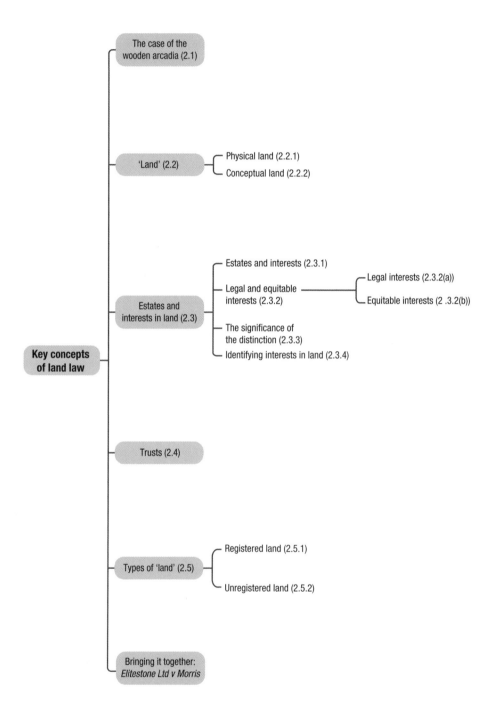

Chapter 2

Key concepts of land law

Key concepts

- **Chattel** – property other than land.
- **Equitable interests** – the interests recognised by the courts exercising their equitable jurisdiction; historically binding only on persons who had notice of them.
- **Fixture** – an object that is treated as part of the land upon which it is situated.
- **Legal estates** – the two types of interest listed in section 1(1) of the LPA 1925 and the basis of land ownership in England and Wales.
- **Legal interests** – the interests listed in section 1(2) of the LPA 1925.
- **Trust** – an equitable doctrine dividing the legal ownership from the beneficial ownership.

2.1 The case of the wooden arcadia

For most of the twentieth century, Holtsfield, near Swansea in South Wales, was the site of a village of wooden chalets or bungalows. The chalets were built as holiday homes before the Second World War, but over the course of time, people began to occupy them on a permanent basis. One such person was David Morris, who, in 1971, acquired the chalet on Lot 6. This was a two-bedroom wooden structure that rested on, but was not attached to, a foundation of concrete blocks. There he lived, in return for the payment of an annual fee to the owner of the site, renewing and replacing his home as required.

Elitestone Ltd purchased Holtsfield in 1989 with a view to redeveloping the land as executive housing. Meanwhile, the company agreed to renew the annual agreements with the residents, but at a much higher fee than that charged previously. A massive campaign followed in an attempt to preserve the chalets on Holtsfield and the way of life of their residents. (At the time of writing, most of the campaign group's website was still visible at www.tlio.org.uk/holtsfield/)

There are a number of legal aspects to the Holtsfield saga. For example, should the chalets be preserved, or should a new development be allowed (planning law)? Were the chalets fit for human habitation (environmental health law)? From a land law perspective, the question was whether Mr Morris and his fellow residents had any interest in the land they occupied that was binding upon Elitestone Ltd as the owners of the field. Indeed, did they have any interest in the land at all, or merely the right to occupy their chalets until the end of the annual agreement? The answer given by the House of Lords (*Elitestone Ltd v Morris* [1997] 1 WLR 687 (HL); see Section 2.6) reflects the way in which different aspects of land law (both case law and statute law) interact in any given case, but it also demonstrates the centrality of the key concepts of land law that are discussed in this chapter.

- What is land?
- What types of interest can be enjoyed in land?
- When will such rights be binding on any third parties to whom the land is transferred (and not just between the original parties)?

2.2   'Land'

2.2.1   Physical land

At common law, 'land' means the soil, the rocks beneath and the air above. Section 132(1) of the Land Registration Act (LRA) 2002 provides that:

'Land' includes
- buildings and other structures,
- land covered with water, and
- mines and minerals, whether or not held with the surface.

Land, therefore, includes things growing on the land and buildings 'attached' to it. In the case of freehold land, it also includes the airspace above the surface of the land necessary to allow the reasonable enjoyment of the surface of the land and any buildings on it (*Bernstein of Leigh (Baron) v Skyviews & General Ltd* [1978] QB 479 (QB)). There is no similar assumption in favour of a tenant. The extent of the land included in the tenancy depends upon the precise wording of the lease (*Rosebery Ltd v Rocklee Ltd* [2011] L & TR 21 (Ch)). The owner of the surface of the land also owns the strata beneath the surface (including any minerals) unless the strata have been separated from the surface in some way. Precisely how far down ownership can extend remains undetermined, but according to the Supreme Court case of *Bocardo SA v Star Energy UK Onshore Ltd* [2011] 1 AC 380 (SC) it is not limited to the depth necessary for the reasonable enjoyment of the surface. Lord Hope (DPSC) considered the old Latin brocard *cuius est solum, eius esty usque ad coelum et ad infernos*, which means, 'whoever owns the soil, it is theirs up to heaven and down to hell'. He concluded:

> In my opinion the brocard still has value in English law as encapsulating, in simple language, a proposition of law which has commanded general acceptance. It is an imperfect guide, as it has ceased to apply to the use of airspace above a height which may interfere with the ordinary user of land: *Baron Bernstein of Leigh v Skyviews & General Ltd* (at [26]).

The general rule is that whatever is attached to the land becomes part of it. Traditionally, all objects fixed to the land have been referred to as 'fixtures'. Objects not attached to the land are 'chattels'. However, in *Elitestone Ltd v Morris* [1997] 1 WLR 687 (HL), Lord Lloyd distinguished a thing which is a fixture from one which is 'part and parcel of the land'. According to Lord Lloyd, both count as land, but the term 'fixture' should be confined to objects that can, in certain circumstances, be detached from it. This terminology is closer to the everyday meaning of the word 'fixture' (it avoids, for example, having to describe a building as a fixture). However, there is little evidence of it having been widely adopted since *Elitestone v Morris* (see Luther (2008) 28 LS 574).

There are a number of circumstances in which it is important to determine whether an object is a chattel or a fixture (or 'part and parcel of the land'); the main examples are set out in Table 2.1.

The status of a particular object is a question of fact in every case. In *Elitestone v Morris* (the facts of which are set out in Section 2.1), the House of Lords held that it was necessary to ask the two questions identified by Blackburn J in *Holland v Hodgson* (1871–72) LR 7 CP 328 (ExCh).

- **First, to what degree was the item annexed (attached) to the land?**
  Normally, an object has to be fixed to the land to some degree if it is to be a fixture. However, in *Elitestone v Morris*, the House of Lords said that this was not

Table 2.1 The significance of the distinction between fixtures and chattels

Circumstances	Comment
I am buying or selling the land.	In most cases, everything to be included with the land will be set out in a detailed list as part of the contract for sale. In the absence of such a list, however, the courts will have to decide (see, for example, *Berkley v Poulett* [1977] 1 EGLR 86 (CA)).
I have granted a mortgage over my land.	If I default on my mortgage, what objects can I remove from my house? All the fixtures automatically pass to the lender (see, for example, *Botham v TSB Bank plc* (1997) 73 P & CR D1 (CA)).
My interest in the land is limited.	If, for example, I have a lease of the land rather than owning the freehold. Special rules apply to tenants wishing to remove trade fixtures, ornamental and domestic fixtures, and agricultural fixtures.
My claim is dependent upon my having an interest in land.	As in *Elitestone Ltd v Morris* [1997] 1 WLR 687 (HL).

required because the chalet was heavy enough to rest on the ground by its own weight.

▶ **Second, for what object or purpose had it been annexed?**

The purpose of annexation is an objective question to be determined on the facts. It is not affected by what the parties thought or agreed between themselves about the status of the object. In *Elitestone v Morris*, the fact that the chalet could not be removed without destroying it demonstrated sufficient purpose of annexation. It is important to remember, however, that the court is usually concerned to determine the intention at the date the object was installed, not the date of trial. *Mew v Tristmire* [2012] 1 WLR 852 (CA) concerned two houseboats resting on piers sunk into the foreshore. According to Patten LJ:

> Although it is unlikely that they could now be removed without breaking up, that is not material to the question whether they became affixed to the land. That question has to be answered by reference to their condition at the time when they were placed on to the supporting structures (at [21]).

The form of the test for purpose of annexation will depend upon the nature of the objects concerned. For example, in *Botham v TSB Bank plc* (1997) 73 P & CR D1 (CA) (see Haley, 1998), the main factors determining the purpose of annexation of bathroom and kitchen equipment were whether the items were a lasting improvement, intended to be permanent (fixture) or merely temporary (chattel), and whether they could be removed without damaging the fabric of the building (chattel).

When considering whether a thing (other than a building) is a fixture or a chattel, the law now puts greater emphasis on the purpose of annexation. However, the degree of attachment provides important evidence about the nature of the intention behind any annexation. As Lord Lloyd explained in *Elitestone v Morris*:

> the intention of the parties is only relevant to the extent that it can be derived from the degree and object of the annexation (at 993).

For example, in *Chelsea Yacht & Boat Co Ltd v Pope* [2000] 1 WLR 1941 (CA) the Court of Appeal held that attaching a houseboat to the river wall by ropes and detachable connections providing electricity and other services was not sufficient to establish that the houseboat was intended to be part of the land.

2.2.2 Conceptual land

It has already been noted that the law of England and Wales sometimes treats land as a physical entity, but that more often it divides land up into a number of abstract rights and interests (see Sections 1.1 and 1.3.3). The definition of 'land' in section 205(1)(ix) of the Law of Property Act (LPA) 1925 combines both of these elements:

> 'Land' includes land of any tenure, and mines and minerals ... buildings or parts of buildings ... and other corporeal hereditaments, also ... a rent, and other incorporeal hereditaments, and an easement right, privilege, or benefit in, over, or derived from land.

The term 'corporeal hereditaments' is an ancient way of referring to the land and the fixtures, while 'incorporeal hereditaments' are the invisible interests in land, such as mortgages and easements (rights of way, for example). Thus, both a person who buys a lease (that is, becomes a leaseholder or a tenant) and a person who buys a right of way over his neighbour's land are buying land.

2.3 Estates and interests in land

2.3.1 Estates and interests

It has already been mentioned that the land lawyer views every piece of land as potentially fragmented into an infinite number of interests (Section 2.2.2; see also Bright, 1998). For historical reasons, he sees people owning an abstract estate or interest in land, not the land itself. The lesser interests are carved out of the major ones (see Section 1.3.1 and Figure 1.1). The major interests are called the 'estates'. This word 'estate' has a long lineage; it means 'an interest in land of some particular duration' (Megarry and Wade, 2012, § 3–001). However, today it is only necessary to know that there are now two legal estates:

> Law of Property Act 1925
> s 1(1) The only estates in land which are capable of subsisting or of being conveyed or created at law are:
> (a) An estate in fee simple absolute in possession [a freehold];
> (b) A term of years absolute [a lease].

The term 'interest in land' is significant to land lawyers because it shows that the rights and duties of the people concerned are not merely personal or contractual. These rights and duties are attached to the land itself, and they automatically pass to anyone who buys or inherits the land. Interests in land can be transferred to other people and bind third parties. In lawyers' vocabulary, interests in land are 'property'.

2.3.2 Legal and equitable interests

Not all rights over land are interests in land. For example, a right to use someone else's land may be permissive or a contractual licence that binds the grantor, but does not attach to the land (see Chapter 3). Particular rights over land are only capable of being interests in land if they have been recognised as such by the courts or by Parliament (see Section 1.3.1). The division between the courts of common law and the courts of equity has given rise to two types of interest in land: *legal* interests and *equitable* interests.

2.3.2(a) Legal interests

The courts of common law recognised various estates and interests in land. Because property rights in land automatically affect anyone who subsequently acquires that land, the courts of common law restricted the classes of proprietary interests to rights that were relatively certain and easily discoverable. In most cases, this required certain formalities to be complied with when the rights were created, although the doctrine of *adverse possession* (see Chapter 13) and the acquisition of easements by *prescription* (see Section 8.5.3) are significant exceptions to this rule.

The interests that are now capable of existing at law are set out in section 1 of the LPA 1925:

(1) The only estates in land which are capable of subsisting or of being conveyed or created at law are:
   (a) An estate in fee simple absolute in possession [a freehold];
   (b) A term of years absolute [a lease].
(2) The only interests or charges in or over land which are capable of subsisting or of being conveyed or created at law are:
   (a) An easement, right, or privilege in or over land for an interest equivalent to an estate in fee simple absolute in possession or a term of years absolute [rights of way, for example];
   (b) A rentcharge in possession issuing out of or charged on land being either perpetual or for a term of years absolute [a periodical payment secured on land, but which does not arise out of a lease or a mortgage];
   (c) A charge by way of legal mortgage;
   (d) … and any other similar charge on land which is not created by an instrument [effectively repealed];
   (e) Rights of entry exercisable over, or in respect of, a legal term of years absolute [a lessor's right to end a lease].

Section 1(3) of the LPA 1925 provides that 'All other estates, interests, and charges in or over land take effect as equitable interests.'

It must be emphasised that LPA 1925 does not say that the estates and interests listed there *are* legal, merely that they *may* be.

2.3.2(b) Equitable interests

Historically, equity has recognised that there are circumstances in which a person with a very strong moral right to a parcel of land might find that his right does not meet the strict requirements of the common law. For example, the interest may have been created without complying with the necessary formalities. Most legal interests must now be created by deed and completed by registration. Writing alone is usually sufficient to create an express equitable interest, although it will usually be necessary to protect an equitable interest by some form of registration if it is to be binding on third parties (see Sections 15.7 and 16.3). The distinction between creation and registration will, for all practicable purposes, become obsolete if electronic conveyancing is ever extended to cover such interests (but see Sections 12.2 and 12.6).

Equity also recognises that there are some circumstances in which a person should be given an interest in land even when no formalities have been complied with. This can be illustrated by the well-known case of *Bull v Bull* [1955] 1 QB 234 (CA). A son and mother both contributed to buying a house on the outskirts of London, but only the son's name appeared on the conveyance (the deed), so he was the legal owner. He then married and, since his wife and his mother could not get on with each other, tried to evict his mother. The Court of Appeal held that he could not simply turn her out. She had a share of the equitable title because of her contribution to the purchase, so the son held the legal title on behalf of the equitable owners (himself and his mother). Another way to express this is to say that the son is a trustee for himself and his mother; they share the 'beneficial' interest (see Section 2.4).

Equity has also been prepared to recognise a limited number of interests in land that have never been recognised at law. One of the most important examples of these is the *restrictive covenant*, which first became enforceable against third parties as a property right in the nineteenth century (see Chapter 9). More recently, the rights arising out of proprietary estoppel (see Section 14.4) have been recognised as having proprietary status (see LRA 2002, s 116).

2.3.3 The significance of the distinction

There are two main reasons why it is important to know whether a particular interest is 'legal' or 'equitable'. The first is that equitable interests depend on equitable remedies, which, in turn, are more to do with trying to prevent the harm than putting a price tag on the loss that occurs. Equitable remedies are at the discretion of the court. The court of equity, being 'a court of conscience', only grants a remedy if the claimant has behaved fairly. Legal remedies, on the other hand (damages, for example), are available 'as of right'. A claimant is entitled to damages if his strict legal rights have been infringed, whether or not this is fair. Thus, in *Tse Kwong Lam v Wong Chit Sen* [1983] 1 WLR 1349 (PC) (see Section 7.5.2(b)), the Privy Council refused to set aside an improper sale of mortgaged land by a lender because the borrower had been 'guilty of inexcusable delay' in bringing the action. The borrower was, however, entitled to monetary damages (a legal remedy). The principles used by the courts in determining whether or not it is equitable to grant a remedy are summed up in the so-called maxims of equity (see, for example, *Hanbury & Martin's Modern Equity*, 2012, §§ 1–024 to 1–036).

The second reason to distinguish between legal and equitable interests is much less significant than it used to be. Historically, the courts could not bring themselves to enforce equitable rights against a completely innocent and honest legal purchaser. Prior to 1925, the rule was that the owner of an equitable interest in land would lose it if someone paid for the legal estate, in good faith and without notice (or 'Equity's Darling': see Section 16.2.2). This rule, known as the 'equitable doctrine of notice', 'has no application in registered land' (per Mummery LJ *Barclays Bank plc v Boulter* [1998] 1 WLR 1 (CA) at 10; see also (2001) Law Com No 271, para 5.16). Even in unregistered land, it only applies in a highly modified form.

2.3.4 Identifying interests in land

When you read land law problems, it is crucial to develop an instinct for the various interests so that you can immediately say, for example, 'This looks like an easement.' The first question to ask in problem solving is therefore:

▷ What legal or equitable interests may exist here?

The main possibilities are considered in Parts II and III of this book, and further tools are available on the companion website. If the rights being claimed do not fall within any of the categories of property interests, they may amount to some form of licence (see Chapter 3).

2.4 Trusts

One of the advantages of dividing land into a number of separate interests is that it is a convenient way of regulating the use of the same parcel of land by a number of people. For example, the freehold of a block of flats will be owned by the landlord. The individual tenants will each have a lease of their flat, giving them ownership of that flat for the duration of their lease. The tenants will also have the right to use the corridors and other common parts of the block of flats (easements). The different types of interest in land allow the ownership of the land to be divided up physically and over time (for the duration of a lease, for example). The doctrine of the *trust* allows ownership of land to be divided in yet another way: legal ownership can be separated from the right to enjoy the land or any income generated by it. An example can be found in the case of *Bull v Bull* [1955] 1 QB 234 (CA) (see Section 2.3.2(b)), where a trust arose because the son and mother both contributed to the purchase of the house. Despite this, only the son's name appeared on the title deeds. Consequently, the son was the sole legal owner of the land. The Court of Appeal had to decide whether his rights as legal owner entitled him to evict his mother. It was held that the mother's contribution to the purchase price meant that the beneficial entitlement to the house was divided between her and her son. He held the legal title on trust for himself and his mother and had, therefore, to respect his mother's rights in the land. This is shown diagrammatically in Figure 2.1.

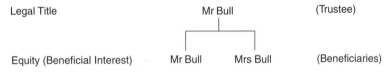

Figure 2.1 The trust relationship in *Bull v Bull* [1955] 1 QB 234 (CA)

The history of how the courts of equity developed the trust is a long one. (For more detail, consult a textbook on equity and trusts, such as Martin, 2012.) In the simplest form of a trust, however, a settler transfers the legal title to trustees to hold for the benefit of the beneficiary or beneficiaries (Figure 2.2).

The trust is a useful and very common device by which land can be shared. Sections 34–36 LPA 1925 provide that any land that is transferred to two or more people is automatically held on trust (the legal owners holding as trustees for themselves as beneficiaries; see Chapter 10). The duties of a trustee are contained in the general rules of equity and in statute. In the case of trusts of land, most of the relevant

Figure 2.2 The trust

rules are contained in the Trusts of Land and Appointment of Trustees Act 1996 (see Chapter 11).

Entitlement to land as the beneficiary of a trust is an equitable interest in the land in its own right (see, for example, *Williams & Glyn's Bank Ltd v Boland* [1981] AC 487 (HL)). When considering a land law problem, it is important to consider whether there are any beneficial interests in the land concerned.

The framers of the 1925 reforms to land law were concerned that beneficial interests seriously compromised the free marketability of land because such interests would not necessarily be readily apparent either from the title documentation or from an inspection of the property. They chose the doctrine of overreaching in an attempt to balance the interests of buyers (and the economic importance of keeping the process of transferring land relatively quick and cheap) with the interests of beneficiaries.

Provided that the buyer of any legal estate in land pays the purchase price to at least two trustees (or a trust corporation), any beneficial interests under a trust in that estate are automatically detached from the land and attached to the purchase price (see LPA 1925, ss 2 and 27). The doctrine of overreaching is considered in more detail in Section 11.6.1.

When considering whether a buyer is bound by any trust affecting the land, it is important to ask:

▶ Has the beneficial interest been overreached into the proceeds of sale?

2.5   Types of 'land'

There are a number of legal interests in land and, in a kind of parallel universe, many equitable interests. As a general rule, anyone who buys or inherits land owns it subject to any interests, legal and equitable, which have been created by previous owners of the land. However, this rule has numerous exceptions. The detailed rules depend upon whether title to the land concerned is registered.

Since 1925, all titles to land in England and Wales are either 'unregistered' or 'registered'. Although people often refer to 'registered land' (and the main statute is the Land Registration Act 2002), it is a person's *title* to the land which is registered, not the land itself.

One of the aims of the 1925 legislation was that ultimately every title to land would be registered in a central registry (see Chapter 15). By the middle of 2013, some 23 million titles in England and Wales were registered, amounting to about 82 per cent of the total area of the land. Up-to-date figures can be found in the publications available from the Land Registry's website www.gov.uk/government/organisations/land-registry.

Registered and unregistered land involve two distinct systems of conveyancing, each with its own set of rules for determining how interests in land are created and transferred and how disputes about those interests are resolved. These rules will be explained in detail as they become relevant in the chapters that follow (and especially in Chapters 15 and 16). For the moment, however, it is useful to identify some of the main differences between the two systems. The meaning and significance of these differences should become more apparent as your study of land law progresses. The main differences are set out in Table 2.2.

It is very important to apply the correct set of rules (registered or unregistered) when addressing a land law issue, not least because the two sets of rules occasionally

Table 2.2 A comparison between unregistered and registered title

	Unregistered	Registered
Underlying nature	Private	Public
Basis of title (ownership)	Possession	Entry in Land Register Title is guaranteed by the State.
Evidence of title	Title deeds	Official copy of the register
Types of interest	Legal estates Legal charges Other legal interests Equitable interests	Registrable estates Registrable charges Interests completed by registration Interests subject to registration Interests capable of overriding the register
Discovery of interests in the land	Deeds Land Charges Register Notice (including inspection of the land)	Register Inspection of the land for interests capable of overriding the register

produce different results. Therefore, one important question to ask when faced with any land law issue is:

▶ Is the title to the land concerned registered or unregistered?

2.5.1 Registered land

When title to land is registered, the question of whether a particular interest will affect someone acquiring the land will be determined by the rules set out in the LRA 2002.

The aim of the LRA 2002 is for as many interests as possible to be entered on the register of title to the estates affected. Any interest that appears on the register will normally be binding on whoever acquires the estate concerned (provided that that interest actually exists, of course). However, it would be unjust, and impracticable, to insist that every interest in the land must be registered if it is to be enforceable against the owner of the land. Consequently, the LRA 2002 lists a limited number of interests that are capable of binding the owner of a registered estate even though they do not appear on the register of title. These interests are commonly referred to as being capable of *overriding* the register. Some of these interests are legal, others equitable.

Consequently, if title to the land is registered, it is necessary to ask:

▶ Is this interest entered on the register, and, if not, does it override the register?

The rules relating to registered land are considered in Chapter 15.

2.5.2 Unregistered land

If title to the land is unregistered, the effect of a particular interest depends upon whether it is legal or equitable. Legal rights are effective against anyone in the world, but equitable rights are only 'good' against certain people. That is to say, an equitable interest may bind some people, but not others. As part of the reforms directed at making conveyancing simpler, the number of legal rights to land was strictly limited in

1925 to those listed in sections 1(1) and 1(2) of the LPA 1925 (see Section 2.3.2(a)). The most important of these are:

- the two legal estates (LPA 1925, s 1(1));
- easements and profits (LPA 1925, s 1(2)(a)); and
- charges by way of legal mortgage (LPA 1925, s 1(2)(c)).

Legal rights over unregistered land automatically bind anyone who subsequently acquires an estate or any other interest in the land. Whether or not any equitable interests in unregistered land will bind a purchaser now depends upon detailed rules, most of which are found in the Land Charges Act 1972. These rules are a significant modification of the traditional doctrine of notice, but they preserve the significance of the distinction between legal and equitable interests. Consequently, when a land law problem concerns unregistered land, it is necessary to ask:

- Is this interest legal or equitable?

The rules relating to unregistered land are considered in Chapter 16.

2.6 Bringing it together: *Elitestone Ltd v Morris*

Elitestone Ltd owned the freehold of Holtsfield and brought possession proceedings against Mr Morris and the other residents. To successfully resist these proceedings, Mr Morris needed to establish that he had an interest in the land occupied by his chalet and that this interest was binding upon the freeholder.

- One possibility was that he occupied the land as an annual licensee (see Chapter 3). This would not give him an interest in the land, and any such rights would terminate at the end of the present licence period.
- The alternative was that Mr Morris had an annual lease of Lot 6. If he could establish this, he would have an interest in the land (a lease is capable of being a legal estate; see LPA 1925, s 1(1)(b)). This in itself would not protect Mr Morris beyond the end of the present year of the lease. By definition, the leasehold estate can only be enjoyed during the term of the lease.
- If Mr Morris had an annual lease of a *dwelling house*, he would be protected by the provisions of the Rent Act 1977, which would entitle him to a new lease at the end of each year at a fair rent. However, the lease of a plot of land alone would not be sufficient.
- It is not possible to have a lease of a chattel. Consequently, Mr Morris would only have a lease of a dwelling house if his chalet formed part of the land that he was leasing. His case turned, therefore, on whether the chalet was a chattel or a fixture.

At first instance, the Assistant Recorder held that the chalet was part of the land, but the Court of Appeal reversed his decision. The House of Lords held that a house built in such a way that it could not be removed except by destroying it could not have been (objectively) intended to be a chattel and must, therefore, have become part and parcel of the land (distinguishing this case from *Deen v Andrews* (1986) 52 P & CR 17 (QB), where a substantial, but moveable, greenhouse had been held to be a chattel).

Summary

2.1 Many types of law are relevant to how land is used and shared. This book is primarily concerned with the interests that can be enjoyed in land and their rules.

2.2 'Land' means the physical land and includes any interests in the land. Land also includes any objects that are attached to the land (traditionally known as 'fixtures'). Whether an object is a 'fixture' is a question of fact, discernible from the degree of annexation of the object and the purpose of its annexation.

2.3 Many interests are capable of existing in a piece of land. The two major interests are the two legal estates. All other interests are carved out of a legal estate. Interests can be legal or equitable. Historically, legal interests would bind anyone who owned the land, while equitable interests would not bind a buyer of a legal estate in good faith for value without notice.

2.4 Trusts allow the ownership of a particular estate in land to be divided between trustees and beneficiaries. The trustees own the legal title to the land, but it is the beneficiaries who are entitled to enjoy the land. Trusts are very important in land law, especially where an estate in land is owned by more than one person. However, interests under trusts can be overreached in certain circumstances.

2.5 Title to land may be either registered or not yet registered (unregistered). The appropriate rules for determining whether a particular interest binds the present owner of the land depend on whether the land is registered or unregistered.

Exercises

2.1 Complete the online quiz on the topics covered in this chapter on the companion website.

2.2 Read *A Tale of Three Students* on the companion website. Use the questions identified in Sections 2.3 to 2.5 (summarised later) to determine how the principles and rules discussed in this chapter are relevant for the three friends.

> Questions to ask when approaching a land law problem
> - What legal or equitable interests may exist here?
> - If the interest is a beneficial interest under a trust, has it been overreached?
> - Is title to the land concerned registered or unregistered?
> - If the title is *registered* (see Chapter 15):
>   - is the interest entered on the register?
>   - if not, does it override the register?
> - If the title is not yet registered (see Chapter 16):
>   - is the interest legal?
>   - if the interest is equitable, does it fall within the scope of the Land Charges Act 1972?
>
> An interactive version of these questions can be found on the companion website.

2.3   What are legal estates? Why are they so significant in modern English land law? How do they differ from other types of interest in land?

2.4   Waheeda has bought Jack's house. When she first viewed the house, she was particularly taken with the garden, which contained an ornamental pond with a statue of a mermaid set on a plinth in its centre. She was also pleased that she would be getting a large garden shed which rested on a concrete base.

When she moved in, she was horrified to discover that Jack had taken away both the statue and the shed. The fitted carpets in the house had also been removed. Waheeda checked the contract for the sale, but found that it made no mention of any of these items.

Advise Waheeda, who also tells you that she cannot understand how Jack managed to remove the shed, since he would have had to dismantle it completely to do so.

You can find suggested answers to exercises 2.3 and 2.4 on the companion website.

Further reading

Bright, 'Of Estates and Interests: A Tale of Ownership and Property Rights' in Bright and Dewar (eds), *Land Law Themes and Perspectives* (Oxford University Press 1998) 529

Haley, 'The Law of Fixtures: An Unprincipled Metamorphosis?' [1998] Conv 137

Hayton, 'The Development of Equity and the "Good Person" Philosophy in Common Law Systems' [2012] 76 Conv 263

Luther, 'The Foundations of *Elitestone*' (2008) 28 LS 574

Martin, *Hanbury & Martin's Modern Equity* (19th edn, Sweet & Maxwell 2012)

Chapter 3 follows overleaf.

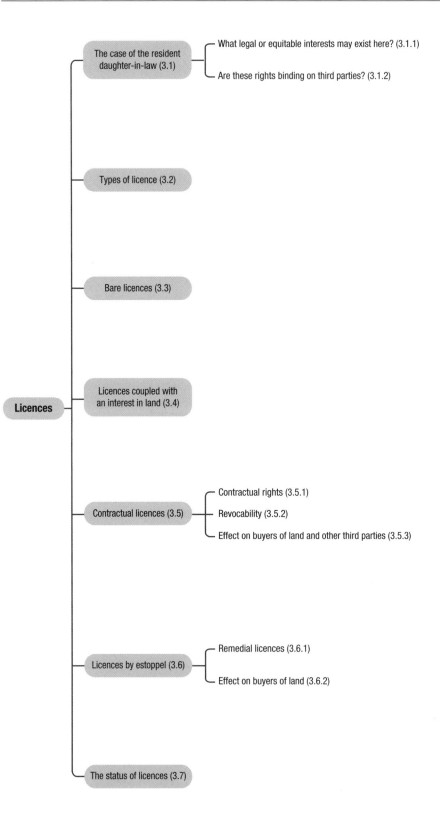

Licences

Key concepts

▶ **Estoppel** – an equitable interest arising out of the claimant's detrimental reliance upon an expectation encouraged by the defendant.
▶ **Licence** – permission to enter onto land.

3.1 The case of the resident daughter-in-law

In 1936, Mr Errington senior bought 27 Milvain Avenue in Newcastle as a home for his son, who had recently married the defendant (Mary Errington). He paid £250 in cash (which he told Mary was a present) towards the house and borrowed the balance of £500 from a building society on the security of the house. The house was conveyed into the name of Mr Errington senior, and he also took the mortgage from the building society in his sole name. However, he handed the building society book to Mary, telling her not to part with it and that the house would belong to her and her husband when they had paid the last instalment on the mortgage.

When Mr Errington senior died some nine years later, legal title to the house passed to his widow (also called Mary Errington). The daughter-in-law continued to occupy the house and to pay the instalments of the mortgage. The mother then claimed possession of 27 Milvain Avenue.

The question before the Court of Appeal in *Errington v Errington & Woods* [1952] 1 KB 290 (CA) was:

> What is the result in law of these facts? (per Denning LJ at 295)

3.1.1 What legal or equitable interests may exist here?

The various legal and equitable interests that are recognised in land have been introduced in Chapter 2 (see, especially, Section 2.3) and will be explored in more detail in Part II. All three members of the Court of Appeal in *Errington* rejected the conclusion of the County Court judge that a special form of lease had been created. (The ingredients required for a lease are considered in Chapter 5.) If the case were to be decided today, it would almost certainly be treated as a possible example of an interest arising by way of proprietary estoppel (see Chapter 14). However, the doctrine of estoppel was much less developed at the date of *Errington*, and the Court of Appeal felt that its only alternative was to hold that the daughter-in-law occupied the house as a licensee.

3.1.2 Are these rights binding on third parties?

One of the characteristics of the interests in land recognised by the law or at equity (and considered in Part II) is that they are binding on third parties. However, the younger Mary Errington did not have such an interest. What protection, if any, should her licence give her against her mother-in-law's claim for possession of 27 Milvain Avenue?

It is important to recognise from the outset that there is no single correct answer to this question. (For the answer in the context of *Errington* see Section 3.5.3.) The status of licences is just one example of a wider problem: How can one reconcile the need for certainty (reflected in the closed list of property interests, for example) with the flexibility needed to reflect the wishes of the parties and the needs of justice in a particular case? Other examples of this tension can be found throughout this book. (See, for example, Sections 11.5, 11.6 and 12.4.5.)

3.2 Types of licence

A person who has a licence to be on another's land has that person's permission to be there; in other words, a licence prevents someone from being a trespasser.

Licences cover a huge variety of activities. A fan at a football match is a licensee, as is a secretary working in an office, a customer in a shop, a paying guest in a hotel, and perhaps a cohabitee sharing her lover's house. Licences may last for a few minutes or for life, and are found within both family and commercial settings. For example, a licence may be created deliberately or accidentally instead of a lease (see Chapter 5) or in place of an easement (such as a right of way) if the necessary formalities have not been complied with (see Chapter 8). It is hardly surprising that there are several types of licence and that the rights and remedies of licensees differ widely.

Licences can be divided into four main categories:

1. bare licences;
2. licences coupled with an interest in land;
3. contractual licences; and
4. licences by estoppel.

This chapter considers each type of licence in turn, and, in particular, the extent to which they might be interests in land or whether they are merely personal rights. The distinction is important, since property rights attach irrevocably to the land, are sold along with the land and, if protected in the appropriate way (see Chapters 15 and 16), will bind a purchaser of the burdened land and benefit the purchaser of any dominant land.

3.3 Bare licences

A bare licence arises when the landowner gives permission for another person to be on her land. This may be express, such as an invitation to a friend to come in and have a cup of coffee, or implied, such as for a postal worker delivering letters. Such licences are gratuitous (that is, given without consideration) and can lawfully be revoked whenever the landowner wishes. The licensee must then leave within a reasonable time, or she becomes a trespasser and may be physically removed. The licensee cannot transfer this kind of licence to another person. Neither will this type of licence bind someone who buys the land from the licensor.

3.4 Licences coupled with an interest in land

When a person owns a *profit à prendre* (a legal interest giving her the right to take something from another person's land; see Sections 8.2 and 8.8), she will be unable to exercise the right without a licence to go onto the land. So, for example, the owner of a profit of piscary (the right to take fish) automatically has a licence to cross the grantor's land in order to get to the river. This form of licence cannot be revoked and will continue for as long as the interest exists, binding third parties in the same way as the *profit*.

3.5   Contractual licences

3.5.1   Contractual rights

A contractual licence is created wherever a person has permission to be on another's land as part of a contract between them. Examples include the fan at the football match and the paying guest in the hotel. The rights of a contractual licensee depend upon the terms of the contract. Lord Greene MR stated that:

> A licence created by a contract … creates a contractual right to do certain things which otherwise would be a trespass. It seems to me that, in considering the nature of such a licence and the mutual rights and obligations which arise under it, the first thing to do is to construe the contract according to ordinary principles (*Winter Garden Theatre (London) Ltd v Millennium Productions Ltd* [1946] 1 All ER 678 (CA) at 680).

It is often assumed that a contractual licence is worth less than a lease. This may be true in regard to the licensee's security if the land is sold, and, in general, licences do not attract the statutory protection afforded to leases. However, there are occasions when it is more beneficial to be a licensee than a tenant under a lease. For example, in *Wettern Electric Ltd v Welsh Development Agency* [1983] QB 796 (QB), a company held the licence of factory premises which were so badly constructed and became so unsafe that the licensee company had to leave. The licensee company successfully sued for breach of an implied term that the premises would be fit for their purpose. This term could not be implied into a contract for a lease, not being one of the 'usual covenants' (see Section 6.2.4). However, in a licence, the ordinary rules of contract law applied. Judge Newey QC explained that:

> The sole purpose of the licence was to enable the plaintiffs to have accommodation in which to carry on and expand their business … If anyone had said to the plaintiffs and the defendants' directors and executives at the time when the licence was being granted: 'Will the premises be sound and suitable for the plaintiff's purposes?' they would assuredly have replied: 'Of course; there would be no point in the licence if that were not so.' The term was required to make the contract workable (at 809).

Contractual licences are common and are generally created expressly. However, in the 1970s, the Court of Appeal used the device of the implied contractual licence to solve certain types of family dispute, such as those in *Errington v Errington & Woods* [1952] 1 KB 290 (CA) and *Tanner v Tanner (No 1)* [1975] 1 WLR 1346 (CA). In *Tanner*, Miss MacDermott (who changed her name to Mrs Tanner) had moved from her Rent Act-protected tenancy into a house bought by Mr Tanner, to live there with their twin children. Mr Tanner then formed a relationship with another woman and tried to evict Mrs Tanner. The Court of Appeal held that Mrs Tanner had a contractual licence which could not be revoked until the twins reached the age of 18. However, since she had already been rehoused following the decision at first instance (which had gone against her) she was awarded £2,000 to compensate her for her loss. This contractual analysis, with the accompanying traditional contractual requirements of consideration and the intention to create a legal relationship, has proved highly problematic when applied to family and domestic arrangements. Today, such cases are usually argued on the basis of a common intention constructive trust (see Section 14.3) or an estoppel (see Sections 3.6 and 14.4).

3.5.2　Revocability

There has been continuing debate on whether a contractual licence can be revoked by the licensor. In *Hurst v Picture Theatres Ltd* [1915] 1 KB 1 (CA), for example, a cinema customer was physically removed because the owner (wrongly) believed he had not paid for his ticket. The Court of Appeal decided that the licensor should not have turned the licensee out and that the licensee was entitled to damages for false imprisonment and breach of contract. The decision was based on the argument that the equitable remedies of specific performance of the contract and an injunction to prevent the breach would, in theory, have been available to the customer, who therefore was seen by equity as having a right to remain in the cinema. Consequently, he could not be a trespasser.

In the *Winter Garden Theatre* case [1946] 1 All ER 678 (CA) and [1948] AC 173 (HL), the theatre owner attempted to revoke a licence allowing a theatre company to produce plays and concerts in the theatre, although there was no provision in the contract for him to do this. The House of Lords stated that whether a contractual licence could be revoked depended entirely on the construction of the contract. In this case, the licence was not intended to last forever and could therefore be determined by the theatre owner on reasonable notice.

Verrall v Great Yarmouth BC [1981] QB 202 (CA) is a clear example of a case in which a contractual licence could not be revoked. Following a change in its political control, a local council tried to revoke a licence to use a hall for a two-day conference which it had previously granted to an extreme-right-wing political organisation. It was held that the council could not do so. Damages for breach of contract would not be a sufficient remedy, since no alternative venue was available, so the Court of Appeal unanimously held that the contract should be specifically enforced. Lord Denning MR said:

> An injunction can be obtained against the licensor to prevent [the licensee] being turned out. On principle it is the same if it happens before he enters. If he had a contractual right to enter, and the licensor refuses to let him come in, then he can come to the court and in a proper case get an order for specific performance to allow him to come in (at 216).

Where a person is occupying premises as her residence under a contractual licence she will enjoy additional rights by virtue of the Protection from Eviction Act 1977 (see also Section 6.2.1(c)). In most cases, the licensor will not be entitled to recover possession of the premises without either a court order or the licensee's consent, even if the licence has expired (s 3(2B)). If the licence is a periodic one, then the licensee will be normally be entitled to four weeks' written notice before the licence can be determined (s 5(1A)).

3.5.3　Effect on buyers of land and other third parties

If it is correct that in some circumstances a licence cannot be revoked, then it is necessary to consider the effect of such a licence on a purchaser of the land from the licensor. Has an irrevocable licence now become an interest in the land to which it relates, thus binding third parties, or does the traditional view prevail, that a licence is merely a personal right?

King v David Allen & Sons Billposting Ltd [1916] 2 AC 54 (HL) is an example of the traditional approach. The licence in this case was to fix advertising posters to the licensor's wall. The licensor then granted a long lease of the building, a cinema, and the leaseholder prevented the licensee from fixing the posters. The House of Lords held that the licensor was liable to pay damages for breach of contract. Although the cinema leaseholder was not a party to the case, Lord Buckmaster LC several times referred to the licence as a purely personal right and not an interest in land. Consequently, the licence did not bind the cinema leaseholder.

However, in *Errington v Errington & Woods* [1955] 1 KB 290 (CA), the facts of which are set out in Section 3.1, the Court of Appeal held that an arrangement between a father and his daughter-in-law was a contractual licence that could not be revoked so long as one of the licensees kept to their side of the bargain, and that it would bind a purchaser who had notice of it:

> The couple were licensees, having a permissive occupation short of a tenancy, but with a contractual right, or at any rate, an equitable right to remain as long as they paid the instalments, which would grow into a good equitable title to the house itself as soon as the mortgage was paid ... contractual licences now have a force and validity of their own and cannot be revoked in breach of contract. Neither the licensor nor anyone who claims through him can disregard the contract except a purchaser for value without notice (per Denning LJ at 296, 298).

In later years, it was Lord Denning's view that equity would enforce a contractual licence against anyone who ought fairly to be bound by it. In *Binions v Evans* [1972] Ch 359 (CA), for example, a contractual licence permitting a widow to remain in a cottage for the rest of her life bound, under a constructive trust, buyers of unregistered land who had agreed to take the land subject to her rights:

> Wherever the owner sells the land to a purchaser, and at the same time stipulates that he shall take it 'subject to' a contractual licence, I think it plain that a court of equity will impose on the purchaser a constructive trust ... It would be utterly inequitable that the purchaser should be able to turn out the beneficiary (per Denning MR at 368).

The view of Denning LJ in *Errington*, that contractual licences can bind third parties, was discredited in *Ashburn Anstalt v WJ Arnold & Co* [1989] Ch 1 (CA). However, the Court of Appeal in *Ashburn Anstalt* approved Lord Denning's imposition of a constructive trust in the later case of *Binions v Evans*. In that case, the constructive trust was necessary to protect the licensee against unconscionable dealing by the new legal owners, who had expressly agreed to uphold her rights. Nevertheless, in *Ashburn Anstalt*, the court took a restrictive view on the use of constructive trusts in such situations, since:

> The court will not impose a constructive trust unless it is satisfied that the conscience of the estate owner is affected. The mere fact that that land is expressed to be conveyed 'subject to' a contract does not necessarily imply that the grantee is to be under an obligation, not otherwise existing, to give effect to the provisions of the contract (per Fox LJ at 25).

3.6　Licences by estoppel

3.6.1　Remedial licences

The circumstances in which detrimental reliance on an expectation encouraged by the legal owner will give rise to an equity (the doctrine of proprietary estoppel) are considered in Chapter 14. An interest arising by way of estoppel will be satisfied by a remedy designed to do minimum justice between the parties and compensate the claimant for the detriment she has suffered. This remedy may sometimes be the award of an estate in the land, as in *Pascoe v Turner* [1979] 1 WLR 431 (CA) (see Section 14.4.2). However, the award of a licence for the claimant to remain on the land is not uncommon. For example, in *Inwards v Baker* [1965] 2 QB 29 (CA), a son was encouraged to build a bungalow on his father's land by the father's promise that the son could remain on the land. The son built the bungalow, but when the father died his heirs claimed the land. The Court of Appeal held that, since the father would have been estopped from going back on his promise, and the heirs were in the same position as the father, the son's equity should be satisfied by the award of a licence to stay on the land. Similarly, in *Greasley v Cooke* [1980] 1 WLR 1306 (CA), a maid who had lived in the house for many years was awarded an irrevocable licence to continue to occupy it for as long as she wished (see Section 14.4.2).

3.6.2 Effect on buyers of land

It is evident that Lord Denning felt that estoppel rights were capable of binding a buyer of the land. In *Inwards v Baker*, for example, he said:

> any purchaser who took with notice would clearly be bound by the equity (at 37).

He followed this in *ER Ives Investment Ltd v High* [1967] 2 QB 379 (CA). While a block of flats was being built, it was discovered that the foundations trespassed onto Mr High's land. Mr High agreed, unfortunately not by deed, that the foundations could remain in return for him being allowed to drive over the developer's land. He then built a garage on his own land at the end of the drive. The block of flats then changed hands, and the new owners tried to prevent Mr High using the drive. Lord Denning held that since the earlier owner of the flats would have been estopped from denying Mr High a right to use the drive belonging to the flats, the successors in title to that earlier owner were also bound by that right.

In *Re Sharpe (a bankrupt)* [1980] 1 WLR 219 (Ch), a woman lent £12,000 to her nephew to buy a maisonette on the basis that they would live there together. He became bankrupt, and the trustee in bankruptcy, having contracted to sell the maisonette, sought a possession order against her. Although the case was decided on the basis that the woman had a contractual licence to remain in the property until the loan was repaid, Browne-Wilkinson J said:

> If the parties have proceeded on a common assumption that the plaintiff is to enjoy a right to reside in a particular property and in reliance on that assumption the plaintiff has expended money or otherwise acted to his detriment, the defendant will not be allowed to go back on that common assumption and the court will imply an irrevocable licence or trust which will give effect to that common assumption (at 223).

This licence was binding on the trustee in bankruptcy. Although the judge was not required to express a view on the position of the purchaser from the trustee, he thought that it was possible that the rights of a purchaser without express notice of the contract would have prevailed over those of the licensee.

In unregistered land, whether a licence by estoppel binds a purchaser will usually depend upon whether the purchaser had notice of the equity (as in *ER Ives Investments Ltd v High*). In registered land, section 116 of the Land Registration Act (LRA) 2002 provides that an equity by estoppel is capable of binding purchasers, provided, of course, that it is combined with actual occupation (Sched. 1, para 2 and Sched. 3, para 2 LRA 2002; see Section 15.8.2).

3.7   The status of licences

If one thing is clear about licences, it is that there is not one answer to the questions 'Are licences interests in land?' and 'Are they property?' Probably the best conclusion to be drawn from the brief summary in this chapter is that licences are not in themselves interests in land. However, licences combined with a recognised interest in land, usually an estoppel, will benefit from the proprietary character of that interest.

The twentieth-century story of licences is an excellent illustration of how the law changes in response to changing social and economic values and concerns. Not that long ago, a number of academics and judges believed that twentieth-century land law was well on the way to developing the contractual licence into a new type of interest in land, in a process equivalent to the development of the restrictive covenant in the nineteenth century. For example, in 1984 Sir Robert Megarry could write:

> The courts seem to be well on their way to creating a new and highly versatile interest in land which will rescue many informal and unbusinesslike transactions, particularly within families, from the penalties of disregarding legal forms. Old restraints are giving way to the demands of justice (Megarry and Wade, 1984, 808).

For some, such licences were symbols of a new form of property, a right to share, which would take its place beside the traditional private and exclusive property rights. However, in *Ashburn Anstalt v WJ Arnold & Co* [1989] Ch 1 (CA) the Court of Appeal held that the circumstances in *Errington v Errington & Woods* [1952] 1 KB 290 (CA) could not give rise to an interest in land:

> A mere contractual licence to occupy land is not binding on a purchaser of land even though he has notice of the licence (*Ashburn Anstalt* per Fox LJ at 15).

To hold otherwise would be to ignore earlier binding decisions of the House of Lords (including *King v David Allen & Sons Billposting Ltd* [1916] 2 AC 54 (HL)). Consequently, section 34–019 of the 2012 edition of Megarry and Wade reads very differently from its predecessor (quoted earlier). The 'old restraints', such as the need for certainty of conveyancing and its formal processes, appear to have reassumed their importance, albeit that the equity raised by a proprietary estoppel retains its proprietary character. The history of licences is an important reminder to the land lawyer that she must be prepared to look beneath the surface of the law when asked to comment on or to evaluate any particular rule.

Summary

3.1 Licences are a mechanism, like interests in land, that allow a person to enjoy rights over land. Historically, however, they have not been recognised as proprietary rights.

3.2 A licence is a permission to be on land; it may be a bare licence or one coupled with an interest in the land, such as a *profit à prendre*, or it may arise through contract or estoppel.

3.3 A bare licence can be revoked at any time.

3.4 A licence coupled with an interest in land will last as long as the interest in question.

3.5 Whether a contractual licence can be revoked depends on the terms of the contract.

3.6 An estoppel licence may be awarded by the court when a person acts to her detriment in reliance on a promise that she will gain an interest in land. Licences by estoppel and licences that give rise to a constructive trust may bind a buyer of land.

Summary cont'd

3.7 Despite attempts to raise contractual licences to proprietary status during the latter half of the twentieth century, it now seems to be accepted that licences cannot bind a third party unless they are combined with a recognised interest in land, such as a *profit à prendre*, constructive trust or estoppel.

Exercises

3.1 Complete the online quiz on the topics covered in this chapter on the companion website.

3.2 Are licences property?

3.3 John and Linda are the registered proprietors of a large house. When they bought it 15 years ago, it was very rundown, and they did not have the time or money to renovate it by themselves. They therefore agreed with Hannah and Joshua (Linda's sister and brother-in-law) that they would move in and help with the work; they said Hannah and Joshua would be able to make their home there. Hannah won £15,000 in the lottery and lent it to John and Linda so they could pay for a new roof. Joshua gave up his job to work on the house and look after John and Linda's children. He has been in hospital since falling off a ladder while mending one of the chimneys last year.

John and Linda are now going to separate. They have transferred the land to Damien, who has been registered as proprietor. Advise Hannah and Joshua.

You can find suggested answers to exercises 3.2 and 3.3 on the companion website.

Further reading

Anderson, 'Of Licences and Similar Mysteries' (1979) 42 MLR 203

Battersby, 'Contractual and Estoppel Licences as Proprietary Interests in Land' [1991] Conv 36

Dewar, 'Licences and Land Law: An Alternative View' (1986) 49 MLR 741

McFarlane, 'Identifying Property Rights: A Reply to Mr Watt' [2003] Conv 473

Part II

The estates and interests

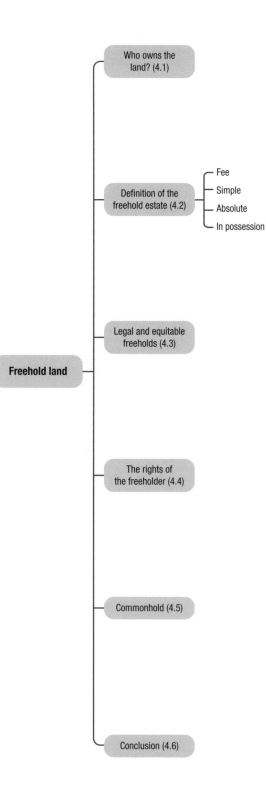

Chapter 4

Freehold land

Key concepts

▶ **Commonhold** – a statutory form of registered freehold that can be used to divide the ownership of a building or estate with shared common parts.
▶ **Freehold** – the most complete form of ownership of land recognised by English law.

4.1 Who owns the land?

Is it true that only the monarch can own land in England and Wales? This is the sort of question that is sometimes asked in pub quizzes and of the occasional land lawyer at certain types of party. Unfortunately, there is not a simple 'yes' or 'no' answer, and, even more unfortunately, many partygoers are not prepared to linger long enough to discover the full truth. One fairly concise answer to the question can be found on the Crown Estate's website (www.thecrownestate.co.uk/about-us/faqs/escheats-faqs/ accessed 18 October 2014):

> Under our legal system, the monarch (currently Queen Elizabeth II), as head of state, owns the superior interest in all land in England, Wales and Northern Ireland – even freehold land is not owned outright, as the monarch has a superior interest. This is not usually relevant, though it can become relevant if freehold land becomes ownerless.

Any attempt to answer the question will, of course, have to examine what is meant by the word 'ownership'. Some of the relevant issues were introduced at Section 1.3 as part of the discussion of the meaning of the word 'property'. Linked to this is the question of how the various rights that are normally accorded to an owner are distributed between the monarch (as outright owner) and the immediate owner. If the immediate owner has effective control of the land, does the monarch's superior interest really matter?

Since 1925, English law has recognised two main 'ownership' interests in land that can be enjoyed by those people who are not head of state: the freehold and the leasehold (Law of Property Act (LPA) 1925, s 1(1); see Section 2.3.1). All other interests in land are granted out of these estates (rather than over the land itself). Of the two legal estates, the superior is the freehold. This chapter considers what a freehold estate comprises, and what rights are incident to holding such an estate. Leases are considered in Chapters 5 and 6.

4.2 Definition of the freehold estate

There used to be many different legal estates, with different rules about inheritance and transfer. Detailed accounts of the history of the doctrine of estates can be found in the early chapters of major land law texts. (See, for example, Cheshire, 2011, 48–60; Megarry and Wade, 2012, ch 3.) Only two legal estates now remain:

▶ *a freehold* is a holding for an indefinite period (providing there is someone able to inherit the land under a will or through the rules of intestacy on the freeholder's death);

▶ *a leasehold* is a holding for a fixed time (the maximum possible duration of the lease must be certain when the lease is granted; the detailed rules, including the possibility of periodic tenancies, are considered in Section 5.4.2).

Because of the reforms of 1925, the legal freehold estate is the basic concept of land-ownership in both registered and unregistered land.

The 'fee simple' is the only surviving legal freehold estate; its proper name is *fee simple absolute in possession*. Each of these words has a particular significance.

fee	This word comes from 'fief' (*feudum* in Latin), the basic concept of the feudal system. By the sixteenth century, a fee had come to be recognised as an estate that could be inherited. It did not automatically return to the feudal landlord when the tenant died.
simple	The fee is 'simple' because it does not suffer from the complications of the fee tail (also known as the 'entail'). The fee simple can be inherited by anyone the owner wishes. The fee tail has to pass to a direct descendant (for example, a child or grandchild), and it can be restricted to, for example, only male children (a 'tail male'). It has not been possible to create new entails since 1997 (Trusts of Land and Appointment of Trustees Act 1996, Sched. 1, para 5), but entails created before 1997 remain valid.
absolute	The word 'absolute' distinguishes this fee simple from others that are limited in some way. One type of limited fee is the 'fee simple upon condition'. An example is where a mother gives land to her son, but if he marries a solicitor, the land will go to his cousin. A conditional fee must be distinguished from another type of fee, the 'determinable fee simple'. Determinable fees are created by words such as 'until he marries a solicitor'. The difference is very subtle but important. Although only the fee simple absolute can be a legal estate (LPA 1925, s 1(1)), a special exception was made in 1926 for conditional fees simple (LPA 1925, s 7(1), as amended). Conditional fees can now be legal, but the other limited fees simple (including determinable fees) can only exist in equity.
in possession	All interests in land can be 'in possession', 'in remainder' or 'in reversion'. 'In possession' means that the owner is entitled to enjoy the interest now by occupying the land or collecting the rent (LPA 1925, s 205(1)(xix)); the other two mean that the owner will have the right to enjoy the interest after another interest (for example, an interest for life) has ended. In the example above, the son has a conditional fee simple in possession, and the cousin has a fee simple absolute in remainder. However, if the mother gave land to her son on the condition that it would return to her if he married a solicitor, the mother would have a fee simple absolute in *reversion*.

4.3   Legal and equitable freeholds

Of all the possibilities raised above, only the fee simple absolute in possession can be a legal estate (subject to the exception for conditional fees), because of section 1 of the

LPA 1925 (see Section 2.3). The fee tail, therefore, can only be equitable, that is, held behind a trust.

4.4 The rights of the freeholder

In theory, at common law the owner can do whatever he likes with his land (subject, of course, to any interests such as mortgages, easements and restrictive covenants that have already been granted). In 1885, Challis wrote that ownership of the fee simple 'confers … the lawful right to exercise over, upon, and in respect of the land, every act of ownership which can enter into the imagination' (Challis, 1911, 218).

However, even then this was not true. For example, the law of tort could be used to prevent a landowner unreasonably interfering with his neighbour's enjoyment of his land (the doctrine of nuisance). In the old case of *Christie v Davey* [1893] 1 Ch 316 (Ch), Mrs Christie, one of the claimants, was a music teacher who taught some pupils at her home. Mr Davey, who occupied an adjoining house, complained about the frequent music practices. Shortly after Mr Davey's complaint, a series of unusual and loud noises began from within his house, which significantly interfered with the comfort of Mrs Christie's pupils. Mr Justice North granted an injunction requiring Mr Davey to cease from his vindictive noise-making. He was:

> persuaded that what was done by the Defendant was done only for the purpose of annoyance, and in my opinion it was not a legitimate use of the Defendant's house to use it for the purpose of vexing and annoying his neighbours (at 327).

North J refused to impose a similar injunction on Mr and Mrs Christie as he considered that their use of their house did not constitute actionable nuisance. However, he did suggest instrument practice should finish by 11 o'clock each evening (at 328).

Today, legislation has imposed great limitations on the owner of land, so that, for instance, he cannot prevent aeroplanes from flying above his land and may not mine coal, demolish a listed building, kill protected species or pollute water; he must also observe building regulations and licensing laws. The Town and Country Planning Acts impose probably the best-known limitation on landowners. When the Act of 1947 established the foundations of our present system of planning law, it was suggested by some that the fee simple had been destroyed by the powers taken by the government to control land use. Few people would say so now, since most landowners appreciate the fact that the value of their land is maintained for them by the local authority, which can forbid or permit their neighbours to open an amusement arcade or a garage, for example.

4.5 Commonhold

Although freehold is the most extensive of the two estates, it has its limitations. Historically, English law has been highly suspicious of so-called 'flying freeholds', that is, a freehold estate that does not include the surface of the land. Further, as will become evident in Chapter 9, in freehold land it is frequently not possible to enforce covenants against successors of the original covenantor. However, being able to enforce a covenant against a successor in title will be very important in certain circumstances. Consider, for example, the owner of a flat in a block of flats. In order to protect the structural integrity of his own property he, or his lessor, might wish to seek to enforce a repairing covenant against his neighbour. Until recently, the only answer has been for all the flats in the block to be held on long leases, since, as is explained in Chapter 6, leasehold covenants are enforceable against successors in title.

However, the use of leases in this situation is not without its own difficulties. The most obvious is that because a lease runs for a defined period it is a diminishing asset (see Section 5.2). A lease will often become unmarketable well before its term is due to expire because mortgage lenders are unwilling to lend on leases with less than 60 years to run. A further difficulty may be the inability of the tenants to get the lessor to manage the building and carry out his obligations to repair and maintain the common parts while keeping the tenants' financial contributions at a reasonable level. These problems have been addressed at various times by Parliament, but no entirely satisfactory solution has been found. The latest attempt is found in Part 2 of the Commonhold and Leasehold Reform Act 2002, which gives qualifying tenants of long residential leaseholds the right to take over management of the property from the lessor, even if the latter is not at fault.

In the final decades of the twentieth century, there was considerable discussion about proposals to introduce a new form of land holding called 'commonhold', based on strata title in Australia and condominium title in the United States. After a good deal of uncertainty and procrastination, these proposals were enacted in the Commonhold and Leasehold Reform Act 2002. Part 1 of the Act, which came into force on 27 September 2004, introduced the 'freehold estate in commonhold land' to English law.

A property to be owned on a commonhold basis (for example, a block of flats or an industrial estate) is registered at the Land Registry by the freehold owner as a 'freehold estate in commonhold land'. The property is divided into 'units', each held by the unit owner on a freehold basis. The owner of each unit becomes a member of the Commonhold Association, a private company limited by guarantee, which owns and has responsibility for the upkeep of the common parts of the building. Under the regulations in the Commonhold Community Statement (CCS), each unit owner has obligations (for example, to maintain his unit in good repair and to contribute to the commonhold expenditure) binding on his successors and enforceable by the Association – a kind of private local community law. The enforcement of the rules in the CCS takes place initially through an internal complaints procedure, and then, depending on regulations introduced through secondary legislation, through some form of mediation or arbitration or through an ombudsman, before finally moving towards formal legal proceedings.

The advantage of the commonhold scheme is that all the obligations in the CCS are binding on all unit holders at all times, so there is no longer any need to use the unsatisfactory device of a long lease in order to buy an interest in a shared building. The scheme should also remove the associated problems of 'unreasonable and oppressive behaviour by unscrupulous landlords' (Commonhold and Leasehold Reform Consultation Paper, Cm 4843, 2000, 107) and the difficulties of getting mortgage finance in the later years of a lease. Of course, as the Law Commission has remarked, the scheme will not solve the problems by itself: neighbours will not always cooperate, and buildings cannot be repaired for ever. Nevertheless, commonhold offers land developers a new flexibility when building new blocks of flats or developing industrial areas. Despite this, the years since 2004 have seen only a handful of commonhold schemes actually established. It seems to be a case of developers and the banks, which provide the mortgage finance for developments and the purchase of individual flats, preferring the devil they know. (Or, perhaps, their lawyers doing so.) For commentary on and detailed criticism of the implementation of commonhold, see Clarke (2002).

4.6 Conclusion

In English land law, the predominant method of owning land is to hold the freehold estate. At this point, the ancient historical roots of modern English land law show through the ground: the origins of freehold land can take lawyers straight back to the conquest of England by William of Normandy in 1066. In theory, all the land in England and Wales is still owned by the Crown, with individuals holding interests in the Queen's land. However, although we may use the same words as lawyers in the eleventh or fifteenth centuries, the meaning and context are quite different. Our forebears might recognise the terms, but they would not understand our law.

This is just one illustration of how land law has developed and continues to develop in response to changing social, economic and political conditions. Whenever a case or statute appears to result in inappropriate or merely technical rules, it is worth taking a step back from the law to consider the conditions in which those rules first developed. One of the tasks of the lawyer is to consider whether and how those rules can be used to meet contemporary needs – or whether the time has come for them to be replaced and to campaign accordingly.

Summary

4.1 The basic unit of ownership in modern land law is the legal fee simple.

4.2 'Fee simple absolute in possession' means an interest in land which can be inherited by anyone, is not restricted by some future event and is enjoyed at the moment.

4.3 Other types of fee can only exist as equitable interests.

4.4 Although it has been asserted that the owner in fee simple absolute in possession has unlimited powers over his land, both common law and statute have greatly restricted his freedom of action.

4.5 A new form of landownership, commonhold (a special type of freehold estate), was introduced in 2004, but it has not been widely adopted.

Exercises

4.1 Complete the online quiz on the topics covered in this chapter on the companion website.

Further reading

Bright, 'Of Estates and Interests: A Tale of Ownership and Property Rights' in Bright and Dewar (eds), *Land Law Themes and Perspectives* (Oxford University Press 1998) 529

Burn and Cartwright, *Cheshire and Burn's Modern Law of Real Property* (18th edn, Oxford University Press 2012) 48–60

Further reading cont'd

Clarke, 'The Enactment of Commonhold – Problems, Principles and Perspectives' [2002] Conv 349

Challis, *The Law of Real Property, Chiefly in Relation to Conveyancing* (3rd edn by Sweet, Butterworth 1911)

Harpum, Bridge and Dixon, *Megarry & Wade: The Law of Real Property* (8th edn, Sweet & Maxwell 2012) ch 3

Chapter 5 follows overleaf.

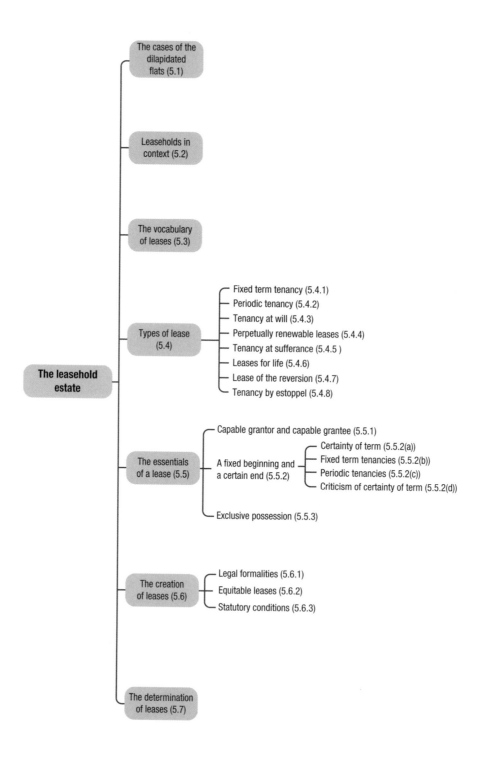

The leasehold estate

- The cases of the dilapidated flats (5.1)
- Leaseholds in context (5.2)
- The vocabulary of leases (5.3)
- Types of lease (5.4)
  - Fixed term tenancy (5.4.1)
  - Periodic tenancy (5.4.2)
  - Tenancy at will (5.4.3)
  - Perpetually renewable leases (5.4.4)
  - Tenancy at sufferance (5.4.5)
  - Leases for life (5.4.6)
  - Lease of the reversion (5.4.7)
  - Tenancy by estoppel (5.4.8)
- The essentials of a lease (5.5)
  - Capable grantor and capable grantee (5.5.1)
  - A fixed beginning and a certain end (5.5.2)
    - Certainty of term (5.5.2(a))
    - Fixed term tenancies (5.5.2(b))
    - Periodic tenancies (5.5.2(c))
    - Criticism of certainty of term (5.5.2(d))
  - Exclusive possession (5.5.3)
- The creation of leases (5.6)
  - Legal formalities (5.6.1)
  - Equitable leases (5.6.2)
  - Statutory conditions (5.6.3)
- The determination of leases (5.7)

The leasehold estate

Key concepts

- **Certainty of term** – the rule requiring that maximum possible duration of a lease must be ascertainable with certainty at the beginning of the lease.
- **Exclusive possession** – the right to exclude other people, including the landlord, from the land.
- **Lease** – a contractual arrangement giving rise to the relationship of landlord and tenant.
- **Tenancy** – another word for 'lease'.

5.1 The cases of the dilapidated flats

Oval House is a three-storey Victorian mansion block typical of those found in Rushcroft Road, London SW2. The London Borough of Lambeth purchased many of the properties in the area in the 1970s, intending to level them to make way for a new residential development. However, the scheme was delayed, and many of the buildings were occupied by members of a 'vibrant squatting community' (something of its story was told, at the date of writing, at www.urban75.org/brixton/features/rushcroft.html). In 1986, the council agreed that London & Quadrant Housing Trust could use Oval House to provide short-term accommodation for people in urgent need of housing. The agreement between the council and the Trust was called 'a licence'. There was no question of it being a lease: in these circumstances, a lease could only have been created with the express consent of the Secretary of State under section 32(3) of the Housing Act 1985 and no such consent was obtained.

In early 1989, the Trust agreed to allow Mr Bruton to occupy a flat in Oval House. The terms were similar to those that the Trust had used many times before.

> Occupation of short-life accommodation at 2, Oval House, Rushcroft Road, SW2 on a temporary basis. As has been explained to you, the above property is being offered to you by [the Trust] on a weekly licence from 6 February 1989. The trust has the property on licence from [the council] who acquired the property for development ... and pending this development, it is being used to provide temporary housing accommodation. It is offered to you on the condition that you will vacate upon receiving reasonable notice from the trust, which will not normally be less than four weeks. You understand and agree that while you are living in the property, you will allow access at all times during normal working hours to the staff of the trust, the owners and agents for all purposes connected with the work of the trust.

Perhaps unsurprisingly, the flats were in a relatively poor state of repair. The only reason that they were available for the Trust to use to help the homeless at all was the fact that they were due to be demolished. However, in 1995, Mr Bruton brought proceedings in the Lambeth County Court, claiming that the Trust was in breach of a covenant (implied by virtue of the Landlord and Tenant Act 1985, s 11) to keep the premises in repair. As section 11 only applies to leases, the case turned on whether the Trust's agreement with Mr Bruton created a lease or a contractual licence. The main issues, therefore, were:

- What are the ingredients of a lease?
- Which of these ingredients distinguish a lease from a contractual licence?
- Were all the ingredients required for a lease present in Mr Bruton's case?
- What was the significance of the fact that the agreement with Mr Bruton described itself as a 'licence'?
- Could the Trust grant a lease to Mr Bruton when it did not own the freehold or have a lease of the land itself? (The Trust only had a licence to use the land, which is not a property interest; see Chapter 3.)

These questions were answered by the House of Lords in *Bruton v London & Quadrant Housing Trust* [2000] 1 AC 406 (HL) and in a number of related cases, including *Kay v Lambeth LBC* [2006] 2 AC 465 (HL).

5.2 Leaseholds in context

A lease was originally a contract for the occupation of land. It was only in the sixteenth century that leases were recognised as interests in land, so that the rights and duties of the parties were no longer merely contractual, but became attached to the land. Now leaseholds are one of only two interests that are capable of being legal estates in land (LPA 1925, section 1(1); see Section 2.3). However, much of the law of leases is still based on contract law, albeit with overarching statutory provisions controlling residential, business and agricultural tenancies. As Lord Browne-Wilkinson explained in the case of *Hammersmith & Fulham LBC v Monk* [1992] 1 AC 478 (HL) at 491:

> In certain cases a contract between two persons can, by itself, give rise to a property interest in one of them. The contract between a landlord and a tenant is a classic example. The contract of tenancy confers on the tenant a legal estate in the land: such legal estate gives rise to rights and duties incapable of being founded in contract alone.

At times, the courts have tended to emphasise the proprietary nature of leases (as in *Street v Mountford* [1985] AC 809 (HL)). More recently, judges have favoured a more contractual approach, as in *Bruton v London & Quadrant Housing Trust* [2000] 1 AC 406 (HL), on which see Section 5.1 and Section 5.5.1, and *National Car Parks Ltd v The Trinity Development Co (Banbury) Ltd* [2002] 2 P & CR 18 (CA) (see Section 5.5.3).

The commercial advantages of the lease are obvious. A landowner can let other people use her land for a certain period of time (for example, to farm, mine for gravel or live there) in exchange for a regular income. She can make rules about the kinds of things that are (or are not) to be done on the land, and, at the end of the period, she will get the land back. The wealth of the powerful landowning families came, to a large extent, from rental income. Great cities such as London were developed in the eighteenth and nineteenth centuries through building leases. The ancestors of the Duke of Westminster owned large estates in London and granted long leases to speculative builders, subject to strict rules about the density and type of housing. The builders made their profit, the Dukes enjoyed the rent, and at the end of the period the valuable housing estates reverted to the descendants of the first Duke. Thus, London and other cities grew through the carefully planned, high-quality developments of far-sighted landowners – and also, of course, through get-rich-quick rented slums.

Today, leasehold arrangements are still very important. In financial terms, the most significant use of leases is in the business world – for office blocks and factory units, for example. In addition, most flats are bought on long (often 99-year) leases. This overcomes the problems associated with flying freeholds (that is, freehold titles that do not include the surface of the ground) and the enforcement of positive freehold covenants (see Chapter 9). However, long leases have their own problems. In particular, they are diminishing assets. Parliament has intervened (not particularly successfully so far) to give owners of long residential leases of houses the right to extend the period of their leases or, in the case of houses, to buy the freehold (the Leasehold Reform Act 1967 as amended and Part II of the Leasehold Reform, Housing and Urban Development Act 1993). Long leaseholders of flats can join together to acquire the freehold of their block by forming a 'right to enfranchise' company and following the procedure set out in Part I of the Leasehold Reform, Housing and Urban Development Act 1993.

Another problem with leases is that lessors tend to have significantly more power than their tenants or potential tenants. For example, it may be very important for a small business trading from rented premises to be able to renew its lease of those premises. Consequently, the lessor may feel able to demand a higher rent when the lease is due for renewal than she might have been able to charge to a new tenant. Parliament has intervened to protect such tenants with a complex set rules contained in Part II of the Landlord and Tenant Act 1954 and its accompanying regulations. Many residential tenants are also vulnerable to the interests of more powerful lessors, especially those who rent their homes because they are unable to climb onto the so-called property ladder. Short leases for housing have been greatly affected by Acts of Parliament since 1915 because of the social and economic importance of decent housing for the community as a whole. Statutes on rent control, security of tenure and repairs (latterly the Rent Act 1977) were intended to protect poor tenants with little bargaining power. The details of these statues, and especially the rules that apply to public-sector residential accommodation, fall outside the scope of this book (and most land law courses). The post-war consensus about the need to protect the security of private residential tenants ended in the 1980s. Statutory protection was reduced (especially by the Housing Act 1988), partly in order to revitalise the private rented sector. Public authorities became less able to provide adequate housing for those excluded from home ownership, and the responsibility in this area was transferred mainly to housing associations. These changes, together with a healthy economy, helped stimulate the so-called buy-to-let market, with lenders eager to provide mortgages to support it. Such lending was quickly curtailed as a response to the financial crisis that hit the British economy and property market at the close of the first decade of the twenty-first century. In many cases, lessors fail to obtain the lender's consent to their leases, with the result that the tenant is at considerable risk of losing his home if the lessor defaults on her mortgage payments, even if the tenant has consistently paid the rent and observed the terms of the tenancy. The Mortgage Repossessions (Protection of Tenants etc) Act 2010 (which came into force on 1 October 2010) seeks to help such tenants by ensuring that they are allowed a reasonable amount of time to find alternative accommodation.

In 2006, the Law Commission published proposals (which included a draft Bill) to replace the present complicated statutory regime of residential tenancies with a much simpler system of occupation contracts based on a consumer protection approach, as in much of the rest of Europe (2006 Law Com 297). The proposals applied to any agreement conferring the right to occupy premises as a home (clause 1(2)(a) of the draft Bill), termed 'occupation contracts'. Had the reforms been introduced, they would have removed the significance of the lease/licence distinction in the residential sector, a distinction that has taken up considerable judicial time (see, in particular, Section 5.5.3).

Despite all its faults, the lease is an instrument of enormous flexibility. For example, leases:

▶ can control housing development, providing both long- and short-term housing;
▶ can provide for the changing needs of businesses;
▶ provide a common and convenient means of holding agricultural land; and
▶ allow land to be used to provide an income and raise capital.

5.3 The vocabulary of leases

There are several words to describe a lease, including 'tenancy', 'letting', 'demise' and 'term of years absolute' (see Section 5.5). All these words have the same meaning, but lawyers tend to use 'tenancy' and 'letting' for a short period and 'lease' or 'demise' for a long one. The word 'term' can refer to one of the covenants or conditions set out in the lease, but it is also used to refer to the duration of the lease (as in 'term of years absolute').

The following fictional story, which is not untypical of the type of problem questions used to assess this area of law, will help to illustrate some of the other important terms relating to leases.

> Louise let the basement flat in her house to Teresa, for three years, at £500 per month. Teresa decided to live elsewhere and sold ('assigned') her lease to Ahmed, who then rented the flat to Sam for six months. Then Louise decided to move, and sold her whole house (including the freehold, the 'reversion', of the flat) to Robert.

This story is shown diagrammatically in Figure 5.1. Such diagrams are very useful for sorting out the characters in a problem on leases. In this book, leases (including subleases) are always shown as vertical lines, and assignments as horizontal lines. Setting out the chain of events in a diagram, even in a fairly simple case or problem question, can help avoid confusing assignments with grants of leases and subleases.

▶ Louise owned the freehold; she is the original lessor (landlord, owner of the freehold, owner of the freehold reversion).
▶ Robert is the new lessor (assignee of the freehold reversion).

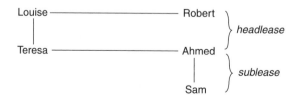

Figure 5.1 Assigning and subletting – an example

- Teresa is the original tenant (lessee, owner of the lease).
- Ahmed is the current tenant (lessee, owner of the headlease, tenant's assignee, assignee of the headlease). He is also the lessor in the middle, the *mesne* (pronounced 'mean') landlord.
- Sam is the subtenant (sublessee, owner of the sublease).

The difference between an assignment and a sublease is important:

- An assignment is the transfer of the whole of a person's interest in the land. In the example above, Teresa assigned her lease when she sold the whole of her remaining interest to Ahmed (shown by a horizontal line in Figure 5.1).
- A sublease is created when a tenant grants a separate lease to a third party. In the example above, Ahmed created a sublease when he sold Sam a lesser period than he himself owned (shown by a vertical line in Figure 5.1). A sublease must terminate at least a day before the end of the term of the headlease.

5.4 Types of lease

There are several different types of lease. Although this chapter is mainly concerned with fixed term tenancies and periodic tenancies, it is important to be able to recognise other types of tenancy when they occur (as the case of *Mexfield Housing Co-operative Ltd v Berrisford* [2012] 1 AC 955 (SC), considered at Section 5.5.2, illustrates).

5.4.1 Fixed term tenancy

A lease granted for a specific period of time and which will terminate at the end of that period.

5.4.2 Periodic tenancy

A 'periodic tenancy' is a lease for a specific period that can be continually repeated until one side gives notice bringing it to an end. A weekly or monthly period is common for furnished accommodation, and a yearly period for agricultural tenancies. If a person uses land and regularly pays money to the owner, then, provided the tenant has exclusive possession (see Section 5.5.3), the common law implies a periodic tenancy unless the parties intended something else. The period of the tenancy is decided by the period by which rent is assessed, not necessarily by the period of payment (*Richardson v Langridge* (1811) 4 Taunt 128). Thus, if the rent is '£1,000 per year, payable monthly', there is an implied legal yearly tenancy. For a more detailed consideration of periodic tenancies, see Cheshire (2011, 204–18).

5.4.3 Tenancy at will

A tenancy at will is, in some respects, similar to a licence. The 'tenant' has exclusive possession of the land, but either side can end the arrangement at any time, and it is not an estate in land. Tenancies at will can be created expressly or by implication, typically where the tenant has moved into possession, or is holding over at the end of the lease while the terms of a new lease are being negotiated.

The circumstances giving rise to an implied tenancy at will can be very similar to those creating an implied periodic tenancy (see Section 5.5.2(c)). The distinction is important because whereas periodic tenants have the protection of various statutory schemes, tenants at will do not. In many cases, the question of rent will be decisive. In *Banjo v Brent LBC* [2005] 1 WLR 2520 (CA), Mr Banjo originally occupied his house under a long lease and continued in occupation after the lease had expired. The Court of Appeal held that this was a tenancy at will and not an implied periodic tenancy because, as Chadwick LJ observed:

> Mr Banjo paid no rent after the end of the contractual term of the long lease; and, so far as appears from the evidence, the Borough did not demand (or take any steps to enforce) payment of rent (at [18]).

However, payment of rent is not conclusive, as according to Nicholls LJ in *Javad v Mohammed Aqil* [1991] 1 WLR 1007 (CA):

> The law will imply, from what was agreed and all the surrounding circumstances, the terms the parties are to be taken to have intended to apply (at 1012).

Erimus Housing Ltd v Barclays Wealth Trustees (Jersey) Ltd [2014] 2 P & CR 4 (CA) arose following protracted negotiations for a new tenancy after an original lease had expired in October 2009. The tenant had remained in occupation and paid rent. Although the terms of a new lease were eventually agreed, it was never completed and the tenant had indicated at several times that it intended to vacate the premises before the end of the term of the new lease. According to Patten LJ at [23]:

> When a party holds over after the end of the term of a lease he does so, without more, as a tenant on sufferance until his possession is consented to by the landlord. With such consent he becomes at the very least a tenant at will … The payment of rent gives rise to no presumption of a periodic tenancy. Rather, the parties' contractual intentions fall to be determined by looking objectively at all relevant circumstances.

Where the parties are negotiating the form of a new lease, as here, the usual inference will be that the parties did not intend to enter into any type of contractual arrangement, such as a periodic tenancy, that would be inconsistent with the ongoing negotiations.

5.4.4 Perpetually renewable leases

The perpetually renewable lease differs from the periodic tenancy (see Section 5.4.2) because the lease continues as long as the tenant chooses, with the lessor unable to give notice in any circumstances. This kind of arrangement was formerly common in agricultural lettings with absentee lessors, but is anomalous within the 1925 structure of land ownership. Since 1925, all new leases of this type are automatically converted into a lease for 2,000 years, with special rules for giving notice (see Schedule 15 of the LPA 1922). The courts now lean against interpreting a renewal clause as being perpetual. (See, for example, *Marjorie Burnett Ltd v Barclay* (1980) 258 EG 642 (Ch), where Nourse J held that a right to renew with a further right of renewal gave the tenant the right to renew twice, rather than perpetually.)

5.4.5 Tenancy at sufferance

Tenancy at sufferance arises if a tenant remains in occupation ('holds over') after the lease has expired, without the lessor's agreement. The lessor can evict the tenant at any time, but if she accepts rent, the tenant becomes a tenant at will or even a periodic tenant.

5.4.6 Leases for life

Before 1926, there were two types of lease: the term of years absolute and the lease for life (or until marriage), and both could exist as legal estates. By section 1 of the LPA 1925, only the first of these can now be legal, but because some people with legal leases for life or until marriage would have suddenly found themselves to be merely equitable lessees on 1 January 1926, section 149(6) of the LPA 1925 converts their interests into legal leases for 90 years, provided that rent is payable (as, for example, in *Mexfield Housing Co-operative Ltd v Berrisford*). Such a lease can be determined by one month's notice following the death or marriage.

5.4.7 Lease of the reversion

Where a lessor creates a lease of her remaining interest, she is leasing the reversion. This is also called a 'concurrent lease'. The tenant of the reversion has the right to collect rent and enforce other covenants against the tenant of the lease. Note that a *lease of the reversion* is not the same as a *reversionary lease* (see Section 5.5.2(a)).

5.4.8 Tenancy by estoppel

If a person attempts to grant a lease that she could not grant because she had no title, she is estopped from subsequently denying her tenant's rights against her. This is part of the ordinary principle of estoppel. Such a tenancy is personal and does not create an estate in land. However, if the lessor subsequently gains the legal title, then the tenant is automatically 'clothed' with the legal lease (this is known as 'feeding the estoppel'). For judicial comment on tenancies by estoppel, see Lord Hoffmann's speech in *Bruton v London & Quadrant Housing Trust* [2000] 1 AC 406 (HL).

In the *Bruton* case, the Trust expressly granted a licence rather than a tenancy; however, because its terms included all the ingredients characteristic of a tenancy, Mr Bruton was held to have a non-estate lease (see Section 5.5.1). In *Kay v Lambeth LBC* [2006] AC 465 (HL), the House of Lords had to consider whether a 'Bruton-style' non-estate lease was binding on the council as the owner of the freehold in the block of flats. The tenancy could not have been binding on the council when it was originally created, as the council did not grant it, and neither was it carved out of any estate granted by the council to the Trust. However, in 1995, after the grant of the tenancy to Mr Bruton, the council had granted the Trust a legal lease of the block of flats. This legal leasehold estate in the land was enough to 'feed the estoppel' implicit in the non-estate lease to Mr Bruton, converting Mr Bruton's tenancy into a legal estate. Unfortunately for Mr Bruton, however, his estate was subject to the terms of the 1995 lease. (The Trust could not give Mr Bruton a greater estate than they themselves owned.) In 1999, the council terminated the lease to the Trust, automatically determining any lesser estates dependent upon it, including those held by Mr Bruton and the other tenants of the flats. Consequently, the occupiers of the flats had no estate that they could enforce against the council, although they might have had an action in damages against the Trust if they could demonstrate that it was in breach of its obligations under the tenancies.

5.5   The essentials of a lease

It will often be of significant importance to the parties whether the relationship between them is an interest in the land or merely a contractual right to use the land. Normally, only a lease will be attached to the land so as to automatically bind any third party who acquires the freehold reversion. However, not all leases are interests in land. In *Bruton v London & Quadrant Housing Trust* [2000] 1 AC 406 (HL), the House of Lords held that it was possible to create a purely contractual (or 'non-estate') lease that is not binding on third parties (see Section 5.5.1). Such contractual leases share this characteristic of licences while also affording the occupier of the land many of the statutory rights enjoyed by tenants. In practice, non-estate leases are very rare. In most cases, the lawyer's task is to determine whether a particular relationship is a lease or a mere licence. Licences are considered in detail in Chapter 3, and a number of more unusual types of lease have been explained at Section 5.4.

The full title of a leasehold estate in the 1925 legislation is 'a term of years absolute'. This term is defined at great length in section 205(1)(xxvii) of the LPA 1925, but most of the rules about what does and does not constitute a lease are to be found in the case law.

A term of years absolute requires:

▶ a capable grantor and a capable grantee (see Section 5.5.1);
▶ a fixed beginning and an end date that is capable of being fixed (see Section 5.5.2); and
▶ exclusive possession to be given to the tenant (see Section 5.5.3).

Section 205(1)(xxvii) of the LPA 1925 defines a term of years absolute as existing 'whether or not at a rent'. Although it is usual for a rent and/or a premium to be paid by the tenant, there is no requirement for consideration if the lease is created by a deed (see *Ashburn Anstalt v WJ Arnold & Co* [1989] Ch 1 (CA)). A premium is an upfront capital sum paid by the tenant to the lessor. For example, the tenant of a long lease of a flat will usually pay a premium at the beginning of the lease, instead of a monthly rent, as is usual with shorter residential tenancies.

5.5.1   Capable grantor and capable grantee

The requirement for a capable grantor and capable grantee is not usually a problem. A minor (person under the age of 18) may not hold a legal estate in land (LPA 1925, s 1(6)). The law also restricts the rights of those unable to deal with their own affairs because of mental illness or deterioration to create or transfer legal estates in land. The power of corporate bodies to grant and accept leases will depend upon whether they are given the necessary powers by their memorandum and articles of association (in the case of a limited company) or by statute (in the case of local authorities and government-created agencies).

Prior to the case of *Bruton*, it was generally thought that a lessor could only grant a lease if that lease were capable of existing as a legal estate. This required the lessor to own an estate in the land greater than the lease being granted (based on the principle of *nemo dat quod non habet* – no one can give something which they do not have). However, in *Bruton*, the House of Lords held that it was possible to create a purely contractual (or non-estate) lease. As Blackburne J (sitting in the Court of Appeal) explained in the case of *Islington LBC v Green* [2005] EWCA Civ 56 at [10]:

> The relationship of landlord and tenant is not dependent on whether the lease or tenancy creates an estate or other proprietary interest which may be binding on third parties. Whether a lease creates a proprietary interest in turn will depend upon whether the landlord has an interest out of which he has granted it.

In *Bruton*, Mr Bruton had brought an action against the Trust, based on the covenants for repair that are implied into leases (but not licences) by section 11 of the Landlord and Tenant Act 1985. (The facts are set out in detail in Section 5.1.) Having decided that the agreement satisfied all the other requirements for a lease (the main issue was whether exclusive possession had been granted; see Section 5.5.3), the House of Lords concluded that Mr Bruton had a tenancy of the flat even though he held no legal estate in the land. Consequently, section 11 applied to the arrangement between Mr Bruton and the Trust. While non-estate tenancies like Mr Bruton's may have significant implications for the original parties, their impact on third parties is much more limited, since they do not constitute proprietary interests (see *Kay v Lambeth LBC* [2006] 2 AC 465 (HL), considered in Section 5.4.8).

5.5.2 A fixed beginning and a certain end

5.5.2(a) Certainty of term

The period of a lease (its term) can be anything from a few hours to thousands of years. It must, however, be certain. The term does not need to start on the date of the document creating it; it can be set to start up to 21 years in the future (LPA 1925, s 149(3)). Such a lease is called a 'reversionary lease'. However, whenever the term begins, its maximum duration must be ascertainable at the outset (although the terms of the lease may allow for it to end ('determine') earlier; see Section 5.7).

Many leases will state a fixed beginning and a fixed end, but even where this is not the case, the facts may be fitted into the definition of a 'term of years absolute'. As Lord Greene MR explained in *Lace v Chantler* [1944] KB 368 (CA) at 370:

> A term created by a leasehold tenancy agreement must be expressed either with certainty and specifically or by reference to something which can, at the time when the lease takes effect, be looked at as a certain ascertainment of what the term was meant to be.

The present requirements for certainty of term were recently summarised by Lord Neuberger MR in the Supreme Court case of *Mexfield Housing Co-operative Ltd v Berrisford* [2012] 1 AC 955 (SC) at [33]:

(i) an agreement for a term, whose maximum duration can be identified from the inception can give rise to a valid tenancy;

(ii) an agreement which gives rise to a periodic arrangement determinable by either party can also give rise to a valid tenancy;

(iii) an agreement could not give rise to a tenancy as a matter of law if it was for a term whose maximum duration was uncertain at the inception;

(iv) (a) a fetter on a right to serve notice to determine a periodic tenancy was ineffective if the fetter is to endure for an uncertain period, but (b) a fetter for a specified period could be valid.

5.5.2(b) Fixed term tenancies

Prudential Assurance Co Ltd v London Residuary Body [1992] 2 AC 386 (HL) concerned an attempt by a London council to grant a lease of a piece of land until it was 'required by the council for the purposes of the widening of Walworth Road and the street paving works rendered necessary thereby'. Confirming previous authorities, including *Lace v Chantler*, the House of Lords held that there was insufficient certainty about the date of the end of the lease, and therefore it could not be a valid term of years absolute. However, it went on to hold that there was, instead, a lease 'from year to year' (a periodic legal tenancy; see Section 5.5.2(c)) which the council's successor in title could end by giving six months' notice (as is usual under a yearly tenancy).

5.5.2(c) Periodic tenancies

Although a 'periodic tenancy' is theoretically a lease for a specific term, in practice the term is continually renewed until one side gives notice bringing it to an end. In *Mexfield Housing Co-operative Ltd v Berrisford* [2012] 1 AC 955 (SC) the Supreme Court had to consider whether there was sufficient certainty of term for Ms Berrisford to have a periodic tenancy. The agreement was expressed to be from month to month, but it also provided that Mexfield could not terminate Ms Berrisford's occupancy except in very limited circumstances. The Court of Appeal decided that there was no lease because the maximum term of the agreement was rendered uncertain by the limitations on Mexfield's right to terminate it. The Supreme Court agreed that Ms Berrisford's lease did not satisfy the certainty requirements for a periodic tenancy. However, the Court was persuaded of the existence of a common law rule (albeit a rather ancient and obscure one) that converts an attempt to grant a lease to an individual for an uncertain term into a lease for life. Such leases for life are, in turn, converted into leases for a fixed term of 90 years by section 149(6) of the Law of Property Act 1925 (see Section 5.4.6). Consequently, Ms Berrisford had been granted a 90-year lease.

This result seems to reflect the original intentions of the parties in *Mexfield*, but this may not always be the case. Further, it is not clear whether the reasoning in *Mexfield* is limited to attempts to grant periodic tenancies. If it also applies to attempts to grant fixed term leases, the results of both *Lace v Chantler* and *Prudential Assurance Co Ltd* (see Section 5.5.2(b)) would be different if decided today. What is clear, however, is that the rule cannot be used unless the original tenant is an individual; it was never possible to create a lease for life in favour of a company.

5.5.2(d) Criticism of certainty of term

Although well established in English law, the rule requiring certainty of term has attracted considerable judicial criticism because of the way in which it limits the contractual freedom of the parties for little apparent benefit. For example, Lord Browne-Wilkinson concluded his speech in the *Prudential* case with the following words:

> This bizarre outcome results from the application of an ancient and technical rule of law … No one has produced any satisfactory rationale for the genesis of this rule. No one has been able to point to any useful purpose that it serves at the present day (at 396).

His comments were echoed by Lord Neuberger MR some twenty years later in *Mexfield*. However, Lord Neuberger went on to set out six reasons (at [35]–[37]) why the Supreme Court could not simply jettison the rule. It is unlikely that the law will be reformed without the intervention of Parliament. The certainty-of-term requirement remains, therefore, a potential stumbling block for those who do not seek legal advice and those, as in *Mexfield*, seeking to give effect to arrangements highly sensitive to the tension between the proprietary and the contractual characteristics of leasehold estates (see Section 5.2).

5.5.3   Exclusive possession

If a person occupying another's land does not have exclusive possession (the right to keep the owner out), she is not a tenant under a lease but only a licensee. The word 'licensee' describes anyone who has a permission to be on land. These 'non-interests-in-land' are the subject of Chapter 3. A licence can be created by contract, with a regular payment of what looks like rent, in which case it may closely resemble a lease. However, licences are merely personal rights: they cannot usually be transferred to third parties and are unlikely to bind a buyer of the land.

The difference between a lease and a licence is 'notoriously difficult' (*Bridge* [1986] Conv 344), and there are hundreds of pages of judgments devoted to explaining the difference. Historically, the distinction was very important in the residential sector because many residential tenants had significant statutory rights. The Rent Act 1977, or its equivalent, gave protection of their occupation and the right to claim a fair rent. 'Mere licensees' enjoyed neither of these statutory protections, although certain terms are implied into licences (see Section 3.5.1). However, this difference is no longer of such importance. Lessors are unlikely to try to create a licence rather than a lease, since the Housing Act 1988 introduced the form of short-term residential tenancy known as the 'assured shorthold' tenancy with effect from 15 January 1989. Assured shorthold tenancies allow the lessor to receive a market rent and considerably limit the tenant's statutory security. The case law nevertheless remains relevant to commercial agreements, to any occupation agreements made before 15 January 1989 and in cases where an occupier must hold a lease in order to gain the benefit of a statute (as, for example, in *Bruton*).

The decision of the House of Lords in *Street v Mountford* [1985] AC 809 (HL) was a milestone in the case law on the lease/licence distinction. Mr Street (a solicitor) let Mrs Mountford live in his house in return for a weekly payment. In a written agreement, headed 'Licence', she accepted rules about visitors and heating, and eviction if the 'licence fee' was more than a week late. Mr Street reserved the right to enter the house to inspect it. Such agreements had formerly been assumed to be licences; in this case, the agreement between Mr Street and Mrs Mountford clearly stated that it was not intended to create a tenancy protected under the Rent Act 1977. Despite this, the House of Lords held that this was a weekly tenancy, thus allowing Mrs Mountford to claim the protection of the Rent Act.

Lord Templeman was clear that an occupier of residential land must be either a tenant or a licensee, and that:

> The tenant possessing exclusive possession is able to exercise the rights of an owner of land, which is in the real sense his land albeit temporarily and subject to certain restrictions. A tenant armed with exclusive possession can keep out strangers and keep out the landlord (at 816).

The normal test of a tenancy is the factual question of 'exclusive possession' rather than the expressed intention of the parties:

> The occupier is a lodger [licensee] if the landlord provides attendance or services which require the landlord or his servants to exercise unrestricted access to and use of the

premises ... If on the other hand residential accommodation is granted for a term at a rent with exclusive possession, the landlord providing neither attendance nor services, the grant is a tenancy ... The manufacture of a five-pronged implement for digging results in a fork even if the manufacturer, unfamiliar with the English language, insists he intended to make and has made a spade (per Lord Templeman at 817–18, 819).

The case was held to apply to all occupation agreements, including shops and agricultural land. It soon became clear, however, that multiple occupation, as is common in rented flats, posed different problems. In *AG Securities v Vaughan* and *Antoniades v Villiers* [1990] 1 AC 417 (HL), the House of Lords held, in the first of this pair of cases heard together, that a group of four people who shared a flat could not be tenants, because they had independent agreements that did not confer a right of exclusive possession on any occupant but merely a right to share the flat with others. Further, because the agreements had been made with the four occupants on different dates and had different terms and rents, they could not be construed as a joint tenancy, which would be necessary for them to co-own a legal estate in the land (see Sections 10.3 and 10.4). Consequently, the four occupants were merely licensees. In the second case, however, a 'Licence Agreement', which seemed to give the owner the right to sleep in the tiny flat with a cohabiting couple, was held to be a tenancy. The term looked as if it denied exclusive possession to the couple, but it was held to be a sham, inserted into the agreement merely in order to avoid giving Rent Act protection to the occupants, and it therefore had no effect.

These cases, and the many subsequent decisions, cannot provide all the answers. Essentially, the question is whether the agreement itself gave exclusive possession to the tenant (or the tenants jointly) so that they had the right to keep the owner out. However, it is often impossible to decide what the agreement means, or whether a term in it is a sham, without looking at the facts of the whole case. Thus, the House of Lords decided in *Westminster City Council v Clarke* [1992] 2 AC 288 (HL) that a person given temporary accommodation by a local council did not have a tenancy but only a licence. Lord Templeman held that this was 'a very special case' (at 302), quite different from private lettings. He held that there was no exclusive possession here because of the purpose of this agreement. A term that the occupant could be moved at any time to another room (thereby denying the occupant the degree of control characteristic of a tenant) was not a sham, because the council needed it in order to fulfil its statutory duty to vulnerable people.

The decision in *Clarke* may be compared with that in *Bruton* (see Sections 5.1 and 5.5.1). Despite the very clear wording of the licence agreement (and the fact that the Trust did not hold a legal estate in the land), the House of Lords found that Mr Bruton had exclusive possession of his flat. He was, therefore, a tenant and not a mere licensee. Lord Hoffmann stated:

> There is nothing to suggest that he was to share possession with the trust, the council or anyone else. The trust did not retain such control over the premises as was inconsistent with Mr Bruton having exclusive possession, as was the case in *Westminster City Council v. Clarke*. The only rights which it reserved were for itself and the council to enter at certain times and for limited purposes. As Lord Templeman said in *Street v. Mountford* ... such an express reservation 'only serves to emphasise the fact that the grantee is entitled to exclusive possession and is a tenant' (at 413–14).

The principle in *Street v Mountford*, that the status of an agreement depends upon the substantive rights granted by it and not the labels used within it, does not mean that the wording of the agreement is irrelevant, especially in cases where both parties have equal expertise and bargaining power. In *National Car Parks Ltd v The Trinity Development Co (Banbury) Ltd* [2002] 2 P & CR 18 (CA) Arden LJ observed:

> the court must look to the substance and not to the form. But it may help, in determining what the substance was, to consider whether the parties expressed themselves in a particular way ... It would in my judgment be a strong thing for the law to disregard totally the parties' choice of wording and to do so would be inconsistent with the general principle of freedom of contract and the principle that documents should be interpreted as a whole (at [28]).

In *Clear Channel UK Ltd v Manchester City Council* [2005] EWCA Civ 1304, Clear Channel was given the right to erect large advertising signs within various plots of land owned by the council. In each case, the agreement identified the general site of the signs, without defining the specific land on which the signs were to be erected. The Court of Appeal held that for exclusive possession to exist, the extent of the land concerned must be capable of precise definition. Although this was sufficient to decide the issue, Jonathan Parker LJ went on to say:

> the fact remains that this was a contract negotiated between two substantial parties of equal bargaining power and with the benefit of full legal advice. Where the contract so negotiated contains not merely a label but a clause which sets out in unequivocal terms the parties' intention as to its legal effect, I would in any event have taken some persuading that its true effect was directly contrary to that expressed intention (at [29]).

Both Arden LJ and Jonathan Parker LJ emphasised that they had no intention of undermining the principles of *Street v Mountford*. However, at least in the case of a commercial agreement, an examination of the agreement as a whole would now seem to include considering the labels that the parties have chosen to use to describe their agreement.

5.6 The creation of leases

5.6.1 Legal formalities

The rules for the creation of legal interests in land are examined in detail in Section 12.5. Briefly:

- ▶ no formalities are required to create a legal lease for a term not exceeding three years, provided that it takes effect in possession and is at the best rent reasonably obtainable (LPA 1925, ss 52 and 54(2));
- ▶ a deed is necessary to *create* any other legal lease; and
- ▶ a lease for a term exceeding seven years (and certain other types of lease) will only be legal estates if registered at the Land Registry (Land Registration Act (LRA) 2002, s 4(1) and s 27(2)(b); see Section 15.5).

A deed is always required to *assign* a legal lease, even a lease falling within section 54(2) (see *Crago v Julian* [1992] 1 WLR 372 (CA) referred to in Section 12.5.1(c)). If there is no deed where one is needed (or the registered land procedure is not followed), then only an equitable interest will be created or transferred.

5.6.2 Equitable leases

Between the original parties, an equitable lease is probably as good as a legal lease. In *Walsh v Lonsdale* (1882) 21 Ch D 9 (CA), there was an equitable seven-year lease of a mill (see Section 12.3). Since the tenant had moved in and was paying a yearly rent, there was possibly also an implied legal periodic yearly tenancy. The Judicature Acts of 1873 and 1875 (now see Senior Courts Act 1981, s 49(1)) required that where the rules of equity and the common law conflicted on the same matter, the equitable rules should prevail. The landlord of the mill was therefore able to enforce the 'rent in advance' term in the equitable seven-year lease against the tenant.

An equitable lease can effectively be converted into a legal lease through the equitable remedy of specific performance (see *Walsh v Lonsdale*) provided that it complies with any formalities required by section 2 of the Law of Property (Miscellaneous Provisions) Act 1989 (see Section 12.4) and the LRA 2002 (see Chapter 15). However, it should be remembered that, while the behaviour of a claimant is not relevant if she is seeking a legal remedy, equitable remedies are discretionary. In particular, a successful claimant must come to equity 'with clean hands', willing and able to perform her side of the bargain (see *Wilkie v Redsell* [2003] EWCA Civ 926 and Section 12.4.4).

Walsh v Lonsdale was followed in *R v Tower Hamlets LBC, ex p von Goetz* [1999] QB 1019 (CA). Miss von Goetz had a ten-year assured shorthold tenancy of a house. Although a written contract had been agreed (so the requirements of section 2 of the Law of Property (Miscellaneous Provisions) Act 1989 were satisfied), no deed had ever been executed. The council argued that this equitable lease could not attract a renovation grant under the Local Government and Housing Act 1989, since, in its view, such leases had to be legal. In rejecting the council's appeal, Mummery LJ stated that Miss von Goetz had:

> for all practical purposes an interest as good as a legal interest … [and that] if she asked the grantors for a deed to perfect the legal title, there is no ground on which that could be refused (at 1023, 1025).

As indicated above, the terms in the equitable lease will normally prevail as between the original parties. However, this may not be the case if either the lease or the freehold is assigned. The most important rule here is that legal interests bind the world, but equitable interests are subject to the doctrine of notice and its statutory replacements (see Chapters 15 and 16). In addition, depending on the date of its creation, the rights and duties in an equitable lease may not pass with the land (see Sections 6.3.5 and 6.4.5). Whether an equitable lease is as good as a legal lease is an ancient essay question; a useful discussion on this issue is provided in Cheshire (2011, 217–20).

5.6.3   Statutory conditions

Generally, the parties to a lease are free to agree what terms they wish, although the common law will imply certain terms deemed characteristic of the relationship between lessor and lessee. Certain types of lease are also subject to terms implied by statute, such as the repairing obligations imposed on lessors of residential accommodation by section 11 of the Landlord and Tenant Act 1985. (See, for example, *Bruton v London & Quadrant Housing Trust* [2000] 1 AC 406 (HL) and Section 6.2.2.)

Part 4 of the Equality Act 2010, which came into force on 1 October 2010, prohibits owners of property discriminating on the grounds of disability, race, religion or belief, sex, sexual orientation or gender reassignment when choosing a tenant. The Act also requires lessors to make or allow reasonable adjustments to premises required to make it easier for people with disabilities to use them. The only common exceptions concern small houses or flats where the lessor lives on the premises and does not employ any-one to manage them. The 2010 Act simplifies and strengthens anti-discrimination law, which was previously contained in a number of pieces of legislation (including the Sex Discrimination Act 1975, the Race Relations Act 1976 and the Disability Discrimination Act 1995). Such discrimination is a tort, and the victim can take action for damages, an injunction and/or a declaration (see Part 9 of the Equality Act 2010).

5.7 The determination of leases

Since all leases must be only for a limited period, sooner or later they must end ('determine'). This happens through:

- *forfeiture* (where the lessor repossesses the land following the tenant's breach of covenant; see Sections 6.5.1(c) and 6.5.2(a));
- *expiry* (when the period ends);
- *notice* (for example, a month's notice for monthly periodic tenancies, half a year's notice for yearly tenants, or as specified in the lease);
- *surrender* (where the tenant gives up the lease with the agreement of the lessor); there can be no unilateral surrender (see *Barrett v Morgan* [2000] 2 AC 264 (HL));
- *frustration* (very rarely: for example, where there is some physical catastrophe); for discussion of the principles involved, see *National Carriers Ltd v Panalpina (Northern) Ltd* [1981] AC 675 (HL);
- *repudiatory breach* (rarely, but where the lessor is in fundamental breach of her obligations under the lease, it may be possible for the tenant to accept this breach and walk away from the lease; see *Hussein v Mehlman* [1992] 2 EGLR 287 (CC) and Section 6.5.2(b)); or
- *merger* (where the tenant obtains the freehold); certain tenants have the right under statute to extend their long lease or to buy their freehold – the main example being tenants of houses held on long leases at a low rent. When a number of his tenants exercised their rights under the Leasehold Reform Act 1967 to claim the freehold of their leases, the Duke of Westminster in *James v UK* (1986) 8 EHRR 123 argued unsuccessfully that his rights to his property under ECHR Article 1, Protocol 1, had been violated (see Section 1.4). The European Court of Human Rights found that the provisions of the 1967 Act, intended to provide a measure of protection for certain tenants against the diminishing value of their leases (see Section 5.2), were not disproportionate.

Summary

5.1 Leases sit at the boundary between contract law and property law. It is often important to determine whether a particular relationship is a lease or a licence.

5.2 Leases are common because of the flexibility they offer. They are socially and economically important.

5.3 Care must be taken to use the correct vocabulary when considering leases and any transactions involving them.

5.4 There are a number of types of lease. Care must be taken to identify a lease correctly as different rules apply to different types of lease.

Summary cont'd

5.5 The main ingredients of a lease are:

- ▶ a capable grantor and a capable grantee;
- ▶ a fixed beginning and a fixed end; and
- ▶ exclusive possession.

5.6 No formalities are required to create a lease not exceeding three years, provided it is at a market rent and takes effect in possession. Legal leases exceeding three years must be created by deed. Leases exceeding seven years will only be legal leases if completed by registration at the Land Registry. The terms of a lease are those agreed by the parties, together with any implied by statute.

5.7 There are a number of ways, in addition to expiry of the term, in which a lease may be determined.

Exercises

▶ **5.1** Complete the online quiz on the topics covered in this chapter on the companion website.

▶ **5.2** Read *Three Students Revisited* on the companion website. Using the ingredients identified in Section 3.4, decide whether Charlie has a lease or a licence.

5.3 '[It] is common ground (a) that whether a contractual relationship governing the use and occupation of land creates a tenancy or a licence depends not on the label which the parties have applied to it but rather on their substantive rights and obligations under it; and (b) that for a tenancy to exist the occupier must have the right to exclusive possession of the land in question' (*Clear Channel UK Ltd v Manchester City Council* [2005] EWCA Civ 1304 at [11] (Parker LJ)). Discuss.

5.4 Pilbeam owns a house in London, which he converted into three one-bedroom flats some years ago. He granted Yasmin a lease of Flat 1 until she got married. The tenant of Flat 2 is Javed, who was told by Pilbeam that he could have a lease until his parents come over from Pakistan. Six months ago, Pilbeam rented Flat 3 to Brenda on a one-year 'licence agreement' in which Brenda agreed that Pilbeam could sleep there whenever he stayed in London. The three occupants all pay their rent monthly.

Advise Pilbeam whether Yasmin, Javed and Brenda have leases of their flats and, if so, what kinds of lease.

▶ You can find suggested answers to exercises 5.3 and 5.4 on the companion website.

Further reading

Bridge, '*Street* v. *Mountford* – No Hiding Place' [1986] Conv 344

Bright, 'The Uncertainty of Certainty in Leases' (2012) 128 LQR 337

Hinojosa, 'On Property, Leases, Licences, Horses and Carts: Revisiting *Bruton v. London & Quadrant Housing Trust*' [2005] 69 Conv 114

Lower, 'The Bruton Tenancy' [2010] 74 Conv 38

Morgan, 'Leases: Property, Contract or More?' in Dixon (ed.), *Modern Studies in Property Law: Volume 5* (Hart 2009) 419

Roche, 'The Madwoman in the Attic: Freeing Landlord-Tenant Law' [2011] 75 Conv 444

Chapter 6 follows overleaf.

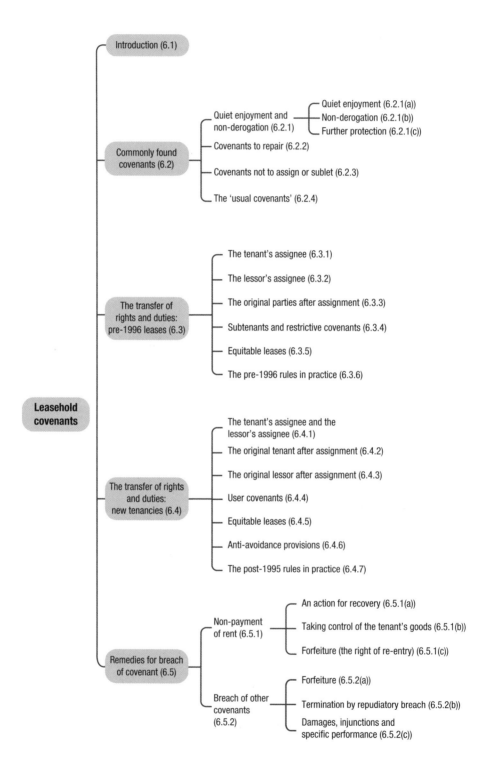

Leasehold covenants

Key concepts

- **Covenant** – a promise made in a deed.
- **Forfeiture** – the right of a landlord to re-enter the land subject to a lease following a breach of covenant by the tenant.
- **New tenancy** – a tenancy granted on or after 1st January 1996 (see section 1(3) of the Landlord and Tenant (Covenants) Act 1995).
- **Privity of contract** – the relationship between the original landlord and the original tenant; this contractual relationship continues even if one or both of them has assigned the lease.
- **Privity of estate** – the relationship between the landlord for the time being and the tenant for the time being.

6.1 Introduction

The previous chapter examined the characteristics of different kinds of lease and how they can be created and ended. A properly drafted business lease or long residential lease will be lengthy and detailed and probably devoted mostly to the obligations of the tenant. On the other hand, some short leases, especially of residential tenancies, may not even be in writing, and any express agreement may have gone no further than to stipulate the amount of rent payable and the frequency with which the tenant should pay it. Even the simplest of leases, however, will contain many more terms than this, and it is fundamental that the parties should understand:

- their obligations under the lease;
- when assignees are bound by, or can enforce, these obligations; and
- the remedies which are available to either party in case of the other's breach.

It is the automatic transfer of both parties' rights and duties under the lease (the fact that covenants 'run with the land') which makes leases so useful. Anyone who buys either the lease or the reversion takes the benefits and burdens of covenants in the lease. 'Benefit' means a right to sue, and 'burden' a liability to be sued. Thus, a person who buys the freehold and becomes the new landlord can sue for the rent; one who buys the lease can sue for repairs. This is also the main reason almost all flats in England and Wales are sold by means of leases, rather than freehold. Only certain negative freehold covenants are enforceable against successors in title of the original covenantor (see Chapter 9). Mortgage lenders would be unlikely to lend money to buy a flat or a maisonette if it were not possible to force the owners of the neighbouring flats to maintain their premises, thus ensuring the continuing value of the lender's security. The Landlord and Tenant (Covenants) Act 1995 has revolutionised this area of the law for leases granted after 1995, but the old rules still apply to the thousands of leases (and contracts for leases) made before that date.

It is probably the technicality of this area of law that is most off-putting, at least so far as the rules that determine liability after assignment are concerned. In most cases, however, it is relatively easy to reach a satisfactory result, provided that the relevant rules are applied systematically. The basic rules are set out in Sections 6.3 and 6.4 and are illustrated by worked examples on the companion website 🐾. Before considering these rules, however, some of the most common and most important covenants will be examined.

6.2 Commonly found covenants

'Covenant' is the general name given to promises made in a deed (see Section 12.5.1). In this chapter, it is also used to refer to the obligations entered into by the parties to an oral lease (see Section 5.6.1). Covenants may be express (written or spoken) or implied (either by common law or by statute). The covenants commonly found in leases are listed below, before the most important of them are considered in more detail.

Common leasehold covenants

By the lessor
- not to derogate from his grant;
- to allow the lessee quiet enjoyment;
- to repair.

By the tenant
- to pay rent (sometimes also land taxes and/or a service charge);
- to repair;
- to permit the lessor to enter to inspect (or repair);
- to insure;
- not to alter the structure;
- not to assign or sublet without permission;
- to use the premises only for a specific purpose (such as a dwelling);
- not to deny the landlord's title.

6.2.1 Quiet enjoyment and non-derogation

Quiet enjoyment and non-derogation are the essence of the lease: if they are not expressed in the lease, they are implied by common law. The two promises are very closely connected. Whether the covenants have been breached is a question of fact.

6.2.1(a) Quiet enjoyment

'Quiet enjoyment' does not mean keeping quiet, but refers to the tenant's right to take possession as promised and to be able to enjoy all aspects of that possession without interference. The lessor promises not to interfere with the tenant's enjoyment of the land – that is, to allow the tenant to enjoy exclusive possession (see Section 5.5.3).

In *Browne v Flower* [1911] 1 Ch 219 (Ch), the tenants of a ground-floor flat complained that a new outside staircase, which ran alongside their bedroom windows, invaded their privacy. As regards the covenant for quiet enjoyment, Parker J said:

> there must be some physical interference with the enjoyment of the demised premises and … a mere interference with the comfort of a person using the demised premises by the creation of

a personal annoyance such as might arise from noise, invasion of privacy, or otherwise is not enough (at 228).

The House of Lords considered the nature of the covenant for quiet enjoyment in *Southwark LBC v Tanner* [2001] 1 AC 1 (HL) (also known as *Southwark LBC v Mills*). The tenant in a local authority block of flats complained that, due to inadequate sound insulation, she could hear all the sounds made by their neighbours and that this was causing her tension and distress. Lord Hoffman said:

> The flat is not quiet and the tenant is not enjoying it. But the words cannot be read literally … The covenant for quiet enjoyment is … a covenant that the tenant's lawful possession of the land will not be substantially interfered with by the acts of the lessor or those lawfully claiming under him (at 10).

When the flats were built in 1919, there had been no statutory requirement that they should be soundproofed. Each tenant had accepted the flat in the physical condition in which she had found it and subject to the rest of the building being used as flats. The House of Lords held that there had been no substantial interference with the tenant's possession (her ability to use the flat in an ordinary lawful way) and thus no breach of the landlord's covenant to allow her quiet enjoyment. In addition, both Lord Hoffmann and Lord Millett (who gave the substantial speeches in the case) expressed concern that the resource implications on the local authority would have been unsustainable had they found in favour of the tenants, since it would have cost over a billion pounds to bring all their premises up to modern building standards. Interestingly, Lord Hoffmann had not allowed himself to be influenced by similar factors (albeit affecting another type of social landlord) a year earlier when deciding *Bruton v London & Quadrant Housing Trust* [2000] 1 AC 406 (HL).

6.2.1(b) Non-derogation

The lessor also promises not to take back what he has given. In *Browne v Flower*, Parker J held that derogation from grant only occurs if property is rendered:

> unfit or materially less fit to be used for the particular purpose for which the demise was made (at 226).

As the rooms could still be used as bedrooms if the tenants drew the curtains, the tenants failed to establish a breach of covenant in regard to either quiet enjoyment or non-derogation of grant.

In *Harmer v Jumbil (Nigeria) Tin Areas Ltd* [1921] 1 Ch 200 (CA), land was leased expressly for the storage of explosives. The landlord then decided to build on his neighbouring land, which would have made this storage illegal. The tenant was able to prevent the landlord erecting the building as doing so would have amounted to a breach of his covenant not to derogate from his grant. In the more recent case of *Platt v London Underground Ltd* [2001] 2 EGLR 121 (Ch), London Underground was held to be in derogation from its grant of a lease of a kiosk located near the south exit to Goodge Street station. This particular exit was only opened to the public during the morning rush hour, thereby discouraging trade at the kiosk for a substantial part of the day. However, Mr Platt's victory was somewhat limited because he also had a lease of a second kiosk at the main exit to the station. Neuberger J held that London Underground were entitled to take into account any increased profits made at the second kiosk (resulting from the closure of the south exit) by way of set-off against any damages due to Mr Platt.

6.2.1(c) Further protection

In leases of residential accommodation, these common covenants are reinforced by section 1 of the Protection from Eviction Act 1977, amended by section 29 of the Housing Act 1988. The section allows a local authority to prosecute a lessor for the crime of harassment where he 'does acts likely to interfere with the peace or comfort of the residential occupier' or refuses any facilities (such as the electricity supply) knowing or believing that this will discourage the occupier from enforcing his rights. This section protects residential licensees as well as tenants.

An example is provided by *Cardiff City Council v Destrick*, unreported, 14 April 1994. A landlord cut off the gas and electricity to a flat rented by a couple with a young baby. He was charged with the offence of doing an act with intent to cause the occupier to leave (Protection from Eviction Act 1977, s 1(3)), and also with doing an act which was likely to make the occupier leave (s 1(3A)), but was acquitted of both charges. He argued that he had had no intention to force them out (it was summer, not winter) and, further, that it was reasonable (under section 1(3B)) to act as he did because the tenants were behind with their payments. The magistrates agreed with him. On appeal, the court recognised that Parliament's intention was to protect residential tenants by ensuring that if a lessor wants an eviction, he must go to court and may not rely on self-help or 'indulge in harassment'. However, the court found that the magistrates' decision had not been so irrational that it should be overruled. This case may have opened a useful escape route for lessors, but it will be a question on the evidence of the reasonableness of the lessor's conduct in every case.

Section 27 of the Housing Act 1988 also creates a tort of unlawful eviction with the potential for substantial damages to be awarded against the landlord. *Tagro v Cafane* [1991] 1 WLR 378 (CA) is 'a cautionary tale for landlords who are minded unlawfully to evict their tenants by harassment or other means' (per Lord Donaldson MR, at 236). Mr Cafane harassed his tenant and eventually 'totally wrecked' her room and possessions. Miss Tagro was awarded £31,000 damages, assessed by virtue of section 28 of the Act on the difference between the value of the premises with the tenant in occupation and their value with vacant possession. The recent trend is towards the award of much lower damages, perhaps reflecting a landlord's ability more easily to end tenants' possession lawfully under the assured shorthold regime.

6.2.2   Covenants to repair

At common law, a furnished dwelling must be fit for habitation at the start of the lease (although no such covenant is implied into leases of other kinds of property). A well-known breach of this implied covenant occurred in *Smith v Marrable* (1843) 11 M & W 5, 152 ER 693 (Ex), where a house was leased and found to be full of bugs.

The only statutory provision which requires the lessor of a dwelling to keep it fit for human habitation at the start and throughout the lease is section 8 of the Landlord and Tenant Act 1985. However, the section applies only to tenancies let at a very low rent and, since there are probably very few of these tenancies left, it is nowadays very much a dead letter.

The covenant to repair the property is fundamental to the lease of a building or part of a building. Whether the burden of this covenant falls on the landlord or the tenant will depend on the kind of property and the length of the lease. If there is nothing expressed in the lease, under common law a periodic tenant with a year's term or less will normally be required to use the premises in a 'tenant-like manner'. This is a vague expression, but Lord Denning MR has given some examples. A weekly tenant must, for example, clean windows and unblock sinks:

> In short, he must do the little jobs about the place which a reasonable tenant would do. In addition, he must, of course, not damage the house ... But ... if the house falls into disrepair through fair wear and tear or lapse of time, or for any reason not caused by him, then the tenant is not liable to repair it (*Warren v Keen* [1954] 1 QB 15 (CA) at 20).

Sections 11–14 Landlord and Tenant Act 1985 impose a duty on the lessor of any dwelling (for a term granted for less than seven years) to keep the external structure in repair and certain items in proper working order, including installations for the supply of water, gas and electricity and for sanitation and space and water heating. This is a complex area of law, but the courts have tended to interpret these requirements as not putting an obligation on the landlord to correct some design defect in the building's structure so long as the structure was not itself in a state of disrepair. An example might be a design fault that caused excessive condensation and thus made the premises unfit for human habitation. However, if the various installations do not perform as they should, they are not in proper working order, and the landlord is liable. In *O'Connor v Old Etonian Housing Association Ltd* [2002] Ch 295 (Ch), water pipes which had been working properly failed to provide a proper supply when the water pressure dropped. The Court of Appeal held that the Housing Association would be in breach if the drop in pressure was foreseeable, unless the reason for it was temporary and external, such as a drought.

The lessor's liability under sections 11–14 is subject to his being given notice that remedial work is needed and having a reasonable opportunity to carry it out (*O'Brien v Robinson* [1973] AC 912 (HL)).

6.2.3   Covenants not to assign or sublet

Theoretically, tenants have an unlimited right to assign or sublet. In practice, a tenant often covenants not to assign or sublet, since the lessor needs to be able to protect his reversionary interest against unsuitable assignees or subtenants. This covenant may be 'absolute', in which case the lessor can prevent the tenant from assigning or subletting, however unreasonable this may be. If the covenant is 'qualified' (that is, the tenant has agreed not to assign or sublet without the landlord's consent), section 19(1) of the Landlord and Tenant Act 1927 provides that the consent cannot be unreasonably withheld, 'notwithstanding any provision to the contrary'. The Landlord and Tenant Act 1988 places the burden of proof on the lessor to show that the refusal of consent was reasonable (s 1). Section 22 of the Landlord and Tenant (Covenants) Act 1995 amended these rules for new commercial leases by inserting a new section 19(1A) into the 1927 Act. In the case of non-residential leases made after 1 January 1996, lessors and lessees can agree the circumstances under which consent to assignment may be given or refused. Where they have done so, the courts may not inquire into the reasonableness of any refusal of consent. This provision has had significant implications in the commercial sector, but it does not affect non-business or pre-1996 leases.

If the consent is withheld, the tenant is placed in a difficult position. He can take a chance that the refusal is unreasonable and assign or sublet regardless, but if he wrongly assigns or sublets, he may lose his lease (see Section 6.5.2). If he is not sure whether the lessor is being reasonable, he can go to court for a declaration, but the delay may lose him the prospective assignee or subtenant.

By statute, it is unreasonable to refuse consent on the grounds of a person's sex, race or disability unless the lessor lives on the premises (Equality Act 2010, s 34). Otherwise, whether a refusal is reasonable is a question of fact in every case. As Lord Denning MR remarked:

> no one decision will be a binding precedent as a strict rule of law. The reasons given by the judges are to be treated as propositions of good sense – in relation to the particular case – rather than propositions of law applicable to all cases (*Bickel v Duke of Westminster* [1977] QB 517 (CA) at 524).

A useful test can be found in *International Drilling Fluids Ltd v Louisville Investments (Uxbridge) Ltd* [1986] Ch 513 (CA), where it was said to be a question of whether the lessor's decision was one 'which might be reached by a reasonable man in the circumstances', provided the refusal was connected to the lessor/lessee relationship. Reasonable refusals include the unsatisfactory references of the proposed tenant and the fact that a subletting would create a tenancy protected by statute.

In *Jaison Property Development Co Ltd v Roux Restaurants Ltd* (1997) 74 P & CR 357 (CA), Aldous LJ quoted with approval from the judgment of Warrington LJ in *Houlder Bros & Co Ltd v Gibbs* [1925] Ch 575 (CA):

> When you look at the authorities … this, at any rate, is plain, that in the cases to which an objection to an assignment has been upheld as reasonable it has always had some reference either to the personality of the [proposed] tenant or to his proposed user of the property (at 585).

The Court of Appeal was faced with an interesting issue in *Olympia & York Canary Wharf Ltd v Oil Property Investments Ltd* (1995) 69 P & CR 43 (CA), where the lessor refused leave to an assignee of the lease who wanted to sell it to the original tenant. The reason for refusal was that the original tenant had the personal right to end the lease (and this would reduce the value of the lessor's interest by £6 million). The Court held that this was a reasonable ground to refuse consent to assignment.

In *Ashworth Frazer Ltd v Gloucester City Council* [2001] 1 WLR 2180 (HL), the House of Lords considered the status of a landlord's refusal to consent to an assignment where the landlord thought that the proposed assignee would probably be in breach of a user covenant in the lease. Approving the approach in *International Drilling Fluids Ltd*, the Court held that reasonable lessors:

> need not confine their consideration to what will necessarily happen … they may have regard to what will probably happen (per Lord Rodger at [70]).

6.2.4   The 'usual covenants'

The phrase 'usual covenants' is a technical expression, quite different from the list of common covenants above. This set of covenants is implied into a lease if the lease states that the parties will be bound by the 'usual covenants', or if the lease is silent as to most matters (as is common in short periodic tenancies). These 'usual covenants' are also implied in a contract for a lease, unless the parties intend otherwise. The 'usual covenants' are listed below, although other covenants may be 'usual' in certain circumstances (for example, because of local or trade customs).

The 'usual covenants'

By the lessor
- quiet enjoyment and non-derogation from grant;
- right of re-entry for non-payment of rent.

By the tenant
- to pay rent;
- to pay land taxes;
- to repair (or to allow access to the lessor to repair).

6.3   The transfer of rights and duties: pre-1996 leases

The enforceability of a covenant in a pre-1996 lease depends upon the rules of privity of contract and privity of estate:

Privity of contract	the original parties are liable to each other for the whole of the term of the lease, even after they have assigned their interest to a third party.
Privity of estate	the relationship between the landlord for the time being and the tenant for the time being. The covenants included in this relationship are regulated by common law and sections 141–42 of the Law of Property Act (LPA) 1925 (see Sections 6.3.3).

6.3.1   The tenant's assignee

When the lease is assigned, the benefit and the burden of the leasehold covenants will pass to the new tenant provided:

- there is 'privity of estate' and
- the covenant 'touches and concerns' the land.

(*Spencer's Case* (1583) 5 Co Rep 16a, 77 ER 72 (QB)).

Privity of estate	means that there is a current legal relationship of landlord and tenant between the parties. A sign of privity of estate is that one person pays rent to the other; therefore there is no privity of estate between a head lessor and a subtenant (see Figure 6.1).

The phrase 'touches and concerns' originated in the sixteenth century and is used by the courts to decide whether promises ought, as a matter of public policy, to be attached to the land. It is 'notoriously difficult to propose a definition of "touching and concerning" which is not flawed by circularity' (Gray and Gray, 2009, para 4.5.44). The basic question is whether the promise really affects the parties in their roles as lessor and tenant, or whether it affects them in their personal capacity. In Cheshire's terms (2011, 304), the promise must be 'reasonably incidental to the relation of landlord and tenant'. In *P & A Swift Investments v Combined English Stores Group plc* [1989] AC

632 (HL), Lord Oliver identified the following working test for whether the covenant touches and concerns the land:

> (1) the covenant benefits only the reversioner [lessor] for time being, and if separated from the reversion ceases to be of benefit to the covenantee; (2) the covenant affects the nature, quality, mode of user or value of the land of the reversioner (3) the covenant is not expressed to be personal, that is to say neither being given only to a specific reversioner nor in respect of the obligations only of a specific tenant (4) the fact that a covenant is to pay a sum of money will not prevent it from touching and concerning the land so long as the three foregoing conditions are satisfied (at 642).

All the commonly found covenants considered in Section 6.2 touch and concern the land. For more examples of covenants which touch and concern the land, and of covenants that do not, see Cheshire (2011, 305–7).

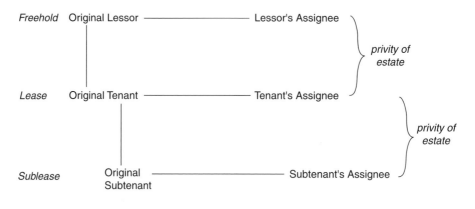

No privity of estate between Headlessor and Subtenant

Figure 6.1 Privity of estate

6.3.2 The lessor's assignee

Where the freehold reversion (or headlease) is sold, the common law has been superseded by sections 141–42 of the LPA 1925.

LPA 1925, s 141   the lessor's assignee will be able to enforce the benefit of all the covenants which 'have reference to the subject matter of the lease'.

LPA 1925, s 142   the lessor's assignee will be bound by the burden of all covenants which 'have reference to the subject matter of the lease'.

The phrase 'have reference to the subject matter of the lease' means the same thing as 'touch and concern the land' (see Section 6.3.1).

6.3.3 The original parties after assignment

As already indicated, the original lessor and lessee have promised to obey the covenants for the whole term of the lease. The doctrine of privity of contract means that they may continue to be liable to each other even after one or both of them have assigned their interest in the lease. The liability to be sued for unpaid rent and service charges can be a continuing worry for the original tenant of an expensive commercial lease, especially in times of recession. Although the original tenant and the original lessor can still be sued after they have assigned their interest, they generally cannot sue. This rule is based on the common law principle that a person cannot be sued by two parties for the same breach of covenant (see *Re King* [1963] Ch 459 (CA)).

Liability of original parties after assignment

Following assignment by the original tenant:
- the original tenant remains liable on the tenant's covenants and can be sued by the original landlord if the assignee (or any subsequent assignee) breaches those covenants;
- however, the original tenant can no longer sue for breach of the lessor's covenants.

Following assignment by the original lessor:
- the original lessor remains liable to the original tenant for breaches of covenant committed by any assignee of the reversion;
- however, the original lessor can no longer sue the tenant.

It is possible that the right to sue the original tenant passes automatically to the lessor's assignee under section 141 of the LPA 1925, without the need for express assignment. The editors of Megarry and Wade identify three cases where this interpretation of section 141 seems to have been assumed, but they concede that there is no reasoned authority to support it (Megarry and Wade, 2012, §§ 20–016).

As a further protection, when a business lease is assigned, the landlord will probably insist that the proposed new tenant obtain a guarantor (a 'surety'). If the new tenant fails to pay the rent, the guarantor may also be sued for it.

The question may arise as to whether the original tenant is liable for subsequent variations or extensions of the lease. In *City of London Corporation v Fell* [1994] 1 AC 458 (HL), the House of Lords offered 'a meagre crumb of comfort to the unfortunate original tenant' (Bridge, 1994). It held that the original tenant was not liable for rent unpaid by a later assignee of the lease in the case of a tenancy which was extended after the end of the term under the provisions of Part II of the Landlord and Tenant Act 1954. The Court of Appeal in *Friends' Provident Life Office v British Railways Board* [1996] 1 All ER 336 (CA) found that an original tenant was not bound by later variations of the lease between the lessor and an assignee of the lease unless the variation had been envisaged in the terms of the original lease (an example being the increased rent payable under a rent review clause).

The potential difficulties faced by the original tenant in leases created before 1 January 1996 have been addressed, to some extent, by the Landlord and Tenant (Covenants) Act 1995. The decision in *Friends' Provident* is now translated into a statutory provision (s 18) which applies to all leases. By section 17 of the Act, a lessor intending to sue the original tenant for money unpaid by the current tenant must give a 'problem notice' to the original tenant within six months of the original payment falling due. If no section 17 notice is given, the original tenant escapes all liability for that debt. If the rent is in the course of being reviewed at the date of the section 17 notice, the landlord will have to serve a second notice covering any increase in the rent within six months of the new rent being determined (*Scottish & Newcastle plc v Raguz* [2008] 1 WLR 2494 (HL)). An original tenant who pays the sums due is now entitled by section 19 to an 'overriding lease'. This places him between the lessor and the current tenant, thus gaining some potential relief in exchange for his ongoing liability. He may, for example, take steps to terminate the lease and either occupy the premises or assign the overriding lease with vacant possession.

If the original tenant is sued, the common law provides that he can claim an indemnity from the current tenant (*Moule v Garrett* (1871–72) LR 7 Ex 101 (ExCh)). If the present tenant is not worth suing (as is likely in such circumstances), the original tenant can choose to sue the person to whom he assigned his interest, provided that the assignment was made for valuable consideration (under the covenant implied into assignments of unregistered leases by section 77 of the LPA 1925 and transfers of registered leases by paragraph 20 of Schedule 12, Land Registration Act 2002). A well-advised tenant will normally seek an express indemnity from his assignee, rather than rely on section 77.

6.3.4 Subtenants and restrictive covenants

A head lessor does not have a relationship of privity of contract or privity of estate with any subtenant of the land. This can cause a significant problem to head lessors where their immediate tenant refuses to take action against a subtenant. However, a head lessor may be able to sue a subtenant for breach of a restrictive (negative) covenant under the rule in *Tulk v Moxhay* (1848) 2 Ph 774, 41 ER 1143 (Ch) (see Chapter 9). Thus, in *Hemingway Securities Ltd v Dunraven Ltd* (1996) 71 P & CR 30 (Ch) a head landlord was able to prevent a subtenant from taking a sublease in breach of a covenant between the head landlord and its immediate tenant. In addition, there are two statutory provisions that may enable a head landlord to benefit from a term in the underlease, provided that the underlease makes appropriate provision for him to do so. Section 56 of the LPA 1925 allows covenants to be made with persons who are not party to the deed concerned (see *Amsprop Trading Ltd v Harris Distribution Ltd* [1997] 1 WLR 1025 (Ch)). Alternatively, section 1 of the Contracts (Rights of Third Parties) Act 1999 allows a third party named in, or identifiable from, the contract to enforce a term in it if there is express provision for him to do so, or if the term purports to confer a benefit on him, and nothing in the contract rebuts this presumption. Consequently, if a subtenant breached a covenant in the sublease, and this covenant was made for the benefit of the head landlord (by name) 'or whomever was for the time being the owner of the freehold reversion', both the head landlord and his assignee could enforce the covenant against the subtenant (see *Amsprop Trading Ltd*). Both of these provisions are discussed in more detail in Section 9.7.

6.3.5 Equitable leases

There are different rules for equitable leases because in such cases, there is no privity of estate, since this depends on a *legal* relationship. Due to the wording of sections 141 and 142, the benefits and burdens of all covenants which touch and concern the land pass to any lessor, whether legal or equitable. As far as the equitable tenant is concerned, the benefit of covenants which touch and concern may pass, but it seems that the burden may not (but see Section 6.4.5 for equitable leases made after 1995).

6.3.6 The pre-1996 rules in practice

Figure 6.2 summarises how the pre-1996 rules apply to a case where the leasehold estate and the reversion have both been assigned twice.

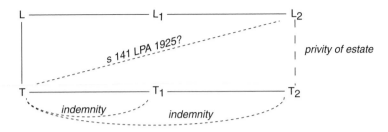

Figure 6.2   Applying the rules for pre-1996 leases

6.4 The transfer of rights and duties: new tenancies

On 1 January 1996, the Landlord and Tenant (Covenants) Act 1995 came into force. Described as 'a statute without precedent … [which] will have an untold impact on … commercial leases in this country' (Bridge, 1996), the Act was passed as a result of a Law Commission Report ((1988) No 174), the commitment of a single MP, and the lessor and lessee lobbies (see Davey, 1996). The negotiations around the new law resulted in a series of hurriedly drafted provisions to effect compromises between the lessor and lessee lobbies.

The rules that apply to post-1995 leases are set out below.

6.4.1 The tenant's assignee and the lessor's assignee

The 1995 Act sets out new rules that regulate the transmission of the burden and benefit of covenants contained in leases granted after 1995. Sections 2 and 3 effectively abolish the test of 'touch and concern'. All landlord covenants and tenant covenants (the obligations of whoever is the landlord and the tenant at the time) automatically pass whenever the lease or freehold is assigned, unless they are specifically expressed to be 'personal'.

In *BHP Petroleum Great Britain Ltd v Chesterfield Properties Ltd* [2002] Ch 194 (CA), the question arose as to whether the original landlord or its assignee should be liable for carrying out remedial work on defects on the premises. Since the covenant was expressed to be a personal obligation on the part of the original landlord, the liability did not pass to the assignee, and the original landlord was held liable for the duration of the lease.

6.4.2 The original tenant after assignment

Section 5(2) provides that any tenant who assigns the whole of his lease:

▶ is released from the tenant covenants of the tenancy and
▶ ceases to be entitled to the benefit of the landlord covenants of the tenancy, as from the assignment.

Any expressly personal covenant will continue to be binding on the original tenant throughout the term of the lease (see *BHP v Chesterfield* at [61–62]).

In leases where the landlord's consent to an assignment of the lease is required, the landlord can insist that the assigning tenant guarantees that the assignee will perform the tenant covenants (s 16). If an 'authorised guarantee agreement' (or AGA) is entered into, the assigning tenant will remain liable until his assignee transfers the lease to a further assignee with the consent of the landlord. A tenant cannot be required to guarantee a subsequent assignee under section 16. In *K/S Victoria Street v House of Fraser (Stores Management) Ltd* [2012] Ch 497 (CA) the Court of Appeal considered whether a landlord can insist that the tenant's guarantor acts as the guarantor of the tenant's assignee. The Court concluded that the clause in this particular lease fell foul of the anti-avoidance provisions in section 25 of the 1995 Act (see Section 6.4.6). However, according to Lord Neuberger, there is no objection to achieving exactly the same outcome simply by requiring the guarantor to be party to a valid 'authorised guarantee agreement' (at [53]).

6.4.3   The original lessor after assignment

When a lessor assigns his reversion, he must still perform his covenants under the lease. He may, however, apply to the tenant to release him. If the tenant refuses consent, the former lessor may apply to the court to be released from the covenants (ss 6–8), provided that those covenants are not personal to the original lessor (*BHP v Chesterfield*). It is important that the tenant should have some say in whether the assigning landlord is released. An insolvent or reluctant lessor would be less likely to be able to perform his covenants, and in such circumstances the tenant would probably want the existing lessor to continue to be bound.

6.4.4   User covenants

Section 3(5) of the 1995 Act allows head lessors to enforce restrictive covenants directly against any person 'who is the owner or occupier of any demised premises to which the lease relates'. Thus, a head lessor can enforce a user covenant against a subtenant without the need to resort to the rule in *Tulk v Moxhay* or the Contracts (Rights of Third Parties) Act 1999 (see Section 6.3.4).

6.4.5   Equitable leases

The definition of 'tenancy' for the purposes of the 1995 Act expressly includes 'an agreement for a tenancy' (s 28(1)). Consequently, the rules for leases granted after 1995 apply to equitable leases in the same way that they apply to legal leases.

6.4.6   Anti-avoidance provisions

Section 25 of the 1995 Act declares void any provisions of a lease that are designed 'to exclude, modify or otherwise frustrate the operation of any provision' of the Act. In *K/S Victoria Street v House of Fraser*, the Court of Appeal held that a provision requiring the tenant's guarantor to guarantee the liability of an assignee was void by virtue of section 25. The fact that the particular terms reflected a genuine agreement between the parties for sound business reasons did not save them. As Lord Neuberger MR explained at [21]:

> If it were otherwise, it would mean, for instance, that a landlord, when granting a tenancy, could require a guarantor of the tenant's liabilities, on every assignment of the tenancy, to guarantee the liability of each successive assignee. Such an obligation ('a renewal obligation') would plainly be wholly contrary to the purpose of section 24(2), as it would enable a

well-advised landlord to ensure that any guarantor was in precisely the position in which it would have been before the 1995 Act came into force.

Despite these anti-avoidance provisions, it is still possible for a lessor to effectively sidestep sections 6–8 of the Act. In *London Diocesan Fund v Avonridge Property Co Ltd* [2005] 1 WLR 3956 (HL) Avonridge had acquired the headlease of seven shop units (the London Diocesan Fund was the head landlord) before subletting six of them for substantial premiums, but nominal rents. Avonridge covenanted with its subtenants that it would pay the rent due under the headlease, 'but not, in the case of Avonridge Property Co Ltd only, so as to be liable after the landlord has disposed of its interest in the Property'. Avonridge had then assigned the headlease to a Mr Phithwa, who promptly disappeared, leaving unpaid the rent due under the headlease. The subtenants were granted relief from the forfeiture of the headlease (see Section 6.5.1(c)) on condition that they pay the rent arrears and take new leases of their individual units at market rents. The subtenants brought proceedings against Avonridge on the grounds that Avonridge had not complied with sections 6–8 of the 1995 Act. The majority of the House of Lords held that section 6 was not relevant and that Avonridge was not, therefore, liable for the non-payment of rent by its assignee. Lord Nicholls explained:

> Whatever its form, an agreed limitation of liability does not impinge upon the operation of the statutory provisions because … the statutory provisions are intended to operate to relieve tenants and landlords from a liability which would otherwise exist. They are not intended to impose a liability which otherwise would be absent. They are not intended to enlarge the liability either of a tenant or landlord (at [19]).

This reasoning could be applied to almost all covenants made by landlords. Consequently, a careful draftsperson should be able to minimise the future exposure of an original lessor. Whether tenants accept such limitations will depend upon their relative bargaining power (and the quality of their legal team).

6.4.7 The post-1995 rules in practice

Using the rules contained in the 1995 Act to establish the rights and duties of the parties to a post-1995 lease requires a similar approach to that taken to pre-1996 leases (see Section 6.3.6), except that greater attention needs to be paid to the circumstances of each assignment and the negotiations between the parties. The practical effect of many of the 1995 Act rules will depend on the relative negotiating strengths of the parties, especially after *London Diocesan Fund v Avonridge*, which will, in turn, be influenced by the state of the property market.

Figure 6.3 summarises how the rules in the 1995 Act apply to a case where the leasehold estate and the reversion under a post-1995 lease have both been assigned twice. A systematic exposition of this example is available on the companion website.

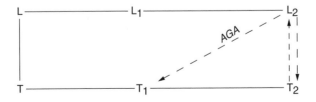

Figure 6.3 Applying the rules for post-1995 leases

6.5   Remedies for breach of covenant

The important question for a practical lawyer is always 'What remedy is available?' A lease is a contract, and, in general, contractual remedies are available. There are also remedies particular to leases. The rules are complicated, and only the briefest details of the main remedies are given here. For historical reasons, there are differences between the lessor's remedies for the tenant's breach of the covenant to pay rent and his remedies for the tenant's breach of other covenants. First, however, it is necessary to distinguish between covenants and conditions.

Condition	The promise is called a 'condition', or is clearly intended to be a condition of the lease.	The lessor can automatically take possession of the land if the condition is broken (known as 'repossession', 're-entry' or 'forfeiture').
Mere covenant	Other promises contained in the lease.	The lessor can forfeit the lease or give notice to quit only if there is a clause to that effect.

If the usual covenants are implied (see Section 6.2.4), then there will be a provision for forfeiture for non-payment of rent but not for breach of any other covenant.

It is also important to be aware of the doctrine of waiver. If a lessor accepts rent knowing of a breach of covenant or condition, he will be taken to have waived his right to take action for the breach. Any lessor who wants to enforce a forfeiture must avoid any action by which he indicates to the tenant that the lease will continue. However, there is no waiver if the lessor did not know of a breach when he indicated the continuance of the lease.

6.5.1   Non-payment of rent

The possible remedies are an action for recovery of rent, distress and forfeiture. The lessor can choose only one of these at a time.

6.5.1(a) An action for recovery

An action can be brought for recovery of arrears of rent. Only the past six years of rent can be recovered (Limitation Act 1980, s 19).

6.5.1(b) Taking control of the tenant's goods

Since 1066, a lessor has been able to enter the premises between sunrise and sunset and 'levy distress': she, or a certified bailiff, can take the tenant's belongings and sell them if the rent is not paid within five days.

In its Report No 194 (1991), the Law Commission concluded that distress for non-payment of rent is 'wrong in principle', and recommended its abolition. There are also concerns that levying distress may be in breach of the rights protected by the Human Rights Act 1998:

> The ancient (and perhaps anachronistic) self-help remedy of distress involves a serious interference with the rights of the tenant under article 8 of the European Convention for the Protection of Human Rights and Fundamental Freedoms to respect for his privacy and home and under article 1 of the First Protocol to the Convention to the peaceful enjoyment of his possessions. The human rights implications of levying distress must be in the forefront of the

mind of the landlord before he takes this step and he must fully satisfy himself that taking this action is in accordance with the law (per Lightman J, *Fuller v Happy Shopper Markets Ltd* [2001] 1 WLR 1681 (Ch) at [27]).

The common law right to levy distress for rent was abolished with effect from 6th April 2014, when Part 3 of the Tribunals, Courts and Enforcement Act 2007 (TCEA) came into force (section 71). A commercial lessor may now take advantage of the new statutory remedy of commercial rent arrears recovery (CRAR), provided that the lease is evidenced in writing (s 74). CRAR allows a lessor to recover rent arrears (but not arrears in respect of service charges or other payments (s 76(2)) by taking control of the tenant's goods. To ensure that the remedy is proportionate, a landlord cannot use CRAR until the arrears amount to least seven days' rent (see s 77(3), (4) and Regulation 52 of the Taking Control of Goods Regulations.

6.5.1(c) Forfeiture (the right of re-entry)

The right to re-enter makes it sound as if the lessor can just barge in, but, although he may physically re-enter commercial property, such re-entry must be peaceable and without the use of force, or he will commit an offence under section 6 of the Criminal Law Act 1977, as amended. The House of Lords in *Billson v Residential Apartments Ltd (No 1)* [1992] 1 AC 494 (HL) criticised the use of this self-help remedy, and it is usually safer for the lessor to go to court for an order for possession, particularly in the light of potential claims under the Human Rights Act 1998. Where the premises are residential, and the tenant is in occupation, under section 2 of the Protection from Eviction Act 1977, the lessor *must* apply to the court for a possession order before re-entering.

Before the lessor may proceed to forfeit the lease for non-payment of rent, he must issue a formal demand for payment, although most carefully drafted leases will contain a term permitting the lessor to forfeit the lease for non-payment of rent 'whether formally demanded or not'. If the lease contains such a term, or if the rent is six months or more in arrears, no formal demand is necessary before seeking to forfeit the lease.

Once the lessor has gone to court, the tenant might be able to claim 'relief' against forfeiture for non-payment of rent under section 212 of the Common Law Procedure Act 1852 (in the High Court) or section 138 of the County Courts Act 1984 (in the county court). This is exactly what it sounds like: very simply, if the tenant pays the arrears and costs, he may be reinstated. The rules here are intricate and somewhat illogical because of the interplay of equity, common law and statute.

6.5.2 Breach of other covenants

General remedies for breach of a tenant's covenant are forfeiture (available only to the lessor) or damages or an injunction. Although a tenant cannot forfeit the lease when the lessor is in breach, a tenant might be able to use contract law to repudiate a tenancy where the lessor is in fundamental or repudiatory breach of a significant covenant (see Section 6.5.2(b)).

6.5.2(a) Forfeiture

This remedy is only available to the lessor if it is included in the lease. If there is a forfeiture clause, the lessor must give notice to the tenant by section 146 of the LPA 1925. Section 146 notices do not apply in respect of non-payment of rent.

The section 146 notice must specify:

- the specific breach complained of;
- the remedy (if the breach is capable of remedy); and
- the compensation (if appropriate or required).

The purpose of the section 146 procedure is to give tenants an opportunity to remedy their breach, if this is possible, so that they do not lose their lease through forfeiture. It is, therefore, important to know which breaches can be remedied and which cannot.

The traditional view had been that the breach of a positive covenant could be remedied by the tenant simply performing whatever it was the lease required him to do, and some negative covenants could be remedied by ending the activity which was causing the breach, and promising to comply with the lease thereafter. The issue of remediability was examined in *Expert Clothing Service & Sales Ltd v Hillgate House Ltd* [1986] Ch 340 (CA). In this case, it had been agreed that the tenant should convert the premises, but, because of lack of money, the tenant had not even begun the work by the date by which the conversion should have been completed. Expert Clothing issued a section 146 notice, claiming that the breach was irremediable. The Court of Appeal stated that the purpose of section 146 was to give the tenant 'one last chance', and that whether a breach was capable of remedy depended, not on the nature of the breach, but rather on the nature of the harm caused to the lessor and whether financial compensation would be sufficient.

In *Savva v Hussein* (1997) 73 P & CR 150 (CA), the tenants were in minor breach of covenants not to put up signs or to alter the premises. On the question of whether such breaches were capable of remedy, Staughton LJ stated:

> When something has been done without consent, it is not possible to restore the matter wholly to the situation which it was in before the breach. The moving finger writes and cannot be recalled. That is not to my mind what is meant by a remedy; it is a remedy if the mischief caused by the breach can be removed. In the case of a covenant not to make alterations without consent or not to display signs without consent, if there is a breach of that, the mischief can be removed by removing the signs or restoring the property to the state it was in before the alterations (at 154).

Akici v LR Butlin Ltd [2006] 1 WLR 201 (CA) concerned an alleged breach of covenant by the tenant by sharing possession of the premises. Neuberger LJ felt that there were very few breaches not capable of remedy:

> In principle I would have thought that the great majority of breaches of covenant should be capable of remedy, in the same way as repairing or most user covenant breaches. Even where stopping, or putting right, the breach may leave the lessors out of pocket for some reason, it does not seem to me that there is any problem in concluding that the breach is remediable (at [65]).

The lessor is not disadvantaged in such circumstances, because the lessor is entitled to 'compensation in money ... for the breach' under section 146(1).

A wrongful subletting is irremediable, as is using the premises for immoral purposes in breach of covenant (see *Rugby School (Governors) v Tannahill* [1935] 1 KB 87 (KB)). However, where the immoral activity is being carried out by a subtenant, the tenant's breach may be remediable, provided that the tenant acts immediately to evict the immoral subtenant (*Patel v K & J Restaurants Ltd* [2011] L & TR 6 (CA)).

If the tenant does not, or cannot, remedy the breach within a reasonable time, the lessor can go to court for a possession order. Again, the tenant (or subtenant) can apply for relief under section 146(2) of the LPA 1925, even if the breach is considered irremediable. Paragraphs [82] to [90] of the judgment in *Patel v K & J Restaurants Ltd* provide a useful illustration of when and how the court will exercise its discretion to grant relief from forfeiture and the type of conditions that it may impose upon the tenant. In *Billson v Residential Apartments Ltd (No 1)* [1992] 1 AC 494 (HL) (see Section 6.5.1(c)), the House of Lords held that a tenant can apply for relief whether or not the lessor has actually re-entered the land, provided there is no final court order granting possession. Here the tenant was carrying out building work in breach of covenant, so the landlord served a section 146 notice and then re-entered by changing the locks. Since there was no court order granting possession at this stage (and the re-entry had been peaceable, so there had been no breach of the criminal law; see Section 6.5.1(c)), the House of Lords sent the case back to the trial court for a decision as to whether relief was to be granted.

If the lease is forfeit, any sublease will also disappear, since its existence depends on the headlease. Therefore, section 146(4) of the LPA 1925 allows the subtenant to apply for relief; if he is successful, he steps into the shoes of the tenant but cannot gain a term longer than his original sublease. Mortgagees of the leasehold interest can also apply for relief, remedy the breach and add the cost of doing so to the mortgage debt.

In an attempt to prevent abuse of the section 146 procedure by lessors, especially when attempting to forfeit the lease against leaseholders who are unable or unwilling to pay unreasonable service charges, sections 168 and 169 of the Commonhold and Leasehold Reform Act 2002 prevent most lessors of residential leases over 21 years from issuing a section 146 notice unless either the leaseholder has admitted the breach of covenant, or the lessor has established the breach to the satisfaction of a leasehold valuation tribunal. If the breach consists of arrears of service charges, the lessor must also show that the charges are not excessive. Even if the tribunal is satisfied as to the breach, the leaseholder may not be served with the section 146 notice for a further 14 days.

6.5.2(b) *Termination by repudiatory breach*

It is a general rule of contract law that a contract may be terminated if one of the parties breaches its terms in such a way as to make it clear that they no longer intend to be bound by the contract. Some older cases cast doubt on whether this remedy applies to leases, but since the county court decision in *Hussein v Mehlman* [1992] 2 EGLR 287, the list of circumstances in which it has been granted has been growing steadily. In *Hussein,* a rented house was uninhabitable due to the lack of repair; the tenant not only won damages but also was entitled to end the lease because of the fundamental nature of the landlord's breach of covenant. Since *Hussein,* the Court of Appeal has, on a number of occasions, accepted that repudiation by a tenant can be appropriate, although in none of the cases is the Court of Appeal's decision dependent upon this. For example, in *Chartered Trust plc v Davies* (1998) 76 P & CR 396 (CA), the lessor allowed the occupier of a neighbouring unit to obstruct access to the defendant's unit. The Court of Appeal dealt with this as a case of derogation from grant, but Henry LJ concluded his judgment by noting:

> The trial judge found this to be a repudiation of the lease – a substantial interference with the tenant's business driving him to bankruptcy. That was a judgment he was entitled to come to on the evidence he heard (at 409).

This is a welcome extension of contractual principles. However, despite appearing to be similar to the lessor's remedy of forfeiture, it is, by its very nature, clearly limited to cases where the lessor has breached a fundamental term of the lease. It is not clear whether the remedy is also available for the lessor in the case of a tenant's repudiatory breach. It seems unlikely, since that would mean that an uncompromising lessor could avoid the statutory and common law protection available to tenants (see Section 6.5.2(a)). Without deciding this question, the Court of Appeal in *Reichman v Beveridge* [2007] 1 P & CR 20 (CA) held that there was no obligation on a lessor to minimise the tenant's liability under the lease by accepting the tenant's repudiatory breach of contract.

6.5.2(c) Damages, injunctions and specific performance

Damages and/or an injunction may be appropriate remedies for some breaches, and are available to both lessor and lessee. Specific performance was once thought to be available only to the tenant in cases of the lessor's breach of his repairing covenant; *Rainbow Estates v Tokenhold* [1999] Ch 64 (Ch) extended this remedy to the lessor 'in appropriate circumstances'. Such circumstances will be rare. In *Rainbow Estates*, the lease had no provision for the landlord to forfeit the lease for the tenant's breach or even to enter the premises to carry out the repairs himself. Specific performance will not usually be available if damages are an appropriate remedy, but here the property was a listed building in serious disrepair, and the condition of the premises was continuing to deteriorate; an award of damages would not have helped the landlord. The traditional reason for the courts' reluctance to order specific performance in these circumstances, that the order would need continuing supervision by the court, was not seen as presenting a difficulty if there was a clear definition of the work to be done.

The House of Lords took the orthodox approach to specific performance in *Co-operative Insurance Society Ltd v Argyll Stores (Holdings) Ltd* [1998] AC 1 (HL), in which it refused to make an order preventing Safeway from closing one of its stores, despite the company having contracted with its landlord, the owner of a shopping mall, to keep it open. Lord Hoffmann distinguished the performance of repairing obligations in a lease from the obligation to continue in a business relationship.

At present, tenants often have very serious problems in persuading their lessors to carry out repairs; one rationale for the introduction of 'commonhold' has been the need to address the problems faced by tenants in rundown blocks of flats (see Section 4.5). Although tenants can seek the remedies discussed above, if they hold a comparatively insecure assured shorthold tenancy they may be reluctant to bring an action against their lessor, knowing that renewal or extension of their tenancy would probably be unlikely. An alternative remedy could be to pay for the repairs themselves and deduct the cost from the rent without becoming liable for non-payment (a 'right of set-off'; see *Lee-Parker v Izzet (No 1)* [1971] 1 WLR 1688 (Ch)).

Instead of relying on contractual provisions within the lease (whether set out in the lease or implied by statute), sometimes the residential tenant's best solution is to get the local authority to take action. Part 1 of the Housing Act 2004 gives local authorities the power to take steps against the lessor to ensure that residential accommodation is brought up to a reasonable standard.

Summary

6.1 The rules relating to leasehold covenants are the product of the need to balance the demands of landlords, tenants and wider society. They are highly technical but in most cases can be applied successfully provided that the issues are approached systematically.

Summary cont'd

6.2 Commonly found leasehold covenants include the lessor's covenants for quiet enjoyment and non-derogation from grant, covenants to repair and the tenant's covenant not to assign or sublet without consent.

6.3 The relevant rules for determining whether a party can enforce or is bound by a particular covenant depend upon the date of the lease. If the lease was granted before 1996 (or pursuant to a contract made before 1996):

▶ its covenants automatically run with the land if there is privity of estate, and the covenant touches and concerns the land;

▶ the original tenant remains liable on all the covenants but may claim an indemnity from his assignee or the current tenant; and

▶ the original tenant is entitled to an overriding lease when he has paid money due by the current tenant.

6.4 Leases made after 1995 fall within the rules contained in the Landlord and Tenant (Covenants) Act 1995:

▶ all covenants run with land unless they are expressed to be personal;

▶ the original tenant ceases automatically to be liable for any breach after assigning the lease (but can be liable under an 'authorised guarantee agreement');

▶ the original lessor may remain liable, unless he obtains a release from the current tenant or from the court.

6.5 There are a number of remedies available to landlords and tenants in addition to the usual contractual remedies:

(a) Remedies for non-payment of rent are normally forfeiture, CRAR or an action for recovery.

(b) Remedies for breaches of other covenants by the tenant include forfeiture, damages and injunction.

(c) A tenant may have the right to repudiate the lease in certain circumstances.

(d) A tenant of residential property may be able to involve the local authority if the lessor is in breach of his repairing covenant.

Exercises

6.1 Complete the online quiz on the topics covered in this chapter on the companion website.

6.2 Consider the advantages and disadvantages of using long leases to regulate the ownership of a number of residential flats making up a single building. How, if at all, do the changes introduced by the Commonhold and Leasehold Reform Act 2002 assist the lessor and the tenants in this situation?

6.3 Four years ago, Ronald granted a six-year lease of a house to Alan. Alan covenanted that he would pay the rent on time, would paint the exterior every three years and would not use the premises for illegal or immoral purposes. Ronald reserved the right to re-enter the premises for breach of any covenant.

The following year, Ronald sold his freehold reversion to Keegan. Two years ago, Alan assigned his lease to Jane.

Keegan has found out that Jane has been smoking cannabis in her house, that she has allowed her friend Sally to use it for prostitution (much to the annoyance of the next-door neighbour) and that she has not painted the house at all. She is five months in arrears with her rent. Four months ago, the roof began to leak badly whenever it rained, and the bedroom ceiling has collapsed as a result. Keegan has steadfastly refused to carry out any repairs, and Jane is obliged to live on the ground floor.

Jane wants to know what she can do about the state of the house and whether Keegan can evict her. Advise her.

You can find suggested answers to exercises 6.2 and 6.3 on the companion website.

Further reading

Bridge, 'First Tenant's Liability in the Lords' (1994) 53 CLJ 28

Bridge, 'Former Tenants, Future Liabilities and the Privity of Contract Principle: The Landlord and Tenant (Covenants) Act 1995' (1996) 55 CLJ 313

Davey, 'Privity of Contract and Leases – Reform at Last' (1996) 59 MLR 78

Dixon, 'A Failure of Statutory Purpose or a Failure of Professional Advice?' [2006] 70 Conv 79

Chapter 7 follows overleaf.

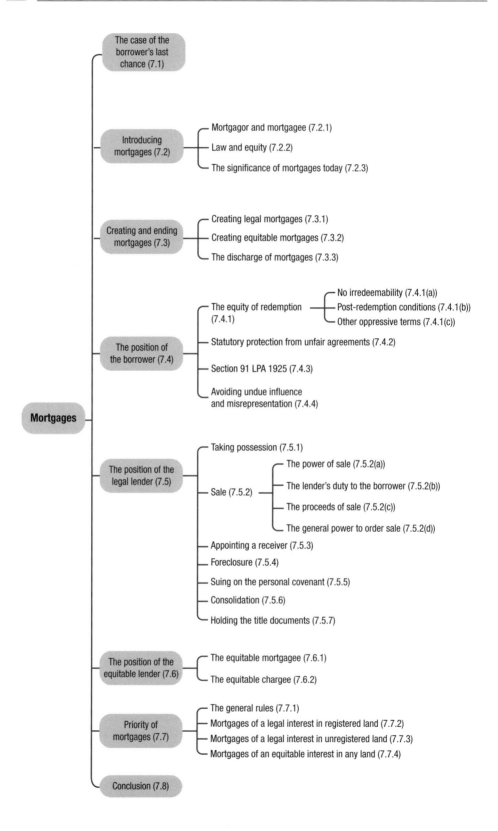

Mortgages

- The case of the borrower's last chance (7.1)

- Introducing mortgages (7.2)
  - Mortgagor and mortgagee (7.2.1)
  - Law and equity (7.2.2)
  - The significance of mortgages today (7.2.3)

- Creating and ending mortgages (7.3)
  - Creating legal mortgages (7.3.1)
  - Creating equitable mortgages (7.3.2)
  - The discharge of mortgages (7.3.3)

- The position of the borrower (7.4)
  - The equity of redemption (7.4.1)
    - No irredeemability (7.4.1(a))
    - Post-redemption conditions (7.4.1(b))
    - Other oppressive terms (7.4.1(c))
  - Statutory protection from unfair agreements (7.4.2)
  - Section 91 LPA 1925 (7.4.3)
  - Avoiding undue influence and misrepresentation (7.4.4)

- The position of the legal lender (7.5)
  - Taking possession (7.5.1)
  - Sale (7.5.2)
    - The power of sale (7.5.2(a))
    - The lender's duty to the borrower (7.5.2(b))
    - The proceeds of sale (7.5.2(c))
    - The general power to order sale (7.5.2(d))
  - Appointing a receiver (7.5.3)
  - Foreclosure (7.5.4)
  - Suing on the personal covenant (7.5.5)
  - Consolidation (7.5.6)
  - Holding the title documents (7.5.7)

- The position of the equitable lender (7.6)
  - The equitable mortgagee (7.6.1)
  - The equitable chargee (7.6.2)

- Priority of mortgages (7.7)
  - The general rules (7.7.1)
  - Mortgages of a legal interest in registered land (7.7.2)
  - Mortgages of a legal interest in unregistered land (7.7.3)
  - Mortgages of an equitable interest in any land (7.7.4)

- Conclusion (7.8)

Mortgages

Key concepts

- **Equity of redemption** – the rights of the mortgagor in the land subject to the mortgage, in particular, the right to recover the mortgaged land upon payment of moneys due.
- **Mortgage** – the transfer of property to secure the repayment of moneys lent by a debtor (the 'mortgagor') to his creditor (the 'mortgagee').
- **Mortgagee's powers** – the powers given to a mortgagee either expressly in the mortgage deed or, if not excluded by the deed, by Part III of the LPA 1925.

7.1 The case of the borrower's last chance

In early 1990, Mrs Norgan was in serious danger of losing her home, a period farmhouse in Wiltshire which she shared with her husband and their five sons. By May of that year, the arrears of interest on her £90,000 mortgage amounted to over £7,000. These arrears were set to double by the end of the year. The mortgage lender had lost patience and applied to the county court for an order allowing it to take possession of the mortgaged house and land.

The mortgage itself dated back to 1986. Mr Norgan, needing additional capital for his business, sold his half-share in the matrimonial home and its eight acres of land to his wife, making her the sole owner. She had financed the transaction by means of a building society loan of £90,000, to be repaid at the end of 22 years from the proceeds of various investments. In the meantime, Mrs Norgan would pay the interest that accrued on the outstanding capital by monthly instalments. The house and land were provided as security for the loan. In practice, the payments were met from the joint funds of Mr and Mrs Norgan, so when Mr Norgan ran into business difficulties, neither he nor his wife was able to keep up the payments due to the building society.

At the hearing in November 1990, the district judge made a possession order in favour of the building society, but suspended it for 28 days to allow Mrs Norgan to arrange to refinance the loan. The loan was not refinanced, and there followed a series of hearings in which the building society sought permission to enforce the possession order, and the Norgans sought to persuade the court to continue to suspend it. Mrs Norgan managed to obtain housing benefit that would cover future interest payments, but by September 1993 there were still considerable arrears outstanding, and a district judge refused to suspend the possession order any further. Mrs Norgan appealed, first to a judge of the county court and then to the Court of Appeal. By the time the matter reached the Court of Appeal in 1995, there was considerable dispute about the amount owing in arrears (in addition to the original £90,000 loan). The building society calculated the figure at £29,000; Mrs Norgan at half that figure. The total value of the mortgaged land was said to be in the region of £225,000. The building society wanted to repossess the house, presumably to sell it with vacant possession at auction. If it were to do this, the building society would recover all the sums that were owing to it, and the balance of the proceeds of the sale would be returned to Mrs Norgan. Mrs Norgan, along with her family, wanted to continue to live in the family home.

The case of *Cheltenham & Gloucester Building Society v Norgan* [1996] 1 WLR 343 (CA) was concerned with such questions as:

- Should Mrs Norgan be given any further time to pay off the arrears?
- If so, how long and on what conditions?
- How long should a lender be forced to wait before being allowed to enforce its security?

However, beneath these issues lie deeper tensions that illustrate how land simultaneously fulfils several functions. The same parcel of land may be used by one person as a home (with, perhaps, the hope that it is also a good capital investment, increasing in value), while for another it is the security against a loan (an investment of a different sort). The different demands of these various functions (shelter, security, direct or indirect investment) make it difficult to balance the competing interests when a dispute occurs.

- How can the courts recognise the commercial and contractual reality of mortgage agreements, while at the same time protecting the vulnerable?
- How should the law balance the interests of those living on the land with the commercial interests of lenders and the need for a buoyant property market, especially if there are beneficiaries (or, as was the case in *Norgan*, children) who were not parties to the mortgage?
- Should the law intervene to protect people who mortgage their land for the benefit of another? For example, the purpose of the transfer of the house and the mortgage in the *Norgan* case was to raise funds for Mr Norgan's business. Would the outcome have been different if, instead of transferring his share in the family home to his wife, Mr Norgan had simply persuaded her to agree to a joint mortgage of the house to guarantee his business overdraft?
- How can the interests of various lenders be balanced where there is more than one mortgage over a particular interest in land, but insufficient equity to redeem them all?

7.2   Introducing mortgages

Lawyers today use the word 'mortgage' in two senses:

- firstly, to describe the relationship between a landowner and a money-lender (the landowner creates a charge over the land in favour of the lender); and
- secondly, to refer to the interest granted as security (the charge).

According to Lindley MR in *Santley v Wilde* [1899] 2 Ch 474 (CA), a mortgage is:

> a conveyance of land ... as security for the payment of a debt or the discharge of some other obligation for which it is given (at 474).

To put it more succinctly, traditionally a mortgage is a transfer of land as security for a loan. Technically, a *mortgage* (which involves the transfer of a legal estate to the lender) should be distinguished from a *charge* (which gives the lender rights in the land but no estate). However, the terms are now widely treated as being interchangeable, not least because of the terminology of the LPA 1925 (see Section 7.3.1).

Mortgage relationships have existed since Anglo-Saxon times, but their form has changed a good deal since then, modified by equity and, more recently, by the intervention of Parliament. Many of the rules are relatively straightforward. However, the language and the concepts are not always quite as they might appear at first sight, resulting in a mismatch of expectation and theory that can be somewhat disconcerting. Consequently, it is essential to keep hold of the rules while exploring the theory. As far as the language is concerned, perhaps the easiest way to assimilate the technical terms is to try to explain them to your most tolerant friend.

7.2.1 Mortgagor and mortgagee

Contrary to the way most people talk, the mortgage is the interest in the land exchanged for the money, not the money being borrowed. When the letter arrives to say that a bank or a building society will lend the money to buy a house, the pedantic borrower should not say, 'They're giving me a mortgage!,' but rather, 'They're letting me grant them a mortgage.' Thus:

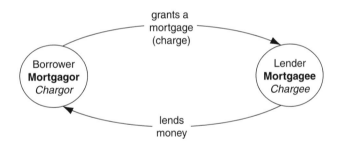

7.2.2 Law and equity

Historically, a mortgage secured a legal debt repayable on a specific date. If the loan was repaid on this date (the legal date of redemption) the mortgaged land would be returned to the borrower. If not, the lender was entitled to keep the land as well as sue the debtor for the unpaid debt. In the seventeenth century, equity began to soften this harsh common law approach by intervening to ensure that lenders were not allowed to take unconscionable advantages over borrowers. In particular, equity allowed borrowers to recover their land after the legal date of redemption had passed. This right, known as the 'equity of redemption', is the basis of modern mortgage lending and is considered in Section 7.4. It might be expected that the date of legal redemption would become irrelevant, but this is not so. The legal date of redemption (usually six months after the date of creation of the mortgage) continues to be the trigger for a number of the remedies available to the lender (see Section 7.5).

The equity of redemption is not linked to the legal or equitable status of the mortgage itself. (See Section 7.3.2 for examples of when equitable mortgages may be created.) The equity of redemption is as essential to legal mortgages as it is to equitable ones.

7.2.3 The significance of mortgages today

It has already been noted how this area of land law illustrates very clearly the way in which land simultaneously fulfils several functions. For many, land is an asset to be mortgaged in order to raise finance for commercial enterprise. The mortgage is also the device by which many people become landowners – the bank or the building society lends money to buy land, which itself provides the security for the loan. Such mortgages are known as 'acquisition mortgages'. Often these two objectives are combined: many small businesses are financed by means of a mortgage on the home of the owner of the business. Most homeowners hope that their land is also an investment that will appreciate in value. Unfortunately, this is not always the case, as the slump in property values in the early 1990s, followed by another less than a decade into the twenty-first century, demonstrate. Some borrowers find that they end up owing more than their land is worth, in which case they are said to be in 'negative equity'.

7.3 Creating and ending mortgages

7.3.1 Creating legal mortgages

Charge by way of legal mortgage (the legal charge; see section 87 of the LPA 1925) is the only way of mortgaging registered land (LRA 2002, s 23(1)(a)). It is also almost universally the method used for creating charges over unregistered land. Charges by way of legal mortgage are simply created by the execution of a deed and can be used for mortgages of either freehold or leasehold land.

Under section 85 of the LPA 1925, it is still possible to create a mortgage by *demise* of freehold land where the title to that land has not yet been registered. A lease is granted to the lender subject to a provision that the lease will come to an end when the debt is repaid (*cesser on redemption*). In a similar way, by section 86, a long lease of land which has yet to be registered can be mortgaged by *subdemise* (the creation of a sublease). In practice, neither *demise* nor *subdemise* is used to create mortgages today. They are more complex than using the charge and can only be used where the land concerned is unregistered.

The grant of a first legal mortgage over an unregistered freehold will trigger compulsory first registration of the land (LRA 2002, s 4(1)), regardless of what method is used to create it.

Before 1925, legal mortgages were created by transferring the estate to the lender, subject to its promise to reassign it to the borrower when the debt was paid. Any attempt to create a mortgage in this way by the owner of an unregistered legal estate will now create a 3,000-year lease (or a sublease) instead (LPA 1925, ss 85(2), 86(2)). A registered proprietor cannot create a legal mortgage in this way (LRA 2002, s 23(1)(a)).

7.3.2 Creating equitable mortgages

It is important to know whether a mortgage is legal or equitable because, as well as the lesser security of equitable interests if the land is sold, the remedies of the lender may be different.

An equitable mortgage may arise:

▶ where the borrower has only an equitable interest in the land, such as a beneficial interest under a trust (see Chapter 12). This equitable interest is mortgaged by assigning it in writing to the lender, who will promise to reassign it when the debt is repaid. Before 1925, this was also the means by which legal estates were mortgaged (see Section 7.3.1).

▶ where, in unregistered land, there has been an attempt at creating a legal mortgage by means of a forgery. In this situation, the mortgage will only be effective against the equitable interest of the forger and not against the interests of any innocent co-owner (see *First National Securities Ltd v Hegarty* [1985] QB 850 (CA)).

▶ where there is a contract for a legal mortgage under section 2 of the Law of Property (Miscellaneous Provisions) Act 1989, or by estoppel. An equitable mortgage, therefore, will come into existence before its conversion into a legal mortgage through the execution of a deed (see Section 12.3). Before the 1989 Act, an equitable mortgage could be created by depositing the title deeds or land certificate with the lender in exchange for the loan, since this was seen as part performance of an oral contract. Now that part performance has been abolished, this method of creating a mortgage is obsolete, as confirmed by *United Bank of Kuwait plc v Sahib* [1997] Ch 107 (CA).

7.3.3   The discharge of mortgages

A mortgage is ended when the lease, sublease or charge is removed from the title to the property.

▶ In registered land, the mortgage can be discharged electronically or by sending a form to the Land Registry.

▶ Normally, in unregistered land, the borrower obtains a signed receipt on the mortgage document, and (in the case of a first charge) the title deeds are returned to the land owner. In the case of a mortgage by a long lease, repayment of the loan means that the lease becomes a satisfied term.

7.4   The position of the borrower

Over the centuries, both policymakers and lawyers seem to have accepted that borrowers are inevitably vulnerable to exploitation by lenders. Lenders are almost always in the stronger negotiating position and, it is argued, have little interest in the relationship beyond personal profit. Consequently, the borrower has been given special rights to protection against oppression by a mortgagee, especially in relation to the terms of the contract. Many of these rights are creations of equity, while others have been introduced by statute. Those that relate directly to the borrower are dealt with in this section. Rights that arise when the lender's powers are exercised are examined in the context of these powers in Section 7.5.

7.4.1   The equity of redemption

As mentioned in Section 7.2.2, mortgage agreements normally specify a contractual date for the repayment of the loan (the legal date of redemption), usually six months from the date of the loan. Where it is fair to do so, equity refuses to enforce this contractual date. Instead, the lender is required to accept the money even though the legal date of redemption has passed, thereby creating an equitable right to redeem.

Historically, equity looks at the substance of an agreement and not at the name given to it. If the effect of an agreement is to create a loan on the security of land, equity will recognise the transaction as a mortgage and protect the borrower, following the maxim 'once a mortgage, always a mortgage'. The rules are summarised in the expression that there must be 'no clogs or fetters on the equity of redemption' and are explained below. However, it must be noted that some of the older cases reflect a different financial world, and, furthermore, one in which the House of Lords was bound to follow its own earlier decisions. It is becoming evident that modern judges will attempt to find a way around inconvenient precedents by, for example, applying general contractual doctrines such as duress and restraint of trade, rather than considering whether a term amounts, in mortgage law theory, to a 'clog'.

7.4.1(a) No irredeemability

Equity will not allow a lender to enforce a promise that prevents a borrower from ever redeeming the mortgage. For example, *Samuel v Jarrah Timber & Wood Paving Co Ltd* [1904] AC 323 (HL) concerned a mortgage of company stock (a debenture). In the mortgage deed, the borrower gave the lender an option to purchase; the lender could therefore choose to buy the stock from the borrower, thus preventing the borrower from redeeming the mortgage. The House of Lords declared the option void because it made the equitable right to redeem 'illusory'. The decision was made very reluctantly (in 1904, the House could not reverse its own decisions) as their Lordships felt that this arrangement, made by two large companies, was quite different from the kind of case for which the rule had been established:

> The directors of a trading company in search of financial assistance are certainly in a very different position from that of an impecunious landowner in the toils of a crafty money-lender (per Lord Macnaghten at 327).

In *Jones v Morgan* [2002] 1 EGLR 125 (CA), the Court of Appeal struck out a term in a mortgage agreement that purported to give the lender a right to buy a half-share in the mortgaged land. In an ordinary contract, the term would have been valid, but since the term was contained within a mortgage agreement, the doctrine of clogs and fetters applied because, again, the Court found itself bound by precedent. However, the doctrine received considerable criticism in the case:

> the doctrine of a clog on the equity of redemption is, so it seems to me, an appendix to our law which no longer serves a useful purpose and would be better excised (per Lord Phillips MR at [86]).

If the option to purchase is seen as a separate agreement from the mortgage agreement, it will be enforced. In *Reeve v Lisle* [1902] AC 461 (HL), a mortgage of a ship was created and, some 12 days later, the mortgagor granted the lender an option to purchase it. The court did not see this as a clog, since the later agreement could be separated from the mortgage, and the option was held to be enforceable. Whether there is a separate agreement is not always easy to determine. For example, in *Jones v Morgan*, Pill LJ dissented from the majority judgment, holding that the right to buy the half-share was a separate agreement and that it was not, therefore, a clog on the equity of redemption.

In *Warnborough Ltd v Garmite Ltd* [2003] EWCA Civ 1544, the Court of Appeal had the opportunity of reviewing the law on the extent to which an option to purchase amounts to a clog on the equity of redemption. Jonathan Parker LJ stated that:

> the mere fact that, contemporaneously with the grant of a mortgage over his property, the mortgagor grants the mortgagee an option to purchase the property does no more than raise

the question whether the rule against 'clogs' applies: it does not begin to answer that question ... the court has to look at the 'substance' of the transaction in question: in other words, to inquire as to the true nature of the bargain which the parties have made (at [73]).

He went on to state that where the original seller of the property was also both mortgagee and the grantee of the option, as in the *Warnborough* case, there would be a strong likelihood that the transaction would be held to be one of sale and purchase rather than one of mortgage, and so the doctrine of clogs would not apply.

An agreement which postpones the equitable right to redeem so that it effectively becomes meaningless is likely to be void. This happened in *Fairclough v Swan Brewery Co Ltd* [1912] AC 565 (PC), where Mr Fairclough held a 17-year lease of a hotel. His landlord was the Swan Brewery, which lent him money on the security of his lease. The contractual date of redemption was fixed for a few weeks before the lease was due to expire. As the equitable right to redeem does not arise until the contractual date has passed, the mortgage was effectively irredeemable, and the promise was therefore held void. However, in *Knightsbridge Estates Trust Ltd v Byrne* [1939] Ch 441 (CA); [1945] AC 613 (HL), a case between two large companies, the contractual date for redemption of the mortgage (for £310,000) was set 40 years in the future. Given the reluctance of the courts to intervene when the parties are of equal bargaining power, and also the fact that the land was freehold, both the Court of Appeal and the House of Lords held that the term was enforceable. This was, in the words of Sir Wilfred Greene MR in the Court of Appeal:

a commercial agreement between two important corporations, experienced in such matters, and has none of the features of an oppressive bargain (at 455).

7.4.1(b) Post-redemption conditions

Another of equity's concerns was the unfair advantage taken by a lender who sought to restrict the borrower's commercial activities, such as requiring a shopkeeper mortgagor to buy wholesale goods only from the mortgagee. These kinds of agreement are known as 'solus agreements' and are common between oil companies and filling stations, and between breweries and publicans. Equity had declared void any terms in a mortgage agreement which would prevent the borrower from freely enjoying his land after he has repaid all the money. An example of this is *Noakes & Co Ltd v Rice* [1902] AC 24 (HL), where the owner of a 26-year lease of a pub mortgaged it to a brewery, promising he would buy liquor only from the lender for the whole term of the lease. The House of Lords held that the promise was ineffective: the lender could not prevent him regaining his property free of ties when he repaid the loan. In *G&C Kreglinger v New Patagonia Meat & Cold Storage Co Ltd* [1914] AC 25 (HL), however, the House of Lords decided that a collateral promise that the borrower would sell his sheepskins to no one but the lender for five years, regardless of when the loan was repaid, was valid. This was not a clog on the equitable right to redeem. The mortgage agreement was a commercial arrangement on reasonable terms between two companies at arm's length, and, after redemption, the mortgagor would be able to enjoy the land in the same state as it had been before the mortgage. Nowadays, the courts tend to apply the contractual doctrine of restraint of trade to this kind of issue (see *Esso Petroleum Co Ltd v Harpers Garage (Stourport) Ltd* [1968] AC 269 (HL)).

7.4.1(c) Other oppressive terms

Equity developed rules against other clogs on the equity of redemption, and declared void any other 'unconscionable or oppressive terms' in the mortgage. In *Multiservice*

Bookbinding Ltd v Marden [1979] Ch 84 (Ch), the bookbinding company granted a mortgage as security for a loan of £36,000. The interest rate was linked to the Swiss franc, because the pound was very unstable. The fluctuation in the money markets meant that the borrower would have to pay £45,000 in interest. Browne-Wilkinson J held that this may have been unreasonable, but it was not oppressive or unconscionable. For a promise to be struck out, it must be shown that the objectionable terms were imposed 'in a morally reprehensible manner ... which affects [the mortgagee's] conscience' (at 110). Again, the court showed its reluctance to intervene in a commercial agreement between equals.

Many mortgage agreements permit the lender, at its discretion, to vary the interest rate payable by the borrower. The Court of Appeal in *Paragon Finance plc v Nash* [2002] 1 WLR 685 (CA) protected the borrower against the arbitrary exercise of this discretion by holding that such agreements contain an implied term that the interest rates 'would not be set dishonestly, for an improper purpose, capriciously or arbitrarily' (per Dyson LJ at [36]). In a later case concerning the same lender (*Paragon Finance plc v Pender* [2005] 1 WLR 3412 (CA)), a differently constituted Court of Appeal decided that there was nothing in this implied term that prevents a lender from increasing the interest rate above that of most of its competitors, provided that the decision to do so is a genuinely commercial one.

7.4.2   Statutory protection from unfair agreements

The vast majority of first mortgages of residential property will fall within the provisions of the Financial Services and Markets Act 2000, which came into force on 31 October 2004. This Act imposes a code of practice on mortgage lenders designed to promote transparency and preclude extortionate charges being imposed. A lender in breach of the Code may find itself subject to disciplinary action by the Financial Services Authority, and the borrower may have an action for damages under section 150 of the Act. However, breaching the Code does not make the mortgage void or limit the mortgagee's remedies (Financial Services and Markets Act 2000, s 151(2)).

Until April 2008, most other mortgages granted by individuals fell within sections 137–40 of the Consumer Credit Act 1974, regulating extortionate credit bargains. Mortgagors could ask the courts to reopen a credit bargain if the payments were 'grossly exorbitant' or 'grossly contravene[d] ordinary principles of fair dealing'. Sections 137–40 have now been repealed and replaced by a new scheme allowing the court to intervene if it finds that the relationship between the creditor and the debtor arising out of a credit agreement is unfair to the debtor (Consumer Credit Act 2006, ss 19–22).

Like sections 137–40, the new scheme applies to agreements between an individual borrower (including an individual in the course of business) and anyone who lends money. It does not apply to first legal charges over residential land regulated under the Financial Services and Markets Act 2000 (see above), but will apply to many second mortgages. Many second mortgages are arranged for purposes such as home improvements or securing a business loan, but sometimes they are an act of desperation by a defaulting borrower, and here in particular that the borrower needs protection.

Under section 140A of the Consumer Credit Act 1974 (as amended), the court may decide that the relationship is unfair to the debtor because of one or more of:

(a) any of the terms of the agreement or of any related agreement;
(b) the way in which the creditor has exercised or enforced any of his rights under the agreement or any related agreement; and
(c) any other thing done (or not done) by, or on behalf of, the creditor (either before or after the making of the agreement or any related agreement.

If satisfied that an agreement is unfair, the court has considerable powers to intervene on behalf of the borrower. It may, for example, alter the terms of the agreement or order repayment or the return of property (s 140B). However, the courts seem to be as unwilling to intervene in credit agreements under section 140A as they were to use their earlier powers under sections 137–40. This is possibly because the more needy (and therefore weak) the borrower, the more justified is the lender in imposing a high interest rate: the interest rate must, it is argued, reflect the degree of risk being taken by the lender. The counter-argument, that if the borrower defaults, the lender can realise the security of the land, appears to hold little attraction.

7.4.3 Section 91 LPA 1925

There may be circumstances, especially when the value of land has been falling, when the mortgagee might seek to prevent a sale of the mortgaged land, despite the borrower being unable to repay the loan. Where there is negative equity, the borrower may be keen to sell the land to repay as much of the debt as possible in order to prevent the interest due on the loan from spiralling upwards. The lender may be equally keen to prevent a sale, leasing out the land in the meantime in the hope that it might increase in value at some point in the future. This situation arose in *Palk v Mortgage Services Funding plc* [1993] Ch 330 (CA), where the borrower had found a buyer for the land, but the price was about £50,000 less than the mortgage debt at that point. The interest on the debt was accumulating at a rate of £43,000 a year, and an annual rent would not have been more than about £13,000. The mortgagee argued that it could prevent a sale if the price were less than the amount needed to repay the debt in full. Mrs Palk claimed, however, that under section 91 of the LPA 1925 (originally intended to facilitate sales in foreclosure proceedings), the court has discretion to order a sale of mortgaged property. Here the Court of Appeal held for Mrs Palk: any borrower, even one suffering with a negative equity, can ask the court to order a sale because the court has an 'unfettered discretion' under section 91 to prevent 'manifest unfairness'.

7.4.4 Avoiding undue influence and misrepresentation

The question of mortgages entered into because of undue influence and misrepresentation has been raised in a large number of cases since the increase in family home repossessions which occurred in the early 1990s, when interest rates were high and the value of property was falling.

In a typical undue influence case, a lender seeks to repossess a home because of arrears, and one of the joint borrowers then claims to have signed the mortgage deed or stood surety for the loan because the other misused his (it is often the husband) influence over her, exploiting the relationship of trust that existed between them. It is important to distinguish undue influence from misrepresentation.

Undue influence is concerned with the abuse of a relationship of trust and confidence by the husband exercising control over the will of the wife in order to procure her consent to the guarantee. In a case of misrepresentation, that consent has been procured not by the exercise of some form of pressure or domination but by the making of a false statement which the wife in the relationship of trust has relied upon (per Patten LJ, *Royal Bank of Scotland plc v Chandra* [2011] EWCA Civ 192 (CA), at [32]).

In both situations, the question for the court is not whether one party acted towards the other unconscionably or in breach of trust, but whether the lending institution had notice of the undue influence or misrepresentation, or was in some other way responsible for it. If the lender did not take steps to ensure that the signature was properly obtained without any undue influence or misrepresentation, the mortgage will be void as far as the injured party is concerned.

The facts of two House of Lords cases are typical of the kinds of situation where a lender might be fixed with notice of the undue influence of the borrower. In the first of the cases, *Barclays Bank plc v O'Brien* [1994] 1 AC 180 (HL), Mr O'Brien was the sole legal owner of the matrimonial home, but his wife had an equitable share in it. He told her he was borrowing £60,000 on a mortgage for three weeks to save his business, so she signed all the surety forms at the bank without reading any of them and without any independent advice. In fact, the loan was for £135,000. Within six months, the repayments were seriously in arrears, and the bank sought possession. Mrs O'Brien successfully argued that her agreement to the mortgage was the result of her husband's misrepresentation about the size of the loan being secured on the house, and that the bank had constructive notice of this, giving rise to her right to set the mortgage aside.

In the second case, *CIBC Mortgages v Pitt* [1994] 1 AC 200 (HL), the facts were fairly similar, but here Mrs Pitt, the wife, was a joint legal owner of the home. As joint legal owner she could be presumed, on the facts, to be benefiting financially from the mortgage loan (its purpose was expressed to be to pay off an outstanding mortgage and to buy a second home, but the husband really wanted the money in order to play the stock market), and therefore the bank was not put on notice to take steps to protect her position.

After a series of undue influence cases in the lower courts, the House of Lords reviewed this area of the law in what is now the leading case on undue influence: *Royal Bank of Scotland plc v Etridge (No 2)* [2002] 2 AC 773 (HL). The questions were these:

▶ what are the requirements that need to be met in order to prove that undue influence has occurred?
▶ under what circumstances is a lender put on notice that there may have been undue influence?
▶ if the lender is on notice, what steps must it take to avoid any subsequent claim by the innocent joint borrower or surety?

The answers to the second and third questions will depend upon whether the transaction took place before or after the House of Lords' decision in *Etridge*.

Pre-Etridge transactions

1 The lender is placed on inquiry in situations where the surety trusted the debtor to deal with her financial affairs or where both were living together in a close emotional relationship.

2 In such circumstances:

> the bank will ordinarily be regarded as having discharged its obligations if a solicitor who was acting for the wife in the transaction gave the bank confirmation to the effect that he had brought home to the wife the risks she was running by standing as surety (per Lord Nicholls at [80]).

3 Additional steps may be required, especially where the lender was aware that the guarantor's circumstances made her particularly vulnerable to exploitation. (See, for example, *National Westminster Bank plc v Amin* [2002] UKHL 9, per Lord Scott at [24].)

Post-Etridge transactions

1 The lender will be on inquiry in all cases where the relationship between the debtor and the surety is non-commercial.

2 In such circumstances:

> The furthest a bank can be expected to go is to take reasonable steps to satisfy itself that the wife has had brought home to her, in a meaningful way, the practical implications of the proposed transaction. This does not wholly eliminate the risk of undue influence or misrepresentation. But it does mean that a wife enters into a transaction with her eyes open so far as the basic elements of the transaction are concerned (per Lord Nicholls at [54]).

3 The bank will be considered to have taken these reasonable steps if:

- it tells the wife or other person in a non-commercial relationship to the debtor that it requires her to consult a solicitor of her choice (who may be the family solicitor, but who must be acting for her);
- it provides the necessary financial information to allow the solicitor properly to advise the borrower (if the debtor will not allow such confidential information to be passed on, the transaction will not be able to proceed); and
- it obtains written confirmation from the solicitor that the documents and the practical implications of the arrangement (that is, that she risks losing her home if the mortgage payments are not met) have been explained to the borrower.

If the bank has reason to believe that the wife is not acting of her own free will, it must inform the solicitor of this.

The case of *Hewett v First Plus Financial Group plc* [2010] 2 P & CR 22 (CA) demonstrates the consequences of a lender still failing to take these relatively simple steps. At the time that he asked his wife to sign the mortgage, Mr Hewett failed to disclose to her that he was having an extra-marital affair (indeed, he had taken great pains to stress his commitment to his family). The Court of Appeal held that this amounted to undue influence on the facts of the case. The lender conceded that it had failed to take the steps, outlined in *Etridge*, that were necessary to protect it from being affected by Mr Hewett's conduct. Consequently, it could not enforce its legal charge against what was now Mrs Hewett's home. However, the lender still had an equitable charge over Mr Hewett's beneficial interest in the land (see Section 7.3.2). This meant that Mrs Hewett's home (although not her share of it) was still at risk as the lender could seek an order for the sale of the land under section 14 of the Trusts of Land and Appointment of Trustees Act 1996 (see Section 11.5).

This complex area of mortgage law indicates the sort of policy tensions which can arise in land law and how the courts deal with them. It is important that lenders are able to lend money on the security of property without being concerned that their security will be lost, and at the same time it is just as important that the rights of more vulnerable owners are protected. (See also, for example, *Williams & Glyn's Bank Ltd v Boland* [1981] AC 487 (HL), *City of London Building Society v Flegg* [1988] AC 54 (HL), discussed at Section 11.6.1.)

7.5   The position of the legal lender

The lender (mortgagee) has remedies to enforce the payment of the money due to it, together with certain other rights. Some of these rights (such as the right to take possession) are characteristic of all mortgages. Others may be granted by the terms of the mortgage deed or implied under the provisions of Part III of the LPA 1925.

The legal mortgagee's most important rights are to:

1. take possession of the property;
2. sell the property;
3. appoint a receiver;
4. foreclose;
5. sue on the personal covenant;
6. consolidate;
7. hold the title deeds if the land is still unregistered; and
8. exercise rights in connection with a series of mortgages ('tacking' – see Section 7.7.1).

The lender does not have to choose only one of these remedies: it is possible to pursue several at the same time.

These remedies date from a time when mortgages were not so commonly used for home buying. Over the years, they have been adjusted by statute to protect the security of home buyers, just as tenants' security has been protected to some extent by modern legislation.

7.5.1   Taking possession

Historically, a mortgagee had a lease of the land. Even today, when mortgages are almost invariably created by 'charge by deed expressed to be by way of legal mortgage', the mortgagee is treated as if it has a lease (LPA 1925, s 87(1)). Consequently, a lender has the right to:

> go into possession before the ink is dry on the mortgage unless there is something in the contract, express or by implication, whereby he has contracted himself out of that right (*Four-Maids Ltd v Dudley Marshall (Properties) Ltd* [1957] Ch 317 (Ch) at 320 per Harman J).

Usually, of course, the lender will not want to take possession unless the borrower fails to pay. It might seem extraordinary that the lender has the right to move in as soon as the mortgage deed is signed. Although it was once common for the mortgagee to take possession of the land at the beginning of the mortgage, in practice this now only happens if the borrower defaults. The lender will then probably want to sell the property with vacant possession (but see below for other remedies) and will generally obtain a court order before taking possession. A court order is not always necessary, but, unless the lender is sure that the premises are unoccupied, it is the safest way of ensuring that there is no breach of section 6 of the Criminal Law Act 1977, which makes it an offence to use or threaten violence to gain entry into premises.

At common law, once a legal mortgagee is entitled to possession, 'the court has no jurisdiction to decline the order or to adjourn the hearing whether on terms of keeping up payments or paying arrears, if the mortgagee cannot be persuaded to agree to this course' (per Russell J, *Birmingham Citizens Permanent Building Society v Caunt* [1962] Ch 883 (Ch), 912). However, where the mortgaged property is (or includes) a home, section 36 of the Administration of Justice Act 1970 (as amended by section 8 of the Administration of Justice Act 1973) gives the court the discretion to postpone an order giving the lender possession if the borrower is likely to be able to pay his arrears 'within a reasonable period'. A number of cases have therefore focused on the issue of when the court might exercise its section 36 discretion; some have concerned the defaulting borrower's likelihood of finding employment and repaying arrears, and others the chances of her being able to sell the land within a reasonable period.

Perhaps the most important case is that of *Cheltenham & Gloucester Building Society v Norgan* [1996] 1 WLR 343 (CA), the facts of which are set out at Section 7.1. The Court of Appeal had to consider what would amount to a reasonable period for the purposes of its section 36 discretion. In the years before *Norgan*, a period of two years had become fairly established in judgments as the normal standard. The Court of Appeal held that 'a reasonable period' was not limited to any particular length of time. In *Norgan*, the mortgage term was to end 13 years from the time of the claim for a possession order, and the Court held that this could be a reasonable period within 'the logic and spirit of the Act' (at 353). However, given the significant dispute about the size of the arrears, the Court felt that it could only comment on the principle of the matter. The case was effectively referred back to a lower court to decide whether it could reschedule the debt over the whole repayment period. In theory, such a rescheduling from the outset of the mortgagor's difficulties should avoid the continuing struggle and repeated orders and delays in repossession proceedings that characterised the proceedings in *Norgan* (see also *Cheltenham & Gloucester plc v Krausz* [1997] 1 WLR 1558 (CA), referred to at Section 7.5.2(d)).

A borrower is only entitled to apply for relief under section 36 if an action for possession has been brought. *Ropaigealach v Barclays Bank plc* [2000] QB 263 (CA) was a relatively rare example of a case where the lender did not obtain a court order for possession. In this case, the borrowers had moved elsewhere, and the house subject to the mortgage was standing empty. The Court of Appeal concluded, albeit reluctantly, that the borrowers were not entitled to section 36 relief in such circumstances. To allow relief in these circumstances would effectively prevent a mortgagee from taking possession without first obtaining a court order, which went beyond what Parliament had enacted in section 36. It has been suggested that this result contravenes the borrower's rights under Articles 6 and 8 and Article 1, Protocol 1 of the European Convention on Human Rights (ECHR) (see Rook, 2001, 199), although this line of argument was rejected by Briggs J in the recent case of *Horsham Properties Group Ltd v Clark* [2009] 1 WLR 1255 (Ch) (see Section 7.5.2(a)).

7.5.2 Sale

7.5.2(a) The power of sale

Although the mortgagee has no power of sale at common law, there is a statutory power of sale provided by the LPA 1925. All mortgages that satisfy the conditions set out in section 101 of the LPA 1925 benefit from the statutory power of sale, except insofar as it is modified or excluded by the terms of the mortgage (as, for example, in *Ropaigealach*, where different conditions were substituted for those set out in section 103 of the LPA 1925 (see below)).

There are two sets of conditions that must be satisfied before a lender can exercise its power of sale under the LPA 1925. The power must have *arisen* under section 101, and it must have become *exercisable* by virtue of at least one of the conditions in section 103 being satisfied.

Section 101: The power of sale *arises* if:

- the mortgage is made by deed (s 101(1)); and
- the deed contains no provision excluding the statutory power (s 101(4)); and
- the contractual date for redeeming the mortgage has passed (that is, the mortgage money has become due; s 101(1)(i)).

On most domestic mortgages, the contractual date of redemption is usually set six months after the creation of the mortgage.

Section 103: The power of sale becomes *exercisable* if:

- the default continues three months after a notice requiring payment is served; or
- interest is two months in default; or
- the borrower has broken another term of the mortgage.

Although the lender only has a charge (or a long lease or sublease), he may sell the borrower's whole interest as soon as one of the conditions in section 103 has been fulfilled (LPA 1925, ss 88–9). Under the provisions of the LPA 1925, the lender does not need a court order to sell the land. In most cases, the lender will first obtain a court order granting possession before proceeding with the sale, but this is not a legal requirement. In *Horsham v Clark*, the lender sold the mortgaged property without first obtaining possession of it from the borrower. A sale under section 101 overreaches the interest of the borrower in a similar way to the overreaching of beneficial interests when the proceeds are paid to two trustees (see Section 11.6.1). This is a neat way of avoiding the court's discretion to postpone possession orders under section 36 of the Administration of Justice Act 1970. Section 36 did not apply in *Horsham v Clark*, because the person seeking possession was not a mortgagee. Consequently, the new owner was able to obtain possession of the property from the borrowers. The mortgagee's actions in *Horsham v Clark* are highly unusual, and the Council of Mortgage Lenders voluntarily issued guidance to its members, directing them not to exploit the decision in *Horsham*. As to whether a court order should be required to authorise a sale, this is exactly what was suggested in the Ministry of Justice's response to *Horsham v Clark*, Consultation Paper CP55/09 *Mortgages: Power of Sale and Residential Property* (issued at the end of 2009). If the suggestions are adopted, mortgagees of owner-occupied residential properties would in future need the approval of the court before exercising a power of sale (through the existing procedure for a possession order or by a new form of order approving sale). However, the scope of the proposals is limited: they would not, for example, apply to mortgages over a dwelling house securing a business debt.

The exercise of the power of sale against the family home can have distressing effects on the family, but any attempt to invoke ECHR Article 8 (the right to respect for a person's private and family life and home) will not succeed, since the Article cannot be used 'to diminish the contractual and proprietary rights of the mortgagee under the mortgage' (per Lord Scott, *Harrow LBC v Qazi* [2004] 1 AC 983 (HL) at [135]; see also *Horsham v Clark*).

7.5.2(b) The lender's duty to the borrower

Although the lender may choose when to sell and does not have to wait for an upturn in the market, when it does sell it is under a duty to the borrower to take reasonable care to get the best price reasonably obtainable 'on the day'.

In a Privy Council case from Hong Kong, *China & South Seas Bank v Tan* [1990] 1 AC 536 (PC), there was a mortgage loan of $HK30 million on the security of shares. Mr Tan, as surety for the mortgage, undertook to repay all the moneys owed by the debtor. When the repayment became due, the shares were worth enough to repay the debt, but by the time the mortgagee decided to exercise his power of sale, the shares were worthless. Mr Tan argued that the mortgagee owed him a duty of care to sell as soon as possible, but this was rejected:

> If the creditor chose to exercise his power of sale over the mortgaged security he must sell for the current market value but the creditor must decide in his own interest if and when he should sell. The creditor does not become a trustee of the mortgaged securities (per Lord Templeman at 545).

In another case from Hong Kong, *Tse Kwong Lam v Wong Chit Sen* [1983] 1 WLR 1349 (PC), Tse had granted a mortgage to Wong in 1963 on a large development in Hong Kong. Three years later, he was in arrears, and the land was sold at auction to the only bidder, a company owned by the lender and his wife and children. This in itself would not necessarily have been relevant, but the lender could not show that:

> he protected the interests of the borrower taking expert advice as to the method of sale, as to the steps which ought reasonably to be taken to make the sale a success and as to the amount of the reserve [minimum price] (per Lord Templeman at 1359).

The normal remedy in such a case is for the sale to be set aside, but here the Privy Council did not do so, because the borrower had been 'guilty of inexcusable delay'; he had not pursued the matter for many years. He won the alternative remedy of damages, the difference between the price which was obtained and the price which should have been obtained.

An example of where the lender was negligent in exercising its power of sale is *Cuckmere Brick Ltd v Mutual Finance Ltd* [1971] Ch 949 (CA). In this case, the lender had failed to advertise to prospective purchasers the full extent of the planning permission which attached to the property. The price paid for the land was almost certainly lower than what would have been obtained had the value of the planning permission been taken into account. The Court of Appeal held that the mortgagee had failed to meet the duty that it owed to the mortgagor to take reasonable care to obtain a proper price. As a result, the lender was liable to the mortgagor for any shortfall between the price obtained by the lender and the true value of the land.

7.5.2(c) The proceeds of sale

Once the land is sold, the lender is under a duty to account to the borrower. It must also take care to protect the interests of others. The lender must apply the proceeds in the order set out in section 105 of the LPA 1925.

Section 105: The order of application of the proceeds of sale:

▶ any prior mortgages, unless the property was sold subject to them;
▶ the expenses of the sale;
▶ the capital and interest due under the mortgage;
▶ any second or subsequent mortgages; and
▶ the borrower.

Although the lender is not a trustee of its power of sale, it is, by virtue of section 105, a trustee of the proceeds of sale and must act in good faith.

A buyer from a mortgagee must check that a power of sale exists, but need not make sure that it has actually become exercisable (LPA 1925, s 104(2)). However, if she knows of, or suspects, any 'impropriety', she might not get a good title. For this reason, she would be wise to ensure that the mortgagee has taken reasonable care; otherwise, she might lose the land and have to try to get the purchase price back from the mortgagee (see Megarry and Wade, 2012, § 25–016).

7.5.2(d) The general power to order sale

In addition to the power given mortgagees by section 101 of the LPA 1925, courts have the general power to order sale at the instance of any 'person interested' by virtue of section 91 of the LPA 1925. The court's general power to order sale may be employed as an alternative to foreclosure (see Section 7.5.4) and can also be used at the request of the borrower (see Section 7.4.3). Occasionally, as in *Target Home Loans Ltd v Clothier* [1994] 1 All ER 439 (CA), the courts will postpone a possession order to allow the borrower, rather than the lender, to sell the property, since the borrower is likely to get a higher price. However, following the Court of Appeal decision in *Cheltenham & Gloucester plc v Krausz* [1997] 1 WLR 1558 (CA), it is unlikely that the courts will take this line in cases where the value of the property is less than the balance owed (what is referred to as 'negative equity').

7.5.3 Appointing a receiver

A lender can appoint a receiver – who manages the land – in the same circumstances in which it has the power of sale (LPA 1925, s 101). This can be very convenient in a commercial mortgage, for example, if the land is let to tenants, and the mortgagee wants the rents to pay off interest which is due. The advantage of appointing a receiver rather than going into possession is that a mortgagee in possession is personally liable to the borrower for any loss, but if it appoints a receiver, the receiver must pay for her own mistakes. This is because, by section 109 of the LPA 1925, the receiver is deemed to be the agent of the mortgagor (the borrower). In *Medforth v Blake* [2000] Ch 86 (CA), the Court of Appeal considered that the duties owed by a receiver to a borrower and others interested in the equity of redemption (see Section 7.4.1) are not confined to a duty of good faith but extend to managing the property with due diligence, subject to trying to create a situation whereby the debt can be paid off. In *Silven Properties v Royal Bank of Scotland plc* [2004] 1 WLR 997 (CA), the Court of Appeal confirmed that the receiver's duty to manage the property does not require him to go so far as to undertake its improvement in order to increase its value. The receiver's primary duty is to effect the repayment of the secured debt.

7.5.4   Foreclosure

Once the legal date of redemption has passed, a foreclosure order is theoretically available from the court. However, these equitable orders are rarely, if ever, sought today. A foreclosure order transfers legal and equitable title in the land to the lender, free from all the borrower's rights in the land (including the right to redeem the mortgage). An order is only granted if the court is clear that the borrower will never be able to repay, but even when an order has been granted, the court has the power to reopen the foreclosure (see *Campbell v Holyland* (1877–78) LR 7 Ch D 166 (Ch)). Any application for a foreclosure order will now almost certainly result in the court making an order for sale pursuant to its powers under section 91 of the LPA 1925 (see Sections 7.4.3 and 7.5.2(d)).

7.5.5   Suing on the personal covenant

If the amount realised on the sale of the mortgaged land is insufficient to cover the amount owed to the lender, the borrower remains personally liable to the lender for the shortfall, and the lender may sue him for the outstanding sum. During the recession of the 1990s, many borrowers left their homes and handed over the keys to lenders in the expectation that this would bring their indebtedness to an end. However, when, due to falling house prices, the proceeds of sale were insufficient to meet the mortgage arrears, the unfortunate borrowers found themselves being sued for the balance.

The right to sue on the personal covenant to repay the mortgage debt must be exercised within 'twelve years from the date on which the right to receive the money accrued' (Limitation Act 1980, s 20). Initially, this date is the contractual date of redemption set by the mortgage, but the 12-year period recommences each time any payment of capital or interest is made and if written acknowledgement of liability is given by the mortgagor (Limitation Act 1980, ss 29, 30). The limitation period for interest due under the mortgage (as opposed to the capital debt) is six years from the date that the interest fell due (Limitation Act 1980, s 20(5)).

In *West Bromwich Building Society v Wilkinson* [2005] 1 WLR 2303 (HL) the lender obtained an order for possession of the borrowers' home in 1989, selling it a year later and leaving a shortfall of nearly £24,000. In 2002, the lender began proceedings for nearly £47,000 (the initial shortfall and the interest on it since 1990). The lender argued that section 20 did not apply, and that even if it did, the limitation period did not start running until after the land had been sold, when the total shortfall would be known. The House of Lords rejected both arguments. Section 20 applies to all actions derived from a mortgage, even if the lender has sold the land concerned. The effect of the wording of this particular mortgage, combined with sections 101 and 103 of the LPA 1925, was that the whole of the mortgage advance fell due as soon as the borrowers had defaulted, and the lender made demand for payment. Consequently, the 12 years began to run in 1989, with the result that the action was statute barred.

The borrower's liability on his personal covenant can have very serious consequences for himself and for others. In *Alliance & Leicester plc v Slayford* (2000) 33 HLR 66 (CA), a lender had been unable to get an order for possession against a borrower due to the wife of the borrower having a very small equitable interest in the house that was not subject to the mortgage. The lender decided to sue on the borrower's personal covenant to repay, which would have had the eventual effect of making the borrower bankrupt. The trustee in bankruptcy could then apply for sale of the house under section 14 of the Trusts of Land and Appointment of Trustees Act 1996 and would almost certainly succeed (see Section 11.5.4). Although the lender would lose its priority over the bankrupt borrower's unsecured creditors, at least by these means it would get some of its money back. The wife, however, would lose her home, despite the mortgage having earlier been declared void against her. In somewhat forthright language, the trial judge stated that the mortgagee's tactic amounted to an abuse of the process of the court. The Court of Appeal had little difficulty in finding for the mortgagee: it was not an abuse for it to employ any or all of the legal remedies available to it.

7.5.6 Consolidation

In rare cases, where the mortgagee has lent money on mortgages granted by the same borrower over different pieces of land, he has a right to consolidate them. This means that he may join the various mortgages together; he can refuse to allow the borrower to redeem one of the mortgages without redeeming any others. Consolidation can be useful if one piece of land is not sufficient security for the debt. The right arises when the power is contained in the mortgage itself, and is exercisable only when the contractual date for redemption has passed. There are a number of technical rules, very clearly explained in Megarry and Wade, 2012, §§ 25–055 to 25–070.

7.5.7 Holding the title documents

The first legal mortgagee of unregistered land is entitled to hold the deeds, which are returned to the borrower on redemption. This is a very effective way of ensuring that the land is not sold without the lender's knowledge, as any attempt to sell the legal estate will require the seller to produce the title deeds. Of course, the title deeds will not be available to any second or subsequent mortgagee, which must protect its interest by registering a Class C(i) land charge under the Land Charges Act 1972 (see Section 16.3.2(a)). All first legal mortgages created after March 1998 will trigger the first registration of the land (see Section 15.3.1).

If the title is registered, any charge is protected by entry on the register (see Section 15.3.4). Prior to 13 October 2003, the Land Registry issued a charge certificate to the mortgagee each time a new mortgage was registered. Charge certificates have not been issued since the LRA 2002 came into force, although the registration of a new legal charge will prompt the issue of a new 'title information document' (see Section 15.3.1).

7.6   The position of the equitable lender

Both equitable mortgagees and equitable chargees can sue on the borrower's personal promise to pay, but apart from this, their rights differ.

7.6.1   The equitable mortgagee

Unless an equitable mortgage has been made by deed, there is no automatic power to sell or appoint a receiver (LPA 1925, s 101). However, the mortgagee can obtain a court order for sale using section 91 of the LPA 1925. If there is a deed, the equitable lender generally has the same remedies as a legal lender, but it must be careful to draft the document to give it the right to sell the legal estate. It is not clear whether it has an automatic right to go into possession.

7.6.2   The equitable chargee

The rights of 'a mere equitable chargee' are fewer than those of other lenders. This kind of lender has only the remedy of sale or appointment of a receiver, both by order of the court.

7.7   Priority of mortgages

7.7.1   The general rules

The rules about priority in mortgages come into play when there are several mortgages of one piece of land. If the borrower defaults, and the land is not worth enough to pay back all the debts, then one or more of the lenders may lose money. The priority rules determine which of the lenders is to be unlucky. There have been few cases in the past hundred years on priorities, but some land lawyers greatly enjoy creating and solving priority puzzles, especially those concerning three or more mortgages. The basic rules are stated very briefly here; for further details see, for example, Megarry and Wade, 2012, ch 26.

There are also special rules about the situation where several mortgages exist on one piece of land and a mortgagee owns two or more of them. In these circumstances, the mortgagee may be allowed to 'tack'. It is convenient to illustrate this with a fictional example. Suppose Oliver purchased his flat with the help of a mortgage from Ceele Bank plc. A few years later, he granted a second mortgage to Klayton Finance Ltd to secure a loan to his business. Finally, when Ceele Bank lent Oliver yet more money this loan was also secured (by a third mortgage) on the flat. If Ceele Bank decides to enforce its charges, it may tack its mortgages, that is, it may jump over Klayton's second mortgage by attaching the third mortgage to the first (Compare consolidation of mortgages at Section 7.5.6.).

7.7.2   Mortgages of a legal interest in registered land

In registered land, the general rule is that, once a mortgage or charge has been protected on the Register, it will defeat all later mortgages as well as earlier mortgages which have not been so protected. Thus, the first mortgage entered on the Register ranks first, and the remainder rank according to the date of their registration (LRA 2002, s 48).

7.7.3 Mortgages of a legal interest in unregistered land

The rules relating to the priority of mortgages in unregistered land are now mainly of historic interest: all new first mortgages of freeholds and long leases since 1998 will have triggered first registration of the land (see Section 15.3.1). Mortgages in unregistered land must be protected either by the deposit of title deeds or by registration as a land charge (see Section 16.3.2(a)). Where a mortgage has to be registered as a C(i) land charge (legal mortgage) or a C(iii) land charge (equitable mortgage of a legal estate), its priority is ranked according to the date of registration, not the date of its creation. Briefly, subject to fraud or negligence, any legal mortgage with deposit of title deeds takes priority over all mortgages except any earlier mortgage which was properly registered. Any mortgage without deposit of title deeds is subject to (a) any earlier mortgage with deposit of deeds, and (b) any other mortgage which was properly registered.

7.7.4 Mortgages of an equitable interest in any land

In the rare case where the interest mortgaged is an equitable interest under a trust, the mortgages rank according to the order in which notice of the mortgage was received by the trustees, whether the title is registered or unregistered (LPA 1925, s 137).

7.8 Conclusion

The law of mortgages demonstrates the tensions that exist between the various approaches to ownership of land, especially where the same land is being used as a home and as security for a loan. The case of *Royal Bank of Scotland plc v Etridge (No 2)* (see Section 7.4.4) is an example of how the courts have decided where to draw the line between commercial expediency and the need to protect the vulnerable. Institutional lenders will be alerted more frequently than before to the possibility that undue influence may have taken place, but it will not be difficult for them to discharge their obligations. The use of the mortgage of family property remains such an important source of capital for small businesses that any shift in the balance towards the further protection of the wife would tend to limit that source of financial provision. Equally, if the restrictions on lenders are eased too much, the consequences will be unacceptable for vulnerable and emotionally involved occupiers who have been persuaded by their partners in financial difficulties to agree to a risky mortgage loan.

The law of mortgages also illustrates very clearly the difference between legal rules and what really happens: in every part of this area of law, theory and practice diverge. There is no reason why the rules need to be so complex. The anachronistic theoretical foundations and the miscellaneous protections offered by a random combination of common law and equitable and statutory rules should easily be replaced by new interests in land that simply provide security for the loan – as proposed by the Law Commission in 1991 (Law Com No 204). The fact that Parliament has not acted upon the Law Commission's proposals suggests, however, that behind the façade of unchanging concepts and rules, the law and those who use it have proved flexible enough to provide an adequate response to social and economic change. Problems may arise, especially when the economic climate is particularly harsh, but to date it has proved possible to adjust the existing system rather than replace it. Much of this adjustment is achieved voluntarily through the Council of Mortgage Lenders (see www.cml.org.uk/cml/home) with the occasional direct intervention by Parliament (as, for example, with the Mortgage Repossessions (Protection of Tenants etc) Act 2010).

Summary

7.1 Mortgages are very important to the ownership and utilisation of land. However, the different demands made of land (and of these various functions – e.g., shelter, security, direct or indirect investment) make it difficult to balance competing interests when a dispute occurs.

7.2 Lawyers today use the word 'mortgage':

- ▶ to describe the relationship between a landowner and a money-lender (the landowner creates a charge over the land in favour of the lender); and

- ▶ to refer to the interest granted as security (the charge).

7.3 Legal mortgages are made by deed and must usually be completed by registration. Equitable mortgages may be of a legal or equitable interest. Legal interests may be mortgaged equitably by a contract to grant a legal mortgage or by equitable charge. Equitable interests can also be mortgaged by conveyance and reconveyance.

7.4 The borrower's rights include:

- ▶ the right to redeem the mortgage (the equitable right of redemption);

- ▶ the equitable right not to have the equitable right to redeem restricted; and

- ▶ equitable rights (reinforced by statute) not to have to suffer unconscionable or oppressive terms.

The lender must take care to avoid being fixed with the undue influence or the misrepresentation of a mortgagee over a surety where there is a non-commercial relationship between the two.

7.5 The legal lender has a number of remedies available. The most important are:

- ▶ the right to take possession of property (mortgagors of residential premises are given limited protection by statute); and

- ▶ the power of sale.

7.6 Equitable mortgagees and chargees may have fewer rights than legal lenders.

7.7 Where there is a succession of mortgages, the rules of priority (which differ depending on the type of land and the type of mortgage) are applied to decide in what order the lenders should have their money repaid.

Exercises

7.1 Complete the online quiz on the topics covered in this chapter on the companion website.

7.2 Critically discuss the extent to which the law protects a mortgagor from being unjustifiably dispossessed of his or her home by a mortgagee, and consider whether these safeguards are adequate in modern economic conditions.

7.3 Clayton owns a freehold shop with a flat above, where he lives with Emily, who has an equitable share in the land. For some years, he has run a business selling computer games from the shop. A couple of years ago, a rival company set up nearby and took away most of

Clayton's trade. Last year, in order to clear his previous mortgage and his other debts and to provide a financial restructuring of the business, he borrowed £150,000 on mortgage from Sharks Ltd, who gave him documents for Emily to sign. Emily signed them but she did so without reading them when Clayton told her that they were 'just something about my will'. The interest rate was set at 5 per cent above the bank rate.

The restructuring has not worked out, and in the past six months Clayton has been unable to make any repayment. There is little or no equity in the property. Advise Emily.

You can find suggested answers to exercises 7.2 and 7.3 on the companion website.

Further reading

Brown, 'The Consumer Credit Act 2006: Real Additional Mortgagor Protection?' [2007] 71 Conv 316

McMurtry, 'Mortgage Default and Repossession: Procedure and Policy in the Post-*Norgan* Era' (2007) 58 NILQ 194

Rook, *Property Law and Human Rights* (Blackstone Press 2001)

Thompson, 'The Cumulative Range of a Mortgagee's Remedies' [2002] Conv 53

Chapter 8 follows overleaf.

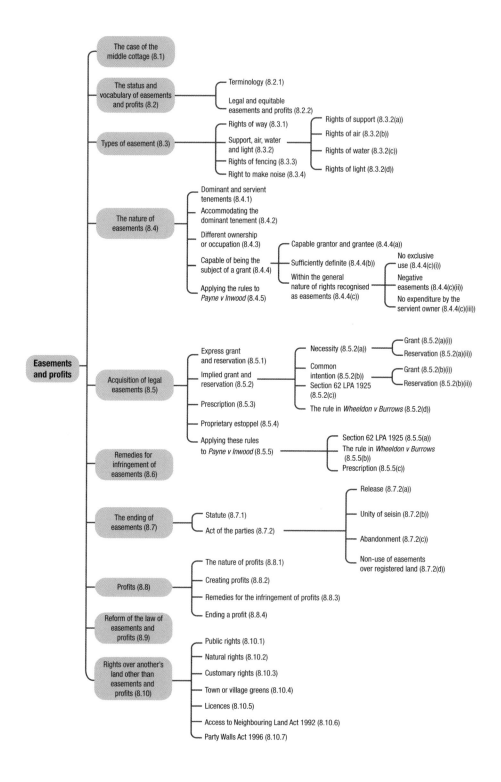

Easements and profits

Key concepts

▶ **Dominant tenement** – the land which benefits from an easement or profit.
▶ **Easement** – a right to do something on land belonging to someone else.
▶ *Profit à prendre* – a right to take something from someone else's land.
▶ **Servient tenement** – the land over which an easement or profit is exercised.

8.1 The case of the middle cottage

Teign Valley Road runs north–south through Christow, a small village on the edge of Dartmoor. To the east side of the road is a terrace of cottages known as Teign Terrace. Figure 8.1 shows a simplified plan of three cottages, Nos 1, 1A and 2, at the northern end of the terrace.

Each of the cottages has a small yard to the rear. The yard to the central cottage (No 1A) can only be reached by passing through the cottage itself or by a path through the garden and yard to No 1 (X–Y on Figure 8.1). Y marks the front gate onto the road, and X marks a gate in the wall dividing the rear yards of Nos 1 and 1A. Gate X was installed by Mr Tucker, the owner of No 1, in 1964 'as a means of facilitating friendly social visits by him to his neighbour at No 1A'. This use continued until Mr Tucker's death in 1969.

Miss Cutler purchased No 1A in May 1970. However, she wanted more room, so when No 1, the larger of the two cottages, came on the market a year later, she bought it. For a week in October 1971, Miss Cutler owned both cottages. No 1A was then conveyed to Miss Winning, and ultimately to Mr and Mrs Payne.

The gate in the wall seems to have been largely forgotten or ignored during the years after 1969. When Miss Cutler owned No 1A, she seems to have believed that she had a right to have coal delivered via the path and gate, and the particulars of sale of No 1A in 1979 referred to 'the side and rear access from adjoining property'. Mr and Mrs Leigh, who owned No 1A from 1979 to 1981, did not use the path or the gate, but their successors, Mr and Mrs Payne, did.

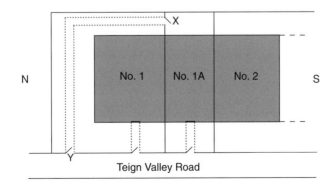

Figure 8.1 Teign Terrace

In 1989, Mr and Mrs Inwood purchased No 1 from Miss Cutler, and in December 1991 they obstructed gate X and refused to allow Mr and Mrs Payne to use the path from the road.

The question that the Court of Appeal had to determine in *Payne v Inwood* (1997) 74 P & CR 42 (CA) was whether the rights claimed by Mr and Mrs Payne amounted to an interest in the land owned by Mr and Mrs Inwood.

English law has long recognised easements and profits (*profits à prendre*) as property interests enjoyed over someone else's land.

- ▷ *Easements* are rights to do something on land belonging to someone else (for example, to use it to gain access to your land, as claimed by Mr and Mrs Payne).
- ▷ A *profit à prendre* is a right to take something from another's land (such as firewood or gravel).

In medieval times, profits were very nearly as important as the fee simple; the rules concerning them were settled centuries ago and have changed little. Easements are also ancient, but they only achieved their present form within the past hundred years or so, after the enclosures of commonly held rural land and the rapid growth of towns and cities. Easements are now much more important than profits. New profits are rarely created these days, having largely been replaced by contractual licences (see Chapter 3). Both profits and easements are generally liable to be affected by decisions in the law of tort, and this chapter illustrates some of the interrelationships of contract, tort and land law.

Easements and profits (such as the right of way claimed by Mr and Mrs Payne) can add significantly to the value of the land that benefits from them. Indeed, it may be impossible to use any buildings on the land without them (the right to run and use gas and water pipes, drains and electric cables, for example). The essential problem for the judges in this area of land law (which is hardly touched by the 1925 legislation) is to balance at least two conflicting demands. If they increase the value of land (for example, by allowing the Paynes a right to walk through their neighbour's garden), this will decrease the value of the other land by reducing privacy and restricting what may be done there (in *Payne*, the path ran through the gardens and past the kitchen windows of cottage No 1). It is important that anyone being granted rights over land can rely upon those rights being secure, but it is equally important that such rights do not unduly burden the subject land, preventing the exercise of other valuable rights. As well as these tensions between the interests of private landowners, and between them and the general public interest in the market in land, there is also the tension between private landownership and public access to land. Most public rights of access to land are not easements, but creations of statute (most recently the Countryside and Rights of Way Act 2000) and largely fall outside the scope of this chapter (but see Section 8.10).

Questions about easements or profits usually boil down to two main issues:

1. Is the right claimed *capable* of being an easement or profit (see Sections 8.4 and 8.8.1)?
2. If so, has an easement or profit actually been created in this case (see Sections 8.5 and 8.8.2)?

These are the two questions that had to be addressed in order to decide what rights, if any, Mr and Mrs Payne enjoyed over their neighbours' land.

8.2 The status and vocabulary of easements and profits

8.2.1 Terminology

Easements and profits have a vocabulary appropriate to their great age. Perhaps the most important distinction to grasp is that between the 'dominant tenement' and the 'servient tenement'.

- The land over which the right is exercised is *burdened* by the easement or profit; it is known as the *servient tenement*.
- An easement must benefit (*accommodate*) another piece of land. The land that benefits from the easement is known as the *dominant tenement*. A profit may, but does not have to, benefit a dominant tenement (see Section 8.8.1).

It is important to realise from the outset that the terms 'servient tenement' and 'dominant tenement' refer to the land and not to the person owning it.

It is also important, for the reason explored as part of Section 8.5, to distinguish between the creation of an easement by grant and creation by reservation of an easement.

- A *grant* of an easement is where the seller gives a right over a part of his land to a person buying another part of it.
- *Reservation* is where he reserves for himself a right over a part of his land which he is selling.

8.2.2 Legal and equitable easements and profits

Easements and profits can be both legal and equitable (see Section 2.3).

A legal easement or profit must be:

- for the proper length of time; and
- created by deed or by implication or by long use; and
- registered if it falls within the scope of section 27(2)(d) of the Land Registration Act (LRA) 2002.

An easement or profit can only be legal if it is to last forever, like a fee simple, or for a period of time with a fixed beginning and end, like a lease (Law of Property Act (LPA) 1925, s 1(2)(a)). Consequently, if the right is granted for an indefinite but limited time, such as 'until I sell my house' or 'for your life', it cannot be a legal easement (see Section 5.5.2).

An easement or profit will be equitable if

- it fails to meet any of the requirements for legal status; or
- the grantor owns only an equitable estate in the land.

Whether an easement or profit is legal or equitable has a fundamental bearing on whether a successor of the owner of the dominant tenement will be able to enforce it and, equally, whether it will be binding on a successor of the servient owner. In unregistered land, a legal interest binds the world, but equitable easements and profits need to be protected under the Land Charges Act 1972 (see Section 16.3). The rules in registered land are more complicated, not least because of the transition between the LRA 1925 and the LRA 2002 (see Section 15.8.3). It should be noted, however, that easements or profits created expressly since 13 October 2003 will only take effect at law once they have been entered in the Register of the servient title (LRA 2002, s 27(2)(d)). All equitable easements must be protected by an entry on the relevant Title Register.

8.3 Types of easement

The Land Registry estimates that some 65 per cent of freehold titles are subject to one or more easements. These easements comprise a wide variety of types of right, some more common than others. The categories of easement are not fixed. It is still possible to create new types of easement, but any new easement must fit the general character of those easements that are already recognised (see, for example, the concerns about when a right to park can amount to an easement, discussed in Section 8.4.4(c)).

This section briefly considers some of the main types of easement. A more detailed examination of the various species of easements and profits can be found in Megarry and Wade, 2012, ch 30.

8.3.1 Rights of way

Rights of way are, perhaps, the most commonly encountered easements. It is important not to confuse the rights enjoyable under such easements with public or permissive rights of way granted to the public in general.

An easement of way can be general, or it may be restricted in some way. For example, it may exclude the use of vehicles or may only be exercisable at certain times of day. Many of the cases involving easements of way claimed by implication or prescription are concerned with the extent of any rights that have actually been exercised. The servient tenement holder has no right to alter the route of an easement of way once it has been acquired, even if the proposed new route is no less convenient (see *Greenwich Healthcare NHS Trust v London & Quadrant Housing Trust* [1998] 1 WLR 1749 (Ch)).

8.3.2 Support, air, water and light

The categories of support, air, water and light are considered together because many of the easements falling within them do not conveniently fit the definition of an easement that is assumed for much of this chapter (see Section 8.4). Most easements give the owner of the dominant tenement the right to do something on someone else's land. These so-called negative easements give the dominant tenement holder the right to take or receive something from the servient land. Despite this anomaly, they have long been recognised as easements (see Section 8.4.4(c)(ii)). In its 2008 consultation on *Easements, Covenants and Profits à Prendre* (Law Com CP No 186), the Law Commission raised the possibility of abolishing negative easements, but this proposal was not among the recommendations made in the report that followed in 2011 (see paras 3.81 and 5.94–9 of Law Com 327, 2011).

8.3.2(a) Rights of support

All land has a natural right of support from neighbouring land but this right does not extend to the support of any buildings on that land (see Section 8.10.2). However, it is also possible to acquire an easement of support for buildings. Indeed, such easements may be very important. For example, semi-detached houses are usually mutually dependent for support.

8.3.2(b) Rights of air

There is no natural right to the air that passes across a neighbour's land. It is, however, possible to acquire an easement of air, provided that the passage of the air is confined to a defined channel (see, for example, *Cable v Bryant* [1908] 1 Ch 259 (Ch)). *Hunter v Canary Wharf Ltd* [1997] AC 655 (HL) concerned not a right to air, but interference to television reception caused by a new building. The House of Lords refused to recognise the existence of an easement to receive television signals and the local residents' claim for compensation failed.

8.3.2(c) Rights of water

The natural right to water is limited to that flowing naturally in a definite channel (see Section 8.10.2). A wide variety of easements relating to water are recognised at law. Some, such as the right to take water from the servient land or to water cattle at a pond, are negative easements. Others, such as a right to receive or discharge water through a pipe running through the servient land, are examples of the more conventional type of easement.

8.3.2(d) Rights of light

English law does not recognise a general right to light, or the right to enjoy a particular view (see Section 8.4.4(b)). However, it is possible to enjoy an easement of light in respect of the light that is received through a particular window or other aperture. The dominant tenement is entitled to enough light through the aperture to render occupation of a dwelling house 'comfortable according to the ordinary notions of mankind' or to enable the dominant tenement holder to continue to beneficially carry on his business from the premises (see *Colls v Home & Colonial Stores Ltd* [1904] AC 179 (HL)).

It is easier to acquire a right of light than it is to acquire other types of easement under the Prescription Act 1832 (see Section 8.5.3), not least because there is no need to show that the use has been enjoyed as of right. The Rights of Light Act 1959 contains a number of other provisions that apply only to this type of easement, including a procedure to allow the temporary interruption of such rights by screens or hoardings.

8.3.3 Rights of fencing

The right to require a neighbour to fence his land and keep those fences in good repair can be very valuable, especially in rural communities. This right is a somewhat 'spurious easement' because it requires positive action and expense by the owner of the servient tenement. It can pass under section 62 of the LPA 1925 (see *Crow v Wood* [1971] 1 QB 77 (CA)). Unusually, however, it cannot be created by express grant, but can be expressly created by means of an express covenant (see Megarry and Wade, 2012, § 30–022).

8.3.4 Right to make noise

The recent case of *Lawrence v Fen Tigers Ltd* [2014] AC 822 (SC), concerned the disturbance caused by the amount of noise generated by motor sports at the defendant's stadium. According to Lord Neuberger PSC at [33]:

> the right to carry on an activity which results in noise, or the right to emit a noise, which would otherwise cause an actionable nuisance, is capable of being an easement. The fact that

the noise from an activity may be heard in a large number of different properties can fairly be said to render it an unusual easement, but … one can characterise a right to emit noise in relatively conventional terms in the context of easements, namely as 'the right to transmit sound waves over' the servient land.

8.4 The nature of easements

It is easy to give examples of easements. However, it is much more difficult to find an adequate generic definition. In order for a right to be classified as an easement, it must comply with the four traditional requirements listed by Dr Cheshire in his *Modern Real Property* in 1925, and reviewed by Lord Evershed MR in one of the leading cases on easements, *Re Ellenborough Park* [1956] Ch 131 (CA).

The four requirements for an easement:

1. There must be a dominant and a servient tenement.
2. The easement must accommodate the dominant tenement.
3. The dominant and servient tenements must be owned or occupied by different people.
4. The easement must be capable of being the subject of a grant.

In *Ellenborough Park*, owners of houses near the park (in a square near the sea at Weston-super-Mare) had been granted the right to use it 'as a leisure garden', but during the Second World War it had been taken over by the government. By statute, individual landowners were entitled to compensation if they had been deprived of a legal right, and the only possible such right was an easement. They were eventually successful in persuading the Court of Appeal that the right to enjoy the park could amount to an easement.

If the right being claimed is, in the judges' view, not capable of being an easement, it will be only a licence. The significance of this is that, while an easement is a property right, attached to the land and passing automatically with it on assignment, a licence is seen as a personal right rarely binding third parties and thus probably neither passing to a new owner of the land nor burdening a successor of the licensor (see Chapter 3).

8.4.1 Dominant and servient tenements

Clearly in *Ellenborough Park*, there was a servient tenement (the park) and there were dominant tenements (the houses). Sometimes, however, this is not so obvious. In *Miller v Emcer Products Ltd* [1956] Ch 304 (CA), a tenant had an easement to use the landlord's lavatory. The dominant and servient tenements were not two plots of land, but the freehold estate and a leasehold estate in the same land; the tenant had the dominant tenement, and the landlord the servient.

In *London & Blenheim Estates Ltd v Ladbroke Retail Parks Ltd* [1994] 1 WLR 31 (CA), the Court of Appeal held that there can be no easement if the dominant land is not in the possession of the grantee and if the grantor does not own the servient land at the time that the purported easement is created. In this case, an option was claimed for an easement to park cars on land owned by the grantor. At the time the option was granted, the claimant did not own the land which was to benefit from it. When he eventually acquired this land and attempted to exercise the option, the grantor had sold the land to be burdened to someone else, who was able to argue that the claim to an easement could not succeed.

An easement cannot, therefore, exist in gross; it must be appurtenant to (that is, it must benefit) a dominant tenement. This requirement seems to have been adopted during the nineteenth century under the influence of Roman law, and reflects judicial concern to preserve certainty with respect to rights over land:

> If one asks why the law should require that there should be a dominant tenement before there can be a grant, or a contract for the grant, of an easement sufficient to create an interest in land binding successors in title to the servient land, the answer would appear to lie in the policy against encumbering land with burdens of uncertain extent (*London and Blenheim Estates Ltd* per Peter Gibson LJ at 37).

Sturley (1980) argues that the authority for requiring a dominant tenement is very weak. He claims that allowing easements to exist in gross (that is, to allow easements which are not attached to benefiting land), such as the right to land a helicopter on distant land, would not now unduly burden titles but could encourage maximum utilisation of land. However, this argument was recently rejected by the Law Commission (see paragraph 2.24 of *Making Land Law Work: Easements, Covenants and Profits à Prendre* (Law Com 327, 2011)).

8.4.2 Accommodating the dominant tenement

Just as in the pre-1996 law of leases, where the covenant must 'touch and concern' the land (see Section 6.3.1), the test is whether the claimed easement benefits the land itself and not merely the landowner. In *Ellenborough Park*, the Court of Appeal found it difficult to decide whether the easement touched and concerned (or 'accommodated' or benefited) the dominant tenement. Earlier cases had been divided on whether the right to use a garden could accommodate land, but Lord Evershed MR concluded that it is 'primarily a question of fact'. In this case, the dominant tenements did benefit from the garden, although it might have been different if they had not been family homes. In the case of *Mulvaney v Gough* [2003] 1 WLR 360 (CA), the right to tend a communal garden was held 'clearly' to benefit the dominant tenement.

In *Hill v Tupper* (1863) 2 H & C 121, 159 ER 51 (Ex) the claim to an easement failed because it did not accommodate the dominant tenement. The owners of the Basingstoke Canal leased part of the canal bank to Mr Hill and granted him the sole right to hire out pleasure boats. A local publican then also rented out boats, and Mr Hill tried to stop him, arguing that the publican was interfering with his easement. The court found that the exclusive right to hire out boats benefited Mr Hill's business rather than his land. Consequently, it was a personal right only. Although this right entitled him to bring an action against the canal owners for breach of covenant, it could not be an easement. Since Mr Hill's rights did not amount to an interest in the land, he had no direct cause of action against the publican. In contrast, in *Moody v Steggles* (1879) 12 Ch D 261 (Ch), the right to hang a pub sign on neighbouring land was held to be an easement. Fry J refused to accept that it was possible to distinguish between the tenement and the business of the occupant of the tenement:

> It appears to me that that argument is of too refined a nature to prevail, and for this reason, that the house can only be used by an occupant, and that the occupant only uses the house for the business which he pursues, and therefore in some manner (direct or indirect) an easement is more or less connected with the mode in which the occupant of the house uses it (at 266).

Although the right to erect the sign benefited the business, it also benefited the land, given the way in which the land was used and had been used for many years.

In the recent case *Polo Woods Foundation v Shelton-Agar* [2010] 1 P&CR 12, Warren J had to consider whether a certain degree of benefit had to be proved in order for a right (in that case a *profit à prendre*) to accommodate the dominant tenement. He concluded that:

> there is no test of real or appreciable benefit to the dominant tenement which has to be passed before a right claimed can be said to 'accommodate' it or to establish the necessary connection or nexus between the right and the dominant tenement … Such a test is not to be found in the long line of cases leading up to *Re Ellenborough Park*, nor in the cases thereafter. Instead, the courts have attempted in different language to describe what is meant by accommodation whilst recognising that question to be one of fact depending largely on the nature of the alleged dominant tenement and the nature of the right granted (at [53]).

8.4.3 Different ownership or occupation

People cannot have rights against themselves. If both tenements come into the hands of one person, the easement is ended ('extinguished by unity of seisin'; see Section 8.7.2(b)). If what was formerly an easement continues to be used by the owner of both tenements, for example, to cross one field to get into the next, this still looks like an easement, but is not because of unity of seisin. Rather, it is what is known as a quasi-easement and might one day come back to life (see Section 8.5.2(d)).

8.4.4 Capable of being the subject of a grant

The requirement that the easement be capable of being the subject of a grant is not altogether clear. In theory, it means that the right claimed must be capable of being conveyed in a deed, and this in turn means that a number of rules need to be satisfied if the right is to be an easement.

8.4.4(a) Capable grantor and grantee

There must be a capable grantor and a capable grantee. Both parties must be the owners of the pieces of land which are to become the dominant and servient tenements (see *London & Blenheim Estates Ltd*), and both must be legal persons.

The principle of *nemo dat quod non habet* (no one can give something which they do not have) applies to easements. Consequently, an easement granted by a tenant will not normally be binding on the title to reversion. However, in the rather unusual circumstances of *Wall v Collins* [2007] Ch 390 (CA), the Court of Appeal decided that such easements are not 'attached' to the leasehold interest out of which they are created and may, therefore, continue to exist for the remainder of the original term of the lease if the lease is brought to a premature end. The Court of Appeal denied that an easement is attached to an estate as such. Instead, it is attached to the land that it is intended to benefit rather than a particular estate in that land (in this case, the lease).

> It is the occupier's 'enjoyment' of the bundle of rights, rather than its legal source, which is material (per Carnwarth LJ at [46]).

There are significant problems with this reasoning, which seems to run counter to the principle that underlies the post-1925 system of land law rules (see Section 2.3.1):

> that, in order to take effect at law, an 'easement, right or privilege' must be 'for an interest equivalent to an estate in fee simple absolute in possession or a term of years absolute' (Law Com 327, 2011 at 3.232).

Consequently, one would expect, as a matter of logic, that termination of an estate extinguishes any easement benefiting that estate. The Law Commission has recommended that *Wall v Collins* be reversed. However, the Commission also recognised the practical benefits (rather than the theoretical coherency) of *Wall v Collins*. It suggested that these benefits would be better achieved by a new statutory power rather than the reasoning used in *Wall v Collins* (see Law Com 327, 2011 at 3.251–3.255).

8.4.4(b) Sufficiently definite

The nature and extent of the right must be capable of sufficiently accurate definition. For example, *Aldred's Case* (1610) 9 Co Rep 57b, 77 ER 816 (KB) confirms that the right to a good view cannot amount to an easement, since such a thing is too imprecise to describe. It is, however, possible to protect one's view by using a restrictive covenant. In *Davies v Dennis* [2009] EWCA Civ 1081, a view of the River Thames was held to be protected by a covenant not 'to do or suffer to be done on the Plot or any part thereof anything of whatsoever nature which may be or become a nuisance or annoyance to the owners or occupiers for the time being of the [properties that benefited from the view]'.

8.4.4(c) Within the general nature of rights recognised as easements

To be capable of being an easement, the right concerned must fall within the general nature of the rights that are already recognised as easements. Many categories of easement are well established, and the most important examples are considered at Section 8.3. The list is not closed:

> The category of ... easements must alter and expand with the changes that take place in the circumstances of mankind (per Lord St Leonards, *Dyce v Hay* (1852) 1 Macq 305 (HL) at 212–13).

However, neither is it capable of infinite extension:

> it must not therefore be supposed that incidents of a novel kind can be devised and attached to property at the fancy or caprice of any owner (per Lord Brougham LC, *Keppell v Bailey* (1834) 2 My & K 517, 39 ER 1042 (Ch) at 1049).

Generally speaking, an easement must not give the dominant tenement holder too much control over the servient tenement and must not impose a positive obligation on the owner of the servient tenement. However, these rules have not always been applied strictly, particularly in the older cases, and a number of recognised easements do not easily fall comfortably within them.

8.4.4(c)(i) No exclusive use

The rights claimed as an easement must not 'amount to rights of joint occupation or ... substantially deprive the ... owners of proprietorship or legal possession' (*Ellenborough Park* at 164 (Lord Evershed MR)). This rule should cause relatively little difficulty if the effect of the right being claimed would be to exclude completely the owner of the servient tenement from his land. In such cases, an argument based on adverse possession is more appropriate (see Chapter 13).

In many cases, however, the right being claimed will fall short of exclusive use of the servient land but will nevertheless significantly limit the ability of its owner to enjoy that land. It is not easy to discern a coherent or consistent approach from the decided cases. The right to store goods can be an easement, as in *Wright v Macadam* [1949] 2 KB 744 (CA), provided the servient owner is not excluded and the right is clearly defined.

Similarly, the tenant in *Miller v Emcer Productions Ltd* [1956] Ch 304 (CA) (see Section 8.4.1) succeeded because he would only have been using the lavatory some of the time. However, in *Copeland v Greenhalf* [1952] Ch 488 (Ch), a wheelwright who for many years had used a strip of the claimant's land alongside a road for storing and mending vehicles failed to establish that he had acquired an easement by long use. The absence of any reference in the judgment of Upjohn J (as he then was) to the earlier and binding authority in *Wright v Macadam* has spawned various judicial and academic attempts to reconcile the two decisions. In reality, however, Upjohn J's decision in *Copeland v Greenhalf* rests at least as much on the vague character of the right being claimed (see Section 8.4.4(b)) as on the ouster of the landowner by the rights claimed (see Haley and McMurtry, 2007).

In recent years, the question of whether a right is too extensive to be an easement has repeatedly arisen in the context of car parking. It has now been established that the right to park a car can amount to an easement, provided that the right is sufficiently certain while also allowing the servient owner sufficient use of her land. Such a claim succeeded in *Hair v Gillman* (2000) 80 P & CR 108 (CA), where the defendant had been given permission to park her car anywhere 'on a forecourt that was capable of taking two or three other cars' (see, also, *Moncrieff v Jamieson* [2007] 1 WLR 2620 (HL)).

The issue of what amounts to reasonable use of the servient land came before the Court of Appeal in *Batchelor v Marlow* [2003] 1 WLR 764 (CA). As part of their business activities, Mr and Mrs Marlow had parked vehicles on land owned by Mr Batchelor. At first instance, Nicholas Warren QC declared that the Marlows had acquired an exclusive right to park up to six cars on the land on Mondays to Fridays between 8.30 am and 6.00 pm. It was common ground in the Court of Appeal that the relevant test was that distilled by Judge Paul Baker QC in *London & Blenheim Estates Ltd* [1992] 1 WLR 1278 (Ch) (sometimes referred to as the 'ouster principle'):

> The essential question is one of degree. If the right granted in relation to the area over which it is to be exercisable is such that it would leave the servient owner without any reasonable use of his land, whether for parking or anything else, it could not be an easement though it might be some larger or different grant (at 1288).

The Court of Appeal held that the effect of the rights claimed by the Marlows would be to seriously curtail Mr Batchelor's ability to use his land for significant periods of each week. The fact that Mr Batchelor could sell the land (subject to the Marlows' rights) or park on the land himself or charge others for doing so outside business hours did not amount to 'reasonable use' of his land. Such ownership would, in the words of Tuckey LJ, be merely 'illusory'. There are indications, however, that this test leans too far in favour of the landowner, and Lord Scott took advantage of the Scottish case of *Moncrieff v Jamieson* to criticise it:

> I would, for my part, reject the test that asks whether the servient owner is left with any reasonable use of his land, and substitute for it a test which asks whether the servient owner retains possession and, subject to the reasonable exercise of the right in question, control of the servient land (at [59]).

The Law Commission considered the 'ouster principle' (as applied in *Batchelor v Marlow*) in its recent report, *Making Land Law Work: Easements, Covenants and Profits à Prendre* (Law Com 327, 2011). It concluded that:

> it is hard to see that the principle is particularly useful. Easements will not, of course, normally deprive the servient owner of any reasonable use of the servient land, but if the parties

wish to make such an arrangement (without conferring exclusive possession) it is hard to see why they should not do so (at 3.207).

Consequently, the Law Commission recommended that the 'ouster principle' should be abolished and *Batchelor v Marlow* reversed by statute.

8.4.4(c)(ii) Negative easements

The courts are 'very wary' of creating new kinds of negative easement. In *Phipps v Pears* [1965] 1 QB 76 (CA), a neighbour demolished a house which was built very close to that of the claimant, who claimed he had an easement of 'protection from the weather' with which the neighbour had interfered. This would have been a negative easement, preventing the neighbour from developing his land. In this case, Lord Denning MR defined the difference between positive and negative easements:

> positive easements, such as a right of way, which give the owner of land a right himself to do something on or to his neighbour's land: and negative easements, such as a right of light, which gives him a right to stop his neighbour doing something on his (his neighbour's) own land (at 82).

Of course, a positive easement will, by definition, prevent servient owners doing things on their land which interfere with the exercise of that easement. It is understandable, however, that entirely negative rights should not be capable of being easements, not just because of the policy reasons discussed above, but also because a servient owner might not know that the easement was being acquired (for example, by use over a long period of time; see Section 8.5.3). The right claimed as an easement in *Phipps v Pears* was held not to be an easement of support and, indeed, was not an easement at all because it would 'unduly restrict the enjoyment' of the servient land and prevent its development. Despite this, a small number of negative easements, including rights to light and support, are recognised, but the list is unlikely to be extended.

Restrictive covenants may offer more appropriate solutions in situations like this, but the answer might also be found in the law of tort. In *Bradburn v Lindsay* [1983] 2 All ER 408 (Ch), Mr Bradburn, owner of one of a pair of semi-detached houses, was concerned that the dry rot in his neighbour's derelict house would spread to his own property. The house had to be demolished by the council, and Mr Bradburn claimed damages from his neighbour for loss of support and exposure of the side of his house to dry rot and decay. There was clearly an easement of support, but Mrs Lindsay was under no obligation to maintain it by keeping the wall in repair. Mr Bradburn therefore successfully relied on the torts of negligence and nuisance.

8.4.4(c)(iii) No expenditure by the servient owner

All the easements referred to thus far have been capable of being enjoyed without the owner of the servient tenement having to take any positive action or spend money, and in general this will be the case. There is, however, an exception to this: the easement of fencing, which requires the servient owner to keep in repair her boundary fence if it is used as part of an enclosure to contain livestock on the dominant land. As Lord Denning MR observed in the case of *Crow v Wood* [1971] 1 QB 77 (CA):

> It is not an easement strictly so called because it involves the servient owner in the expenditure of money. It was described by Gale [*Easements*, 11th edn (1932), 432] as a 'spurious kind of easement.' But it has been treated in practice by the courts as being an easement (at 84).

In *Liverpool City Council v Irwin* [1977] AC 239 (HL), the House of Lords dealt with the issue of whether a landlord had to maintain easements of access to the flats in a tower block. The tenants had stopped paying rent because the common parts of the block were in such a bad condition. They had no written tenancy agreement, only a list of rules. Easements to use the passages, lifts and rubbish chutes were implied into the tenancies by the judges, along with an obligation to maintain and repair them:

> there appears to be no technical difficulty in making an express grant of an easement coupled with an undertaking by the servient owner to maintain it. That being so, there seems to be no reason why the easement arising in the present case should not by implication carry with it a similar burden on the grantor (per Lord Edmund-Davies at 268).

This, though, is probably exceptional, since in attempting to achieve a balance between the competing demands of landowners and aware of the need to maintain a healthy property market, the courts do not want to see servient land further burdened.

8.4.5 Applying the rules to *Payne v Inwood*

If Mr and Mrs Payne's right to use the path was an easement, it must meet the four requirements set out in rules in *Re Ellenborough Park.*

1. The dominant tenement is No 1A (the middle cottage owned by Mr and Mrs Payne). The servient tenement (the land over which the right is being claimed) is No 1 (owned by the Inwoods).
2. There seems to be little doubt that the right of way being claimed benefited No 1A. The only other access to the yard was through the house. Although the yard was not landlocked, most people would prefer to have an alternative route over which to bring goods (such as coal) destined for the yard.
3. Different people owned the two cottages at the date that the right was claimed. However, the cottages had been in common ownership for a brief period in 1971. Any easement that existed prior to the period of co-ownership would have been extinguished or converted to a quasi-easement (see Section 8.5.2(d)).
4. Rights of access, such as that claimed by Mr and Mrs Payne, have long been recognised as an important category of easement. The right being claimed was capable of being the subject of a grant.

However, merely establishing that a right is capable of being an easement was not sufficient to establish Mr and Mrs Payne had an interest that was binding on their neighbour. They also had to demonstrate that the right of access had been acquired in such a way as to create a legal easement.

8.5 Acquisition of legal easements

There are a number of ways of acquiring a legal easement. The obvious way is to create one in a deed, but other methods of creation are based on behaving as if such a right already existed, together with a (usually mythical) deed. Legal easements can also be directly created by long usage (compare adverse possession in Chapter 13). Although long user (known as 'prescription') is dealt with as a separate category below, it also usually operates by presuming the existence of a fictional deed granting the easement.

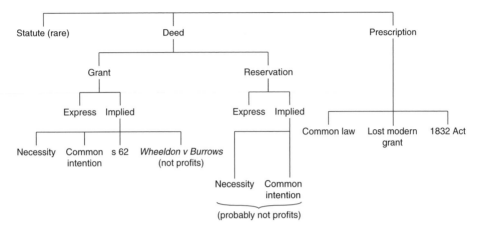

Figure 8.2   Acquisition of easements and *profits* at law.

Figure 8.2 shows the various ways in which legal easements can be acquired. For convenience, it also indicates which of these methods do not apply to *profits*.

Easements can be created by grant or by reservation. A *grant* of an easement is where the seller gives a right over a part of his land to a person buying another part of it. A person *reserves* an easement when he keeps a right over a part of the land that he is selling for the benefit of his retained land. The distinction between *grant* and *reservation* is particularly important when it comes to applying the rules that allow easements to be acquired by implication (see Section 8.5.2). It is much more difficult to reserve an easement than it is to grant one, because the courts are generally unwilling to allow a person to claw back an interest in land that he has transferred to another (what is known as 'derogating' from his grant; see Section 6.2.1(b)).

There is a considerable body of law on the acquisition of easements. Judges tend not to use categories consistently, so in practice they overlap (especially easements of necessity and intended easements). Only the bare outlines of the rules are given here. The main thing is to understand the variety of ways in which these interests can be created and acquired so that you can recognise the circumstances in which one might arise, either to take advantage of it or to avoid it.

8.5.1   Express grant and reservation

Like so many cases, the case of *Payne v Inwood* (1997) 74 P & CR 42 (CA) (the facts are set out at Section 8.1) arose because insufficient attention was given to the importance of a particular right when land was sold. For a short period in 1971, Miss Cutler owned both No 1 and No 1A. If the conveyance of 1A had expressly included a right of way over the path marked 'X–Y' there would have been no doubt that Mr and Mrs Payne had the right to use the path in 1991.

8.5.2   Implied grant and reservation

Much of the law on easements created by implication is based on the old principle of non-derogation from grant (see Section 6.2.1(b)). *Wong v Beaumont Property Trust Ltd*

[1965] 1 QB 173 (CA) is a good example of this. A basement was let subject to the condition that it was to be used as a restaurant, but it could not be used for this purpose without a ventilation duct over the land retained by the lessor. Consequently, it must have been the common intention of the parties that the lease should include such an easement.

8.5.2(a) Necessity

8.5.2(a)(i) Grant

Where land is (at the time of the sale) completely unusable without an easement, the courts may imply one into the deed transferring the land (or granting a lease of it). However, they will not do so if the wording of the deed expressly excludes the grant of such an easement (see *Nickerson v Barraclough* [1981] Ch 426 (CA)).

8.5.2(a)(ii) Reservation

It is possible, but very difficult, to reserve an easement of necessity by implication. In *Adealon International Corp Proprietary Ltd v Merton LBC* [2007] 1 WLR 1898 (CA), the Court of Appeal refused to infer an easement of necessity because at the time of the transfer, the transferor expected to have access to the retained land from the land of a third party. In *Manjang v Drammeh* (1991) 61 P & CR 194 (PC), a person owned land situated between a river and a road. He sold that part of his land by the road but failed to reserve for himself an easement to cross it in order to reach the rest of his land on the bank of the river. The Privy Council refused to imply an easement across the land he had sold, since it was possible for him to get to his retained land by boat, and occasionally in the past he had done so.

8.5.2(b) Common intention

8.5.2(b)(i) Grant

According to Lord Parker in *Pwllbach Colliery Company Ltd* v *Woodman* [1915] AC 634 (HL):

> The law will readily imply the grant or reservation of such easements as may be necessary to give effect to the common intention of the parties to a grant of real property, with reference to the manner or purposes in and for which the land granted or some land retained by the grantor is to be used ... But it is essential for this purpose that the parties should intend that the subject of the grant or the land retained by the grantor should be used in some definite and particular manner (at 646–7).

In the recent case of *Donovan v Rana* [2014] 1 P & CR 23 (CA), Mrs Donovan sold a plot of land adjacent to her house in a the residential suburb of Gravesend in Kent as a building plot. The purchaser covenanted 'to erect within one year from the date [of the transfer] upon the property, the dwelling house to the satisfaction of the Local Authority'. The transfer granted a specific right of way, but was silent as to other easements. Mr and Mrs Rana then acquired the building plot and duly built their new house, which they named 'Shalimar'. During its construction, the contractors dug up land belonging to Mrs Donovan and her husband to connect 'Shalimar' to mains drainage, water, gas, electricity and telephone. They did so without the express permission of Mr and Mrs Donovan, who responded by bringing court proceedings. The Court of Appeal had no doubt that the parties must have intended that the building of a dwelling house on the building plot 'to the satisfaction of the Local Authority' would include the connection to the mains utility services. Indeed, Vos LJ observed (at [29]) that:

> The suggestion that a dwelling-house in such an environment might sensibly be expected by the parties to be constructed without connections to the mains utilities just a few metres away … is, if I may say so, a somewhat optimistic submission.

Both easements of common intention and easements of necessity are based upon implication and the doctrine of non-derogation from grant (see *Wong v Beaumont Property Trust Ltd* above). However, while easements of necessity are normally restricted to the minimum rights needed to gain access to the land, and last only as long as the necessity lasts, easements derived from the parties' intended use of the land will extend as far as is necessary to achieve the parties' expressly intended purpose (*Donovan v Rana* at [33]).

8.5.2(b)(ii) Reservation

It is possible to reserve an easement of common intention by implication, but the courts will not readily infer such easements.

8.5.2(c) Section 62 LPA 1925

Section 62 of the LPA 1925 is a 'wordsaving' provision which, on conveyance, transfers with the land all benefits which are attached to it (see Section 12.5.1(d)). It can be (and frequently is) expressly excluded by the parties. Section 62 operates on the grant of land only and cannot, therefore, be used as the basis of an implied reservation.

Wright v Macadam [1949] 2 KB 744 (CA) (see Section 8.4.4(c)(i)) illustrates the potential of section 62. Here, with her landlord's permission, a tenant was storing coal in a shed; then, when a new lease was granted to her (the 'conveyance'), her licence was converted into an easement. It was an 'advantage … appertaining to the land' and, when section 62 implied it into the deed, it grew into a legal easement and could not be revoked by the landlord. In any problem about a person who lives on land owned by another and has permission to do something extra, and who then receives a grant, the answer will probably involve section 62.

Wright v Macadam was followed in *Hair v Gillman* (2000) 80 P & CR 108 (CA) (also referred to at Section 8.4.4(c)(i)). In this case, a licence to park a car was given to the tenant of land used as a nursery school and was later 'crystallised' into an easement under section 62 when she was granted the freehold. Chadwick LJ felt it to be a matter of regret that a property right binding the servient land could be created unintentionally. He repeated the comments of Tucker LJ in *Wright v Macadam* that such decisions:

> may tend to discourage landlords from acts of kindness to their tenants. But there it is; that is the law (*Wright v Macadam* at 755).

It has been argued that the section should only operate where the dominant and servient tenements are already in separate ownership or occupation. This was stated by a minority in the House of Lords in *Sovmots Investments Ltd v Secretary of State for the Environment* [1979] AC 144 (HL). Although the reasoning in *Sovmots* was accepted by the Court of Appeal in *Payne v Inwood* (see Section 8.5.5), the Court of Appeal has subsequently recognised that a right of way can pass under section 62 where there is no diversity of ownership, provided that the right is continuous and apparent. In *P & S Platt Ltd v Crouch* [2004] 1 P & CR 18 (CA), the owner of a hotel by a river also owned an island in the river on which he had moorings which could be used by the hotel guests. When the hotel was sold, the conveyance did not refer to the moorings, but the new owners argued that they had an easement to use them. Peter Gibson LJ stated that:

> the rights in question did appertain to … and were enjoyed with the hotel, being part of the hotel business and advertised as such and enjoyed by the hotel guests. The rights were continuous and apparent, and so it matters not that prior to the sale of the hotel there was no prior diversity of occupation of the dominant and servient tenancies (at [42]).

A detailed consideration of the case law can be found in Morgan J's judgment in *Wood v Waddington* [2014] EWHC 1358 (Ch) at [101] to [133].

The Law Commission considers section 62, 'a trap for the unwary, as well as being uncertain in its effect and in the extent to which it overlaps with *Wheeldon v Burrows*' (Law Com 327, 2011 at 3.059). It has recommended that section 62 cease to operate to convert permissive rights into easements.

8.5.2(d) The rule in Wheeldon v Burrows

The rule in *Wheeldon v Burrows* (1879) LR 12 Ch D 31 (CA) determines what easements are implied when a landowner sells part of her land. Thesiger LJ stated the rule in this case twice, but unfortunately not consistently. The basic principle is this: where a person sells part of her land which has the benefit of a *quasi-easement* (rights that would be easements but for the fact that the land is in common ownership), the buyer will gain the benefit of the quasi-easement if at the time of the grant:

1. the seller was using the quasi-easement for the benefit of the land she was selling;
2. the use of the quasi-easement was 'continuous and apparent' (such as an obvious track, or a drain which could have been discovered on inspection); and/or
3. the quasi-easement was necessary for the reasonable enjoyment of the land sold.

It is not known whether Thesiger LJ meant conditions 2 and 3 to be alternatives. In many cases, of course, if the quasi-easement (for example, a right of way) satisfies one test, it will also satisfy the other. The third condition does not mean 'essential' (as in easements implied by necessity), but that there can be no reasonable enjoyment of the land without the easement. The requirement that the right be 'continuous and apparent' would appear to preclude the rule in *Wheeldon v Burrows* being used to create profits as it is difficult to see how a profit can satisfy this part of the rule.

In *Millman v Ellis* [1996] 71 P & CR 158 (CA), the Court of Appeal held that Mr Millman had successfully proved an easement under the rule. He had bought a large house from Ellis and also part of Ellis' remaining land; he claimed the right to use the driveway which Ellis had always used to get to the house and which was safer than using the main road. In *Wheeler v JJ Saunders Ltd* [1996] Ch 19 (CA), however, Mr Wheeler had bought part of a farm and claimed an easement to allow him to pass through a gap in a wall southwards to get to a road. It was held that this access was not necessary for the reasonable enjoyment of the house because there was another equally suitable access in the east.

For the rule in *Wheeldon v Burrows* to apply, the land must have been in common occupation immediately prior to the transfer. Common ownership (for example, by a common landlord) is not sufficient (see *Kent v Kavanagh* [2007] Ch 1 (CA)). The rule applies only to the implied grant of an easement and cannot be used to infer a reservation for the benefit of retained land. This was confirmed by the Court of Appeal in *Chaffe v Kingsley* (2000) 79 P & CR 404 (CA).

In some respects, the rule in *Wheeldon v Burrows* and section 62 of the LPA 1925 (see Section 8.5.2(c)) seem very similar. This, and the fact they are often discussed and even pleaded in the alternative (see, for example, *P & S Platt Ltd v Crouch*), can cause considerable confusion, and not only to students. The main differences and similarities between the two rules are summarised in Table 8.1.

8.5.3 Prescription

The use for many years of a right which is capable of being an easement can create a legal easement by 'prescription'. The role of this doctrine was summarised by Elias LJ in *Dewan v Lewis* [2010] EWCA Civ 1382 at [33]:

> As Lord Hoffmann observed in the House of Lords in *R v Oxfordshire CC ex p Sunningwell PC* [2000] 1 AC 335, at 349 D, the purpose of rules of prescription is to 'prevent the disturbance of

Table 8.1 Section 62 of the Law of Property Act 1925 and the rule in *Wheeldon v Burrows* (1879) LR 12 Ch D 31 (CA) compared

LPA 1925, s 62	The rule in *Wheeldon v Burrows*
Effect	
1. Transfers those easements which existed in respect of land previously leased to a tenant when the tenant buys the freehold. 2. Turns rights which were merely licences into easements on a conveyance: the 'legal metamorphosis' (see Tee, 1998).	A purchaser takes as easements any 'rights' that the seller has been exercising and that would have been easements but for the fact that the land was in common ownership and occupation (quasi-easements) – for example, a path.
Differences	
Can only create legal easements. This is because section 62 can only operate where the sale or lease is a 'conveyance' as defined by s 205(1)(ii) LPA 1925.	Can create legal and equitable easements. The rule can operate on both legal and equitable sales and leases.
The dominant and servient tenements may be in separate occupation immediately prior to the sale.	All the land must be owned and occupied by the seller immediately prior to the sale.
The right needs to be 'continuous and apparent' only where the land was in common ownership immediately prior to the sale; see *P & S Platt Ltd v Crouch* [2004] 1 P & CR 18 (CA).	The right must be 'continuous and apparent' and/or necessary for the reasonable enjoyment of the land sold or subject to the lease.
Similarities	
Can be excluded from the conveyance expressly. Can also be excluded by implication (that is, because of the circumstances of the conveyance).	Can be excluded by express words. Can probably be excluded by implication.
Only applies to rights which are capable of being easements.	Only applies to rights which are capable of being easements.
Grant only (not reservation).	Grant only (not reservation).

long established de facto enjoyment.' In English law, the fiction is that at some point a right was conferred on the owner of the dominant tenement. The right must relate to what has in fact been enjoyed.

Prescription may arise if an easement has been used:

- openly;
- as of right;
- without permission; and
- continuously.

by one fee simple owner against another, provided that the right could have legitimately been granted by the landowner (see *Bakewell Management Ltd v Brandwood* [2004] 2 AC 519 (HL)). It is important to note how this differs from the doctrine of implied grant (considered at 8.5.2). Implied grant focuses upon the expected use of the dominant tenement, whereas prescription is based on acquiescence.

There are three forms of prescription: common law, 'lost modern grant' and statutory prescription under the Prescription Act 1832. The requirements for each form of prescription are summarised below. (For a much more detailed consideration see Megarry and Wade, 2012, §§ 28–043 – 28–102.)

Prescription at common law:

- *the claim*: the right has been enjoyed since time immemorial (1189);
- *the proof*: 20 years' continuous user shown, provided that the right could have been exercised in 1189.

Prescription by lost modern grant:

- *the claim*: the right was granted in a deed, but that deed has now been lost;
- *the proof*: user for any 20 years (there is no requirement that the right is still being enjoyed at the date of the commencement of proceedings) provided that the fictitious grant was not impossible.

Prescription under the Prescription Act 1832:

- *the proof*: user as of right (except easements of light) for statutory period of 20 or 40 years immediately prior to proceedings.

The detailed rules are obscure and complex, and there are significant differences among the three forms. In particular, under the 1832 Act, the defendant must demonstrate enjoyment of the right for a period of at least 20 years immediately before the action is brought, whereas in a claim based on lost modern grant, the 20-year period can expire at an earlier time. A detailed summary of the various rules can be found in the first instance judgment of Roth J in *London Tara Hotel Ltd v Kensington Close Hotel Ltd* [2010] EWHC 2749 (Ch) (the Court of Appeal's decision, confirming Roth J's conclusions, can be found at [2012] 1 P & CR 13).

In 1966, the Law Reform Committee recommended the simplification of prescription law (14th Report, Cmnd 3100); it also described the Prescription Act 1832 as 'one of the worst drafted Acts on the Statute Book' (at para 40). Despite this no new statute was forthcoming, and the Law Commission and the Land Registry subsequently proposed (in their 1998 Consultation paper *Land Registration for the Twenty-First Century*, Law Com No 254, paras 10.79ff) that the sole method of acquiring an easement by prescription in registered land should be by the Prescription Act 1832. In its consultation paper on *Easements, Covenants and Profits à Prendre* ((2008) Law Com CP No 186), the Law Commission identified several concerns about the operation of prescription. In particular, at para 4.1.76:

(1) Prescription allows the claimant to get something for nothing.
(2) Prescription may penalise altruism. The claim may well originate from the servient owner's 'good neighbourly' attitude.
(3) Prescription may sometimes operate disproportionately by giving the claimant a proprietary interest in the servient owner's land.

In its 2011 report, *Making Land Law Work: Easements, Covenants and Profits à Prendre* (Law Com 327, 2011) the Law Commission recommended that a new, single statutory method of prescription replace the three methods of prescription presently available. The government has given no indication of any plans to implement this reform.

8.5.4 Proprietary estoppel

Where a claimant has detrimentally relied on an expectation that an easement will be granted, the court may declare that the claimant is entitled to an easement if this is necessary to satisfy the estoppel (as, for example, in *Joyce* v *Epsom and Ewell BC* [2012] EWCA Civ 1398).

8.5.5 Applying these rules to *Payne v Inwood*

Three different possible methods of creation were pleaded during the course of *Payne v Inwood*. All three were ultimately rejected, and Mr and Mrs Payne failed to establish that No 1A had the benefit of an easement over No 1.

8.5.5(a) Section 62 LPA 1925

The main issue before the Court of Appeal was whether an easement was created by virtue of section 62 of the LPA 1925 when Miss Cutler sold the freehold to No 1A in 1971 (see Section 8.5.5(c)). Roch LJ, who gave the only substantial judgment in the Court of Appeal, held that there were two reasons why no easement had been created by section 62:

1. There was no evidence that any licence or other right that could be turned into an easement existed at the date of the 1971 conveyance.

   Section 62 of the 1925 Act cannot create new rights where there has been no actual enjoyment of a facility, call it a liberty, privilege, advantage, easement or quasi-easement, by the owner or occupier of the dominant tenement over the servient tenement (at 47).

2. There was no diversity of occupation of the two parcels of land immediately prior to the 1971 conveyance.

The second reason, based as it is on *dicta* in the *Sovmots Investments* case, can no longer be considered sound (see Section 8.5.2(c)). However, the lack of any right that could be turned into an easement means that the argument based on section 62 would still fail today.

8.5.5(b) The rule in Wheeldon v Burrows

The claim that an easement had been created in 1971 by virtue of the rule in *Wheeldon v Burrows* was rejected by the trial judge, and this decision was not appealed. At first sight, this might seem like a case in which the rule is likely to apply. The problem, however, is establishing that the right was 'necessary to the reasonable enjoyment' of No 1A. The right claimed by Mr and Mrs Payne is very similar to that unsuccessfully claimed by Mr Wheeler in the earlier case of *Wheeler v JJ Saunders* (see Section 8.5.2(d)).

8.5.5(c) Prescription

The claim that an easement had been created under the doctrine of lost modern grant (see Section 8.5.3) was also rejected by the trial judge and not resurrected before the Court of Appeal. The 20-year period began to run when Miss Cutler sold No 1A in 1971; any easement or prescription period before that date was extinguished by Miss Cutler's common ownership of Nos 1 and 1A in 1971 (see Section 8.7.2(b)). In fact, it seems that the route of the path was not blocked until just over 20 years after the 1971 conveyance. Unfortunately, however, there was no evidence that the path had been used for at least the first half of that period.

8.6 Remedies for infringement of easements

The remedies available to the aggrieved owner of an easement are through the self-help remedy of abatement and by means of an action in the courts.

Abatement means that the owner of the easement can go onto the servient tenement and, for example, break a padlock on a gate if this is necessary. However, the courts are wary of abatement, and the dominant owner must choose the least mischievous method and refrain from causing unnecessary damage.

The owner of the easement may claim an injunction and/or damages and/or a declaration against the owner of the servient land. He can also take action against third parties who interfere with his right.

8.7 The ending of easements

Easements and profits may be ended by statute or through an act of the parties, either by release, through abandonment or through unity of seisin.

8.7.1 Statute

There is no statutory provision equivalent to section 84 of the LPA 1925 which allows the Lands Tribunal to discharge or modify a restrictive covenant (see Section 9.9.2). However, there are a number of statutes that allow easements and profits to be terminated. For example, under the Town and Country Planning Act 1990, local authorities may, in the course of development, end easements and profits. They can also be ended under the Commons Registration Act 1965.

In certain circumstances, the provisions of the LRA 2002 will effectively extinguish easements over registered titles (see Sections 8.7.2(d) and 15.8.3).

8.7.2 Act of the parties

8.7.2(a) Release

An easement or profit can be released explicitly by deed. An agreement to release without a deed may be enforceable in equity.

8.7.2(b) Unity of seisin

As stated at Section 8.4.3, a person cannot have an easement or profit against herself, so an easement ends if one person owns both tenements; of course, as indicated earlier, it might be resuscitated under section 62 of the LPA 1925 or under the rule in *Wheeldon v Burrows* (1879) LR 12 Ch D 31 (CA).

One situation that is worthy of special mention is where a leasehold interest is merged with the reversionary freehold title. This may occur when a tenant purchases the freehold to the land that she occupies. Many residential tenants with long leases of residential properties have a statutory right to purchase the freehold title to their homes under the Leasehold Reform Act 1967. One would expect that any easements granted by the tenant would be extinguished by merger of the lease with the freehold estate. However, in *Wall v Collins* [2007] Ch 390 (CA), the Court of Appeal held that such easements were not 'attached to' the leasehold estate and would continue to bind the land (including the freeholder) for the full term of the lease. The considerable problems with this reasoning are discussed at Section 8.4.4(a).

8.7.2(c) Abandonment

If the owner of the easement or profit abandons the right, she cannot later resurrect it. However, the benefit of an easement cannot be lost simply by non-use, even where the period of non-use is substantial. (It was 175 years in the case of *Benn v Hardinge* (1993) 66 P & CR 246 (CA).) For abandonment, there must also be a manifest intention to abandon, and this is very difficult for the servient owner to establish. The owner of the dominant tenement:

> must make it clear that his intention is that neither he nor his successors in title should there-
> after make any use of the right … abandonment is not to be lightly inferred because own-
> ers of property do not normally wish to divest themselves of property unless to do so is to
> their advantage, even if they have no present use for the property in question (per Lloyd LJ,
> *CDC2020 plc v George Ferreira* [2005] EWCA Civ 611 at [24]).

Intention to abandon an easement can be implied because of the circumstances, but rarely is. In the *CDC2020* case, the Court of Appeal refused to infer an intention to abandon a right of way, even when the garages to which it related had been demolished. Similarly, in the much earlier case of *Moore v Rawson* (1824) 3 B & C 332, 107 ER 756 (KB), the Court held that, even where the windows which benefit from an easement of light are blocked up for many years, this only amounts to abandonment if there is no intention to open them up again.

Swan v Sinclair [1925] AC 227 (HL) provides an example of circumstances in which abandonment will be inferred. A number of adjoining houses and their gardens had been sold in 1871. Each garden included part of a strip of land to the rear of the houses that had been designated as the route of a right of way giving access to the back gardens. By the date of the action in 1923, several householders had built fences across the strip of land, and one had changed the level of the strip adjacent to his land by some six feet. The House of Lords was satisfied that any right of way over the strip of land had been abandoned by common consent of the various owners: the right had never been exercised, and no action had been taken to enforce it for over 50 years.

8.7.2(d) Non-use of easements over registered land

Unless protected by registration, a legal easement over registered land may be unenforceable against the new registered proprietor of the servient tenement (LRA 2002, s 29 and Sched. 3, para 3). This statutory provision is entirely independent of the doctrine of abandonment, and its rules are considered in more detail at Section 15.8.3. The Law Commission has recommended that, in registered land, an easement created by implication or prescription should be deemed to have been abandoned if the dominant owner cannot show that it has been used within the previous 20 years ((1998) Law Com No 254, *Land Registration for the Twenty-First Century*, para 5.24).

8.8 Profits

8.8.1 The nature of profits

A profit is the right to take something from someone else's land. For example, there are profits of piscary (fish), turbary (turf), estovers (wood for firewood or other purposes) and pasture (the right to graze as many animals as can be supported through the winter months). Some of these profits are still economically very important to their owners.

The rules on profits are fairly similar to those on easements, except that profits can either:

▶ be *appurtenant* – benefiting a dominant tenement; or
▶ exist *in gross* (without a dominant tenement).

Thus, a person can own a profit to graze a goat on someone else's meadow, even though she owns no land which can benefit.

Where a profit is attached to land, it must accommodate the dominant tenement, just like an easement. In *Bailey v Stephens* (1862) 12 CB (NS) 91, 142 ER 1077 (CP), the owner of a field claimed a profit appurtenant to take wood from a neighbouring copse. It was held that this was not valid because it did not benefit the field. It might have been different if the alleged dominant tenement had been a house, and the wood had been used as firewood.

A profit may be 'sole', where only one person can take the thing, and the owner of the servient tenement is excluded from it. Alternatively, it can be shared with the servient owner and is then known as a profit 'in common'.

The owner of a profit automatically has a licence entitling him to enter the servient tenement in order to exercise his rights (see Section 3.4).

8.8.2 Creating profits

Profits can be acquired in most of the same ways as easements (see Section 8.5). However, because a profit cannot be 'continuous and apparent', *Wheeldon v Burrows* (1879) LR 12 Ch D 31 (CA) probably cannot apply. In addition, the relevant periods under the Prescription Act 1832 are 30 and 60 years for profits, a little longer than those required for easements.

8.8.3   Remedies for the infringement of profits

The remedies for infringement of profits are the same as those for infringement of easements (see Section 8.6), save that a profit gives sufficient degree of possession to enable a profit holder to take action against a third party without the need to prove title to the profit. Thus, the owner of a profit of piscary could win damages from a factory upstream which polluted the river and killed the fish, without having to first prove title to the profit (*Nicholls v Ely Beet Sugar Factory (No 1)* [1931] 2 Ch 84 (Ch)).

8.8.4   Ending a profit

The rules for terminating a profit are the same as those for ending an easement (see Section 8.7).

8.9   Reform of the law of easements and profits

The Law Commission's report, *Making Land Law Work: Easements, Covenants and Profits à Prendre* (Law Com 327, 2011), which has already been referred to in this chapter, is well worth reading, not least for its accessible analysis of the present law. The Commission's main recommendations are:

- the statutory reversal of the decision in *Wall v Collins* [2007] Ch 390 (CA) (see Section 8.4.4(a));
- the statutory abolition of the 'ouster principle' (see Section 8.4.4(c)(i));
- that s 62 of the LPA 1925 no longer be allowed to convert permissive rights into easements (see Section 8.5.2(c));
- a single statutory method of creation by implication be introduced, with no distinction between grant and reservation (replacing the rules considered at Section 8.5.2);
- the introduction of a single statutory method of prescription, to replace the present methods considered at Section 8.5.3; and
- the abolition of prescription and implication as means of creating profits.

There is no indication of when, if at all, Parliament will be invited to consider putting these recommendations into effect.

8.10   Rights over another's land other than easements and profits

Listed below are a number of other interests in land which appear similar to easements or profits, but which are classified differently by lawyers.

8.10.1   Public rights

These are rights which can be used by anyone, such as the right to fish between high- and low-water marks. The most familiar are rights of way, which include roads as well as footpaths, but the 'right' to use a road is now more like a licence, since it can be denied at the discretion of a police officer (see Public Order Act 1986).

The Countryside and Rights of Way Act 2000 provides a limited statutory right of public access to open countryside (the 'right to roam') and is intended to bring about the modernisation of the public rights of way network.

8.10.2 Natural rights

These rights exist automatically and arise out of the nature of land. There is a right to water flowing naturally in a definite channel, but not to water which percolates through the land. All land has a natural right of support from neighbouring land, so you may not dig a large hole in your garden if your neighbour's land consequently collapses. In *Holbeck Hall Hotel Ltd v Scarborough BC* [2000] QB 836 (CA), the council owned land between the sea cliffs and the hotel. Coastal erosion caused part of the hotel to disappear into the sea, and the rest of it had to be demolished. Its owners sued the council in the tort of nuisance. The Court of Appeal stated that a landowner could be liable for not acting to prevent the hazard, but only if it could reasonably be expected to know about it. In this case, the danger could not reasonably have been foreseen by the council, and it was therefore not just and reasonable to impose a liability on it.

There are no automatic rights to light and air, so if such rights are to exist they must amount to easements, unless the tort of nuisance can provide a remedy. The quick-growing bush *Cupressus leylandii* has deprived many landowners of natural light for their gardens and homes and has frequently given rise to heated and even violent disputes. The Anti-social Behaviour Act 2003, Part 8 (most of which came into force on 1 June 2005) provides local authorities with powers to intervene in such neighbourly disputes and to issue remedial notices in certain circumstances.

8.10.3 Customary rights

Sometimes a group of people – for example, the residents of a particular village – have a right which looks like an easement, but it is not because 'the inhabitants of a village' are not a legal person.

8.10.4 Town or village greens

Since 1970, it has been necessary to protect town or village greens by registration under the Commons Registration Act 1965. However, it is possible for land to become a new town or village green if it has been used as such by local inhabitants for a period of not less than 20 years. The Commons Act 2006, when fully implemented, will repeal the 1965 Act, but preserves the requirement for registration and the acquisition of town or village green status by long user.

8.10.5 Licences

See Chapter 3.

8.10.6 Access to Neighbouring Land Act 1992

A particular difficulty can arise for a landowner whose premises are built right up to the boundary with the neighbouring land. In the past, if she did not have an easement to go onto her neighbour's land to repair or maintain her own property, and the neighbour refused to give her permission to do so, there was little she could do except watch her wall crumble away. Now, however, under the Access to Neighbouring Land Act 1992, in cases where it is reasonably necessary to carry out work to preserve her land, and this work can really only be carried out from her neighbour's land to which she cannot otherwise gain access, a landowner may apply to the court for an order to allow her access to carry out the work. The court will not automatically make the order and may impose conditions on the applicant.

8.10.7 Party Walls Act 1996

Extensive rights are given under the Party Walls Act 1996 to landowners who want to go onto the neighbouring property in order to carry out repairs to the party wall, so landowners should use this Act rather than the more restrictive Access to Neighbouring Land Act if it is appropriate to do so. The adjoining owner must first be served with a notice in prescribed form; the person carrying out the works has the right to enter any land (and may break open doors to do so, if necessary, so long as a police officer is present); weatherproofing may need to be provided to protect the neighbouring property, and there may be a requirement to pay compensation for loss or damage caused to the adjoining owner. This Act would have been very helpful to Mr Bradburn in *Bradburn v Lindsay* [1983] 2 All ER 408 (Ch) (see Section 8.4.4(c)(ii)) and exists to prevent exactly that kind of mischief.

Summary

8.1   Easements and profits are property interests enjoyed over someone else's land. Easements are rights to do something on land belonging to someone else. There are two main stages in establishing whether a particular right is an easement or profit:

(a) is the right claimed capable of being an easement or profit; and, if it is,

(b) has an easement or profit actually been created?

8.2   A legal profit or easement must be equivalent to an interest in fee simple or to a lease, and must be created expressly by deed or by implication or by long use; all other profits and easements are equitable.

8.3   Easements include a wide variety of rights over land. Any new type of easement must fit the general character of the easements that are already recognised.

8.4   To be an easement, a claim over another person's land must fulfil the four requirements of *Re Ellenborough Park* [1956] Ch 131 (CA) that is:

- there must be dominant and servient tenements;
- the right must accommodate the dominant tenement;
- the two tenements must be in different ownership or occupation; and
- the right must be capable of being the subject of a grant.

8.5   Easements may be acquired expressly or impliedly, by grant or reservation or by court order. They may also be acquired by prescription.

8.6   Remedies for infringement of an easement or profit are abatement or action.

Summary cont'd

8.7   Easements and profits may be ended by statute, release, abandonment or unity of seisin.

8.8   Profits are rights to take something from another person's land. The rules relating to profits are very similar to those relating to easements. The main differences are that profits may or may not be appurtenant, and may be in common or sole.

8.9   The Law Commission has proposed significant changes to some of the rules governing covenants. Even if these proposals are not implemented, engaging with the reasoning behind them will lead to a deeper understanding of the issues surrounding easements.

8.10   Easements and profits must be distinguished from other claims, such as natural, customary or public rights, from statutory rights and from licences.

Exercises

8.1   Complete the online quiz on the topics covered in this chapter on the companion website.

8.2   Making reference to recently decided cases, consider whether it is possible to create an easement giving the dominant tenement holder joint or exclusive user of the servient tenement.

8.3   Critically compare the ways in which an easement may be created by implication under the rule in *Wheeldon v Burrows* (1879) 12 Ch D 31 (CA) and by operation of section 62 of the Law of Property Act 1925.

8.4   In 1995, Megan sold half her farm to Jeff, but she continued to keep her tractors in a barn on the land she had sold to him. In 2005, she leased one of her remaining fields to Jeff, by deed, for 20 years, giving him permission to use a short-cut to the field across her land 'for as long as he needs to'; he had, in fact, already been using the field and short-cut for several weeks. Last year, Jeff agreed in writing with Megan that the children attending her nursery school could play on his smallest field.

Megan has just died, and her heir, Sam, wants to know whether any of these arrangements will affect him.

You can find suggested answers to exercises 8.2, 8.3 and 8.4 on the companion website.

Further reading

Burns, 'Easements and Servitudes Created by Implied Grant, Implied Reservation or Prescription and Title-by-Registration Systems' in Dixon (ed.), *Modern Studies in Property Law: Volume 5* (Hart 2009)

Haley and McMurtry, 'Identifying an Easement: Exclusive Use, *De Facto* Control and Judicial Constraints' (2007) 58 NILQ 405

Law Commission, *Making Land Law Work: Easements, Covenants and Profits à Prendre* (Law Com 327, 2011)

Smith, 'Centre Point: Faulty Towers with Shaky Foundations' [1978] Conv 449

Sturley, 'Easements in Gross' (1980) 96 LQR 557

Tee, 'Metamorphoses and s.62 of the Law of Property Act 1925' [1998] Conv 115

Xu, 'Easement of Car Parking: The Ouster Principle is Out but Problems May Aggravate' [2012] 76 Conv 241

Chapter 9 follows overleaf.

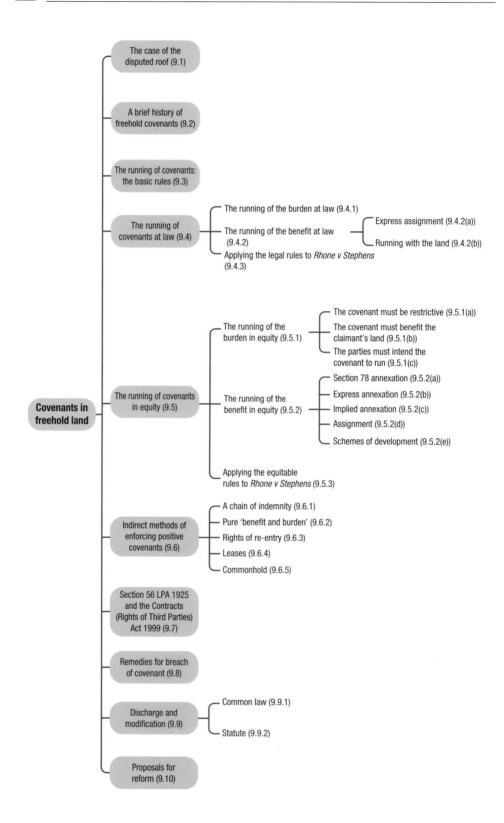

The case of the disputed roof (9.1)

A brief history of freehold covenants (9.2)

The running of covenants: the basic rules (9.3)

The running of covenants at law (9.4)
- The running of the burden at law (9.4.1)
- The running of the benefit at law (9.4.2)
  - Express assignment (9.4.2(a))
  - Running with the land (9.4.2(b))
- Applying the legal rules to *Rhone v Stephens* (9.4.3)

The running of covenants in equity (9.5)
- The running of the burden in equity (9.5.1)
  - The covenant must be restrictive (9.5.1(a))
  - The covenant must benefit the claimant's land (9.5.1(b))
  - The parties must intend the covenant to run (9.5.1(c))
- The running of the benefit in equity (9.5.2)
  - Section 78 annexation (9.5.2(a))
  - Express annexation (9.5.2(b))
  - Implied annexation (9.5.2(c))
  - Assignment (9.5.2(d))
  - Schemes of development (9.5.2(e))
- Applying the equitable rules to *Rhone v Stephens* (9.5.3)

Covenants in freehold land

Indirect methods of enforcing positive covenants (9.6)
- A chain of indemnity (9.6.1)
- Pure 'benefit and burden' (9.6.2)
- Rights of re-entry (9.6.3)
- Leases (9.6.4)
- Commonhold (9.6.5)

Section 56 LPA 1925 and the Contracts (Rights of Third Parties) Act 1999 (9.7)

Remedies for breach of covenant (9.8)

Discharge and modification (9.9)
- Common law (9.9.1)
- Statute (9.9.2)

Proposals for reform (9.10)

Covenants in freehold land

Key concepts

- ▶ **Benefit** – the right to enforce a covenant.
- ▶ **Burden** – the obligation to perform a covenant.
- ▶ **Restrictive covenant** – a negative covenant; one that requires the covenantee to refrain from certain actions.

9.1 The case of the disputed roof

In 1960, Mr Garland decided to divide Walford House, in the Somerset village of Combwich, into two separate dwellings. As the building was roughly L-shaped, it was relatively easily divided between the leg (which became Walford Cottage) and the larger foot (which continued to be known as Walford House). However, the structure of the building meant that the roof of Walford House also covered one end of Walford Cottage.

In August 1960, Mr Garland conveyed Walford Cottage to its new owners, and in the years that followed, both the cottage and the house changed hands several times. By 1984, Mr and Mrs Rhone owned the cottage, and Mrs Barnard owned the house. Unfortunately, Mrs Barnard seems not to have paid too much attention to the part of her roof that protected the cottage, and by the beginning of 1984 Mr and Mrs Rhone were complaining of leaks into one of their bedrooms. Although Mrs Barnard arranged for some repairs to be carried out, the Rhones were not satisfied. Eventually, after being refused access to the roof to carry out further repairs, Mr and Mrs Rhone commenced court proceedings. Not long afterwards, Mrs Barnard died, and responsibility for defending the claim fell to the executrix of her will, Mrs Stephens.

In support of their claim, Mr and Mrs Rhone pointed to the provisions of the original conveyance of Walford Cottage in 1960, and in particular clause 3:

> 3. The vendor [Mr Garland] hereby covenants for himself and his successors in title owner or occupiers for the time being of the property known as Walford House aforesaid to maintain to the reasonable satisfaction of the purchasers and their successors in title such part of the roof of Walford House aforesaid as lies above the property conveyed in wind and water tight condition.

This clause contains a formal promise by Mr Garland that, if effective, gives the owners for the time being of Walford Cottage the right to force the owner for the time being of Walford House to repair the relevant section of the roof and to recover damages if it is not properly maintained. This type of promise is quite different from an easement (considered in Chapter 8). Easements allow landowner A to use land belonging to landowner B. Covenants enable landowner A directly to control what landowner B does on B's land. In many ways, Mr Garland's promise is similar to the sort of covenant that might be found in a lease, but for the fact that both the house and the cottage are freehold land. The rules for determining when leasehold covenants will bind successors in title are based on the doctrines of privity of estate and, latterly, the Landlord and Tenant (Covenants) Act 1995 (see Chapter 6). Like leasehold covenants, freehold covenants arise out of a contract. However, neither privity of estate nor the 1995 Act is applicable to the relationship between the successors to separate freehold titles.

In order to find an answer to a question concerning freehold covenants, it is necessary to establish the relationships of the claimant and the defendant to the promise which has been, or may be, broken. This can be conveniently done using a simple diagram. A vertical line usually represents the promise, with the benefiting person (the covenantee) at the top and the burdened person (covenantor) at the bottom. As with leases, sales of the land are usually shown by horizontal lines. In most cases, it will be easy to identify the original parties to the covenant, as they will be named in the documentation.

In *Rhone v Stephens* [1994] 2 AC 310 (HL), Mr Garland is the covenantor (he made the promise), and the original purchaser of the cottage is the covenantee. The key relationships in the case are summarised in Figure 9.1. The owners of Walford House had clearly failed to keep the roof in good repair. However, whether the Rhones could use the promise made by Mr Garland to force Mrs Stephens to carry out the work depended upon the answers to two questions:

1. Had the burden of the covenant passed to Mrs Stephens?
2. Had the benefit of the covenant passed to Mr and Mrs Rhone?

Figure 9.1   *Rhone v Stephens* [1994] 2 AC 310 (HL)

In order to find the answers to these questions, the rules of law and equity considered in Sections 9.3–9.5 must be applied in turn.

9.2   A brief history of freehold covenants

It has long been possible for the *benefit* of a contract (such as a freehold covenant) to be transferred to a third party. There is also a long-established rule that the burden of a freehold covenant cannot be attached to land so as to bind buyers of that land. This rule is often referred to as the rule in *Austerberry v Oldham Corp*, after the decision of the Court of Appeal in that case ((1885) LR 29 Ch D 750 (CA)). Despite its long pedigree, this rule has a number of disadvantages, something which the courts of equity had begun to address even before the decision in *Austerberry* itself. By the end of the nineteenth century, it was accepted that the *burden* of a freehold covenant could be attached to land (affecting anyone who owned the land), provided that the terms of the covenant were 'restrictive'. Restrictive covenants are promises that prevent the owner from doing something. Even today, restrictive covenants can only be equitable interests. They must be protected by registration (see Sections 15.7 and 16.3), and any equitable remedies for the breach of such covenants are discretionary (see Section 2.3.3).

The nineteenth-century courts were concerned with finding a balance between protecting third-party interests in land and encouraging land development, themes which also run through the law of leases and easements. Perhaps inevitably, therefore, the courts adopted the established policy test of whether the covenant 'touches and concerns' or 'accommodates' the land concerned (see leasehold covenants in Section 6.3.1 and easements in Section 8.4.2). *Tulk v Moxhay* (1848) 2 Ph 774, 41 ER 1143 (Ch) is the first major case in which a court enforced a covenant on freehold land against a successor to the original covenantor. Mr Tulk sold freehold land in Leicester Square in London, and the buyer promised, on behalf of himself and his successors in title, to:

> keep and maintain the said parcel of ground and square garden, and the iron railing around the same in its [present] form and in sufficient and proper repair, as a square garden and pleasure ground, in an open state, uncovered with any buildings, in a neat and ornamental order.

The land changed hands several times, and a later owner decided to build on the garden, although he had known about the covenant before he bought the land and had paid less because of it. In a dramatic decision by the Court of Chancery, Mr Tulk, the original covenantee (the person to whom the promise had been made), successfully enforced the covenant against the later owner. The decision was based on the doctrine of notice and the inequitable consequences that would follow if:

> the original purchaser should be able to sell the property the next day for a greater price, in consideration of the assignee being allowed to escape from the liability which he had himself undertaken (per Lord Cottenham at 778).

In succeeding decisions, equity came to provide a cheap and effective planning law nearly a hundred years before the State seriously took on the control of land use. Many urban areas have their present shape and character because of covenants imposed by careful developers. Nowadays the public restrictions on the use of land (for example, planning law and building regulations) are normally of greater significance, but covenants are still imposed and enforced because they allow for more detailed and individual control than public planning law is able to provide. According to the Law Commission's Consultation Paper 186 (2008), some 79 per cent of registered freehold titles are subject to restrictive covenants. However, although covenants are still among the main legal strategies used to control the use of land, the underlying rules are unnecessarily complex and anachronistic. The LPA 1925 contained a statutory scheme for modifying and discharging obsolete covenants (see Section 9.9.2), together with a number of 'wordsaving' provisions. The benefits of some of the latter have been considerable, due to benevolent interpretation by the courts (see, for example, the discussion of section 78 in Section 9.5.2(a)). However, it is still necessary to track the benefit and the burden using two different sets of rules, and the burden of a positive covenant cannot run under either set. Land lawyers have responded, as they so often do, by making the best of the rules that are available, not least by developing a number of schemes to avoid the rule that the burden of positive covenants cannot pass (see Section 9.6). Inevitably, such schemes tend to add a further level of complexity and even more possible pitfalls for the unwary.

Reform of covenants in freehold land has been considered several times since 1925. In 1984, the Law Commission proposed a new and simple law to govern the running of benefit and burden at law of both restrictive and positive covenants through the creation of two new legal interests in land, 'Neighbour Obligations' and 'Development

Obligations' ((1984) Law Com No 127). This proposal was supplemented in 1991 by the recommendation that a restrictive covenant cease to be enforceable after 80 years unless the owner of the benefit could show it was not obsolete ((1991) Law Com No 201). In 2008, the Law Commission began a fresh consultation on the reform of the law relating to easements, covenants and *profits à prendre* (Law Com CP No 186), which included provisional proposals for a single scheme of 'Land Obligations' to replace covenants. These latest proposals are reviewed in the final section of this chapter.

9.3   The running of covenants: the basic rules

The basic pattern for determining whether a freehold covenant can be enforced is relatively straightforward, provided one remembers that:

- there are two independent sets of rules: *legal* and *equitable*;
- each set of rules is divided into subsets of rules for the passing of the benefit and the burden, respectively;
- the legal and equitable rules in regard to the benefit are similar but not identical; and
- the sets of rules for the burden are quite different.

The sets of rules are largely the result of case law, and different authors tend to classify the contents of each set slightly differently. The statement of the rules that follows seeks to be as simple and accurate as possible. The rules are summarised in Table 9.1.
These rules are considered in more detail in the sections that follow.

Table 9.1   Summary of the rules relating to the running of freehold covenants

	Benefit runs if:	Burden runs if:

At law (see Section 9.4)	1. It is expressly assigned (LPA 1925, s 136); or
	2. a. it benefits the land; and
	   b. the covenantee had a legal estate in the benefiting land; and
	   c. the claimant has a legal estate in the benefiting land; and
	   d. it was intended to run.
		Generally not possible.

In equity (see Section 9.5)	1. It benefits the land; and
	2. a. LPA 1925, s 78 applies; or
	   b. it was expressly or impliedly annexed to the benefiting land; or
	   c. it was assigned to the claimant.
		Under the rule in *Tulk v Moxhay* (1848) 2 Ph 774, 41 ER 1143 (Ch):
		1. it is restrictive; and
		2. it benefited land owned by the covenantee and now owned by the claimant or is part of a scheme of development; and
		3. it was intended to run (LPA 1925, s 79); and
		4. it is protected by registration; and
		5. there is no reason to deny the claimant an equitable remedy.

9.4   The running of covenants at law

9.4.1   The running of the burden at law

As indicated in Section 9.2, the common law did not (and still does not) allow the burden of a freehold covenant to be attached to land so as to bind buyers. In *Austerberry v Oldham Corp* (1885) LR 29 Ch D 750 (CA), the Court of Appeal applied the contractual doctrine that only a party to an agreement can be burdened by it. Over a hundred years later, Lord Templeman had no hesitation in accepting the rule in his speech in *Rhone v Stephens* [1994] 2 AC 310 (HL):

> At common law a person cannot be made liable upon a contract unless he was a party to it … As between persons interested in land other than as landlord and tenant, the benefit of a covenant may run with the land at law but not the burden (at 316–17).

Despite the apparent certainty of this rule, conveyancers have, with the cooperation of the courts, devised a number of indirect methods of enforcing positive covenants. The main examples are briefly explained in Section 9.6.

9.4.2   The running of the benefit at law

In answering the question 'Can the claimant sue at law?' (or 'Has the benefit passed to the claimant at law?'), two separate rules must be examined. The first provides for the express transfer of the benefit of a contract, and the second for the automatic running (implied transfer) of a benefit when the land is sold.

9.4.2(a) Express assignment

Anyone can expressly transfer the benefit of any contract to which she is a party, provided that the covenant is not a purely personal one. Under section 136 of the LPA 1925, the benefit of a promise relating to the use of land can be sold and will be enforceable at law by the buyer, provided that the assignment is in writing and express notice in writing has been given to the covenantor.

9.4.2(b) Running with the land

If there has been no express assignment of the benefit of a covenant, the law allows the benefit to pass automatically with the benefited land if:

1. the covenant benefits the land; and
2. the covenantee had a legal estate in the land when the promise was made; and
3. the claimant now has a legal estate in that land; and
4. the benefit was intended to pass.

For the covenant to benefit the land, it must be shown that the promise affects the land itself rather than its owner; that is to say, it must 'touch and concern' the land (see the discussion of *P & A Swift Investments v Combined English Stores Group plc* [1989] AC 632 (HL) in Section 6.3.1). There is some question about whether it is essential for the original parties to the covenant to have intended that its benefit should pass, as this intention is not included in the requirements set out by the House of Lords in *P & A Swift Investments*. Practically, however, the question is unlikely to be significant because of section 78 of the LPA 1925. This section provides that the benefit of a promise which 'relates to' (that is, touches and concerns) land is deemed to be made not only with the covenantee but also with all his successors in title. Section 78 means that anyone who owns a legal estate in land automatically has the benefit of any covenant made after 1925 which touches and concerns that land. The section is discussed in more detail in Section 9.5.2(a).

The importance of section 78 can be seen in the case of *Smith v River Douglas Catchment Board* [1949] 2 KB 500 (CA). In 1938, the Board promised Ellen Smith that it would maintain the banks of the Eller Brook adjoining her land in Lancashire. She sold the land to John Smith (the first claimant), and he leased it to Snipes Hall Farm Ltd. When the river flooded the land because of the Board's failure to carry out proper maintenance, John Smith and the farm tried to recover their losses from the Board on the ground that the benefit of the covenant had automatically passed to them when they bought the land. It was held that:

1. the covenant did benefit their land;
2. it had been made with a legal owner of the land;
3. the present claimants were both legal owners; and
4. the benefit of the covenant had been intended to run by virtue of section 78 of the LPA 1925.

Both claimants could therefore claim damages for the Board's breach of covenant. The farm, as tenant, succeeded because section 78 enables any legal owner (freeholder or leaseholder) to enjoy the benefit of a covenant relating to the land.

9.4.3 Applying the legal rules to *Rhone v Stephens*

To enforce the covenant at law, Mr and Mrs Rhone must demonstrate that they have the benefit of the covenant and that Mrs Stephens is subject to the burden. There is little doubt that the Rhones have the benefit of covenant, as the promise made by the original covenantor satisfies the requirements set out in *Smith v River Douglas Catchment Board*. However, Mrs Stephens cannot be subject to the burden of the covenant at law because the rule in the *Austerberry* case prevents the burden being transferred at law.

9.5 The running of covenants in equity

9.5.1 The running of the burden in equity

In *Tulk v Moxhay* (1848) 41 ER 1143 (Ch) (the facts of which are set out in Section 9.2), Cottenham LC granted the claimant an injunction allowing him to enforce a covenant against the successor in title of the original covenantor. This appeared to be a straightforward decision. Lord Cottenham believed that if the court had failed to enforce the promise:

> it would [have been] impossible for an owner of land to sell part of it without incurring the risk of rendering what he retains worthless (at 1145).

This is true, although it was, and still is, possible for a landowner to maintain control over the land being sold by granting a long lease (with the appropriate covenants) instead of parting with the freehold. The leasehold covenants would be enforceable against subsequent assignees of the lease.

The decision in *Tulk v Moxhay* turned on the question of notice (see Section 16.2.2). If the purchaser of the affected land was found to have had notice of the burden of the covenant, then equity required that he be bound by it. This potentially opened the way to allowing the burden of all sorts of covenants, as well as other kinds of non-property obligations, to bind successors in title. However, later in the nineteenth century, the judges seem to have thought that the now depressed land market required restrictions on land use to be kept to a minimum in order to encourage purchasers.

They therefore introduced increasingly complex and technical requirements limiting the effect of *Tulk v Moxhay*. Today, the burden of a covenant runs in equity if:

1. it is restrictive; and
2. it benefits land once owned by the covenantee and now owned by the claimant or is part of a scheme of development (see Section 9.5.2(e)); and
3. it was intended to run with the land.

Further, because this is merely an equitable interest:

4. the notice or registration rules must be complied with (these rules are set out in Chapters 15 and 16); and
5. the claimant must have 'clean hands' (that is, the claimant must act fairly; see Section 2.3.3).

9.5.1(a) The covenant must be restrictive

Whether a covenant is 'restrictive' (that is to say, negative) is a question of its substance, not its form. What matters is the real meaning of the covenant rather than what it appears to mean. For example, a covenant to maintain the land uncovered with buildings, although positive in terms of the words used, is negative in substance because the covenantor can comply by doing nothing (that is, without spending money). In reality, it simply requires the covenantor not to build on the land.

The rule that equity will enforce the burden of only those covenants that are restrictive was restated by the House of Lords in *Rhone v Stephens* [1994] 2 AC 310 (HL), the facts of which are set out in Section 9.1.

Lord Templeman reviewed all the authorities and concluded that the rule of restrictive covenants is a rule of property: an owner of land cannot exercise a right which has never been transferred to him. Equity follows the law, and:

> cannot compel an owner to comply with a positive covenant entered into by his predecessors in title without flatly contradicting the common law rule that a person cannot be made liable upon a contract unless he was a party to it. Enforcement of a positive covenant lies in contract; a positive covenant compels an owner to exercise his rights. Enforcement of a negative covenant lies in property; a negative covenant deprives the owner of a right over property (at 69).

He believed that any judicial alteration of the rule now would cause chaos for landowners.

9.5.1(b) The covenant must benefit the claimant's land

The claimant's land (the land once owned by the covenantee) must be identifiable and either benefited ('accommodated') by the covenant or part of a scheme of development (see Section 9.5.2(e)). The point here is that equity will only enforce a restrictive covenant if its purpose is to protect the value and amenity of the covenantee's neighbouring land (an example of a covenant that did not pass this test can be found in the recent case of *Cosmichome Ltd v Southampton City Council* [2013] 1 WLR 2436 (Ch)). The person trying to enforce the covenant need not own a legal estate in the land and need not have bought the whole of the covenantee's land, so long as the part she owns is capable of benefiting from the promise. In *London CC v Allen* [1914] 3 KB 642 (CA), Mr Allen promised the council that he would not build on a strip of land needed for the continuation of a road. The burdened land was ultimately conveyed to Mr Allen's wife, and Mrs Allen proceeded to build on it. It was held, with great regret, that the claimant authority could not enforce the covenant because it had sold the benefiting land. Statutes now provide that local authorities and certain other bodies, such as the National Trust, are exempt from this rule.

In *Dano Ltd v Earl Cadogan* [2004] 1 P & CR 13 (CA), the sixth Earl Cadogan had conveyed some land in 1929 to a local authority, which covenanted with him on behalf of itself and its successors that the land would be used for no other purpose than the housing of the working classes 'so long as such adjoining or neighbouring property or any part thereof forms part of the Cadogan Settled Estate in Chelsea but not further or otherwise'. In the 1960s the Cadogan family rearranged its affairs, and the Settled Estate was ended. Later, Dano Ltd acquired the land from the local authority, received planning permission to build private houses on some of the land and sought a declaration that the covenant was unenforceable. Although the neighbouring land was still in the Cadogan family, it no longer formed part of the 'Cadogan Settled Estate in Chelsea', and on that basis the Court of Appeal held that there was no longer any land capable of benefiting from the covenant, which was therefore unenforceable, despite its philanthropic objectives.

9.5.1(c) *The parties must intend the covenant to run*

This intention will usually be expressed in the document containing the covenant, but if not, it may be implied by section 79 of the LPA 1925. Section 79 does not apply if the covenant was made before 1926. The operation of section 79 can be excluded by demonstrating contrary intention. Usually, such intention will be clearly stated in the wording of the covenant, but the courts can construe the document as a whole in order to determine the intention of the original parties (see, for example, *Morrells of Oxford Ltd v Oxford United FC Ltd* [2001] Ch 459 (CA)). In *Roadside Group Ltd v Zara Commercial Ltd* [2010] EWHC 1950 (Ch), the question was whether a user covenant in a lease was binding on a subtenant as the successor in title of the tenant by virtue of section 79 (see Section 6.3.4). Kitchen J concluded that the user covenant was intended to be interpreted more narrowly than the other covenants in the lease because it alone was worded in the passive voice ('shall not be used' instead of 'not to use'). He went on to hold that reading the words of section 79 into the user covenant would be to broaden its scope beyond the intention of the original parties. This case illustrates the importance of careful drafting and reading when dealing with documents relating to interests in land.

9.5.2 The running of the benefit in equity

Equity also developed its own rules about the running of the benefit of a covenant, based on the legal rules:

▶ the covenant must touch and concern the land of the covenantee; and
▶ the benefit of the covenant must have passed to the claimant.

There are three ways in which the benefit of the covenant may pass to the claimant:

1. by annexation (statutory, express or implied); or
2. by assignment; or
3. under a scheme of development.

9.5.2(a) Section 78 annexation

For the benefit of a covenant to be annexed to the land it is necessary to establish that this was the intention of the original parties. Traditionally this was dependent upon how the court construed the document containing the covenant. However, the decision of the Court of Appeal in *Federated Homes Ltd v Mill Lodge Properties Ltd* [1980] 1 WLR 594 (CA) means that almost all covenants made since 1925 are deemed to be annexed to the land by virtue of section 78 of the LPA 1925.

The facts of the *Federated Homes* case were relatively simple and are shown diagrammatically in Figure 9.2. M Ltd owned a large estate, which was divided into three plots, blue, green and red. They sold the blue land to Mill Lodge Properties, who promised, for the benefit of the green and red land, that they would not build more than 300 houses on it. Both the green and the red land then came into the hands of Federated Homes. There was an unbroken chain of express assignments of the benefit of Mill Lodge's promise with the green land, but not with the red. (The assignment of benefit is discussed in Section 9.5.2(d).)

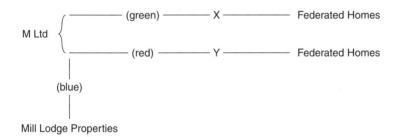

Figure 9.2 *Federated Homes Ltd v Mill Lodge Properties Ltd* [1980] 1 WLR 594 (CA)

Federated Homes successfully claimed an injunction for breach of the covenant when Mill Lodge began building 32 houses more than were permitted under the covenant. The defendant's arguments centred on technical details of the planning permission, but this was decided in the claimant's favour. It then became clear that, as owners of the *green* land with an unbroken chain of express assignments, Federated Homes had the benefit of the covenant and could enforce it against Mill Lodge. However, the judge at first instance went further and said that, under section 62 of the LPA 1925 (by which a conveyance of land transfers all rights which benefit it), Federated Homes could also enforce the covenant as owners of the *red* land.

The Court of Appeal agreed with the judge on the planning issue and the green land, but took a different view on the red land. Rather than section 62, they chose to use section 78 of the LPA 1925 to pass the benefit of the covenant to the claimants. Until then, it had been thought that section 78 was merely a 'wordsaving' provision, but Brightman LJ rejected this interpretation as it seemed to him to 'fly in the face of the wording'.

The widest interpretation of *Federated Homes* is that the benefit of any covenant made since 1925 automatically runs in equity if it touches and concerns the land. This represents the radical obliteration of a century of case law about the annexation or assignment of freehold covenants. Annexation and assignment cases (briefly outlined below) had been lovingly analysed by generations of conveyancers and academics, and the Court of Appeal's decision surprised many commentators.

Although the decision in *Federated Homes* has not been challenged, the courts have had to address two questions not answered in the original case.

1. Is it necessary to identify the land benefiting from the covenant?
2. Can the parties displace the effect of section 78 by expressing a contrary intention?

Both of these questions were addressed by the Court of Appeal in *Crest Nicholson Residential (South) Ltd v McAllister* [2004] 1 WLR 2409 (CA).

Chadwick LJ answered the first question by confirming that the requirement for express annexation (set out in *Marquess of Zetland v Driver* [1939] Ch 1 (CA)) also applied to section 78 cases; that is, the land which is intended to be benefited by the covenant must be sufficiently defined so as to be easily ascertainable. In the earlier case of *Stocks v Whitgift Homes* [2001] EWCA Civ 1732 (not referred to by Chadwick LJ in *Crest*), the Court of Appeal stated that it is not necessary for the covenant to exactly identify the land to be benefited, providing that there is sufficient extrinsic identification evidence to determine the extent of the land concerned.

The second question had already been answered at first instance by Judge Paul Baker QC in *Roake v Chadha* [1984] 1 WLR 40 (Ch). In that case, there was a 50-year-old covenant not to build more than one house per plot on land in a London suburb, and a further clause in the conveyance that the benefit of the covenant would not pass unless it was expressly assigned. All the land changed hands, without an express assignment of the benefit of the covenant, and a later owner of the burdened land wanted to build another house in his garden. Judge Paul Baker QC held that there was nothing in the *Federated Homes* decision that prevented the parties to the covenant preventing it being annexed to the land by section 78 if that was their intention:

> The true position as I see it is that even where a covenant is deemed to be made with successors in title as s.78 requires, one still has to construe the covenant as a whole to see whether the benefit of the covenant is annexed (at 46).

The effect of expressing contrary intention was contentious because, unlike sections 62 and 79 of the LPA 1925, there is no provision in section 78 allowing the parties to negate its effect by expressing their wish to do so. In the *Crest Nicholson* case, Chadwick LJ confirmed the decision in *Roake v Chadha*, explaining that the wording of section 78 means there is no need for it to include the words 'unless a contrary intention is expressed':

> The qualification 'subject to contrary intention' is implicit in the definition of 'successors in title' which appears in section 78(1); that is the effect of the words 'the land of the covenantee intended to be benefited'. If the terms in which the covenant is imposed show … [that the parties did not intend the benefit of the covenant to be annexed to the land] then the owners and occupiers of the land sold off in those circumstances are not 'owners and occupiers for the time being of the land of the covenantee intended to be benefited'; and so are not 'successors in title' of the original covenantee for the purposes of section 78(1) (at [43]).

The same argument does not apply to section 79, because of the specific meaning given to 'successors in title' in section 79(2).

Thus, the effect of *Federated Homes* is to annex the benefit of the covenant to the land (and each and every part of the land) unless the parties have expressed their intention that this should not be the case. There remain, however, a number of additional complications with this simplification of the law. For example, the operation of section 78 is almost certainly limited to covenants made since 1925 (see, for example, the recent case of *Seymour Road (Southampton) Ltd v Williams* [2010] EWHC 111 (Ch), which concerned a pre-1926 covenant). In addition, because of the wording of the section, it may only apply to the running of the benefit of restrictive covenants.

9.5.2(b) Express annexation

In cases where section 78 does not apply, it is necessary to fall back on the old concepts of annexation and assignment created in nineteenth-century cases. When considering whether the benefit of a covenant falling outside section 78 has been annexed to the land, the situation is the reverse of that when section 78 of the LPA 1925 applies. For the benefit of such a covenant to be annexed it must be possible to establish from the original document that this was the positive intention of the parties. The best evidence for this is the use of express words to this effect, similar to those used in *Rogers v Hosegood* [1900] 2 Ch 388 (CA). In 1869, the Duke of Bedford had bought a plot of land in Kensington and had promised not to build more than one house on it. The deed stated that this was:

> with intent that the covenants might so far as possible bind the premises … and might enure to the benefit of the [sellers] … their heirs and assigns and others claiming under them to all or any of their land adjoining or near to the said premises.

The Duke's land passed to Hosegood, who decided to build a large block of flats on it. Rogers, an owner of adjoining land, wanted to prevent the development. The burden of the covenant had clearly passed to Hosegood, so the question was whether the benefit had passed to Rogers. It was held that the benefit had been annexed to his land by the words of the deed, so anyone who subsequently owned that land could enforce the covenant.

9.5.2(c) Implied annexation

If the original document lacks the kind of wording used in the covenant in *Rogers v Hosegood* (see Section 9.5.2(b)), it may be possible for the successor to the covenantee to show that annexation can be implied by considering the wording of the original document in the context of all the surrounding circumstances; see *Marten v Flight Refuelling Ltd (No 1)* [1962] Ch 115 (Ch).

9.5.2(d) Assignment

If there is no annexation, the benefit may still have been passed by a chain of assignments such as existed for the benefit of the green land in *Federated Homes* (see Section 9.5.2(a)). If there is no complete express chain, it may be that there could yet be an implied assignment of the benefit. For this to happen, the covenant must have been intended to benefit the land of the original covenantee, and the successor who is attempting to enforce the covenant must have had the benefit expressly assigned to him. In *Newton Abbot Cooperative Society v Williamson & Treadgold Ltd* [1952] Ch 286 (Ch), a covenant preventing the use of a shop as an ironmongery was not expressed to be for the benefit of the land belonging to the covenantee. The judge, however, was able to look at the surrounding circumstances and found that the covenantee (who herself ran an ironmongery and understandably did not want competition):

> took the covenant restrictive of the user of the defendants' premises for the benefit of her own business of ironmonger and of her property … where at all material times she was carrying on that business (at 297).

When the covenantee died, her heir received the land and the benefit of the covenant, which he could then assign expressly to his successor, who could enforce it.

9.5.2(e) Schemes of development

A final method by which successors in title of the original covenantee might enforce covenants is through what is known as a 'scheme of development'. A scheme of development (or 'building scheme') is another creation of equity and provides a useful method for the modern developer to create and preserve new estates. If the conditions for a scheme are fulfilled, then the burdens (provided the covenants have been protected by registration) and the benefits of restrictive covenants which touch and concern the land run automatically to all owners covered by the scheme, thus greatly simplifying the question of whether one owner can stop another breaching a covenant.

The first known scheme was created in 1767 and upheld in 1866. A large number were created in the nineteenth century and upheld by the courts, but, after 1889, the number of successful schemes began to fall. Strict rules were laid down in the judgment in *Elliston v Reacher* [1908] 2 Ch 374 (Ch), and later judges treated them as if they were part of a statute. According to *Elliston v Reacher*:

- there had to be one seller; and
- the plots must have been laid out in advance; and
- mutual restrictions must have been established for the mutual benefit of the plots; and
- the purchasers of the plots must have known about the intended mutual enforceability.

Between 1908 and the 1960s, only two schemes were successfully enforced in reported cases, but then the climate appears to have changed again, and the rules in *Elliston v Reacher* relaxed. In *Re Dolphin's Conveyance* [1970] Ch 654 (Ch), there was no common vendor, nor were the plots laid out in advance. However, the local authority in Birmingham was prevented from developing the site because it was held that a building scheme had been created and that the proposed development would have been in breach of covenant. Stamp J said that the rules set out in *Elliston v Reacher* were only part of a wider rule, and that a scheme arose because of the existence of 'the common interest and the common intention actually expressed in the conveyances themselves' (at 664). According to *Dolphin's Conveyance*, the requirements for a building scheme are therefore:

- mutually binding covenants
- applying within a clearly defined and commonly understood area.

The question of whether the covenants are sufficiently mutual is concerned with both the content of the covenant (are they all in broadly the same terms) and the awareness of the original covenantors that they were part of a building scheme. In the case of *Small v Oliver & Saunders (Developments) Ltd* [2006] 3 EGLR 141 (Ch), the company had started to build a second house on land forming part of the garden of an existing house that it owned. This house was part of an impressive 'estate' built around a central golf course between 1922 and 1950, and both the house and its garden were subject to a covenant to use the land only as a private residence. Mr Small, who owned a house nearby, argued that the company was in breach of this covenant because it was using one part of the garden to gain access to the other part, where it was building the new house. The judge rejected the claim that there was a building scheme, because Mr Smith was unable to demonstrate that the various people who had originally purchased the houses on the estate had been aware of the reciprocal nature of the obligations contained in the covenants concerned. Mr Smith was, however, able to establish that the benefit of the covenant had been annexed to the land that he himself owned (not that this enabled him to prevent the construction of the new house; see Section 9.9).

With older developments, there are often problems in finding sufficient numbers of the original documents, and often the original owners are beyond recall as well. In cases where common interest and intention cannot be shown from the covenants (as in *Emile Elias & Co Ltd v Pine Groves Ltd* [1993] 1 WLR 305 (PC)), the courts will apply the rules in *Elliston v Reacher*. In *Emile Elias & Co Ltd*, the Privy Council emphasised the necessity for a 'common code of covenants'.

In *Stocks v Whitgift Homes*, [2001] EWCA Civ 1732 a large residential estate of some 440 acres had been developed in the 1920s and 1930s. Some of the estate was clearly intended to be within a building scheme, but there was a good deal of uncertainty about the rest. In finding that no building scheme existed, even among owners of the properties situated within the area originally intended to be part of the scheme, the Court of Appeal stated that:

> the authorities show that [a] number of characteristics must be established. Among them is certainty: otherwise, in relation to each plot of land said to fall within the scheme, the question will continually arise: does it or does it not so fall? More precisely, is it, or is it not subject to mutually enforceable benefits and obligations, and, if enforceable, by and against the owners of which plots? This essential requirement of certainty makes obvious practical sense (per Judge LJ at [110]).

9.5.3   Applying the equitable rules to *Rhone v Stephens*

A return to the facts of *Rhone v Stephens* (see Section 9.1) might help make the application of all these rules clearer. The question was whether Mr and Mrs Rhone had the benefit, and Mrs Stephens the burden, of the promise made by Mr Garland. There was, of course, no building scheme.

A glance at the summary of the rules relating to the benefit and the burden (see Table 9.1) shows that the strictest requirement relates to the running of the burden. This is, therefore, always the place to start in a problem of this kind, since otherwise you may go to all the trouble of tracing the benefit, only to find that the burden cannot run in any event.

To decide whether the burden has passed with the land, it is necessary to apply the equitable rules in *Tulk v Moxhay*, since the burden cannot run at law. It will already be apparent from Section 9.5.1(a) that in this case the covenant is positive in substance.

Consequently, the burden cannot run in equity. This is despite the fact that the other rules in *Tulk v Moxhay* are almost certainly satisfied: the covenant did benefit the land of the covenantee (the original purchaser of the cottage), and there is no evidence of contrary intention to negate the section 79 of the LPA 1925 assumption that it was intended to run.

On the facts of *Rhone v Stephens* it is, therefore, unnecessary to test whether the benefit has passed with the land to Mr and Mrs Rhone. It is important to note, however, that when testing whether the benefit has passed, it is not permissible to mix legal and equitable rules. *Burden and benefit must run in the same medium* (that is, both must run at law, or both must run in equity). In practice, this means that if the burdened land has changed hands, requiring equitable principles to be applied to the burden, then the equitable rules must also be used for the benefit.

9.6 Indirect methods of enforcing positive covenants

There are many circumstances where a covenantee may wish the burden of a positive covenant to bind the successor in title of the original covenantor and where the court's refusal to permit this will cause significant inconvenience (as in *Rhone v Stephens* [1994] 2 AC 310 (HL)). It is not surprising, therefore, that lawyers have devised a number of methods of effectively enforcing positive covenants, although each has its own limitations.

9.6.1 A chain of indemnity

If the original covenantor, and each of his successors in title, obtains an indemnity covenant from the next purchaser, the continuing liability of the original covenantor can be offset by a claim against the landowner in breach of the covenant. It is essential, however, that the 'chain' of indemnity covenants be complete.

9.6.2 Pure 'benefit and burden'

The burden of a positive covenant may bind a successor who wishes to assert the benefit of a covenanted obligation, provided that there is reciprocity between the benefit and burden. The classic illustration of this principle is *Halsall v Brizell* [1957] Ch 169 (Ch) in which Upjohn J held that the purchaser of a house on a residential estate could not enjoy the benefit of use of a private road without performing a freehold covenant to maintain it. However, unlike the doctrine of restrictive covenants (which creates an interest in the servient land), benefit and burden 'gives the third party nothing more than a personal right to enforce the covenant in equity against the registered proprietor' (per Patten LJ, *Goodman v Elwood* [2014] 2 WLR 967 (CA), [35]).

9.6.3 Rights of re-entry (see LPA 1925, s 1(2)(e))

The performance of a positive covenant can be attached to a right of re-entry that becomes exercisable if the covenant is breached. The right of re-entry, but not the covenant itself, would, if annexed to a rentcharge, run with the burdened land.

9.6.4 Leases

Since there is no prohibition on the transfer of a positive leasehold covenant, the land-owner may prefer to grant a lease of the relevant part of his land (with appropriate covenants) rather than sell the freehold.

9.6.5 Commonhold

Under Part 1 of the Commonhold and Leasehold Reform Act 2002, it is possible for a development to be registered at the Land Registry by the freehold owner as a 'freehold estate in commonhold land'. The property is divided into 'units', each held by the unit owner on a freehold basis, with each freeholder owing obligations to the others through the medium of a Commonhold Association. Commonhold is examined in more detail in Section 6.5.

9.7 Section 56 LPA 1925 and the Contracts (Rights of Third Parties) Act 1999

Section 56 of the LPA 1925 may be relevant whenever the person claiming the benefit (or his predecessor in title) owned land nearby at the time the covenant was made. In a sense, it is a legal extension of privity of contract and provides that:

> A person may take ... the benefit of any ... covenant ... over or respecting land ... although he may not be named as a party to the conveyance or other instrument.

This is a way of giving the benefit of a covenant to someone other than those who are named in the deed, provided the covenant purports to be made with him. The section applies if the person alleged to have the benefit of the covenant was identifiable in the covenant agreement and existed at the date of the covenant. The reason for these rules is that it would be unfair if the covenantor were effectively making her promise to everyone in the neighbourhood; she needs to be able to identify, on the day she made the promise, the landowners who might be able to take action against her.

The rules were established in *Re Ecclesiastical Commissioners for England's Conveyance* [1936] Ch 430 (Ch). In that case, the court had to decide whether a large house near to Hampstead Heath in London was subject to a restrictive covenant. The issue was whether neighbouring landowners had the right to enforce it, and this depended on whether the original landowners who had owned the neighbouring land at the time of the covenant could enforce it through section 56. A clause in the conveyance stated that the original covenantor made the promise, 'also as a separate covenant with ... owners for the time being of land adjoining or adjacent to the said land hereby conveyed'. This was held to be enough for section 56 to apply. The neighbours were identifiable from the agreement and were in existence at its date. Their successors in title were able to claim the benefit from them by the usual rules for the running of the benefit, and thus were able to enforce the covenant.

For covenants made after 11 May 2000, the Contracts (Rights of Third Parties) Act 1999 can also be used in this situation. Under section 1 of the Act, a person who is not a party to the contract may enforce it if it purports to confer or expressly confers a benefit on her, so long as the contract identifies her by name, as a member of a class or as answering a particular description, even though she was not in existence when the contract was entered into. From its wording, it seems that operation of the Act is wider than section 56, since it will allow a landowner to enforce the benefit of a covenant even though it is not purported to be made with her and even though she might not have been identifiable when the covenant was created. However, there are unlikely to be a significant number of cases involving covenants using the 1999 Act as the provisions of section 56 of the LPA 1925 will usually be sufficient.

9.8　Remedies for breach of covenant

The equitable nature of restrictive covenants means that the burden of the covenant will need to be registered if it is to be enforced against a successor in title of the original covenantor. The detailed rules are examined in Chapters 15 and 16. Another implication of the rule that the burden of a restrictive covenant runs only in equity is that only equitable remedies are available to the courts when remedying any breach. In principle, therefore, a remedy will only be available if the wrong committed can be solved by an injunction. Further, all equitable remedies are given at the discretion of the court and can be refused if, for example, the claimant has unnecessarily delayed bringing his action or has otherwise acted improperly.

Although the usual remedy for the breach of a restrictive covenant will be a permanent injunction, the court has the power to award damages instead (but not in circumstances where an injunction could not be granted). The circumstances in which damages may properly be awarded in lieu of an injunction were summarised by AL Smith LJ in *Shelfer v City of London Electric Lighting Co (No 1)* [1895] 1 Ch 287. Damages may be given in substitution for an injunction:

1. if the injury to the claimant's legal right is small, and
2. is one which is capable of being estimated in money, and
3. is one which can be adequately compensated by a small money payment, and
4. the case is one in which it would be oppressive to the defendant to grant an injunction (per AL Smith LJ, *Shelfer* at 322–23).

For example, in *Small v Oliver & Saunders (Developments) Ltd* [2006] 3 EGLR 141 (Ch) (see Section 9.5.2(e)), the court took the view that it would be disproportionate to grant an injunction that would effectively prevent the defendant company from completing a nearly finished house. The claimant was awarded £3,270 as damages in lieu of an injunction.

The original covenantor will always be liable in contract law (unless a contrary intention is expressed in the contract), but the remedy against him can only be damages once he has parted with ownership of the burdened land.

9.9　Discharge and modification

Covenants are automatically ended ('discharged') in two ways: by the common law, and under statute. Statute also allows covenants to be modified. The power to discharge or modify covenants is important, because the very existence of the power encourages people to agree to waive covenants. Many cases do not go to litigation; it is often a question of the developer 'buying off' the covenants.

9.9.1   Common law

First, if the same person owns the burdened and benefiting lands, the covenant cannot be enforced: a person does not have rights against herself. However, if the covenant is part of a building scheme, life after death is possible: the covenants revive if the plots come into separate ownership again later.

Second, if the covenant has been abandoned, the courts will not enforce it. This was argued in *Chatsworth Estates v Fewell* [1931] 1 Ch 224 (Ch). In this case, there was a covenant on a house in a seaside resort restricting its use to that of a private dwelling. Thirty years later, the then owner started taking paying guests. The claimants warned him of the breach and asked whether he wished to apply to have the covenant modified or discharged under section 84 of the LPA 1925 (see Section 9.9.2), but he did nothing. When taken to court for the breach, he argued that the claimants had waived breaches by others in the neighbourhood and had therefore abandoned the benefit. The claimants won their injunction to end the breach. Abandonment is a question of fact in every case; here the essential residential character of the area remained, and the claimants could not be expected to conduct inquisitorial examinations into their neighbours' lives in order to see how they were using the land.

In *Shaw v Applegate* [1977] 1 WLR 970 (CA), a café owner in another resort was allowed to keep his amusement arcade, contrary to the covenant, because of the claimant's delay in enforcing it. On the facts, the delay had not meant that the claimants had acquiesced in the breach, which would have made the covenant unenforceable, but an injunction (an equitable remedy – see Section 9.8) was refused on the grounds that the café owner had been lulled into a false sense of security because of the delay, and damages were awarded instead.

9.9.2   Statute

Several statutes authorise the discharge of a covenant; one well-known example is section 237 of the Town and Country Planning Act 1971, which allows a local authority to carry out a development against a covenant, provided it pays compensation. The most important provision, however, is section 84 of the LPA 1925, as amended by section 28 of the LPA 1969.

A statutory power to end freehold covenants was deemed necessary in 1925 because restrictions on land use could 'enclose individual premises and often whole streets and neighbourhoods in a legal straitjacket' (Polden, 1986). There was no discussion of section 84 in Parliament, although it allows the State to destroy private property (the right to enforce the covenant), sometimes without compensation. The question is now whether section 84 is in breach of Article 1, Protocol 1 of the European Convention on Human Rights. This issue has been tested before the European Commission of Human Rights in *S v UK* (1984) (Application No 10741/84). The applicant lost her case there, on the particular facts, but it seems unlikely that any other application, even on different facts, would succeed because of the doctrine of proportionality and the public interest element: 'ensuring the most efficient use of the land for the benefit of the community' (see Dawson, 1986, 126).

Applications under the section are made to the Lands Tribunal, a body which spends much of its time determining land valuations for the purposes of rating and compulsory purchase. In June 2009, the Lands Tribunal joined the new two-tier tribunal system established by the Tribunals, Courts and Enforcement Act 2007 when it became the Lands Chamber of the Upper Tribunal. However, for the time being, at least, it is still referred to as the Lands Tribunal. Appeal on a point of law can be made to the Court of Appeal. Under section 84 of the LPA 25, the Lands Tribunal has the power to modify or discharge any restrictive covenant and some covenants in long leases. There is provision for compensation to be paid in certain cases.

Under section 84, a covenant may be discharged or modified if:

- it should be deemed obsolete due to changes in the character of the property or neighbourhood; or
- it impedes some reasonable use of the land, provided money is sufficient compensation and either (a) 'it provides no practical benefits of substantial value or advantage' or (b) it is contrary to the public interest; or
- the parties agree, expressly or impliedly, 'by their acts or omissions'; or
- it will not injure anyone entitled to the benefit.

The Tribunal must have regard to any planning permissions or local plans, but these are not decisive. There are innumerable cases on section 84, and each turns on its own facts. Two examples are briefly considered here.

Re Bass Ltd's Application (1973) 26 P & CR 156 (Lands Tribunal) concerned an application to use land, restricted to housing, as a lorry park. The owner of the burdened land already had planning permission, and the objectors to the covenant's discharge (the owners of the benefit) already suffered from serious traffic noise. The adjudicator found, from a visit to the site, that, although living close to heavy lorries was far from pleasant, the restrictive covenant still conferred a substantial advantage on the objectors in preventing any increase in the number of lorries, and the application therefore failed. (This case is useful in that it lists the questions which must be asked in an application under section 84.)

In *Re University of Westminster* [1998] 3 All ER 1014 (CA), the University applied to have discharged or modified covenants restricting the use of one of its properties to particular educational purposes. The Court of Appeal upheld the Lands Tribunal's determination: the covenants could be modified to permit the use of the property for the wider educational purposes the University proposed, but they would not be discharged entirely. The parties who had the benefit of the covenants had not objected to the proposal for discharge. However, the Lands Tribunal was not satisfied that they realised the possible effect of discharging them: the University, and any subsequent owner, would be able to use the property for any purpose. On this basis, the Lands Tribunal found that they had not therefore agreed to the discharge of the covenants, as required by section 84(1)(b). Nor was the Lands Tribunal convinced that some reasonable use of the property would be impeded by a failure to allow discharge.

It can be seen, even from this brief review, that the Lands Tribunal has a challenging role. Many different interests are involved in these cases: developers, nearby landowners intent on preserving the status quo, 'expert' planners, the general policy that contracts be respected, the wider public interest in land use and the views of particular political parties (such as the Conservative government's policy of reducing planning restrictions during the 1980s and 1990s). These difficult issues are part of the background of all planning law, private and public.

9.10 Proposals for reform

In its report *Making Land Law Work: Easements, Covenants and Profits à Prendre* (Law Com 327, 2011), the Law Commission identified a number of major defects in the law governing covenants (see para 5.4):

- It is difficult to identify who has the benefit of a restrictive covenant, for two reasons:
  - (a) there is no requirement that the instrument creating the covenant should describe the benefited land with sufficient clarity to enable its identification without extrinsic evidence; and
  - (b) the benefit of a restrictive covenant, being an equitable interest, cannot be registered as an appurtenant interest on the register of title to the dominant land.
- There are differing and complicated rules for the running of the benefit and burden of restrictive covenants.
- The contractual liability between the original parties to a covenant persists despite changes in the ownership of the land; when the land is sold, the original covenantor remains liable.
- Whereas the benefit of a positive covenant can run at law, the burden of a positive covenant does not run so as to bind successors in title.

The Law Commission responded by recommending the creation of the 'land obligation', a new type of legal interest in land to be added to those listed in section 1(2) of the Law of Property Act 1925. Land obligations would differ from freehold covenants in that:

- they could be positive as well as negative;
- both the benefit and burden would be capable of registration; and
- the original parties to the land obligation would not be liable for breaches of it occurring after they parted with the land (compare the rules on leasehold covenants introduced by the Landlord and Tenant (Covenants) Act 1995, considered at Section 6.4).

Only time will tell whether these proposals will fare any better than earlier proposals for reforming the law of covenants.

Summary

9.1 Covenants are interests that enable a landowner to directly control what another landowner does on her own land.

9.2 Many of the rules relating to enforcing covenants were developed by equity in the nineteenth century. Many people consider these rules to be anachronistic and unnecessarily complicated.

9.3 There are separate sets of rules to pass the benefit of a covenant at law and to pass both the benefit and the burden of a covenant in equity (see Table 9.1 in Section 9.3).

9.4 It is possible for the benefit of a covenant to run at law by express or implied assignment. However, it is not possible for the burden of a covenant to run at law.

9.5 It is possible for the burden of a covenant to run in equity if the conditions derived from *Tulk v Moxhay* (1848) 2 Ph 774, 41 ER 1143 (Ch) are complied with, including the requirement that the covenant is negative in effect. The burden of positive covenants cannot run in equity. The rules for the passing of the benefit in equity are distinct from those at law and must be met in their own right.

9.6 Various indirect methods have been developed to enable positive covenants to be enforced against successors in title to the original parties.

9.7 Section 56 LPA 1925 allows a person not named in a deed to be a party to it if he was referred to in the deed and identifiable at that time. The Contracts (Rights of Third Parties) Act 1999 is wider and potentially more helpful.

9.8 Only the equitable remedies are available for breach of a restrictive covenant. The usual remedy will be an injunction, but the court has the power to award damages in lieu of an injunction or to decline to give any remedy where it feels this would be justified on the facts of the case.

9.9 Covenants (except those in building schemes) may be ended at common law if the benefiting and burdened land come into the same hands or if the benefit is abandoned. Section 84 LPA 1925 provides machinery for the discharge or modification of restrictive covenants which have outlived their useful life; each case is decided on its own facts.

9.10 In response to the problems caused by complexity of the rules relating to freehold covenants, the Law Commission has recommended the introduction of a new type of legal interest: the 'land obligation'.

Exercises

9.1 Complete the online quiz on the topics covered in this chapter on the companion website.

9.2 'The law relating to the enforcement of restrictive covenants consists of a complicated mixture of common law, equity and statutory provisions, which makes it difficult to know whether freehold covenants remain enforceable after a transfer of the burdened land or the benefited land to new owners.'

Discuss this statement.

9.3 In 1950, Karen sold part of her large garden in the Chequers Estate to Barry, who built 'The Palace' on it. In 1965, she sold another part of her garden to Phil, who promised her that he would not build more than one house on the land and that he would erect and maintain a fence around the land. The promise was stated to be made 'also with owners for the time being of adjoining land, formerly part of the Chequers Estate'.

In 1990, a council estate was built in the fields neighbouring the estate. Karen died, and her executors sold her remaining land to Yehudi. Rita has bought Phil's land and plans to build a block of flats with an open, unfenced garden.

Who can enforce the covenants, and whom do they bind? What remedies are available to the parties?

You can find suggested answers to exercises 9.2 and 9.3 on the companion website.

Further reading

Dawson, 'Restrictive Covenants and Human Rights' [1986] Conv 124

Gravells, 'Enforcement of Positive Covenants Affecting Freehold Land' (1994) 110 LQR 346

Howell, 'The Annexation of the Benefit of Covenants to Land' [2004] 68 Conv 507

Law Commission, *Making Land Law Work: Easements, Covenants and Profits à Prendre* (Law Com 327, 2011)

Martin, 'Remedies for Breach of Restrictive Covenants' [1996] Conv 329

Polden, 'Private Estate Planning and the Public Interest' (1986) 49 MLR 195

Part III

Sharing interests in land

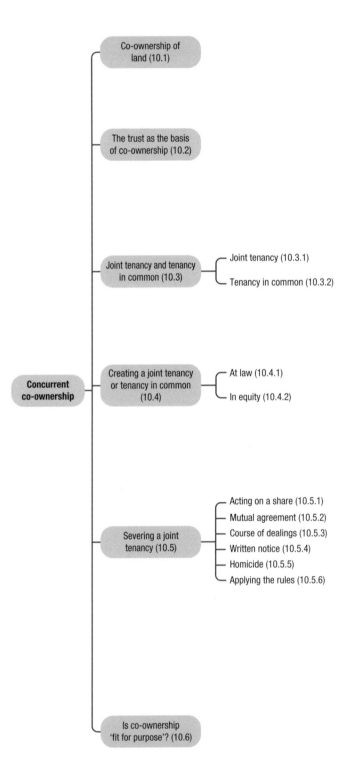

Chapter 10

Concurrent co-ownership

Key concepts

- **Joint tenancy** – a form of co-ownership in which all the co-owners own the whole title to the whole of the land.
- **Severance** – the conversion of a joint tenancy into a tenancy in common.
- **Tenancy in common** – a form of co-ownership in which the beneficial title is divided between the co-owners in separate shares.
- **Trust** – an equitable doctrine dividing the legal ownership from the beneficial ownership.

10.1 Co-ownership of land

There are many ways of dividing ownership of land. Indeed, many of the preceding chapters of this book have been concerned with how the different rights enjoyable over a single parcel of land can be shared among a number of people. Examples include the relationships between a tenant (entitled to possession) and a lessor (entitled to the rent) and between an owner of land and his neighbour who is allowed to use a path over it (an easement). In none of these cases do the various parties share all the rights that accompany the *ownership* of land (or, more strictly, ownership of a particular legal estate in the land). The rights are divided up between the freeholder and those with lesser interests in the land. There are many reasons, however, why people may wish to share ownership of a single legal estate, or, to put it less technically, to be co-owners of the land. The examples below are taken from cases considered either in this chapter or elsewhere in this book.

To provide a family home	*Williams & Glyn's Bank Ltd v Boland* [1981] AC 487 (HL)
	City of London Building Society v Flegg [1988] AC 54 (HL)
	Stack v Dowden [2007] 2 AC 432 (HL)
To provide a home while studying at university	*AG Securities v Vaughan* [1990] 1 AC 417 (HL)
To divide up an inheritance	*Barclay v Barclay* [1970] 2 QB 677 (CA)
To provide premises for a business partnership	*Rodway v Landy* [2001] Ch 703 (CA)
To act as an investment	*Laskar v Laskar* [2008] 1 WLR 2695 (CA)

Shared ownership, especially of the family home, is now so commonplace that it is easy to overlook the serious theoretical and practical issues that arise from it:

- *How to balance the policy that land should be capable of being bought and sold without undue delay or expense with the need to provide sufficient protection for all the co-owners of the land?*
This question is addressed briefly in Section 10.2 and in more detail in Section 11.6.

▶ *What happens if the relationship between the co-owners breaks down? What are the rules for resolving disputes?*

The most important rules are now contained in Part 1 of the Trusts of Land and Appointment of Trustees Act (TOLATA) 1996 (see Sections 11.4 and 11.5).

▶ *What should a co-owner of land actually 'own'? To put it another way, when a co-owner dies, what (if anything) will pass to his heirs?*

There are two main possibilities:

1. Each co-owner owns a proportionate value of the land, which he is free to dispose of as he wishes.
2. The land is not divided between the co-owners. They do not have separable shares, but they together have a single interest in the whole of the land. One consequence of such a doctrine of co-ownership is that no co-owner has a 'share' with which he can deal (or which he can leave to their heirs).

This question forms the subject matter of Sections 10.3–10.6.

There is no single right answer to these questions. The most appropriate answer will depend upon the reason the co-owners are sharing the land and on wider social and economic values. For example, land law has tended to be led by the needs of large landowners and investors. The result is that land law, to put it rather crudely, generally seeks to achieve 'justice through certainty'. However, modern developments in this area of law are largely the result of the growth in landownership by ordinary families. If a family breaks up, those involved will need to resolve the ownership of the family property. The effects of this can be far-reaching, since, as well as providing the family home, which is perhaps the real and symbolic focus of family life, the land may be the most valuable financial asset owned by any family member. Family law tends to be more interested in 'justice in the individual case'. Where the demands of certainty and individual justice diverge, there is bound to be some tension – and possibly confusion.

10.2 The trust as the basis of co-ownership

English law attempts to balance the apparently competing objectives of co-owners by imposing a trust whenever two or more people own land concurrently (see sections 34 and 36 of the LPA 1925). Since 1 January 1997, such trusts are trusts of land as defined by section 1(1) TOLATA 1996. The history of trusts of land and the detailed rules regulating them are considered in the next chapter.

In the simplest form of a trust, a trustee (or trustees) holds (hold) the legal title for the benefit of a beneficiary or beneficiaries (see Figure 10.1 and Section 2.5). However,

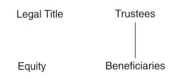

Figure 10.1 A simple trust

in many trusts of land, trustees are also beneficiaries at the same time. This is particularly common where a couple are the legal owners of the family home: they will hold it on trust for themselves as beneficial co-owners.

The detailed rules that regulate the relationships between the various parties concerned with a trust of land are contained in Part I of TOLATA 1996 and form the subject matter of Chapter 11.

10.3 Joint tenancy and tenancy in common

Before 1925, there were four methods of co-owning land, all of which could occur either at law or in equity. Only two methods now survive: *joint tenancy* and *tenancy in common*. A joint tenancy can be legal or equitable, but since 1925, a tenancy in common can only exist in equity (LPA 1925, ss 1(6), 34(1), 36(2)).

10.3.1 Joint tenancy

Blackstone describes the joint tenancy as a 'thorough and intimate union' (Blackstone's Commentaries, ii, 182). The basic principle is that, as far as outsiders are concerned, the owners are regarded as one person. They are united in every way possible, through 'the four unities'.

A joint tenancy requires *the four unities*

▶ Possession: all the joint tenants are entitled to possess the whole of the land.
▶ Interest: they each hold an identical interest (freehold, leasehold).
▶ Title: their interest was obtained by the same document.
▶ Time: their interest vested in them at the same time.

(easily remembered by the acronym PITT)

In *AG Securities v Vaughan* [1990] 1 AC 417 (HL) (see Section 5.5.3), a claim that there was a joint tenancy of a lease of a student flat failed because the claimants had arrived at different times. Indeed, on the facts of the case, Lord Oliver found that none of the four unities was present, not even that of possession.

The basis of joint tenancy is that the joint tenants together own the whole title to the land rather than each having a share in the land. As a consequence, and very importantly, joint tenants enjoy the 'right of survivorship' (*ius accrescendi*). The joint tenants are 'all one person', and if one dies it is as if he had never existed. The survivor(s) still own the whole of the land, and there is nothing for the heirs of the dead joint tenant to inherit. It follows, therefore, that the last survivor among joint tenants will own the whole land absolutely.

The risk involved in the right of survivorship may seem unfair, but in fact it is quite convenient that legal ownership of trust land should not be affected if one co-owner at law dies. In equity, on the other hand, although joint tenancy is possible, the risks can be inconvenient. Equity 'leans against' this form of co-ownership and in favour of the tenancy in common (see Section 10.4.2).

Since a tenancy in common cannot exist at law, the legal title to any co-owned land must be held by the co-owners as joint tenants (LPA 1925, ss 1(6), 34(1), 36(2)).

10.3.2 Tenancy in common

Tenancy in common is often referred to as 'undivided shares'. Although the land is held in separate shares, it has not been physically partitioned.

A tenancy in common:

▶ requires only the unity of possession (although all three of the other unities may also be present); and
▶ does not give rise to any right of survivorship.

When a tenant in common dies, he can leave his undivided share to anyone he pleases. This is the reason tenancy in common is no longer possible at law (LPA 1925, ss 1(6), 34(1), 36(2)). If legal tenancies in common were permitted, a purchaser would have to investigate the individual titles of each tenant in common, adding considerably to the time and expense of conveyancing. With a joint tenancy, there is only one title to investigate. As far as a buyer of land is concerned, the interests shared in equity are 'behind a curtain'. He can overreach all the beneficial interests (whether joint tenancy or tenancy in common) by paying the trustees (who will, of course, be legal joint tenants), providing there is more than one of them (see Section 11.6.1).

10.4 Creating a joint tenancy or tenancy in common

10.4.1 At law

A joint tenancy at law arises whenever a legal interest in land is shared concurrently, that is, whenever land is conveyed into the names of two or more people (LPA 1925, ss 34(2) and 36(1)). However, there can be no more than four legal joint tenants (Trustee Act 1925, s 34(2)). If title to land is conveyed to more than four people, the first four named on the deed who are willing and at least 18 years old and mentally competent will be the legal joint tenants (the trustees). The remainder will be beneficial owners only. There is no restriction on the number of joint tenants in equity.

Any attempt to create a legal tenancy in common will vest the legal title in the purchasers (or the first four of them named in the conveyance if there are more than four) as joint tenants, holding the land on trust for all of the purchasers as tenants in common (LPA 1925, s 34(2)).

10.4.2 In equity

In equity, there may be either a joint tenancy or a tenancy in common, or even a combination of the two.

The starting point in determining whether a person is a beneficial joint tenant or a beneficial tenant in common is the maxim that 'equity follows the law' (see *Stack v Dowden* [2007] 2 AC 432 (HL) at [33], [54] and [109]). Despite this principle, equity has historically inclined against the unpredictability of the right of survivorship. As a result, a beneficial tenancy in common will exist not only where one of the unities is missing, but also if there is a particular reason for inferring that there was no intention to create a joint tenancy.

No intention to create a beneficial joint tenancy can be shown by:

- creating a tenancy in common expressly in the deed; or
- using words which show an intention that the owners should have shares ('words of severance') in the conveyance. Such words include 'equally', 'in equal shares', 'amongst' and 'share and share alike' (see, for example, *Barclay v Barclay* [1970] 2 QB 677 (CA), where land was left 'equally' under an express trust in a will to the testator's five children.)

In addition, there are three circumstances in which equity *presumes* a tenancy in common (although this presumption may be rebutted).

Equity *presumes* a tenancy in common where the co-owners:

1. make unequal contributions to the purchase price, provided that the property was not purchased as a family home (see *Stack v Dowden* and *Jones v Kernott* [2012] 1 AC 776 (SC); but compare *Laskar v Laskar* [2008] 1 WLR 2695 (CA) where the house was purchased as an investment);
2. are business partners or are acquiring the land for businesses purposes; or
3. are lending money on a mortgage.

In each case, the presumption can be rebutted if there has been an express agreement to create a joint tenancy (see *Malayan Credit Ltd v Jack Chia-MPH Ltd* [1986] AC 549 (PC)).

10.5   Severing a joint tenancy

Severance is the conversion of an *equitable* joint tenancy into a tenancy in common and may arise out of the express wishes of one or more of the joint tenants, or by operation of law if certain circumstances occur.

When a joint tenant severs his beneficial interest:

- he becomes a tenant in common in equity with an equal share of the value of the property whenever it comes to be sold;
- the right of survivorship will cease to apply to him, which means that:
  - his beneficial interest will pass to his heirs on his death; and
  - his beneficial interest in the property will not increase automatically on the death of any of the other tenants.

In what follows, it must always be remembered that, because there cannot be a legal tenancy in common, a legal joint tenancy cannot be severed (LPA 1925, s 36(2)). This means that any severance of the beneficial interests will not automatically affect the legal title. When analysing problems concerning co-ownership, it can be helpful to show the various interests diagrammatically, using a single box to show a joint tenancy (see Figure 10.2) and a series of joined boxes for a tenancy in common (see Figure 10.3).

Anything which creates a distinction between equitable joint tenants amounts to a severance.

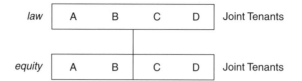

Figure 10.2 Legal joint tenants holding for themselves as beneficial joint tenants

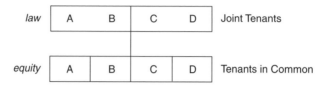
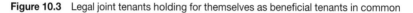

Figure 10.3 Legal joint tenants holding for themselves as beneficial tenants in common

---

Methods of severance

▶ The three methods of severing a joint tenancy of personal property listed by Page Wood vc in *Williams v Hensman* (1861) 1 John & H 546, 70 ER 862 (QB) (see LPA 1925, s 36(2)):
  1. by 'an act of one of the parties interested operating on her own share';
  2. by mutual agreement;
  3. by a 'course of dealing' ('mutual conduct') which shows a common intention to sever.
▶ By notice in writing of immediate severance (created by LPA 1925, s 36(2)).
▶ Where a joint tenant kills another joint tenant (if the right of survivorship operated in such circumstances, the killer would be 'profiting from his own wrong').

It should be remembered that whether severance has taken place always depends on the evidence; each case depends on its own facts. Frequently, the trigger for any dispute will be the death of one co-owner, and the question may arise as to whether there has been a severance of the equitable joint tenancy some time before the death.

10.5.1 Acting on a share

If a joint tenant assigns his share during his lifetime, the assignee will take it as a tenant in common with any remaining joint tenants. Granting a mortgage or charge over his interest will also sever it. However, leaving the interest to a third party by will does not sever the joint tenancy: the right of survivorship means that a joint tenant has no interest to leave by will, provided that at least one other joint tenant survives him (see *Gould v Kemp* (1834) 2 My & K 304, 39 ER 959 (Ch)). The rules are explained in more detail in Megarry and Wade, 2012, §§ 13–038 to 13–041.

Where a joint tenant is declared bankrupt, title to his property is automatically transferred to his trustee in bankruptcy. This amounts to an act on his share by operation of law and will, therefore, sever his equitable interest in the land.

10.5.2 Mutual agreement

Severance by mutual agreement requires the agreement of *all* of the joint tenants. However, the agreement does not have to be capable of specific performance (see Section 12.3). In the words of Sir John Pennycuick in the case of *Burgess v Rawnsley* [1975] Ch 429 (CA):

> The significance of an agreement is not that it binds the parties; but that it serves as an indication of a common intention to sever (at 446).

10.5.3 Course of dealings

Severance by course of dealings differs from that by mutual agreement in that severance will be inferred from the conduct of the parties: there is no need for a meeting of minds between the joint tenants. In *Burgess v Rawnsley*, the Court of Appeal considered the possibility of a course of dealings as well as mutual agreement (see Section 10.5.2). Mr Honick and Mrs Rawnsley met at a Scripture rally. After a few months of friendship, they bought the house in which Mr Honick lived, as joint tenants at law and in equity. Mr Honick thought they were going to get married. However, Mrs Rawnsley merely intended to live in the upper flat. After a year or so, they discovered each other's error and agreed orally that Mr Honick should buy Mrs Rawnsley's share. However, they did not finally agree a price, and nothing more was done before Mr Honick died three years later. Mrs Rawnsley claimed the whole house by right of survivorship. As to a course of dealing between Mr Honick and Mrs Rawnsley, Lord Denning MR said:

> It is sufficient if there is a course of dealing in which one party makes clear to the other that he desires that their shares should no longer be held jointly but be held in common … it is sufficient if both parties enter on a course of dealing which evinces an intention by both of them that their shares shall henceforth be held in common and not jointly (at 439).

The 'course of dealing' argument failed in *Greenfield v Greenfield* (1979) 38 P & CR 570 (Ch). Two brothers owned a house as joint tenants at law and in equity. When each married, they converted the house into two maisonettes, sharing the garden and some bills. When the elder brother died, his widow claimed that the division of the house showed an intention to sever the beneficial joint tenancy and that she had inherited her husband's tenancy in common. Fox J held:

> The onus of establishing severance must be on the plaintiff … It seems to me that on the facts, the plaintiff comes nowhere near discharging that onus. Neither side made clear any intention of ending the joint tenancy. The defendant had no intention of ending it and never thought that he or [his brother] Ernest had ended it (at 578).

10.5.4 Written notice

Neither a unilateral unstated intention to sever nor verbal notice by one party to another has ever been sufficient to sever a joint tenancy. However, the policy of the law as it stands today, having regard particularly to section 36(2), is to facilitate severance at the instance of either party (per Sir John Pennycuick, *Burgess v Rawnsley* [1975] Ch 429 at 448).

Section 36(2) of the LPA 1925 provides that notice in writing of the desire to sever by one joint tenant to another is sufficient to sever the joint tenancy. No agreement from the other joint tenant is required. Nor is it necessary to give the notice in any particular form, provided that it is worded in such a way as to make it clear that an immediate severance is being sought. However, expressing a wish to sever the joint tenancy in the future will not be sufficient (see *Re Draper's Conveyance* [1969] 1 Ch 486 (Ch) and *Harris v Goddard* [1983] 1 WLR 1203 (CA)).

Severance by written notice is a unilateral act. It is not necessary for the other joint tenants to read the notice, provided that the notice has been properly served upon them. In *Kinch v Bullard* [1999] 1 WLR 423 (Ch), a wife suffering from a terminal illness was intending to divorce her husband. They were both the beneficial joint tenants of the matrimonial home, and, since she no longer wanted the right of survivorship to operate, she instructed her solicitors to send him a notice severing the joint tenancy. The solicitors sent the letter by first-class post. However, the husband suffered a serious heart attack before it was delivered. The wife, realising she would lose half the house if her husband died with the joint tenancy having been severed, destroyed the letter as soon as it arrived. Her husband died a week or so later and never learned about the letter. After the wife died the following year, the husband's executors brought an action claiming that the joint tenancy had been severed by the written notice and that they were therefore entitled to the husband's half-share in the property. The case turned upon whether the notice of severance had been properly served. By section 196 of the LPA 1925, a notice is properly served 'if it is left at the last known place of abode or business in the United Kingdom of the … person to be served'. In this case, the court held that service occurred (and the notice became effective) when the letter fell through the letterbox onto the mat. The wife's destruction of the letter failed, therefore, to prevent her severance of the joint tenancy through which otherwise she would have gained the whole of the property by the right of survivorship.

10.5.5 Homicide

The principle that a person should not benefit from his own crime (the forfeiture rule) means that in most cases, a joint tenant will not be allowed to enjoy the benefits of survivorship if he criminally causes the death of another joint tenant. However, as Vinelott J noted in the case of *Re K* [1985] Ch 85 (Ch):

> There is curiously no reported case on the point in England but it has been held in other jurisdictions where the law was similar to English law before 1925 that where one of two joint tenants murders the other while the entire interest vests in the survivor the law imports a constructive trust of an undivided one-half share for the benefit of the next of kin of the deceased other than the offender … Under English law since 1925 the result is more simply reached by treating the beneficial interest as vesting in the deceased and the survivor as tenants in common (at 100).

If there are only two joint tenants to start, the result will be the same whether it is reached by severance or by imposing a constructive trust. The killer-survivor will hold the legal estate on trust for himself and the estate of his victim as equitable tenants in common in equal shares. However, where there are more than two joint tenants at the outset, the choice between automatic severance and the imposition of a constructive trust may be important as the latter allows the court more flexibility in allocating the beneficial entitlement. This issue is considered in some detail in Gray and Gray, 2009, paras 7.4.99–105.

Section 2 of the Forfeiture Act 1982 gives the court the power to modify the effect of this rule in cases other than murder 'where the justice of the case required it'. The

Court of Appeal exercised this power (albeit by a majority) in the tragic case of *Dunbar v Plant* [1998] Ch 412 (CA). Miss Plant and Mr Dunbar attempted to kill themselves following a suicide pact. Miss Plant failed, but Mr Dunbar succeeded. Although the forfeiture rule applies in cases of aiding and abetting a suicide such as this, it was held that, under the particular circumstances of the case, the couple's joint tenancy of their house had not been severed. Consequently, Miss Plant was entitled to the whole of the beneficial interest in the proceeds of sale. (The house had already been sold.)

10.5.6 Applying the rules

Problem questions on severance (such as Exercise 10.3) require a step-by-step analysis of what happens to the legal and equitable ownership. This is, perhaps, most easily done initially with the help of diagrams.

Let us imagine that a group of five people, whom we shall call, Annie, Belinda, Charlie, Dee and Ellen, buy a house as joint tenants in equity, each contributing equally to the purchase price. As they are all over 18 years old, the first four become the legal owners as joint tenants holding on trust for all five. Certain events now take place, each of which may affect the legal ownership or sever the equitable joint tenancy. A description of each event and an analysis of its effect are set out in Figures 10.4–10.7.

This kind of problem question often ends by stating that some of the surviving co-owners now want to sell, and others want to remain in the property, inevitably requiring a discussion of the case law under sections 14 and 15 of TOLATA (see Section 11.5).

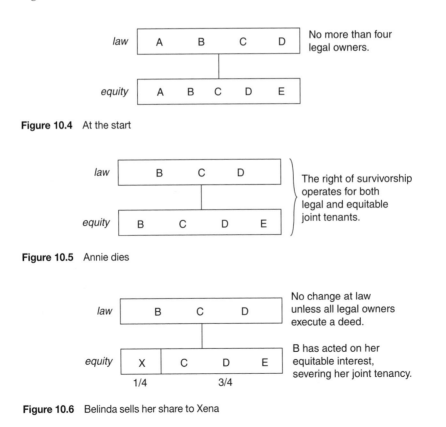

Figure 10.4 At the start

Figure 10.5 Annie dies

Figure 10.6 Belinda sells her share to Xena

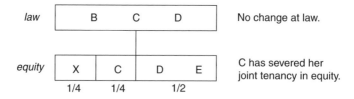

Figure 10.7   Charlie gives written notice of severance to Dee and Ellen

10.6   Is co-ownership 'fit for purpose'?

The rules about severance of an equitable joint tenancy, on which so much may depend, are sometimes uncertain and can result in expensive litigation and injustice. The written notice procedure introduced by section 36(2) of the LPA 1925 addresses many, but not all, of the potential problems, and the procedure is not itself completely free from uncertainty. From time to time, the case is made for simplifying the law. It has even been suggested that the equitable joint tenancy should be abolished in order to avoid 'much troublesome and expensive litigation' (see Thompson, 1987a, b; Prichard, 1987).

In fact, the doctrines of joint tenancy and tenancy in common on the whole work quite well in practice, provided that co-owners are clear as to their motives and properly advised about the two alternatives before they complete the purchase of the land. However, problems can arise if title documents are not drafted as well as they should be. For example, the dispute in *Stack v Dowden* [2007] 2 AC 432 (HL) would have been avoided if the Land Registry standard form of transfer form had been worded differently (see Baroness Hale at [50]).

Summary

10.1 Co-ownership of land is common in England and Wales. However, different people co-own land for different reasons. The legal rules have to try to accommodate and balance the resulting tensions.

10.2 The trust divides the legal title to land (held by the trustees) from the equitable (or 'beneficial') ownership of the land. In England and Wales, all co-owned land is held on trust regulated under the Trusts of Land and Appointment of Trustees Act 1996.

10.3 There are two types of co-ownership: joint tenancy and tenancy in common.

1. Joint tenants share the unities of possession, interest, title and time, and take the risk of the right of survivorship.
2. Tenants in common have 'undivided shares' in the land; the only unity that is essential is the unity of possession.

10.4 Legal title to land may only be shared under a joint tenancy. Equitable co-owners may be joint tenants or tenants in common, depending on whether there have been words of severance, or on the general circumstances of the creation of the trust.

10.5 Equitable joint tenants can sever their tenancy and become tenants in common.

10.6 Co-ownership works relatively well in practice, provided that all the parties are properly advised. However, the rules relating to the severance of a beneficial joint tenancy can sometimes cause confusion and even injustice.

Exercises

10.1 Complete the online quiz on the topics covered in this chapter on the companion website.

10.2 'It is easy to understand a desire to make severance as flexible as possible. On the other hand, this can lead to considerable uncertainty as to property rights' (Smith, *Property Law, Cases and Materials,* 4th edn, Longman 2009, 367).

Critically discuss this statement.

10.3 Uri, Neil and Val work independently as freelance engineers. Three years ago, they purchased the registered freehold of Techno House, intending to use it as a base for their respective businesses as well as their home together.

A couple of months ago, there was a serious disagreement between Neil and the others. Uri and Val refused to speak to Neil, but left him a note demanding that he leave the house immediately. The note concluded by inviting Neil to 'consider his position in relation to our partnership'. Neil went to stay with his brother, Buzz, and made a will leaving all of his property to Buzz.

Last month, Neil wrote to Uri and Val, saying that he was willing to divide his share in the house between Uri and Val if they each paid him £60,000 in return. On receipt of the letter, Uri told Val that he was willing to agree to Neil's proposal, but Val said that she would never do so. However, Val then wrote to Neil offering to pay £120,000 for Neil's share in Techno House. Neil phoned Val to say that he would come round immediately to 'finalise the deal'. When Uri found out, he was very angry. He stormed out of the house, straight into the path of Neil's car. Uri died in the resulting accident.

Were Uri, Neil and Val originally beneficial joint tenants or tenants in common? Assuming that they were originally beneficial joint tenants, what interests, if any, do Neil, Val and Buzz hold in Techno House following Uri's death?

You can find suggested answers to exercises 10.2 and 10.3 on the companion website.

Further reading

Conway, 'Joint Tenancies, Negotiations and Consensual Severance' [2009] 73 Conv 67

Cooke, 'Community of Property, Joint Ownership and the Family Home' in Dixon and Griffith (eds), *Contemporary Perspectives on Property, Equity and Trusts Law* (Oxford University Press 2007) 39

Prichard, 'Beneficial Joint Tenancies: A Riposte' [1987] Conv 273

Tee, 'Severance Revisited' [1995] Conv 104

Thompson (a), 'Beneficial Joint Tenancies: A Case for Abolition?' [1987] Conv 29

Thompson (b), 'Beneficial Joint Tenancies: A Reply to Professor Prichard' [1987] Conv 275

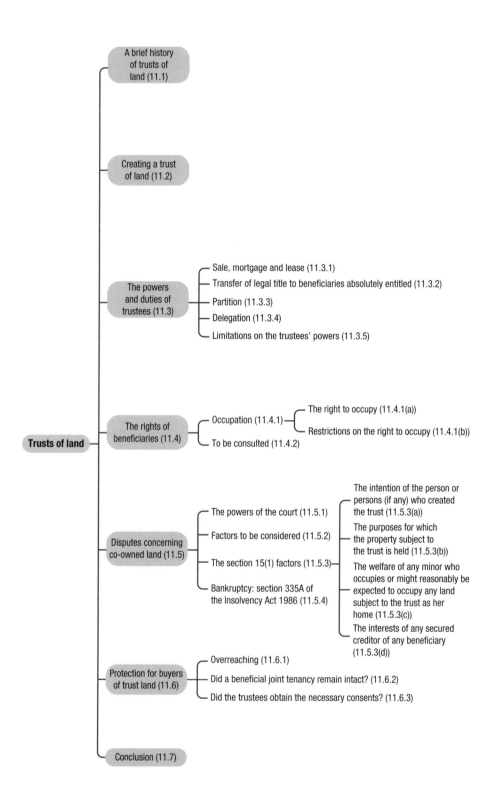

Chapter 11

Trusts of land

Key concepts

▶ **Overreaching** – transferring the beneficial interest from the land that was subject to the trust to the proceeds of sale (or mortgage) of the land.
▶ **Section 15 factors** – the factors listed in section 15 (especially, but not exclusively, those in section 15(1)) of the Trusts of Land and Appointment of Trustees Act 1996 to be taken into account when the court considers a dispute between co-owners.
▶ **Trust** – an equitable doctrine dividing the legal ownership from the beneficial ownership.

11.1 A brief history of trusts of land

The rules regulating co-ownership of land need to be flexible enough to take account of a number of competing, and sometimes changing, interests (see Section 10.1). Since 1925, the law of England and Wales has used the trust as its chosen mechanism to facilitate the different objectives of co-owners while also ensuring that co-owned land can be easily bought and sold. All trusts including land are now regulated under the Trusts of Land and Appointment of Trustees Act (TOLATA) 1996, and most of this chapter is devoted to the rules contained in Part I of that Act. However, some knowledge of the earlier law is necessary. Much of the old law of trusts remains in place beneath TOLATA 1996, and some of the pre-1996 rules will almost certainly be encountered when reading older cases that remain relevant today.

The 1925 legislation recognised two main motives behind the co-ownership of land (and provided two very different types of statutory trust to facilitate them):

1. preventing the fragmentation of the great aristocratic estates; and
2. investment, usually for the purpose of generating income.

The first of these objectives was accommodated by the strict settlement, regulated by the Settled Land Act (SLA) 1925. Settlements under the SLA 1925 are now obsolete and lie outside the scope of this book. For details of the cumbersome and technical rules of strict settlements, see Cheshire, 2011, 432–462 and Megarry and Wade, 2012, appendix. All other co-owned land was assumed to have been acquired for investment purposes and was deemed to be held subject to a statutory 'trust for sale' under the LPA 1925. Consequently, this kind of trust included not only land which was genuinely held for investment purposes, but also land held for commercial purposes (for example, by a partnership of solicitors) and family land (for example, where the co-owned land was the family home).

The trust for sale was never really appropriate for commercial or family property because:

▶ the land was deemed to have been bought mainly as an investment; and
▶ it gave rise to an 'immediate and binding duty' to sell the land (albeit, with a power to postpone sale in order to receive the rental income).

A further problem was the 'doctrine of conversion', which arose out of the principle that 'equity looks on that as done which ought to be done'. Even though the land had not yet been sold, it was treated it as though it had been (the doctrine of conversion). Consequently, the beneficiaries behind a trust for sale did not have an interest in land, but merely an interest in the 'proceeds of sale'. However, a number of cases showed that, although the beneficiaries were in theory only interested in the proceeds of sale, in practice the courts might still recognise their interest as an interest in the land itself. In the well-known case of *Bull v Bull* [1955] 1 QB 234 (CA) (see Section 2.3.2(b)), a son, the sole trustee of the trust for sale and a joint beneficiary under it, wanted to evict his mother (the other beneficiary), but the court held that her interest in the land included a right to occupy it. In *Williams & Glyn's Bank Ltd v Boland* [1981] AC 487 (HL) the House of Lords held that a beneficial interest in land held on a trust for sale could be a sufficient interest to be protected by occupation of the trust land under section 70(1)(g) of the LRA 1925 (now LRA 2002, Sched. 1, para 2 and Sched. 3, para 2).

As the twentieth century progressed, land was, with increasing frequency, bought for owner-occupation rather than income generation. In the minds of most homeowners, sale was merely a possibility at some time in the future, not the main purpose of acquiring the land. Despite this, under the terms of the statutory trust, the trustees had a duty of sale subject to a power only to postpone that sale. Consequently, if the trustees disagreed about what to do with the land, the presumption was in favour of sale even if a majority of the trustees did not want this. Section 30 of the LPA 1925 gave

Table 11.1 The main provisions of Part I of the Trusts of Land and Appointment of Trustees Act 1996

Section 1	Any 'trust of property which consists of or includes land' is a *trust of land* (apart from some very limited exceptions in s 1(3)).
Section 2	No new strict settlements may be created, nor may any be added to an existing strict settlement.
Section 3	The doctrine of conversion does not apply to trusts of land. Note, however, that an interest under a trust for land can still be overreached on sale of the land. (See Section 11.6.1.)
Section 4	If a new trust of land is expressly created as a trust for sale, the trustees will be allowed to postpone sale indefinitely. An express trust for sale will only be appropriate if the main purpose of creating the trust involves the sale of the land (as in *Barclay v Barclay* [1970] 2 QB 677 (CA)).
Section 5	Trusts for sale are no longer implied by statute. Sections 34–36 LPA 1925 are amended so that such trusts are now trusts of land.
Sections 6–9A	TOLATA gives the trustees various powers that they need to deal with the land. (See Section 11.3.)
Section 11	The trustees have a duty to consult with the beneficiaries before making decisions about the land, whether or not such a provision is expressly included in the terms of a trust. (See Section 11.4.2.)
Sections 12–13	Beneficiaries have a right to occupy the land, subject to certain exceptions and provisos (replacing the common law right recognised in *Bull v Bull* [1955] 1 QB 234 (CA)). Section 13 contains rules for dealing with any dispute where two or more beneficiaries are entitled to occupy the land. (See Section 11.4.1.)
Sections 14–15	The statutory scheme for dealing with disputes between people with an interest in trust land, which replaces LPA 1925, s 30. (See Section 11.5.)
Section 16	Protection for buyers of trust land that is not yet registered. (See Section 11.6.3.)

the courts a discretion about ordering sale, and a long line of case law resulted as the courts sought to balance the duty to sell (when one family member wanted to turn the land into money) against the need of the rest of the family to stay in their home.

In the end, and despite the valiant efforts of the courts, the machinery of the trust for sale and its accompanying doctrine of conversion were simply too far removed from the reality of family landowning. In 1989, the Law Commission observed:

> We consider that the present dual system of trusts for sale and strict settlements is unnecessarily complex, ill-suited to the conditions of modern property ownership, and liable to give rise to unforeseen conveyancing complications (Law Com No 181 (1989) at iv).

The result was the Trusts of Land and Appointment of Trustees Act 1996, the main provisions of which are summarised in Table 11.1. TOLATA replaced the old trust for sale with the new 'trust of land'. Since 1 January 1997, all trusts containing land are trusts of land.

11.2   Creating a trust of land

A trust of land may be created expressly, by statute or impliedly.

Express trusts
: An express trust must be evidenced in writing, signed by the person creating it, in order to be enforceable by the beneficiaries (LPA 1925, s 53(1)(b)). It must declare the nature of the beneficial ownership and the terms of the trust.

Statutory trusts
: In the absence of an express trust, whenever a legal estate in land is conveyed to two or more people, a statutory trust of land will be imposed under LPA 1925, sections 34–36.

Implied trusts
: It is also possible for a person to gain a beneficial share in land in circumstances in which there is no express or statutory trust. In certain circumstances, equity will find that the land is co-owned because of the conduct of the relevant parties. These trusts are known as resulting and constructive trusts and are dealt with (alongside proprietary estoppel) in Chapter 14.

11.3   The powers and duties of trustees

The trustees of a trust of land hold the legal title to the land. Their rights and duties are subject to the general law of trusts, the rules contained in TOLATA and the particular provisions (if any) of the trust in question (TOLATA, s 8). The powers of trustees of charitable, ecclesiastical and public trusts continue to be limited in special ways that lie outside the scope of this book.

If the trust is created expressly, the trustees are usually appointed in the trust deed. In the case of implied trusts, the trustees will be the persons who hold the legal title to the land. If there is no trustee (for example, if land is conveyed to a child who by section 1(6) of the LPA 1925 cannot own land), the court can appoint trustees. Part II of TOLATA (ss 19–21) gives beneficiaries a measure of control over their trustees, in that they can require the appointment of a new trustee or the retirement of a current trustee, unless the settlor has expressly specified that the beneficiaries should not have this power.

11.3.1   Sale, mortgage and lease

Section 6(1) of TOLATA provides that the trustees 'have all the powers of an absolute owner': thus, they may sell, mortgage, lease or otherwise deal with the land. It is possible for these powers to be restricted by the terms of the trust (s 8(1)), although it is not possible to exclude the trustees' statutory power to postpone sale (s 4). Section 6(3) of TOLATA expressly gives trustees the power (subject to the terms of the trust) to buy land with trust money as an investment or for occupation by a beneficiary or 'for any other reason'. In exercising these powers, the trustees must 'have regard to the rights of the beneficiaries' (s 6(5)). Section 13 gives the trustees the power to 'exclude or restrict' the entitlement of any of the beneficiaries to occupy the land. This power is considered alongside the statutory right to occupy in Section 11.4.1.

11.3.2 Transfer of legal title to beneficiaries absolutely entitled

Where the beneficiaries are of full age and capacity, the role of trustees may be limited or unnecessary. Consequently, section 6(2) restates the old rule that if such beneficiaries 'are absolutely entitled to the land', the trustees can convey the land to them.

11.3.3 Partition

Subject to the terms of the trust, the trustees may also have the power to divide up ('partition') the land for any purpose, but only if the beneficiaries are adult tenants in common, absolutely entitled, and they all consent (s 7).

11.3.4 Delegation

The trustees may (subject to the terms of the trust) delegate their powers to beneficiaries of full age who are entitled to an interest in possession in the land (s 9). This allows beneficiaries in occupation to carry on the routine management of the land themselves.

11.3.5 Limitations on the trustees' powers

It has already been noted that the trustees must exercise their powers with due regard for the rights of the beneficiaries (see s 6(5)). Trustees of land are also subject to the general duty of care to 'exercise such care and skill as is reasonable in the circumstances', imposed on all trustees by section 1(1) of the Trustee Act 2000.

Section 11 of TOLATA provides that trustees must normally consult the beneficiaries before exercising any of their functions, so far as it is practicable to do so (see Section 11.4.2). It is also possible to make dealings with the trust land subject to the consent of a particular person or persons (ss 8(2) and 10). For example, if a spouse dies and leaves her property to her children, it could be a term of the trust that the property can only be sold with the consent of the surviving spouse, who might well also have the right to live there, thus ensuring that the property remains unsold, at least for a time.

11.4 The rights of beneficiaries

11.4.1 Occupation

The beneficiaries of a trust of land are generally entitled to whatever the trust provides for them. Their rights under the old trust for sale depended on the original purposes of the trust, which posed a conceptual problem for land lawyers, since the purpose of a trust for sale was, in theory, for the land to be sold straight away. Equity, therefore, saw the interests of the beneficiaries as being in the proceeds of sale rather than in the land and was slow to recognise that the beneficiaries might have a right to live there (see Section 11.1). TOLATA, having abolished the doctrine of conversion, also provides a statutory right for beneficiaries to occupy the trust land.

11.4.1(a) The right to occupy

Section 12 of TOLATA states that a beneficiary is entitled to live in the house if:

(a) the purposes of the trust include making the land available for his occupation …
or
(b) the land is held by the trustees to be so available

provided that the land is not 'unavailable or unsuitable for occupation by him'.

In *Chan v Leung* [2003] 1 FLR 23 (CA), the Court of Appeal had to decide whether a large house in Surrey was suitable for occupation solely by Miss Leung, a university student. Jonathan Parker LJ stated that:

> 'suitability' for this purpose must involve a consideration not only of the general nature and physical characteristics of the particular property but also a consideration of the personal characteristics, circumstances and requirements of the particular beneficiary (at [101]).

Despite its size and the expense of its maintenance, the judge did not consider the house unsuitable for Miss Leung, especially as she would only wish to occupy it until the end of her studies. Even if this had not been the case, she had previously been living there with her partner, and the judge 'would have taken some persuading' that it was unsuitable for her now he had left.

11.4.1(b) Restrictions on the right to occupy

Section 13 of TOLATA gives the trustees certain responsibilities in cases where two or more beneficiaries are entitled to occupy the land, as is common in trusts of the family home where adults share beneficial interests.

Where there is more than one beneficiary, the trustees have the power to exclude one or more, but not all, of the beneficiaries from the land (s 13(1)). In exercising this power, the trustees:

- must not act 'unreasonably' (s 13(2));
- may impose 'reasonable conditions' on an occupying beneficiary (s 13(3));
- must take into account the intentions of the creator of the trust, the purposes of the trust and the circumstances and wishes of the beneficiaries (s 13(4)); and
- must not use their powers to prevent anyone already in occupation (whether or not they have a beneficial interest in the land) from continuing in occupation, or in an attempt to induce them to leave (s 13(7)).

Examples of 'reasonable conditions' might include paying expenses relating to the land or paying compensation to a beneficiary who has been reasonably excluded from occupation (ss 13(5), 13(6)).

When determining whether the beneficiary in occupation must pay an occupation rent, the court (and the trustees) are usually governed by the provisions of TOLATA rather than by wider equitable doctrines such as equitable accounting (see *Murphy v Gooch* [2007] EWCA Civ 603 and *Stack v Dowden* [2007] 2 AC 432 (HL) at [93]). However, not all cases fall within the scope of sections 12 and 13 of TOLATA. For example, in the case of *French v Barcham* [2009] 1 WLR 1124 (Ch), Mr and Mrs Barcham were the registered proprietors of their bungalow when Mr Barcham was declared bankrupt in 1994. The couple continued to live in the bungalow until Mr Barcham's trustee in bankruptcy sought an order for its sale in 2006 under section 14 of TOLATA (see Section 11.5.4). The question arose as to whether the trustee in bankruptcy was entitled to any payment from Mrs Barcham for her occupation of the premises for the previous 12 years. Mrs Barcham argued that the Court had no power to award the trustee in bankruptcy compensation because he was not a beneficiary entitled to possession, and, therefore, was not eligible for compensation under section 13 of TOLATA. Blackburne J held that TOLATA did not prevent the Court exercising its wider general equitable jurisdiction in such cases:

> Where the [TOLATA] scheme applies, it must be applied. But where it plainly does not I do not see why the party who is not in occupation of the land in question should be denied any compensation at all if recourse to the court's equitable jurisdiction would justly compensate him (at [20]).

Many cases concern land occupied as a family home. *Rodway v Landy* [2001] Ch 703 (CA) provides an example of the type of difficulties that may arise in a different context. In this case, two doctors in partnership had bought a property together from which to run their practices. They fell out, and one of them sought an order for the property to be sold to her under section 14 of TOLATA (see Section 11.5). The other asked the court to order that, since they were both trustees as well as beneficiaries, they use their powers under section 13 to divide the property in two, allowing one partner exclusive occupation of one part of the property, and the other partner exclusive occupation of the other part. The Court of Appeal was of the opinion that if the building lent itself to division in this way, the trustees were entitled under section 13 to exclude the beneficiaries' entitlement to occupy all of the building. The Court also held that, under section 13(3), the trustees could require the beneficiaries to contribute to the cost of adapting the building. Here, of course, the trustees and the beneficiaries were the same people, so the case also serves as an example of the separation of the roles and functions of trustees and beneficiaries.

11.4.2 To be consulted

Subject to the exceptions in section 11(2), section 11(1) of TOLATA provides that the trustees of land shall in the exercise of any function relating to land subject to the trust:

(a) so far as practicable, consult the beneficiaries of full age and beneficially entitled to an interest in possession in the land, and

(b) shall so far as consistent with the general interest of the trust, give effect to the wishes of those beneficiaries, or (in case of dispute) of the majority (according to the value of their combined interests).

There are, however, certain exceptions. The beneficiaries' right to be consulted may be excluded by the terms of the trust (s 11(2)(a)) and will not normally apply to an express trust created before 1997 (s 11(2)(b)). Neither do the trustees need to consult the beneficiaries if they want to transfer the title to all of the beneficiaries under section 6(2), considered in Section 11.3.2 (s 11(2)(c)).

At first sight, the section 11 right to be consulted seems to transfer considerable power to the beneficiaries. In fact this is not the case, as even the wishes of a majority of the beneficiaries may be ignored if they are inconsistent with the 'general interest of the trust' (s 11(1)(b)). The right of consultation will, in any event, be meaningless in the many cases where the people who are the beneficiaries are also the trustees (as is often the case with co-owned family land).

11.5 Disputes concerning co-owned land

11.5.1 The powers of the court

If the land is sold or mortgaged in breach of trust because the provisions for consultation and the gaining of consents have not been observed, aggrieved beneficiaries can, in theory, sue their trustees. However, in most cases it is more appropriate to resolve any disputes using the mechanism contained in section 14 of TOLATA. The main exception is when a civil partnership or marriage breaks down; in such cases, any co-owned land is normally dealt with by way of a property adjustment order under the Civil Partnership Act 2004 or the Matrimonial Causes Act 1973.

Section 14 gives anyone with an interest in the trust property the right to apply to the court for an order:

(a) relating to the exercise by the trustees of any of their functions … or
(b) declaring the nature or extent of a person's interest in property subject to the trust.

Consequently, section 14 gives the court the power to resolve a wide range of potential disputes upon the application of a wide range of parties, including:

▶ a trustee;
▶ a beneficiary;
▶ a secured creditor (mortgagee);
▶ purchasers of the land who find themselves subject to the interests of a beneficiary whose rights were not overreached; and
▶ the trustee in bankruptcy of a beneficiary.

Many applications under section 14 ultimately come down to the question of whether the land should be sold. However, the court may be required to determine other matters, including a dispute over the allocation of the right to occupy (see, for example, *Rodway v Landy* [2001] Ch 703 (CA), considered in Section 11.4.1(b)).

11.5.2 Factors to be considered

Section 15 lists several matters to which the court is to have regard when determining an application under section 14. The relevant factors vary according to the circumstances, the most significant difference being where the application is made by a trustee in bankruptcy of one of the co-owners. The factors relevant to the most common types of application are summarised in Table 11.2.

Table 11.2 Main factors to be taken into account on an application under section 14 of the Trusts of Land and Appointment of Trustees Act 1996

	Sale by trustee, beneficiary or secured creditor	Sale by a trustee in bankruptcy	Concerning the right to occupy
Main TOLATA factors	The Section 15(1) factors; below	Section 335A of the Insolvency Act 1986 (TOLATA, s 15(4))	The Section 15(1) factors or the factors referred to in section 13(8) if section 13(7) is engaged
Other TOLATA factors	The circumstances and wishes of the majority (according to value) of the beneficiaries of full age (s 15(3))		The circumstances and wishes of beneficiaries with a right to occupy under s 12 (s 15(2))

Although section 15(3) of TOLATA requires the court to have regard to the wishes of any beneficiaries, it is open to the court to override the need for the consent of any particular person (per Chadwick LJ, *Avis v Turner* [2008] Ch 218 (CA) at [35], a trustee in bankruptcy case).

Section 6 of the Human Rights Act 1998 requires the court to take account of any rights under Article 1 of the First Protocol and Article 8 of the European Convention on Human Rights when exercising its powers pursuant to section 14. However:

> it will ordinarily be sufficient for this purpose for the court to give due consideration to the factors specified in section 15 of TOLATA ... I would not rule out the possibility that there may be circumstances in which it is necessary for the court explicitly to consider whether an order for sale is a proportionate interference with the Article 8 rights of those affected, but I do not consider that this will always be necessary (per Arnold J, *National Westminster Bank v Rushmer* [2010] 2 FLR 362 (Ch) at [50]).

11.5.3 The section 15(1) factors

Section 15(1) lists four factors to which the court is to have regard in all cases except for applications by a trustee in bankruptcy. This list is not exhaustive, nor does the section give any indication of how the factors are to be weighted should they conflict in a particular case: that is a matter for the court to determine, and examples are referred to below.

Prior to TOLATA, the court's discretion to make an order concerning co-owned land was exercised under section 30 of the LPA 1925. The discretion under section 30 of the LPA 1925 was more limited than under section 15 of TOLATA because there was a presumption in favour of a sale. (See the explanation of trusts for sale in Section 11.1.) This presumption meant that the court had to begin by determining the underlying purpose of the trust for sale; only if this purpose were still achievable could the court block the trustees' duty of sale. The principles developed under section 30 of the LPA 1925 were highly nuanced by the time TOLATA came into force at the beginning of 1997. Section 15(1) of TOLATA seems to have been intended to place them on a statutory footing, free from the presumption in favour of sale. Consequently, many of the cases decided under section 30 of the LPA 1925 continue to inform the court's deliberations.

Each of the section 15(1) factors is now considered in turn.

11.5.3(a) The intention of the person or persons (if any) who created the trust

This factor is most likely to be referred to where the trust was created expressly and the intention of the settlor is discernible from the document creating the trust. For example, in *Barclay v Barclay* [1970] 2 QB 677 (CA), the trust was created by a will in which the testator directed his bungalow be sold by his executor and the proceeds divided between certain persons. In that case, decided under the old law applicable to trusts for sale, the declared intention that the bungalow be sold was enough to preclude any possibility of the claimant beneficiary having a right to occupy it. However, if a similar case were to be decided under section 15(1), the express intention of the executor would have to be balanced with the other three factors considered below.

11.5.3(b) The purposes for which the property subject to the trust is held

In *Re Buchanan-Wollaston's Conveyance* [1939] Ch 738 (CA) the four owners of a plot of land entered into a mutual deed of covenant under which they agreed that any transaction involving the land required them to act unanimously. Despite the presumption in favour of sale under the old law, the Court of Appeal refused to allow the claimant to rely on equity to escape from a contract that he had entered into freely. Conversely, in *Jones v Challenger* [1961] 1 QB 176 (CA) a house had been bought by a husband and wife as a matrimonial home, but the marriage had broken down, and the wife had left. There were no children, and the Court of Appeal held that the house should be sold because:

> with the end of the marriage, [the] purpose [of the trust] was dissolved and the primacy of the duty to sell was restored (per Devlin LJ, at 183).

In *Bank of Ireland Home Mortgages Ltd v Bell* [2001] 2 FLR 809 (CA) the Court of Appeal agreed with the district judge, who had concluded that the purpose of using the house as a family home ceased, if not as soon as the husband left (never to return), then certainly by the time the bank began possession proceedings a year and a half later.

There seems to be a considerable overlap between the first two factors listed in section 15(1), and the courts often consider the two factors together (as, for example, in *Holman v Howes* [2005] EWHC 2824 (Ch) at [64]; this part of the judgment was not challenged when the case reached the Court of Appeal). The second factor (s 15(1)(b)) is probably a little wider, especially where the purpose of the trust may have evolved over time. In *First National Bank plc v Achampong* [2003] EWCA Civ 487 at [65], Blackburne J tentatively distinguished the original intention that the house provide a *matrimonial* home for the couple from its later purpose as a *family* home for them *and their children*.

11.5.3(c) The welfare of any minor who occupies or might reasonably be expected to occupy any land subject to the trust as her home

In the cases decided under section 30 of the LPA 1925, the courts distinguished between homes purchased merely to provide accommodation for the owners (as in *Jones v Challenger*) and those intended to provide a home for the co-owners and their children. In *Re Evers' Trust* [1980] 1 WLR 1327 (CA), an unmarried couple with three children had bought a house. The man left and applied for an order for sale in order to take out the money he had contributed towards the purchase price. Ormrod LJ found that the underlying purpose of the trust was to provide a family home and, since that purpose still subsisted, albeit without the man, declined at that time to make the order.

Section 15(1)(c) now requires the interests of any children who occupy (or who might be expected to occupy) the trust land as their home to be considered separately from the purpose of the trust. Although there has been relatively little judicial consideration of section 15(1)(c), it does seem clear that the mere presence of children (or grandchildren) living on the land will not be sufficient to make the factor relevant. The court will need to be provided with specific evidence as to how the children's welfare will be affected should an order for sale be granted. As Blackburne J explained in the Court of Appeal case of *First National Bank v Achampong*:

> While it is relevant to consider the interests of the infant grandchildren in occupation of the property, it is difficult to attach much if any weight to their position in the absence of any evidence as to how their welfare may be adversely affected if an order for sale is now made. It is for the person who resists an order for sale in reliance on section 15(1)(c) to adduce the relevant evidence (at [65]).

11.5.3(d) The interests of any secured creditor of any beneficiary

Under the section 30 of the LPA 1925, when the party seeking an order for sale was a creditor, the courts applied the principles based on bankruptcy cases (see Section 11.5.4). The result was that, unless there were exceptional circumstances, the interests of a secured creditor would take precedence over the wishes of the beneficiaries (*Lloyds Bank plc v Byrne* [1993] 1 FLR 369 (CA)).

Under section 15(1), the interests of any secured creditor are only one consideration among several in section 15 to be taken into account by the court. In *Mortgage Corp Ltd v Shaire* [2001] Ch 743 (Ch), a case in which a secured creditor brought an action under section 14 for possession of the trust property following mortgage arrears, Neuberger J held that there was nothing to indicate that the interests of a secured creditor should take precedence over the other factors listed in section 15(1). The court was clear that section 15 was intended to enable the courts to exercise a wider discretion than formerly in favour of families as against secured creditors. With regard to previous authorities, he stated:

> there are obvious dangers in relying on authorities which proceeded on the basis that the court's discretion was more fettered than it now is. I think it would be wrong to throw over all the earlier cases without paying them any regard. However, they are to be treated with caution, in the light of the change in the law, and in many cases they are unlikely to be of great, let alone decisive, assistance (at 761).

Despite *Mortgage Corp Ltd v Shaire*, the Court of Appeal subsequently returned to the previous orthodoxy of *Lloyds Bank plc v Byrne*. In *Bank of Ireland v Bell* [2001] 2 FLR 809 (CA), Peter Gibson LJ explained that although section 15 had increased the scope of the discretion available to the court:

> a powerful consideration is and ought to be whether the creditor is receiving proper recompense for being kept out of his money, repayment of which is overdue (at [31]).

In this case, there was no equity in Mrs Bell's property, the debt was continuing to increase, and her son was almost 18 (minimising the relevance of s 15(1)(c)). The court found little difficulty in ordering sale. In *First National Bank v Achampong* the Court of Appeal adopted the reasoning in *Bell*, despite the presence of infant grandchildren:

> Prominent among the considerations which lead to that conclusion is that, unless an order for sale is made, the bank will be kept waiting indefinitely for any payment out of what is, for all practical purposes, its own share of the property (per Blackburne J at [65]).

Despite the unfortunate consequences for the occupiers, there is a certain logic behind the decisions in *Bank of Ireland v Bell* and *First National Bank v Achampong*, since it is open to a creditor to initiate bankruptcy proceedings, then have the case heard under section 335A of the Insolvency Act 1986 and thus avoid the section 15(1) factors entirely (see Section 11.5.4).

11.5.4 Bankruptcy: section 335A of the Insolvency Act 1986

Section 15(4) of TOLATA provides that where the section 14 application is made by the trustee in bankruptcy of one of the parties the case is considered not under section 15(1–3), but under section 335A of the Insolvency Act 1986.

The court must make such an order 'as it thinks just and reasonable', having regard to:

▷ the interests of the bankrupt's creditors; and
▷ all the circumstances of the case except for the needs of the bankrupt.

Where the trustee in bankruptcy's application relates to a dwelling house that has been the home of the bankrupt or the bankrupt's spouse or civil partner (or former spouse or former civil partner), the court will also have to take into account:

▷ the extent to which the spouse or partner contributed towards the bankruptcy;
▷ the needs and resources of the spouse or partner; and
▷ the needs of any children.

However, by section 335A(3), once a year has passed since the bankruptcy was declared, the court:

> shall assume, unless the circumstances of the case are exceptional, that the interests of the bankrupt's creditors outweigh all other considerations.

From time to time, the High Court is asked to consider whether the exercise of the rights contained in s 335A is compatible with the right to respect of the home and family life under Article 8 of the European Convention on Human Rights. The Court has repeatedly found the section compliant, most recently in *Ford v Alexander* [2012] EWHC 266 (Ch), where Peter Smith J opined:

> the requirements in sub section (2) [of s 335a] and the change of emphasis in sub paragraph (3) do not infringe Article 8(2). They provide a necessary balance as between the rights of creditors and the respect for privacy and the home of the debtor. That balance serves the legitimate aim of protecting the rights and freedoms of others. I am therefore of the opinion that the requirements of section 335A satisfy the test of being necessary in a democratic society and are thus proportionate (at [49]).

The reference to exceptional circumstances in section 335A(3) gave statutory effect to a principle originally developed by the courts. In *Re Citro (Domenico) (a bankrupt)* [1991] Ch 142 (CA), a case heard under the section 30 (LPA 1925) jurisprudence, the Court of Appeal considered the nature of exceptional circumstances. The disruption of losing a home and changing schools is 'not uncommon', and therefore not exceptional. Nourse LJ described this as 'the melancholy consequences of debt and improvidence with which every civilised society has been familiar' (at 157).

Before *Citro*, only in *Re Holliday* [1981] Ch 405 (CA) had the court postponed sale in a bankruptcy case. In *Holliday*, the spouse had made himself bankrupt, the creditors were not pressing for repayment, there were young children, and the wife would have been unable to find accommodation elsewhere in the area with her share of the proceeds of sale. As if that were not enough, the bankrupt had left his wife for another woman. Asking the question 'In all the circumstances of the case, whose voice in equity ought to prevail?', a different Court of Appeal from that in *Citro* felt able to postpone sale for five years.

Under the Insolvency Act 1986, if the court finds that there are exceptional circumstances it may postpone sale or refuse it entirely. It appears that the courts are prepared to offer a measure of protection to the family home in cases where the health of a member of the family who is suffering from a serious or terminal illness would be further prejudiced by a forced removal from her home. For example, in *Re Raval* [1998] 2 FLR 718 (Ch), an order for sale against a paranoid schizophrenic was postponed for a year to allow suitable accommodation to be found for her. In *Claughton v Charalambous* [1999] 1 FLR 740 (Ch), the bankrupt's spouse had severe medical problems, and the house they shared had been specially adapted for her. Jonathan Parker J found that these circumstances were exceptional and confirmed the decision of the county court to suspend the order for sale indefinitely. He seems to have been influenced by the fact that the creditors were unlikely to receive anything from the sale of the property, as its value was less than the costs that would be deducted by the trustee in bankruptcy. However, the likelihood that a bankrupt's creditors will be repaid in full if the sale of the family home is delayed does not to amount to exceptional circumstances (see *Donohoe v Ingram* [2006] EWHC 282 (Ch)).

In *Barca v Mears* [2004] EWHC 2170 (Ch), the defendant raised the question of whether the narrow approach to 'exceptional circumstances' in *Citro* was consistent with the rights protected under Article 8 of the European Convention on Human Rights. Although Mr Nicholas Strauss QC (sitting as a Deputy Judge of the High Court) had no difficulty in deciding that there were no exceptional circumstances in that case, he expressed some concern about the test as formulated by Nourse LJ, because:

> This approach leads to the conclusion that, however disastrous the consequences may be to family life, if they are of the *usual kind* then they cannot be relied on under section 335A; they will qualify as 'exceptional' only if they are of an unusual kind, for example where a terminal illness is involved (at [40]).

11.6 Protection for buyers of trust land

One of the main aims of land law reform in the twentieth century (and, indeed, the twenty-first) has been to ensure that land is freely and conveniently marketable. Beneficial interests are potential traps for buyers and mortgagees because such interests are not necessarily readily apparent from either the title documentation or an inspection of the property itself. The danger of these traps is minimised by a number of important statutory rules. However, although these rules offer increased protection to the buyer or mortgagee, they can only do so by reducing the security of the beneficiaries.

11.6.1 Overreaching

A buyer (including a mortgagee) of land subject to a trust 'shall not be concerned with the trusts' provided that she has satisfied the conditions in sections 2 and 27 of the

LPA 1925. If the conditions are satisfied, the rights of the beneficiaries are automatically 'overreached'. They are detached from the land and attached to the purchase price (or mortgage advance), which is now in the hands of the trustees. If the conditions are not met, any beneficial interests will not be overreached and will be binding on the purchaser.

To satisfy the section 2 and 27 conditions, the purchaser must:

▶ acquire (or take a mortgage over) a legal estate; and
▶ pay the purchase price (or mortgage advance) to at least two trustees or a trust corporation.

It also seems that the trustees must be acting in good faith. In *HSBC Bank plc v Dyche* [2010] 2 P & CR 4 (Ch), Judge Purle QC, sitting as a High Court judge, held that the transfer of a house to Mrs Dyche had been a dishonest breach of trust that had not been authorised by the beneficiary. Consequently, the beneficiary's interest was not overreached by virtue of section 2 of the LPA 1925, even though the purchase price had been paid to two trustees.

Overreaching beneficiaries' interests simply by paying two trustees is very convenient for buyers. In theory, the beneficiaries are happy too because they are entitled to their share of the proceeds in the safe hands of their trustees. Two trustees are less likely to run off with the cash than a single trustee, but this is not unknown. For example, in the case of *City of London Building Society v Flegg* [1988] AC 54 (HL) Mr and Mrs Maxwell-Brown held the land on trust for themselves and Mr and Mrs Flegg. Without the knowledge of Mr and Mrs Flegg, the Maxwell-Browns (the trustees) granted a mortgage of the land to the City of London Building Society. When the Maxwell-Browns failed to keep up the mortgage payments, the question arose as to whether the beneficial interests claimed by Mr and Mrs Flegg were binding on the building society. The House of Lords held that the Fleggs' beneficial interests had been overreached when the mortgage advance was paid to two trustees (Mr and Mrs Maxwell-Brown). Consequently, Mr and Mrs Flegg had no beneficial interest in the land: all that they could do was to try to recover their share of the mortgage advance from the Maxwell-Browns. However, the result would have been very different if the mortgage advance had been paid only to a single trustee, as in the earlier case of *Williams & Glyn's Bank Ltd v Boland* [1981] AC 487 (HL). In *Boland,* the beneficial interest (belonging to Mrs Boland) was not overreached and was binding on the land in the hands of the bank. (See also the unregistered land case of *Kingsnorth Finance Co Ltd v Tizard* [1986] 1 WLR 783 (Ch), discussed in Section 16.5.)

The decision in the case of *State Bank of India v Sood* [1997] Ch 276 (CA), while making sound commercial sense, further prejudices the position of beneficiaries. In breach of trust, two trustees mortgaged a house which they held on trust for themselves and five other beneficiaries. The mortgage secured past indebtedness and future borrowing, and no capital money was paid to the trustees. In a somewhat strained interpretation of section 2 of the LPA 1925, the Court of Appeal held that this was a transaction which enabled the bank to overreach the equitable rights of the beneficiaries despite the fact that no money was paid to the two trustees. The overreaching took effect on the execution of the charge, and at that time the interests of the beneficiaries became attached to the equity of redemption. This decision is consistent with the policy of encouraging free alienability of land and conforms to lending practice, but it removes the protection for beneficiaries, whose interest is transferred to the capital money paid to the trustees. Peter Gibson LJ stated:

> Much though I value the principle of overreaching as having aided the simplification of conveyancing, I cannot pretend that I regard the resulting position in the present case as entirely satisfactory. The safeguard for beneficiaries under the existing legislation is largely limited to having two trustees or a trust corporation where capital money falls to be received. But that is no safeguard at all, as this case has shown, when no capital money is received on and contemporaneously with the conveyance (at 290).

In fact, overreaching is only convenient for beneficiaries if they agree that the money is as good as the land. The Law Commission has recommended (Law Com No 188) that the consent of beneficiaries in occupation should be obtained before overreaching can take place (as is common practice where there is only one trustee), but this recommendation has not been taken up.

11.6.2 Did a beneficial joint tenancy remain intact?

If a buyer is acquiring land formerly owned by joint tenants that is vested in a single surviving tenant, there is always a risk that the beneficial joint tenancy was severed prior to the death of one of the joint tenants (see Section 10.5). If severance occurred, there may be a number of beneficial interests in the land, and these will not be overreached unless a second trustee is appointed.

Section 1 of the Law of Property (Joint Tenants) Act 1964 addresses this problem if title to the land were still unregistered at the date of the transfer. In such cases, the buyer of unregistered land is entitled to presume that the joint tenancy remained unsevered provided that:

- the conveyance states that the seller is solely and beneficially entitled to the land;
- no note or memorandum signed by the joint tenants or one of them has been made on the title deeds recording that the joint tenancy was severed; and
- none of the joint tenants has been adjudged bankrupt. (This can easily be discovered by a bankruptcy search in the Land Charges Register).

There is no similar rule for registered title.

11.6.3 Did the trustees obtain the necessary consents?

Where the terms of the trust make any sale subject to the consent of more than two people, section 10 of TOLATA provides that the purchaser only has to be sure that two have actually consented.

If title to the land was still unregistered at the date of the transfer, the buyer has even greater protection under section 16 of TOLATA:

- she does not need to concern herself with whether the trustees are acting in the interests of the beneficiaries or whether the beneficiaries have been consulted (s 16(1)); and
- she will still get good title to the land, even if the disposition is in breach of trust, so long as she does not have actual notice of that breach (s 16(2)).

As with the 1964 Act, the protection in section 16 is not extended to purchasers of registered land. This prompted some academic discussion as to whether overreaching occurs when a disposition of registered land is made in breach of trust (see Ferris and Battersby [1998] Conv 168). The High Court has now answered this question in the affirmative (see *HSBC Bank plc v Dyche* [2010] 2 P & CR 4 (Ch)).

11.7 Conclusion

The Trusts of Land and Appointment of Trustees Act 1996 provides a coherent conceptual foundation for trusts of land. Although not without its own difficulties, it has extended and clarified the roles of trustees and beneficiaries in relation especially to partition, consultation, rights of occupation and delegation, and it gives beneficiaries limited powers in respect of the appointment of trustees.

Some problems remain, not least for family members when a co-owner faces section 14 proceedings from a secured creditor or a trustee in bankruptcy. Although section 15 of TOLATA and the Insolvency Act 1986 were designed to provide a compromise between the needs of the family and the wishes of the creditors to get at their money, recent cases indicate that in most cases the court will order the home to be sold. Perhaps this is inevitable given TOLATA's heritage. The rules of equity have historically focused on the financial entitlement of individual parties, rather than the purpose of any co-ownership venture or the relationship between the parties (see Cooke, 2007). This is also reflected in equity's preference for tenancy in common over joint tenancy and its willingness to recognise severance (see Sections 10.4 and 10.5), although there is some evidence that this may be changing, at least insofar as family property is concerned (see *Stack v Dowden* [2007] 2 AC 432 (HL)). This can be contrasted with the 'community of property' enjoyed in several European states and the 'homestead legislation' of New Zealand and parts of North America, which are based on very different priorities from those implicit, if not actually embedded, in TOLATA (see Omar, 2006).

Summary

11.1 Trusts containing land are now 'trusts of land' and are regulated by the Trusts of Land and Appointment of Trustees Act (TOLATA) 1996. However, it is important to know something of the rules prior to TOLATA as aspects of pre-TOLATA cases may still be relevant.

11.2 Trusts of land may be created expressly, by statute or by implication.

11.3 The trustees are the persons who hold the legal title to the land. Their duties are contained in TOLATA and the Trustee Act 2000. Subject to the terms of the trust, trustees of land have the powers of an absolute owner of land together with power to transfer the land to adult beneficiaries absolutely entitled, to partition the land and to delegate their powers to beneficiaries.

11.4 Beneficiaries usually have the right to occupy the land, subject to rules to accommodate competing claims. They also have the right to be consulted by the trustees.

11.5 Under a trust of land, any trustee or beneficiary can go to court for an order of sale or otherwise. The court may make such order as it thinks fit, but where a party is bankrupt, the land will probably be sold after a year, unless the circumstances are 'exceptional'.

11.6 When buying land subject to a trust, it is important to pay the price to two or more trustees or a trust corporation to ensure that any beneficial interests are overreached (that is, transferred from the land to the proceeds of sale).

Exercises

11.1 Complete the online quiz on the topics covered in this chapter on the companion website.

11.2 Read *A Matter of Trust* on the companion website. Based on what you have learned from this and the preceding chapter, what further steps would you recommend that Alexia and her co-purchasers take?

11.3 Critically consider whether section 15 of the Trusts of Land and Appointment of Trustees Act 1996 has enabled the courts adequately to balance the interests of the various parties who may be interested in a dispute concerning co-owned land.

11.4 Five friends, Denise, Michael, Florence, Jacob and Ben, who had just graduated and found jobs, bought a house, intending to share it while they established themselves in their new careers. They each contributed £10,000 to the deposit and were equally liable for the mortgage repayments.

Denise decided to leave her job and sail round the world, so she sold her share of the house to her friend Amanda, who has now taken over her mortgage liability.

Florence and Michael became lovers and had a baby. Since the house is large, they want to divide it into two maisonettes, keeping the smaller one for themselves. The others want to keep it as it is.

Ben's business investments have failed, and he thinks he might be made bankrupt.

Discuss the rights of all the parties, and explain what might now happen to the land.

You can find suggested answers to exercises 11.3 and 11.4 on the companion website.

Further reading

Baker, 'The Judicial Approach to "Exceptional Circumstances" In Bankruptcy: The Impact of the Human Rights Act 1998' [2010] 74 Conv 352

Bright, 'Occupation Rents and the Trusts of Land and Appointment of Trustees Act 1996: From Property to Welfare?' [2009] 73 Conv 378

Brown, 'Insolvency and the Matrimonial Home: The Sins of Our Fathers: *In re Citro (a Bankrupt)*' (1992) 55 MLR 284

Cooke, 'Community of Property, Joint Ownership and the Family Home' in Dixon and Griffith (eds), *Contemporary Perspectives on Property, Equity and Trusts Law* (Oxford University Press 2007) 39

Dixon, 'Trusts of Land, Bankruptcy and Human Rights' [2005] 69 Conv 161

Ferris and Battersby, 'The Impact of the Trusts of Land and Appointment of Trustees Act 1996 on Purchasers of Registered Land' [1998] Conv 168

Omar, 'Security over Co-owned Property and the Creditor's Paramount Status in Recovery Proceedings' [2006] 70 Conv 157

Pascoe, 'Section 15 of the Trusts of Land and Appointment of Trustees Act 1996: A Change in the Law?' [2000] Conv 315

Pascoe, 'Right to Occupy under a Trust of Land: Muddled Legislative Logic?' [2006] 70 Conv 54

Part IV

Acquiring interests in land

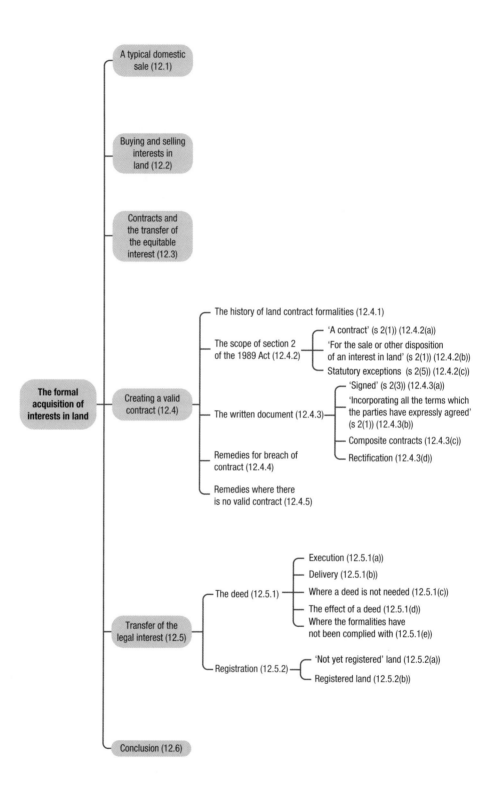

Chapter 12

The formal acquisition of interests in land

Key concepts

- **Completion** – the creation or transfer of a legal estate or interest pursuant to a contract to do so.
- **Disposition** – the creation or transfer of an interest.
- **Estate contract** – a contract for the creation or sale of an interest in land.
- **Exchange** – the exchange of copies of the contract (one usually signed by the seller, the other by the buyer) in order to create a binding contract.

12.1 A typical domestic sale

The most common transaction concerning land is almost certainly the sale and purchase of a freehold title containing a house and garden, combined, in most cases, with the simultaneous grant of a mortgage in favour of a lender who has provided a considerable proportion of the purchase moneys. The process begins when the sellers advertise the house for sale, usually through a firm of estate agents. Traditionally, prospective buyers would have begun their search for a suitable property by looking at the cards in the windows of estate agents; today, they are more likely to use the Internet. Whichever method is used, in due course the buyers will see one or more houses they like and arrange to visit them. Eventually they will make an offer to purchase the house they want, at a price acceptable to the sellers.

Once the buyers' offer has been accepted, the sale is said to be agreed 'subject to contract'. At this stage, neither party is legally bound to honour the agreement; both are free to withdraw without giving any reason for doing so. At this point the transaction usually passes into the hands of lawyers, who will undertake the necessary enquiries and ensure that the required formalities are complied with. The buyers will want to know exactly what is included in the sale and to be sure that both the structure of the house and its title are in order. They will also need to arrange any mortgage finance that is needed, and the lender will also want to satisfy itself that the property is worth the value placed on it. It is the buyers' responsibility to carry out all the checks, searches and enquiries that they and their solicitor or licensed conveyancer feel are necessary. While the enquiries are being made, the lawyers will agree the terms of the formal contract for the sale and purchase of the house. In many cases, the contract will be based on a standard form (either pre-printed or, more usually now, selected from a set of precedents stored on computer or forming part of a conveyancing software package). In some cases, most of the terms of the contract will be the result of substantive negotiation, but most residential transactions incorporate a set of standard conditions published by the Law Society of England and Wales (presently the Standard Conditions of Sale (5th edn)).

This period of pre-contractual enquiries and negotiation is a time of great uncertainty for the buyers and sellers alike. Neither side can be sure of completing the sale. The buyers might fail to get the loan they need to finance the purchase, or they might decide that the house is too expensive. The sellers might receive a higher offer from another prospective buyer or might decide to withdraw the house from the market. Each side would like the other to be bound as soon as possible, but is wary of committing itself too soon. The proposed transaction will only become legally binding on the parties when they exchange signed copies of the contract (see Section 12.4). The buyer will usually be required to pay a deposit when contracts are exchanged.

Reaching the exchange of contracts is a major achievement for anyone involved in buying or selling a house. However, exchange of contracts is not the end of the process, as it does not transfer legal title to the buyers. Traditionally, the contract will set a date some two to four weeks in the future for the transfer of the legal title to the land in return for the payment of the balance of the purchase price. This period allows final checks to be made on the sellers' entitlement to sell the land; deeds of conveyance and mortgage are prepared and executed, and the mortgage advance is transferred to the buyers' lawyers in readiness. Once everything is in place, the transfer of the legal title can be completed. This long-planned-for day can be somewhat frantic, not least because there will often be a chain of completions that need to be coordinated: the buyers are probably selling a house, too, and the sellers will need somewhere to move to before the buyers arrive with all their belongings.

However, even a successful completion day, with the keys released and the various parties installed in their new homes, does not mark the completion of the transfer of legal title. The buyers' lawyers must arrange for the transfer of legal title to be registered: ultimately, legal ownership is not final until the transfer has been recorded at the Land Registry.

Table 12.1 summarises the important steps in a typical conveyance of freehold land, although the order and timescale of events are by no means universal. For example, in

Table 12.1 The main stages in the purchase of a house

Time	Facts	Law	Section
	Advertising the house for sale Buyer makes an offer		
About 8 weeks	Negotiation of price, fittings, etc. Survey and finance arranged Draft contract prepared by seller Buyer checks the details of the property and makes searches and enquiries of the seller and others (such as the Local Authority to check planning, access) Contract agreed by buyer and seller	None of these steps has any legal or equitable implications: there is no contract	12.1
	Contracts signed by both parties are exchanged, and the buyer pays a deposit to the seller	The contract is made Equitable title passes to the buyer	12.4 12.3
Usually between 2 and 4 weeks	Pre-completion searches of title Deeds of conveyance and mortgage are prepared The lender releases the mortgage moneys Completion by execution of the deeds and payment of the balance of the purchase price to the seller		12.5.1
Within 2 months	The transfer and mortgage are sent to the Land Registry for registration The Land Registry completes registration and issues an official copy of the register of title, etc.	Legal title is transferred to the buyer	12.5.2

some parts of the country, it is becoming increasingly common to exchange contracts and complete the transfer of the legal title on the same day.

If the transaction includes a new lease the terms of that lease will need to be negotiated. Buyers who cannot afford to purchase their home outright, even with the aid of a mortgage, may choose to buy a share in a house with friends (see Chapters 10 and 11 for the rules regulating co-ownership). Others may purchase a share in the freehold title and pay rent (usually to a social landlord) on the other share. In recent years, the British government has funded a number of shared equity schemes enabling people to purchase the entire title to their home. Under one recent scheme, the homeowner purchased title to the land from a housing association. The housing association also provided an equity loan covering up to 30 per cent of the purchase price (with the remainder being financed in the conventional way). This loan is interest free for the first five years, but when repaid (on the sale of the house, or earlier), the housing association also receives a proportionate share of any increase in the value of the house since the date it was purchased.

12.2 Buying and selling interests in land

It is important to remember that 'land' includes all interests in land (see Section 2.3) and that:

> 'purchaser' means a purchaser in good faith for valuable consideration and includes a lessee, mortgagee or other person who for valuable consideration acquires an interest in property (LPA 1925, s 205(1)(xxi)).

Therefore, the rules in this chapter control not only sales of freehold land, but also other *dispositions* of interests in land, including, for example, the creation of leases, mortgages and easements, and the assignment of leases. The detailed rules vary, depending upon the nature of the interest concerned and, especially, on whether the interest is legal or equitable.

This chapter focuses on:

- the rules about the creation and enforcement of contracts for the sale of land, *because* unless these rules are observed, there will not be a binding contract between the parties; and
- the rules about deeds and registration, *because* failure to comply with these rules may mean that the buyer does not get the legal interest that he has paid for, but an equitable interest, which may be less secure (for the reasons explained in Section 2.3.3).

Other aspects of the process of buying and selling land will be referred to, but their details belong to courses on conveyancing rather than the study of land law (although the line between what is conveyancing law and what is land law is rather blurred). The term 'conveyancing' is derived from 'conveyance', a word used to describe both the transfer of the property and the document (technically a deed of grant) which brings the transfer about. For many purposes, however, the term 'conveyance' includes not only the transfer of freehold land, but also the granting of mortgages and leases (LPA 1925, s 205(1)(ii)).

The Electronic Communications Act 2000 and Part 8 of the LRA 2002 provided the statutory framework for discarding the printed page in favour of electronic conveyancing, 'the most revolutionary change ever to take place in conveyancing practice' ((1998) Law Com No 254, *Land Registration for the Twenty-First Century*, 1). The original intention was that all stages of conveyancing should be capable of being completed electronically, and contracts and deeds created, signed and communicated to the Land Registry by electronic means in order to have any effect. The first e-charge (electronic mortgage) was signed electronically by the borrower and registered on 29 March 2009 as part of a pilot project using a small number of lenders and conveyancers. However, at the end of June 2011, the Land Registry announced at that it would not be proceeding with the digitisation of other types of transactions (including transfers). The majority of conveyancing looks likely to continue to require the use of paper for the foreseeable future, whether in the form of a written contract or a deed. The main requirements, together with some important exceptions, are summarised in Table 12.2.

As in all areas of land law, the rules on which this chapter focuses are affected by other rules. The most important are those about registered and unregistered land.

Table 12.2 A summary of formalities relating to dealings with land

Type of interest	Basic rule	Significant exceptions
Creation or transfer of a legal estate and legal interest	▶ Deed (LPA 1925, s 52) followed by registration under LRA 2002 (note that all legal interests in land are 'estates in land' for the purposes of LPA 1925, s 52 (see LPA 1925, s 1(4)); or ▶ A limited number of transactions (mainly e-charges or electronic mortgages) may be completed electronically by virtue of the Electronic Communications Act 2000 and Part 8 of the LRA 2002.	▶ Short leases (LPA 1925, s 52(2)(d); LRA 2002, ss 4(2) and 27(2)(b)) ▶ Adverse possession (see Chapter 13) ▶ The doctrine of prescription (see Section 8.5.3)
Creation of a contract creating an equitable interest in the land (see Section 12.3)	▶ Writing satisfying Law of Property (Miscellaneous Provisions) Act 1989, s 2	▶ Short leases, public auctions, certain financial arrangements and resulting implied and constructive trusts (Law of Property (Miscellaneous Provisions) Act 1989, s 2(5); see Section 12.4.2(c)) ▶ Contracts subject to rectification (see Section 12.4.3(d))
Creation of a trust of land	▶ Evidenced in writing (LPA 1925, 53(1)(b))	▶ Statutory trusts of land on co-ownership (see Section 11.2) ▶ Resulting and constructive trusts (see Chapter 14) ▶ Resulting implied and constructive trusts (LPA 1925, s 53(2))
Creation of other types of equitable interest in land	▶ Writing (LPA 1925, s 53(1)(a))	▶ Resulting implied and constructive trusts (LPA 1925, s 53(2)) ▶ Proprietary estoppel (see Section 14.4)
Transfer of equitable interests	▶ Writing (LPA 1925, s 53(1)(c))	▶ Resulting implied and constructive trusts (LPA 1925, s 53(2))

However, legal title can also be obtained by long use, and equitable title by means of a trust. Given the interdependent parts of the land law machine, it is only possible fully to understand the rules about buying and selling land when the rest of land law is also understood.

12.3 Contracts and the transfer of the equitable interest

The outline of a land transaction in Section 12.1, while typical, is not universal. There is no strict requirement to enter into a contract to transfer the land in advance of the transfer itself. For example, many leases, including most short residential leases and some longer business leases, will be granted without first exchanging contracts. It might be wondered why conveyancers normally proceed via exchange of contracts rather than simply proceeding directly to the transfer of the legal interest. The reason is that a considerable number of things need to be done, at considerable expense, to facilitate completion. Today, the main task is to organise the release of funds from the lender. Historically, however, investigating unregistered titles was a much slower and riskier process than most conveyancing today. Buyers did not want to go to the expense of conducting the necessary examinations until they had some assurance that the seller would actually sell them the land. The parties to a sale of land could (and still can) usually feel secure once contracts had been exchanged, because the rules of equity provide that the contract may be specifically enforced during the period before the deed is executed. This remedy is available because 'equity regards as done that which ought to be done'. Since specific performance is an equitable remedy, it is discretionary and will only be ordered if the claimant has behaved properly.

If equity is prepared to grant specific performance of the contract, the sellers become, effectively, trustees for the new equitable right of the buyers to become the legal owners when the contract is completed. As Jessel MR explained in the case of *Lysaght v Edwards* (1875–76) LR 2 ChD 499 (Ch):

> What is the effect of the contract? It appears to me that the effect of a contract for sale has been settled for more than two centuries ... What is that doctrine? It is that the moment you have a valid contract for sale the vendor becomes in equity a trustee for the purchaser of the estate sold, and the beneficial ownership passes to the purchaser, the vendor having a right to the purchase-money, a charge or lien on the estate for the security of that purchase-money, and a right to retain possession of the estate until the purchase-money is paid (at 505–06).

The case of *Walsh v Lonsdale* (1882) LR 21 ChD 9 (CA) (see also Section 5.6.2) provides an example of the rule that an equitable interest in land is created as soon as there is a contract. In this famous old case, Lonsdale made a contract to grant a seven-year lease of a mill to Walsh, but the parties never completed the deed necessary for transfer of the lease, the legal estate. Jessel MR concluded:

> The tenant holds under an agreement for a lease. He holds therefore under the same terms in equity as if a lease had been granted, it being a case in which both parties admit that relief is capable of being given by specific performance (at 14–15).

A written contract for the sale of land is, therefore, an equitable interest in land (called an 'estate contract'). Walsh had a seven-year equitable lease, and one might have expected him to be delighted with this result. Unfortunately for him, it meant that he had to observe all the terms of the lease, including payment of rent in advance, so he owed Lonsdale £1,005.

The trust relationship that is created between the buyers and the sellers allows the sellers to retain some rights to enjoy the land: They can remain in possession of the land and exclude the buyers. However, the seller must take care to keep the land in the same condition as it was when contracts were exchanged. The passing of the beneficial interest in the land to the buyer means that the buyer must observe any obligations attached to that beneficial interest (which is why Walsh had to pay the rent due to Lonsdale). The burden of the risk of damage to the property is also transferred to the buyer at exchange of contracts. This means that the buyer must pay the whole of the purchase price, even if the house has been completely destroyed between exchange and the completion of the legal transfer of the land. However, this rule can cause significant complications (particularly with respect to the insuring of the property between exchange and completion), so it is usual for the contract to reverse it by expressly providing that the seller will retain the risk until completion.

12.4 Creating a valid contract

All of the statutory references in this section are to the Law of Property (Miscellaneous Provisions) Act 1989 unless otherwise indicated.

12.4.1 The history of land contract formalities

It has long been the rule that some form of writing was usually required when entering into a contract to buy and sell land. From the late seventeenth century until 1989, the rule was that a contract for the sale of any interest in land was not enforceable until there was some evidence of it either by writing or by part performance. Over time, the legal rules about what would constitute sufficient written evidence and what counted as part performance of the contract became detailed and confusing. As a result, a completely new set of rules was introduced in section 2 of the Law of Property (Miscellaneous Provisions) Act 1989. These rules apply to all agreements for the sale of any interest in land made after 26 September 1989.

Section 2(1) of the 1989 Act states:

> A contract for the sale or other disposition of an interest in land can only be made in writing and only by incorporating all the terms which the parties have expressly agreed in one document or, where contracts are exchanged, in each.

Section 2(3) of the 1989 Act requires the document or documents to be signed by or on behalf of each of the parties to the contract.

Under section 2 there is no contract until there is a signed document containing all the agreed terms. Although this provided a welcome element of certainty compared to section 2's immediate predecessor (section 40 of the Law of Property Act 1925), judges were, at first, reluctant to find that an unwritten agreement was not a contract merely because of section 2, and sought to hold people to their word. However, a stricter view subsequently emerged, in which the courts were more ready to insist upon compliance with all the formal requirements of section 2 (see Chadwick LJ in *Bircham & Co Nominees (2) Ltd v Worrell Holdings Ltd* (2001) 82 P & CR 34 (CA) at [15] and Biggs J in *North Eastern Properties Ltd v Coleman* [2010] 1 WLR 2715 (CA) at [43]). Partly as a result of this, a number of cases since 1989 concern the non-contractual remedies that may be available when an agreement fails to satisfy section 2 (see Section 12.4.5).

The 1989 Act will not be the final word on land contracts. As has already been noted in Section 12.2, the Electronic Communications Act 2000 and Part 8 of the LRA 2002 provide a statutory framework under which all aspects of conveyancing can be handled electronically. However, there are no plans at present to replace paper contracts.

If an agreement falls within the scope of section 2, there will normally be no contract until there is:

▶ one document or two identical documents (the latter is more usual)
▶ containing all the expressly agreed terms
▶ that has been signed by (or on behalf of) both the buyer and the seller.

12.4.2 The scope of section 2 of the 1989 Act

12.4.2(a) 'A contract' (s 2(1))

The requirements of section 2 are additional to the normal common law rules for the existence of a contract. Consequently the normal prerequisites of a valid contract must be present, including offer, acceptance and consideration and the intention to create a legally binding relationship. Negotiations for the sale and purchase of land frequently include agreements that are expressed to be made 'subject to contract'. Such an agreement is not an enforceable contract, but:

> a transaction in which each side hopes the other will act like a gentleman and neither intends so to act if it is against his material interests (per Sachs J *Goding v Frazer* [1967] 1 WLR 286 (QB) at 293).

Prior to the 1989 Act, it was usual for all pre-contractual negotiations concerning land to be headed 'subject to contract'. This was to prevent an oral agreement accidentally becoming enforceable under the provisions of section 40 of the LPA 1925. Although it is no longer possible to create a valid oral contract, 'subject to contract' remains in common use during negotiations. It has been suggested that its use may have significant consequences for the availability of alternative remedies if section 2 has not been complied with (see Section 12.4.5).

Section 2 only applies to *executory* contracts, that is contracts which have yet to be completed. In *Helden v Strathmore Ltd* [2011] Bus LR 1592 (CA), the claimant sought to set aside a registered legal charge because it attempted to incorporate terms by reference to a document that had never existed. According to Lord Neuberger MR (at [27]):

> Section 2 is concerned with contracts for the creation or sale of legal estates or interests in land, not with documents which actually create or transfer such estates or interests. So a contract to transfer a freehold or a lease in the future, a contract to grant a lease in the future, or a contract for a mortgage in the future, are all within the reach of the section, provided of course the ultimate subject matter is land. However, an actual transfer, conveyance or assignment, an actual lease, or an actual mortgage are not within the scope of section 2 at all.

However, completion of the land element of an agreement that does not comply with section 2 will not rescue any non-land terms that formed part of the agreement (see *Keay v Morris Homes (West Midlands) Ltd* [2012] 1 WLR 2855 (CA)).

12.4.2(b) 'For the sale or other disposition of an interest in land' (s 2(1))

For the purposes of the 1989 Act an 'interest in land' means:

> any estate, interest or charge in or over land (s 2(6), as amended by s 25(2) Trusts of Land and Appointment of Trustees Act 1996).

What is needed for a contract to be a 'contract for the sale or other disposition' of such an interest was considered by Arden LJ, in the case of *Joyce v Rigolli* [2004] EWCA Civ 79. She concluded that:

> for a contract to be one 'for' selling or disposing of land, it must have been part of the parties' purposes ... in entering into such a contract, that the contract should achieve a sale or other disposition of land (at [31]).

In that case, it was held that a boundary agreement did not fall within the scope of section 2 because the primary purpose of the agreement was to demarcate the boundary, albeit that this involved some land being exchanged.

Consequently, section 2 applies not only to the sale and purchase of legal estates, but also to the creation and disposition of other interests in land, including:

▶ the grant of an option to buy land (*Spiro v Glencrown Properties* [1991] 2 Ch 537 (Ch)); and

▶ a contract to create a mortgage (*United Bank of Kuwait plc v Sahib* [1997] Ch 107 (CA)).

However, section 2 does not apply to:

▶ an agreement by the seller not to consider any offers for the land from any other parties for a specific period (a 'lock-out agreement') (*Pitt v PHH Asset Management Ltd* [1994] 1 WLR 327 (CA));

▶ the grant of a right of first refusal (or 'pre-emption') if the landowner decides to sell a particular piece of land. However, any exercise of the right of pre-emption must satisfy section 2 for it to create a valid contact (see *Bircham & Co Nominees (2) Ltd v Worrell Holdings Ltd*);

▶ an agreement about the priority of two mortgages (*Scottish & Newcastle plc v Lancashire Mortgage Corp Ltd* [2007] EWCA Civ 684 (CA)); and

▶ a boundary agreement (*Joyce v Rigolli*; *Yeates v Line* [2013] Ch 363 (Ch)).

Spiro v Glencrown Properties concerned an option to purchase land and raised the question of whether the letter giving notice that the buyer was going to exercise the option and buy the land had to satisfy the section by also containing the seller's signature. Hoffmann J held:

> Apart from authority, it seems to me plain enough that section 2 was intended to apply to the agreement which created the option and not to the notice by which it was exercised ... The exercise of the option is a unilateral act. It would destroy the very purpose of the option if the purchaser had to obtain the vendor's countersignature to the notice (at 541).

The only document which required both signatures was the contract creating the option and, since both parties had signed this, the buyer was entitled to demand enforcement of the contract.

12.4.2(c) Statutory exceptions (s 2(5))

The following types of contract do not have to satisfy the section 2 formalities because of section 2(5):

1. contracts to grant leases of three years or less which take effect in possession and are at the market rent (see LPA 1925, s 54(2) and Section 12.5.1(c));
2. contracts made in a public auction (where the agreement is made in public, with the auctioneer acting for both parties); and

3. contracts regulated under the Financial Services and Markets Act 2000, except for regulated mortgage contracts, regulated home reversion plans and regulated purchase plans. This exception governs investments such as shares, which may include interests in land.

In addition, section 2(5) provides that section 2 has no effect 'on the creation or operation of resulting, implied or constructive trusts'. This allows the courts to mitigate the consequences of the strict requirements of section 2 in some cases by recognising a constructive trust (see Chapter 14). Section 2(5) is silent as to any possible role for proprietary estoppel. The availability of equitable remedies when section 2 has not been complied with is considered in Section 12.4.5.

12.4.3 The written document

Morgan J set out a step-by-step approach to using the principles of section 2(1) when determining the validity of a contract to which they apply in his 'thoughtful judgment' in *Oun v Ahmad* [2008] EWHC 545 (Ch). (It was praised as such by Lord Neuberger MR in *Helden v Strathmore Ltd* [2011] Bus LR 1592 (CA) at [29].)

The *Oun v Ahmad* approach

28. Section 2(1) requires the [signed] written document to incorporate all the terms which the parties have expressly agreed.
29. The first matter to be explored is a question of fact: What were all the terms which the parties had expressly agreed?
30. Once one has found all the terms which the parties have expressly agreed, then one can examine the written document to see if it incorporates all those terms or omits any.
31. If, on examination of the written document, it is found that it does not incorporate all the terms that the parties have expressly agreed, then prima facie there is no binding contract at all. … There cannot be a binding contract for only those terms which have been incorporated, because they are not the complete set of terms which were expressly agreed.
32. The prima facie position may be displaced in two cases, in particular.
33. The first particular case is where there are two separate contracts and not one composite contract …
34. The second particular case is where the written document, which does not incorporate all of the terms expressly agreed, can be rectified to include in the written document all of the terms expressly agreed.

12.4.3(a) 'Signed' (s 2(3))

The written document must be signed by the parties or on their behalf (s 2(3)). Prior to the 1989 Act, the rules about what constitutes a signature were somewhat complex and would have surprised most non-lawyers. Any occurrence of the name of the party who had written or typed the agreement (or on whose behalf it had been written) could be regarded as the signature, even if the party had not written his name on the document with his own hand. Fortunately, the Court of Appeal has held that these rules do not apply to contracts made under the 1989 Act. In the case of *Firstpost Homes v Johnson* [1995] 1 WLR 1567 (CA), Peter Gibson LJ refused to:

> encumber the new Act with so much ancient baggage, particularly when it does not leave the word 'signed' with a meaning which the ordinary man would understand it to have (at 362).

For the purposes of section 2, signature has its ordinary meaning as recognised in the case of *Goodman v J Eban Ltd* [1954] 1 QB 550 (CA):

> In modern English usage, when a document is required to be 'signed' by someone, that means that he must write his name with his own hand on it (per Denning LJ at 561).

Section 2 allows a valid contract to be signed by the parties themselves, or by someone else on their behalf. In the unreported case of *Grunhut v Ramdas* (2002), the signature appeared to be that of the relevant party, but was actually a forgery. It was held, however, that even though the party did not sign it herself, the contract was still valid because (on the facts) she had authorised someone else to sign it on her behalf.

Where the contract is to incorporate terms from another document, it is important that both parties sign the primary document. In *Firstpost Homes v Johnson*, Mrs Johnson agreed orally to sell some farmland to the claimant. The buyer drafted a letter which had his name typed on it as addressee and contained the terms of the contract to sell the land 'shown on the enclosed plan'. He signed the plan but not the letter, and sent both documents to Mrs Johnson, who signed and dated them both. She then died. When the buyer sought to enforce the agreement, Mrs Johnson's personal representatives claimed there was no contract because section 2 was not satisfied. On appeal, it was held that the two documents could not be joined as one, since the plan (the only document signed by both parties) did not incorporate the letter. Enclosing the letter in the same envelope as the plan was insufficient to combine the two documents. In fact, as it was the letter which expressly incorporated the plan, it was the letter which should have been signed by both parties. The buyer's typed name on the letter did not amount to his signature.

12.4.3(b) 'Incorporating all the terms which the parties have expressly agreed' (s 2(1))

To satisfy section 2, all of the expressly agreed terms of the agreement must be written in a single document (or duplicates for exchange) or incorporated into that document by reference to some other document (s 2(2)). Any variation of the terms must also satisfy section 2, as Morritt LJ (as he then was) explained in *McCausland v Duncan Lawrie Ltd* [1997] 1 WLR 38 (CA):

> The choice lies between permitting a variation, however fundamental, to be made without any formality at all and requiring it to satisfy section 2. In my view, it is evident that Parliament intended the latter. There would be little point in requiring that the original contract comply with section 2 if it might be varied wholly informally (at 40).

Section 2(2) allows the terms to be incorporated into a document either by being set out in it or by reference to some other document. In *Courtney v Corp Ltd* [2006] EWCA Civ 518 (CA), a finance company's contract letter expressly incorporated its standard terms and conditions, which were contained in a separate document. The claimant did not read these conditions before signing the contract letter, and subsequently claimed that the contract was invalid. The Court of Appeal held that the express incorporation of the standard conditions was sufficient to satisfy section 2, even if Mr Courtney had not seen or read them.

Where a formal contract is drafted in two parts, all the terms must be recorded identically in each part. This is the most usual way of preparing contracts for the sale of land. The seller signs one copy, and the purchaser signs the other. The contract comes into being when the two copies are exchanged and any deposit paid. It seems that if the two parts of the contract are not identical records of the terms, the formalities of section 2 are not satisfied.

Before section 2 came into force, it was possible to create a valid contract through the exchange of correspondence. The Law Commission proposed that creation of contracts by correspondence should continue ((1987) Law Com No 164, para 4.15). However, section 2 as enacted was significantly different from the draft proposed by the Law Commission. In *Hooper v Sherman* [1994] NPC 153 (CA), the Court of Appeal held that the exchange of two informal letters between the parties, each containing the terms and signed by the senders' solicitors, could amount to an 'exchange of contracts'. The majority in the Court of Appeal held that the letters could be joined together and thus satisfy section 2: all the terms were in writing and signed by both parties. Morritt LJ dissented, however, on the ground that, although these letters would have been enough for section 40 of the LPA 1925, they were not sufficient for the clear terms of the new law. Shortly afterwards, in *Commission for New Towns v Cooper (GB) Ltd* [1995] Ch 259 (CA), a differently constituted Court of Appeal decided that it was not bound by *Hooper v Sherman* for procedural reasons and then went on to agree with the dissenting judgment of Morritt LJ. In *Cooper*, the parties were in dispute as to the terms of payment for building work as part of a complex arrangement of various land agreements. They reached an agreement, subject to the approval of the claimant's directors, the terms of which were included in an exchange of faxes. One side claimed that this amounted to an 'exchange of contracts' for section 2, but the Court of Appeal unanimously held that it did not, because 'exchange of contracts' in section 2(1) refers to the exchanging of identical documents as part of a formal process indicating the intention to enter a contract:

> In my judgment, when there has been a prior oral agreement, there is only an 'exchange of contracts' within section 2 when documents are exchanged which set out or incorporate all of the terms which have been agreed and when, crucially, those documents are intended, by virtue of their exchange, to bring about a contract to which section 2 applies (per Evans LJ at 295).

Thus, it is not sufficient under section 2 for the documentation signed by the parties to confirm a prior oral agreement: the documents must, on proper construction, create the contract itself.

12.4.3(c) Composite contracts

There are two circumstances in which failure to include all of the expressly agreed terms in the written document may not prove fatal to the contract. The first is where the missing term does not relate to the land *and* that term is separable from the terms relating to the land. As Briggs J, sitting in the Court of Appeal, explained in the case of *North Eastern Properties Ltd v Coleman* at [54]:

(i) Nothing in section 2 of the 1989 Act is designed to prevent parties to a composite transaction which includes a land contract from structuring their bargain so that the land contract is genuinely separated from the rest of the transaction in the sense that its performance is not made conditional upon the performance of some other expressly agreed part of the bargain. Thus ... parties may agree to the sale and purchase both of a house and of its curtains and carpets in a single composite transaction. Nonetheless it is open to them to agree either (a) that completion of the purchase of the house is dependent upon the sale of the carpets and curtains or (b) that it is not. They are free to separate the terms of a transaction of type (b) into two separate documents (one for the house and the other for the carpets and curtains) without falling foul of section 2 ...

(ii) By contrast, the parties to a composite transaction are not free to separate into a separate document expressly agreed terms, for example as to the sale of chattels or the provision of services, if upon the true construction of the whole of the agreement, performance of the land sale is conditional upon the chattel sale or service provision.

The Law Commission report which preceded the 1989 Act ((1987) Law Com No 164) suggested that unincorporated terms could be valid if they fell within the doctrine of 'collateral contracts' (that is, contracts 'on the side'). Initially, the courts seemed receptive to this approach, as in *Record v Bell* [1991] 1 WLR 853 (Ch). In this case, an additional term was agreed after the two copies of the contract had been signed. The seller promised that there were no unforeseen burdens affecting the title to the land registered at the Land Registry. The buyer subsequently wished to withdraw from the contract and argued that the extra term meant that section 2(2) of the 1989 Act had not been complied with and that the contract was, therefore, void. Judge Paul Baker QC rejected this argument. He held that there were two contracts: (1) one for the sale of the land, and (2) the agreement to complete this sale in consideration of the seller's extra promise. He went on to hold that the second contract was collateral to the first and did not relate to a disposition of an interest in land. Consequently, neither agreement failed for non-compliance with section 2. The first contained all of its terms in writing, and the second agreement did not need to be in writing as it was not a contract for the disposition of land. However, the courts have subsequently taken a stricter line in respect of collateral contracts. In *Godden v Merthyr Tydfil Housing Association* (1997) 74 P & CR D1 (CA), the Court of Appeal stressed that the existence of a collateral contract was a question of fact based on the commercial reality of the agreement. The relevant test is whether the completion of the land contract is conditional upon the completion of the other terms (see *North Eastern Properties Ltd v Coleman* at [54], quoted above). The court cannot artificially divide what is in reality a single agreement.

12.4.3(d) Rectification

The other method by which a seemingly invalid contract may be saved is the equitable remedy of rectification. The availability of rectification is expressly recognised by section 2(4) of the 1989 Act and has been used by the courts on a number of occasions. When applied in these circumstances rectification will render valid an otherwise void contract. Section 2(4) gives the court the power to specify the date upon which the contract became legally effective.

In *Wright v Robert Leonard Developments Ltd* [1994] EGCS 69 (CA), contracts were exchanged for the sale of a show flat, but the expressly agreed term that the furnishings would be included in the sale was omitted. Although the furnishings were not fixtures and were not, therefore, land within the meaning of section 2(1), the Court of Appeal refused to treat the agreement about the furnishings as separable from the rest of the transaction (see Section 12.4.3(c)). Consequently, the exchange of contracts did not satisfy section 2, and therefore, it would appear, there was no contract. However, the Court agreed that the document could be rectified to include the missing term. Once the missing term was inserted, the contract satisfied section 2.

'Rectification is about setting the record straight' (per Morgan J, *Oun v Ahmad* [2008] EWHC 545 (Ch) at [46]). It is a discretionary remedy which allows the court to correct a mistake in the way in which the terms of the agreement have been recorded in writing. It is not a vehicle for varying or clarifying the terms of the agreement. Peter Gibson LJ summarised the basic requirements to justify rectification in the case of *Swainland Builders Ltd v Freehold Properties Ltd* [2002] 2 EGLR 71 (CA) at [33]:

(1) the parties had a common continuing intention … in respect of a particular matter in the instrument to be rectified;
(2) there was an outward expression of accord;
(3) the intention continued at the time of the execution of the instrument sought to be rectified;
(4) by mistake, the instrument did not reflect that common intention.

In *Sargeant v Reece* [2008] 1 P & CR DG8 (Ch), Edward Bartley Jones QC, sitting in the High Court, reviewed the Court of Appeal cases on the doctrine of rectification and particularly the burden of proof falling on the claimant. He concluded that the claimant does not need to be able to prove the exact form of words that should have been used in the written document, provided that he can establish the substance of the missing term or terms in sufficient detail. The amount and type of evidence needed to do this will depend upon the quality of the document concerned, but will need to be sufficiently convincing to outweigh the evidence of the written contract itself:

> It is not, I think, the standard of proof which is high, so differing from the normal civil standard, but the evidential requirement needed to counteract the inherent probability that the written instrument truly represents the parties' intention because it is a document signed by the parties (per Brightman LJ, *Thomas Bates & Son Ltd v Wyndham's (Lingerie) Ltd* [1981] 1 WLR 505 (CA) at 521).

12.4.4 Remedies for breach of contract

If there is a valid contract, then the buyer or the seller may be entitled to specific performance if the other party defaults, provided that damages would be an insufficient remedy (which will usually be the case, given the unique nature of land). However, specific performance is an equitable remedy available at the discretion of the court. It may be denied, for example, because of the claimant's conduct ('he who comes to equity must come with clean hands'). In *Wilkie v Redsell* [2003] EWCA Civ 926, the Court of Appeal declined to grant a rogue specific performance of his contract to buy land, since, first, there was no evidence that he would be able to pay the purchase price and thus complete his side of the bargain, and, second, he had 'abused the facilities of the court in relation to the very matter in respect of which he [sought] relief' (at [34]) and so did not have clean hands.

Even if a person is entitled to specific performance, the court may award damages instead if it would be fairer to do so – for example, where the land has now been sold to a third party. Under the Law Society's Standard Conditions of Sale, if the buyer refuses to complete, the seller may retain the deposit (a powerful incentive for the buyer), subject always to the courts' statutory discretion to order the return of the deposit pursuant to section 49(2) of the LPA 1925.

Other remedies for the buyer include suing for the restitution of a lost deposit or for misrepresentation. In *McMeekin v Long* (2003) 29 EG 120 (QB), the buyers of a house were awarded £67,000 damages for fraudulent misrepresentation when the sellers deliberately failed to disclose a dispute with their neighbours.

12.4.5 Remedies where there is no valid contract

The requirements of section 2 of the 1989 Act cause no problems in the vast majority of transactions concerning land. The need to satisfy the provisions of section 2 means that the parties can be certain both as to whether they have entered into a binding contract and about the terms of that contract. If section 2 is not satisfied, there are no reciprocal contractual obligations between the parties. As Chadwick LJ observed in *Bircham & Co Nominees (2) Ltd v Worrell Holdings Ltd* (2001) 82 P & CR 34 (CA):

> There are obvious difficulties in the way of a claimant who seeks specific performance of an agreement which, by reason of the provisions enacted in section 2 of the 1989 Act, has no contractual effect (at [15]).

Consequently, if a party spends money or other resources in reliance upon an agreement that has yet to satisfy section 2, he does so at his own risk. Without a valid contract, he cannot force the other party to honour the agreement. As Biggs J (sitting in the Court of Appeal) observed in the case of *North Eastern Properties Ltd v Coleman* [2010] 3 All ER 528 (CA):

> [Section 2] enables parties to land contracts who have changed their minds to look around for expressly agreed terms which have not found their way into the final form of land contract which they signed, for the precise purpose of avoiding their obligations, on the ground that the lack of discipline of their counterparty, or even their own lack of discipline, has rendered the contract void (at [43]).

Equity has long recognised that there are circumstances in which it would be unfair not to provide a remedy to a claimant who has acted to his detriment as a result of the other person's actions simply because of the absence of the signed document.

Prior to section 2, a contract relating to land was merely unenforceable if the formality requirements had not been complied with. However, evidence that the claimant had performed a part of (or had done some other act showing the existence of) the unwritten contract, and that the defendant knew of this, would render the contract enforceable in equity. This is the doctrine of 'part performance'. Although the 1989 Act does not expressly abolish part performance, it is difficult to see how the doctrine can apply within the provisions of section 2. After some initial doubt, the Court of Appeal has now confirmed on a number of occasions that the doctrine of part performance is not applicable to contracts made after 26 September 1989 (see, for example, *United Bank of Kuwait plc v Sahib* [1997] Ch 107 (CA) and *Yaxley v Gotts* [2000] Ch 162 (CA)).

The Law Commission expected part performance to be replaced by proprietary estoppel, although it did not anticipate frequent resort to equity:

> In putting forward the present recommendation we rely greatly on the principle, recognised even by equity, that 'certainty is the father of right and the mother of justice' ((1987) Law Com No 164, para 4.13).

There have been many attempts to summarise the circumstances in which an estoppel can arise. None is perfect, but that offered by Mr Edward Nugee QC, sitting as a High Court judge, in the case of *Re Basham* [1986] 1 WLR 1498 (Ch) is a helpful starting place. The doctrine means that:

> where one person, A, has acted to his detriment on the faith of a belief, which was known to or encouraged by another person, B, that he either has or is going to be given a right over B's property, B cannot insist on his strict legal rights if to do so would be inconsistent with A's belief (at 1503).

The doctrine of proprietary estoppel is a significant area of law in its own right which has recently received considerable attention from the House of Lords in *Cobbe v Yeoman's Row Management Ltd* [2008] 1 WLR 1752 (HL) (a failed s 2 contract case) and *Thorner v Major* [2009] 1 WLR 776 (HL). Proprietary estoppel and the related doctrine of common intention constructive trusts are considered in detail in Chapter 14.

The doctrine of proprietary estoppel will only be relevant if the parties expected to be bound by the terms of their agreement. Consequently, an agreement labelled 'subject to contract' (see Section 12.4.2(a)) will not ordinarily be capable of giving rise to a proprietary estoppel, as the label reveals that neither party expects to be bound by it (see *Haq v Island Homes Housing Association* [2011] 2 P & CR 17 (CA)). In the case of *Cobbe*,

Mr Cobbe, an experienced property developer, orally agreed to purchase a property comprising a number of flats from Yeoman's Row Management Ltd for £12 million. On the basis of this arrangement, he then spent 18 months and a considerable amount of money applying for, and obtaining, planning permission for the proposed development. Immediately after the grant of planning permission, the company demanded £20 million for the flats. In the Court of Appeal, Mr Cobbe successfully argued that the company was estopped from going back on the original agreement. However, the House of Lords held that Mr Cobbe's claim failed. Although reasoning in *Cobbe* was criticised in subsequent case of *Thorner v Major* (also in the House of Lords), *Thorner* does not cast doubt upon the actual outcome in *Cobbe*. Lord Neuberger explained:

> Mr Cobbe's claim failed because he was effectively seeking to invoke proprietary estoppel to give effect to a contract which the parties had intentionally and consciously not entered into, and because he was simply seeking a remedy for the unconscionable behaviour of Yeoman's Row (at [92]).

There is considerable doubt, however, whether the doctrine of proprietary estoppel is ever appropriate in the context of an agreement that fails to be a contract because of failure to comply with section 2. A number of judges have expressed concern that using the doctrine in these circumstances contravenes the intention of Parliament underlying the 1989 Act, not least because estoppel is not one of the exceptions listed in section 2(5) (see Section 12.4.2(c)). In an *obiter* comment in *Cobbe*, Lord Scott expressed his view that:

> proprietary estoppel cannot be prayed in aid in order to render enforceable an agreement that statute has declared to be void. The proposition that an owner of land can be estopped from asserting that an agreement is void for want of compliance with the requirements of section 2 is, in my opinion, unacceptable. The assertion is no more than the statute provides. Equity can surely not contradict the statute … statute provides an express exception for constructive trusts (at [29]).

In *Yaxley v Gotts*, Mr Yaxley, a builder, orally agreed with a friend (Mr Gotts senior) that he would take the ground floor of a house that his friend was about to buy, in return for renovating and rebuilding the house as a number of flats. In fact, the friend's son (Mr Gotts junior) bought the house, but Mr Yaxley carried out the work as he had promised. A few years later, Mr Yaxley fell out with the father and son. They barred him from the premises and denied that he had any right to the ground floor of the house. At first instance, Mr Yaxley, having relied on the father's oral promise (which had apparently been adopted by the son), successfully claimed an interest in the house by virtue of proprietary estoppel and was awarded a 99-year lease of the ground floor. On appeal, Robert Walker LJ (as he then was) was reluctant to find an estoppel in Mr Yaxley's favour for the reason identified above, although he was not prepared to rule out the possibility of estoppel ever being appropriate in circumstances in which section 2 had not been complied with. Instead, he imposed a constructive trust on Mr Gotts. Typically, this type of constructive trust arises where the parties have agreed that A shall have a proprietary interest in property, and A has acted to his detriment in reliance on that agreement. Robert Walker LJ felt able to impose a constructive trust on Gotts because of the provision in section 2(5) that the creation or operation of constructive trusts is not affected by section 2. Beldam and Clarke LJJ, while agreeing with the imposition of a constructive trust, also supported the first instance judge's finding of proprietary estoppel. They were prepared to give much more weight to the views of the Law Commission when interpreting section 2, since the 1989 Act was based on the Commission's report. According to Beldam LJ, the underlying policy behind section 2 was not to prohibit informal agreements relating to land, but to make them void for the purposes of contract law if they did not satisfy the formalities contained in the statute. In *Whittaker v Kinnear* [2011] EWHC 1479 (QB), Bean J preferred the reasoning of Beldam LJ in *Yaxley v Gotts* over the *obiter* comments of Lord Scott in *Cobbe* (not least because Beldam LJ was the Chairman of the Law Commission at the time of the report which gave rise to the 1989 Act).

The House of Lords has yet to decide this question.

12.5　Transfer of the legal interest

12.5.1　The deed

As mentioned already, a deed is normally necessary to transfer a legal estate or interest. When the land is registered, the deed is a Land Transfer form from the Land Registry.

Section 52(1) of the LPA 1925 states:

> All conveyances of land or of any interest therein are void for the purpose of conveying or creating a legal estate unless made by deed.

Before 31 July 1990, a deed was a document that was 'signed, sealed and delivered'. Now, the ancient requirement for a seal is dispensed with. The requirements for a deed are now set out in section 1 of the Law of Property (Miscellaneous Provisions) Act 1989.

A deed is a document which:

- makes clear on its face that it is a deed;
- is validly executed; and
- is delivered.

12.5.1(a) Execution

An individual 'executes' the deed (that is, makes the document his deed) by signing it in the presence of one witness who also signs. Alternatively, the deed can be signed 'at his direction and in his presence' by another person, and in this case there must be two witnesses present who also sign the deed. Different rules apply to corporations, including limited companies.

12.5.1(b) Delivery

A deed is 'delivered' when the grantor (the person executing the deed) does or says something to 'adopt the deed as his own'. In practice, solicitors usually treat a deed as delivered at the moment they add a date to a document which has already been signed and witnessed; this is said to show that they adopt it.

12.5.1(c) Where a deed is not needed

There are a number of circumstances where a legal estate or legal interest can be obtained without a deed.

1. *Short leases* (defined in LPA 1925, s 54(2)): by section 52(2)(d), a lease is legal without any formality (even writing) if it does not exceed three years, the tenant is entitled to occupy the premises from the date of the lease (that is, the lease 'takes effect in possession') and it is at a market rent. There is no need for any special formality, or even writing, for this kind of short lease, because there is little risk that a buyer of the property will be caught unawares – the tenant will be present on the property and paying rent. In addition, the expense and delay in conforming to the formality

requirements of sections 1 and 2 of the 1989 Act would be bound to inhibit the crea-tion of these commonly found leases or would lead to non-compliance. However, somewhat illogically, a deed is still needed to *assign* any lease (to transfer the whole of the legal interest to another person, as opposed to creating a sublease), as shown in *Crago v Julian* [1992] 1 WLR 372 (CA).

2. *Long use*: in unregistered land, using someone else's land for a minimum of 12 years can ensure that the user cannot be defeated by anyone; effectively, he becomes a legal owner. This is known as 'adverse possession'. It is also possible to obtain title to registered land by adverse possession, although the rules are somewhat different. Adverse possession is considered in detail in Chapter 13. Long use of an easement or profit (for example, a right of way or a right to fish) can create a legal right by 'prescription' (see Section 8.5.3).

3. *Personal representatives' assent* (Administration of Estates Act 1925, s 36(1)): if a landowner dies, his land automatically goes to ('vests in') his legal representatives. When they have completed their administration of the estate, they transfer the land to the heir(s). Writing, but no deed, is necessary to do this; it is called an 'assent'.

4. *Trustee in bankruptcy's disclaimer*: where a landowner becomes bankrupt, the land automatically vests in his trustee in bankruptcy. If the land is more trouble than it is worth (for example, a lease with a high rent), the trustee can disclaim it in writing; a deed is not necessary.

5. *Court order*: a court can order land to be transferred.

12.5.1(d) The effect of a deed

The deed transfers not only the interest but also any advantages which belong to the land, unless the parties show that they intend otherwise. Section 62 of the LPA 1925 states:

> A conveyance of land shall be deemed to include and shall by virtue of this Act operate to convey, with the land, all buildings, erections, fixtures, commons, hedges, ditches, fences, ways, waters, water-courses, liberties, privileges, easements, rights, and advantages whatso-ever, appertaining or reputed to appertain to the land, or any part thereof, or, at the time of conveyance, demised, occupied, or enjoyed with, or reputed or known as part or parcel of, or appurtenant to, the land or any part thereof.

Thus, a buyer of land may, by section 62, get the right enjoyed by his predecessor to park his car in his neighbour's drive (see Section 8.5.2(c)). Sections 78 and 79, respec-tively, ensure that he will automatically have the right to enforce, and will be bound by, any valid restrictive covenant over the land (see Sections 9.5.2(a) and 9.5.1(c)).

12.5.1(e) Where the formalities have not been complied with

The formalities described above are necessary for the valid execution of a deed. However, in the case of *Shah v Shah* [2002] QB 35 (CA), a person was induced to rely on what appeared on the face of it to be a deed. A later representation by the executor of the deed that it was invalid since it had not been properly witnessed was unsuccessful, and the executor was estopped from relying on his strict legal rights.

12.5.2 Registration

Almost every sale, transfer, lease or first legal mortgage of land in England and Wales must now be registered at the Land Registry. The main exception relates to leases with less than seven years to run, although it is anticipated that this period will eventually be reduced to three years. The consequences of failing to register the disposition will depend upon whether the land was already registered at the time of the transfer.

12.5.2(a) 'Not yet registered' land

Section 4(1) of the LRA 2002 requires all transfers of freehold and the grant and transfer of leases for a term exceeding seven years to be registered. The grant of a first mortgage will also trigger compulsory first registration. In these circumstances, the legal title to the land is transferred to the buyer on the date set out in the deed of transfer. The buyer has two months within which to apply for registration (s 6); otherwise the legal title will revert to the seller, who will then hold the land on trust for the buyer (s 7). It is the responsibility of the buyer to ensure that the legal title is re-transferred to him and properly registered (s 8). In the meanwhile, the buyer will only have title to the land in equity, and he will not enjoy all the protection afforded to a legal owner. The implications of this are explored more fully in Chapter 15.

12.5.2(b) Registered land

Different rules apply to the transfer of legal title to land that is already registered at the date of the transfer. In this case, there is no two-month window. Section 27 of the LRA 2002 provides that the transfer of registered estates (and the creation of several types of interest over them) will not operate at law until the registration requirements are met. In the gap between completing the transfer deed and completion of its registration (the so-called registration gap) the buyer will have only an equitable interest in the land. Again, the detailed implications of this are considered in Chapter 15.

12.6 Conclusion

The transfer of land is financially and socially so important that it is bound to be the subject of some ritual and, therefore, of technical rules. The present rules are only the latest in a long line of such requirements which have focused on the use of paper and particular forms of documents. At some point in the future, the formal requirements may be electronic. However, the introduction of e-conveyancing has proved more complex, and therefore slower, than anticipated when the LRA 2002 was passed. For the time being, the Land Registry has decided to focus upon increasing the scope of electronic registration of documents rather than increasing the number of types of transactions that can be completed electronically.

Whatever the future of e-conveyancing, the major issues that must be addressed will not change merely because of the availability or otherwise of a new method or new technology. In particular, a compromise must be found between the need for a clear rule and the need to make sure that people do not unfairly take advantage of one another. The requirements of the 1989 Act have a more ruthless simplicity than their predecessors, and cases on section 2 suggest that it does not successfully address all of the tensions between certainty and justice inherent in any system of formalities. The extent to which the formalism of section 2 is reflected in the decisions of the courts may change according to the state of the property market, and according to the attitude adopted by the courts towards proprietary estoppel and constructive trusts. In any event, despite the nature of the rules, many hundreds of thousands of interests in land are successfully conveyed each year. It has yet to be seen whether the rules of e-conveyancing can achieve a better balance.

The rules relating to the buying and selling of interests in land are (and will probably remain) formalistic and detailed, but, in an area where the law is seeking to achieve a simple and certain resolution of complicated and dynamic human relationships, this is hardly surprising. Different legal systems tackle the problem in different ways (compare, for example, the system in Scotland), but none seems to be free from criticism. In any event, most non-lawyers are less concerned about the technicality of the rules than they are with their financial situation and the state of the property market. Rules that do not obviously hinder the market are unlikely to attract much attention or criticism.

Summary

12.1 In England and Wales, dealings with interests in land are typically divided into two main stages. The first stage ends when there is a legally binding contract between the parties. The second stage concludes with the transfer of title to the interest.

12.2 The buying and selling of interests in land usually requires certain formalities (writing, deeds or electronic) to be complied with. The rules are found in statute, supplemented by equity.

12.3 As soon as there is a contract for the sale of an interest in land, the buyer effectively becomes the equitable owner of the land, provided the discretionary remedy of specific performance is available.

12.4 In order for there to be a contract for the sale of an interest in land, normally the agreement must satisfy the terms of section 2 of the Law of Property (Miscellaneous Provisions) Act 1989. In particular, all the terms must be in writing and signed by both sides. If there is no contract, equity may nevertheless enforce the 'agreement' by finding a constructive trust, or under the doctrine of proprietary estoppel.

12.5 A deed, signed, witnessed and delivered, is normally necessary to create or transfer a legal interest in land. It also transfers benefits attached to the land. Most deeds must be registered at the Land Registry for the interest concerned to operate at (or be transferred at) law.

Exercises

12.1 Complete the online quiz on the topics covered in this chapter on the companion website.

12.2 Read *Three Students: A Further Tale* on the companion website. Use the issues considered in this chapter to decide whether there is a valid contract for the sale and purchase of the house.

12.3 Critically consider the justifications for and the disadvantages of requiring dispositions of land and contracts for the dispositions of land to comply with the formalities contained in the Law of Property Act 1925 (as amended), the Law of Property (Miscellaneous Provisions) Act 1989 and the Land Registration Act 2002.

12.4 William owned the freehold of a rather dilapidated house. He agreed to sell it to Ajay for £150,000, and, once contracts were exchanged, Ajay began work on the repairs. Due to a change in his circumstances, William has decided he no longer wishes to sell the house to Ajay. William's solicitor has told him that, since no deed has yet been executed, William can withdraw from the arrangement. It also turns out that Ajay never signed his copy of the contract.

Advise Ajay.

You can find suggested answers to exercises 12.3 and 12.4 on the companion website.

Further reading

Capps, 'Conveyancing in the Twenty-First Century: An Outline of Electronic Conveyancing, and Electronic Signatures' [2002] Conv 443

Critchley, 'Taking Formalities Seriously' in Bright and Dewar (eds), *Land Law Themes and Perspectives* (Oxford University Press 1998)

McFarlane, 'Proprietary Estoppel and Failed Contractual Negotiations' [2005] 69 Conv 501

Owen and Rees, 'Section 2(5) of the Law of Property (Miscellaneous Provisions) Act 1989: a Misconceived Approach?' [2011] 75 Conv 495

Thompson, 'Oral Agreements for the Sale of Land' [2000] Conv 245

Chapter 13 follows overleaf.

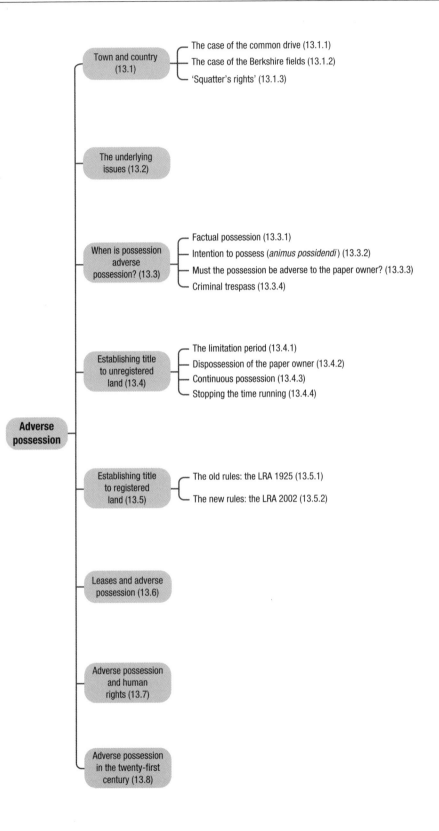

Adverse possession

Key concepts

- **Adverse possession** – the acquisition of title to land by dispossessing the original owner for the requisite period.
- *Animus possidendi* – the requisite intention to possess the land being claimed.
- **Factual possession** – exclusive physical control of the land being claimed; the degree of control required depends upon the characteristics of the land concerned.

13.1 Town and country

13.1.1 The case of the common drive

Numbers 31 and 33 Rosedale Road are neighbouring houses in the suburbs of Epsom, Surrey. When they were built in 1934, the two houses shared a common drive. The owner of each house had title to the half of the drive running alongside her house with an easement to use the half of the drive owned by her neighbour. For convenience, the fence between the houses was built close to Number 33, which gave the impression that the drive actually belonged to Number 31. As it happened, the owner of Number 33 never did use the drive and, from 1952, did not even have access to it. In 1962, the new owners of Number 31 paved the drive and used it for parking their cars. The Williams family moved into Number 33 in 1977 and decided to pursue their apparent legal right, as the 'paper owners', to half the width of the drive.

- The argument in favour of the Williams family was that they were the legal owners of the strip of land (the original title deeds stated it clearly) and they ought therefore to have been entitled to legal protection against trespassers. From their point of view, any rule that prevented them from recovering their half of the drive was a 'cheat's charter' (McCormick, 1986).
- On the other hand, the earlier owners of their house had 'slept on their rights', even later acknowledging that they did not think they owned the strip of land, whereas the owners of Number 31 had used it and repaved it 'at some expense, which went beyond any normal maintenance requirements'.

Should the Williams family be allowed to resurrect so stale a claim?

13.1.2 The case of the Berkshire fields

In 1982, John Graham and his wife purchased Manor Farm at Henwick Manor in West Berkshire, together with some 67 hectares of surrounding land. Mr Graham farmed the land with his son Michael. Four of the fields next to Manor Farm belonged to JA Pye (Oxford) Ltd. Pye hoped to be able to develop its land at some point in the future, but for several years it allowed the occupants of Manor Farm to use the fields as grazing land under the terms of various agreements. The Grahams entered into such an agreement with Pye in February 1983. Pye refused to grant a new grazing agreement for 1984 as it wanted to keep the land free, ready for its application for planning permission to develop the land. However, the Grahams continued to use the land, and in August 1984 they took a cut of hay from the fields in return for a payment to Pye. From September 1984 onwards, the Grahams used all four fields all year round for farming. The Grahams made a number of attempts to contact Pye with a view to regularising the arrangement and would have been happy to pay for the use of the fields had payment been demanded. Pye, however, did not answer their various requests.

In 1997, after farming the fields for over 12 years without any interference from Pye, Michael Graham took the first steps towards protecting the 'squatter's title' that he believed he had acquired over the four fields. Pye objected, but despite some negotiations, no progress had been made towards resolving the dispute when Michael Graham was tragically killed in a shooting accident in February 1998. His widow felt duty bound to continue the claim, and at the beginning of 1999, Pye issued court proceedings in an attempt to reclaim its land. The value of the four fields, assuming planning permission was granted, was now said to be in the region of £10 million.

Who should be entitled to the land?

- There was no doubt that Pye had simply stood by while the Grahams farmed Pye's land for a considerable period of time: and the Grahams had done nothing to hide what they were doing. But is the loss of ownership a proportionate response to Pye's indifference?
- The Grahams had put considerable work into the land over the years. However, they were aware that Pye owned the land and were willing to take the risk that they would lose the benefit of their work. As it was, they had reaped the profits of the land rent-free for over 12 years, and the land was worth far more than the Grahams had ever spent on it.
- How could Mrs Graham's claim be consistent with Article 1 of the First Protocol of the European Convention on Human Rights, 'No one shall be deprived of his possessions except in the public interest and subject to the conditions provided for by law and by the general principles of international law'?

13.1.3 'Squatter's rights'

This chapter investigates the issues which arise when an owner's title is challenged because someone else has been in possession of her land for many years. Such a dispute might concern squatters claiming ownership of a house in a fashionable area or a large area of land with valuable potential for development, and might be worth pursuing to the highest courts. The dispute between Mrs Graham and Pye went to both the House of Lords (*JA Pye (Oxford) Ltd v Graham* [2003] 1 AC 419 (HL)) and the European Court of Justice (*JA Pye (Oxford) Ltd v UK* (2008) 46 EHRR 45). Other claims (perhaps the majority) concern a relatively small area of land, frequently land lying on the boundary between two titles. Such disputes are pursued with no less thoroughness. The Williams took their case as far as the Court of Appeal (*Williams v Usherwood* (1983) 45 P & CR 235 (CA)).

13.2 The underlying issues

Historically, adverse possession is part of the general law of limitation of actions, now contained in the Limitation Act 1980. The basic principle is straightforward: after a certain length of time, a person using land may have a better title to it than anyone else, including the real or 'paper' owner, simply because the law will not permit anyone to remove her. Through adverse possession, a person can effectively become the legal owner of land solely because of her occupation of it.

Many of the justifications offered for the doctrine of adverse possession arise out of the limitations of the traditional, unregistered conveyancing, where there may be considerable uncertainty about who owns a particular parcel of land. The interests of certainty and the market in land require a rule that actions to recover possession may not be brought after a certain length of time has passed. They become 'time barred'; otherwise 'stale claims' will haunt landowners and their purchasers indefinitely. In addition, deeds can get lost, and people can forget what they own, but the land itself remains. If the law did not provide for cases where there is no formal proof of title, areas of land would be 'outside the law' and unmarketable. Adverse possession thus provides a way of curing defective titles in unregistered land, since the paper owner cannot evict the squatter after the required period of possession has passed.

In registered land, the justifications for retaining rules on adverse possession are different but no less compelling. Here, title is not based on possession, as it is in the unregistered system, but on the fact that ownership has been recorded at the Land Registry, which guarantees the title (see Chapter 15). Although the LRA 1925 incorporated the rules that applied to unregistered land with little significant amendment, it is now generally recognised that adverse possession has a much more limited role within the registered title scheme. In their consultation prior to the LRA 2002 ((1998) Law Com No 254, para 10.98) the Law Commission stated that:

> the title that registration confers should be capable of being overridden by adverse possession only where it is essential to ensure the marketability of land or to prevent unfairness ... namely –
> (1) where the registered proprietor cannot be traced;
> (2) where there have been dealings 'off the register';
> (3) in some cases where the register is not conclusive; and
> (4) where an adverse possessor has entered into possession under a reasonable mistake as to his or her rights.

This reasoning is reflected in the new set of rules introduced to govern claims to adverse possession of registered land in the LRA 2002. These rules (examined in Section 13.5) offer the registered proprietor considerable protection against a claim by 'squatters', as she will be given notice of any claim and has the right to object in all but a few circumstances.

Essentially, the argument justifying adverse possession is that if it were not for this doctrine, many pieces of land would be waste, forgotten and unutilised by the paper owner. However, the law of adverse possession inevitably causes problems for people who think that legal title to land – private property, for which the owner has probably 'paid good money' – ought to be protected by the law, come what may. The idea that people can be deprived of their land in such a way certainly raises issues under the Human Rights Act 1998, which are considered in more detail in Section 13.7. In real life, few unregistered titles are perfect, and innumerable difficulties arise when a title needs to be traced to its origin. In most cases, however, it is normally sufficient to prove a good title (the 'root of title') going back only 15 years to satisfy a purchaser of land that has not yet been registered (Law of Property Act 1969, s 23).

In addition to these practical justifications for adverse possession, there are various ethical issues to be considered. The doctrine of adverse possession does not sit comfortably alongside a policy of State protection of private owners (a policy realised, for example, in section 144 of the Legal Aid, Sentencing and Punishment of Offenders Act 2012 which makes it a criminal offence for a person to knowingly live in a residential building as a trespasser). However, it may be equally argued that the public interest lies in supporting industrious and careful squatters who make better use of the land than neglectful paper owners as this encourages the efficient use of land resources (see *Hounslow LBC v Minchinton* (1997) 74 P & CR 221 (CA)).

13.3 When is possession adverse possession?

The most difficult issues in this area of law arise when the courts have to consider what the squatter must do if she is to show that she actually was in adverse possession of another person's land. In *JA Pye (Oxford) Ltd v Graham* [2003] 1 AC 419 (HL), the House of Lords reviewed the law of adverse possession and identified two fundamental elements.

The requirements of adverse possession

1. The possession must be real (or 'factual'): the squatter must act as owner, showing an 'appropriate degree of physical control'.
2. The trespasser must have an intention to possess the land (*animus possidendi*).

13.3.1 Factual possession

The case of *Buckinghamshire CC v Moran* (1988) 56 P & CR 372 (Ch); [1990] Ch 623 (CA) illustrates the sort of behaviour required from the trespasser if she is to be able successfully to claim adverse possession. From 1971, Mr Moran had used as an extension to his garden a patch of land owned by the council which they intended to use for a future bypass. His predecessor had probably done the same since 1967. Mr Moran built a new fence, enclosing the land, and added a new gate and a lock. The council finally noticed him in 1985 and sued for possession. In its analysis of the sort of acts required to constitute factual possession, the Court of Appeal quoted with approval from the first instance judgment by Slade J in *Powell v McFarlane* (1979) 38 P & CR 452 (Ch):

> Factual possession signifies an appropriate degree of physical control ... The question of what acts constitute a sufficient degree of exclusive physical control must depend on the circumstances, in particular the nature of the land and the manner in which land of that nature is commonly used or enjoyed (at 470–71).

Physical control can be shown if the squatter encloses the land or improves it in some way, but trivial acts performed on the land will generally be insufficient to establish factual possession. In *Pye v Graham*, the facts of which are set out in Section 13.1.2, the Grahams kept animals on the land all year round, maintaining and improving it and excluding everyone from it. An occupying owner could not have done more, and the House of Lords found that Mr Graham had clearly been in factual possession of the land.

What acts are required to show 'an appropriate degree of physical control' of residential property such as a house or flat?

> Possession of a flat with a front door which can be locked is obviously different from possession of part of an unfenced moor or hillside. But in either case there must be exclusive

possession, in the sense of occupying and controlling the land in question to the exclusion of others (per Robert Walker LJ, *Simpson v Fergus* (2000) 79 P & CR 398 (CA) at 401).

In *Lambeth LBC v Copercini*, unreported, 1 March 2000, a housing co-operative had squatted in a council-owned property for many years. The judge found clear evidence of factual possession, since the co-operative had decided who should live there, arranged lettings, funded repairs and maintenance, and 'without doubt … treated the property as their own'. In *Ofulue v Bossert* [2009] Ch 1 (CA), [2009] 1 AC 990 (HL) Mr Bossert and his daughter were let into a flat by a former tenant in 1981 and took up residence. At that time, the flat was in so bad a state of repair that the local authority had condemned it as uninhabitable. Mr Bossert spent a considerable amount of time and money repairing the flat and by 1989 estimated its value to be between £150,000 and £200,000. Unsurprisingly, the Court of Appeal found that Bossert's acts were sufficient to amount to factual possession. The Ofulues' appeal to the House of Lords concerned a different issue (see Section 13.3.2).

13.3.2 Intention to possess (*animus possidendi*)

Exactly what constitutes the necessary intention to possess the land has been a contentious issue until relatively recently. It might be thought that a trespasser must show that she intends to become the owner of the land, but, although this may have been the case in the past, it clearly no longer is. The leading case is now *Pye v Graham*, in which Lord Browne-Wilkinson expressly approved the attempts of two earlier judges to explain *animus possidendi*. At first instance in *Buckinghamshire CC v Moran* (1988) 56 P & CR 372 (Ch), Hoffmann J had observed that what is required is:

> not an intention to own or even an intention to acquire ownership but an intention to possess (at 378).

and in *Powell v McFarlane*, Slade J explained:

> *animus possidendi* involves the intention, in one's own name and on one's own behalf, to exclude the world at large, including the owner with the paper title … so far as is reasonably practicable and so far as the process of the law will allow (at 471–72).

It is rare that the court will have direct evidence of an intention to possess the land and exclude the world, but the intention can be inferred from the acts of the trespasser, such as the enclosure of the land by the squatter in *Buckinghamshire CC v Moran* or through otherwise controlling access. Lord Browne-Wilkinson, who gave the leading speech in *Pye v Graham*, stated that:

> intention may be, and frequently is, deduced from the physical acts themselves (at [40]).

Depending on the facts, a person may be deemed to have sufficient intention to possess the land even if she were prepared to accept a licence or a lease from the paper owner, so her claim to adverse possession could still succeed if the licence were not in the end forthcoming. In *Pye v Graham*, Mr Graham admitted that he would have accepted a licence from the paper owners if one had been offered. This was an admission that Lord Diplock thought 'any candid squatter hoping in due course to acquire a possessory title would be almost bound to make' (*Ocean Estates Ltd v Pinder* [1969] 2 AC 19 (PC) at 24) and that did not prevent her from being in possession.

There is a clear difference, though, between a squatter's willingness to recognise the title of the paper owner if asked to do so 'without prejudice' as part of court pleadings (see *Ofulue*) and the written acknowledgement of the paper owner's title. A squatter might make such an acknowledgement by, for example, writing to ask for a lease or a licence to use the land. In claims concerning unregistered land, such an acknowledgement of title is enough to stop time running in the squatter's favour under sections 29–31 of the Limitation Act 1980 (see Section 13.4.4). Sections 29–31 do not apply to cases concerning registered title. However, in cases decided under the LRA 2002, the court will still have to decide whether any acknowledgement (written or otherwise) precludes *animus possidendi* on the part of the squatter.

13.3.3 Must the possession be adverse to the paper owner?

Possession clearly cannot be adverse if it is enjoyed with the paper owner's permission. In the words of Romer LJ:

> if one looks to the position of the occupier and finds that his occupation, his right to occupation, is derived from the owner in the form of permission or agreement or grant, it is not adverse (*Moses v Lovegrove* [1952] 2 QB 533 (CA) at 544).

For example, a mortgagor is in adverse possession as against the mortgagee because her possession is not primarily derived from the mortgage. This will not normally cause any difficulty to the lender because the relevant limitation period will start afresh each time the borrower makes a payment towards the mortgage. However, in *Ashe v National Westminster Bank plc* [2008] 1 WLR 710 (CA), the bank had taken no action since a final payment some 13 years earlier. Consequently, Mr and Mrs Ashe were able to claim the title to the house.

A difficulty has arisen in cases where the paper owner intends to use the land in the future for some particular purpose, but has no present use for it. The uncertainty can be traced back to the judgment of Bramwell LJ in *Leigh v Jack* (1879–80) 5 Ex D 264 (CA), where he said:

> in order to defeat a title by dispossessing the former owner, acts must be done which are inconsistent with his enjoyment of the soil for the purposes for which he intended to use it (at 273).

Subsequently, the courts developed the doctrine of the implied licence to show that the possession is not adverse. In *Wallis's Cayton Holiday Camp Ltd v Shell-Mex & BP Ltd* [1975] QB 94 (CA), a petrol company bought a garage by a proposed new road with the intention of extending the garage if the new road were to be built. Wallis's farmed this land and then used it to enlarge their holiday camp business. Their use of the land totalled just over the necessary 12 years, and they claimed adverse possession of it. They lost by a majority decision in the Court of Appeal. Lord Denning stated:

> When the true owner of land intends to use it for a particular purpose in the future, but has no immediate use for it, and so leaves it unoccupied, he does not lose his title to it simply because some other person enters on it and uses it for some temporary purpose ... his user is to be ascribed to the licence or permission of the true owner (at 103).

This 'heresy', had it been allowed to stand, could have spelled the end of adverse possession in cases where the paper owner had in mind a future use for the land, or at least severely limited its effect. The doctrine of the implied licence was expressly abolished by para 8(4) of Sch 1 Limitation Act 1980. In *Pye v Graham*, Lord Browne-Wilkinson made it clear that the heresy had not survived the 1980 Act:

> The suggestion that the sufficiency of the possession can depend on the intention not of the squatter but of the true owner is heretical and wrong ... The highest it can be put is that, if

the squatter is aware of a special purpose for which the paper owner uses or intends to use the land and the use made by the squatter does not conflict with that use, that may provide some support for a finding as a question of fact that the squatter had no intention to possess the land in the ordinary sense but only an intention to occupy it until needed by the paper owner (at [45]).

The spectre of the *Leigh v Jack* heresy briefly returned in *Beaulane Properties Ltd v Palmer* [2006] Ch 79 (Ch), when Nicholas Strauss QC held that the only way in which the law of adverse possession (under LRA 1925, s 75) could be consistent with the European Convention on Human Rights was to require the squatter's use of the land to be inconsistent with the use of the paper owner. This judgment was rejected by the Court of Appeal in *Ofulue v Bossert* [2009] Ch 1 (CA) as inconsistent with the subsequent decision of the European Court of Human Rights in *JA Pye (Oxford) Ltd v UK* (2008) 46 EHRR 45.

An interesting question arises if the paper owner writes to the squatter granting her a licence to use the land. On the face of it, since the squatter now occupies the land with permission, the possession can no longer be adverse. Indeed, in *BP Properties* Ltd v *Buckler* (1988) 55 P & CR 337 (CA), a case which has been subject to some criticism (see Wallace, 1994), the paper owner wrote to the squatter giving her permission to remain on the land for the rest of her life. The result was that:

> So far as Mrs. Buckler was concerned, even though she did not 'accept' the terms of the letter BP Properties Ltd. would, in the absence of any repudiation by her of the two letters, have been bound to treat her as in possession as licensee on the terms of the letters (per Dillon L at 346).

Although the squatter did not respond to the letters (indeed, probably because she failed to respond), the paper owner was deemed to have ended the adverse possession.

13.3.4 Criminal trespass

On 1 September 2012, it became a criminal offence for a person to live (or intend to live) in a residential building as a trespasser if she entered those premises as a trespasser and knows or ought to know that he or she is a trespasser (Legal Aid, Sentencing and Punishment of Offenders Act 2012, s 144). It was not long before the relationship between this new offence and the ancient doctrine of adverse possession had to be considered by the courts. In *Best v Chief Land Registrar* [2014] 3 All ER 637 (Admin), Ousley J, after considering the arguments from public interest and the legal precedents, held that adverse possession can arise where the act of possession is an offence.

13.4 Establishing title to unregistered land

13.4.1 The limitation period

Section 15(1) of the Limitation Act 1980 provides:

> No action shall be brought by any person to recover any land after the expiration of twelve years from the date on which the right of action accrued to him or, if it first accrued to some other person through whom he claims, to that person.

The section states clearly that the paper owner cannot bring an action if 12 years have passed since the right to do so arose, that is, since the squatter (by definition, a trespasser) moved onto the land with the necessary intention to occupy it (see Section 13.3.2). The statute does not operate to transfer the paper owner's title to the adverse possessor, but, by refusing any remedy, merely ensures that no one can remove her.

Not only can the paper owner not bring an action to recover possession after 12 years, but her title to the land is extinguished after that period (Limitation Act 1980, s 17). It is important to remember that, as the squatter herself is not a 'purchaser' of land, she is, like someone who simply inherits land, bound by all earlier interests in the land, whether they are legal or equitable, and whether or not they were protected by registration or she had notice of them.

By section 38 of the Limitation Act 1980, 'land' means more than just the legal freehold; it includes, for example, equitable freeholds and legal and equitable leases. Consequently, it is possible to obtain title to a long lease by adverse possession as well as title to freehold land (see Section 13.6). There are special rules for adversely possessing Crown land (the limitation period is 30 years) and for special classes, such as between trustees and their beneficiaries (see Megarry and Wade, 2012, § 35–037–35–043 for more details).

13.4.2 Dispossession of the paper owner

In order for time to start running in the squatter's favour, the paper owner must either have been dispossessed of the land or have discontinued possession (Limitation Act 1980, Sched. 1, para 1). It is now clear, following the leading case of *JA Pye (Oxford) Ltd v Graham* [2003] 1 AC 419 (HL), that all that is required is for the squatter to take possession of the land without the permission of the owner.

If a tenancy is an oral periodic tenancy (see Section 5.5.2), time can begin to run in favour of the tenant from the time she stops paying rent, since the tenancy is then deemed to have ended (Limitation Act 1980, Sched. 1, para 5(2)). In *Hayward v Chaloner* [1968] 1 QB 107 (CA), a quarter of an acre of land was let as a garden on such a tenancy to whoever was the rector of a small village. For some 25 years from 1942, no rent was paid, and there was no acknowledgement of the paper owners' title. The then rector decided to sell the land as his own, and the paper owners decided to fight him; they had failed to collect the rent, not because they forgot, but because of 'their loyalty and generosity to the church'. The rector won by a majority decision in the Court of Appeal, although all the judges regretted it:

> The generous indulgence of the plaintiffs and their predecessors in title, loyal churchmen all, having resulted in a free accretion at their expense to the lands of their church, their reward may be in the next world. But in this jurisdiction we can only qualify them for that reward by allowing the [Rector's] appeal (per Russell LJ at 123–24).

13.4.3 Continuous possession

The squatter must prove that she has been in continuous possession throughout the required period. Any interruption to her possession means that the period must begin again. However, the adverse possession need not have been by one squatter. In *Williams v Usherwood* (1983) 45 P & CR 235 (CA) (see Section 13.1.1), there were several different owners of Number 31 who, in succession, adversely possessed the land continuously for the necessary period.

13.4.4 Stopping the time running

A paper owner can bring an action for possession within the limitation period. Of itself, this does not stop time running, but simply means that the paper owner is not time barred. She must, therefore, pursue the action and bring it to a successful conclusion (*Markfield Investments Ltd v Evans* [2001] 1 WLR 1321 (CA)).

The Limitation Act 1980 provides that the period of adverse possession will stop running if the squatter acknowledges in writing the title of the paper owner (ss 29–31). Whether a document amounts to such an acknowledgement depends on the true construction of that document in the context of all the surrounding circumstances (*Allen v Matthews* [2007] 2 P & CR 21 (CA)). In *Edginton v Clark* [1964] 1 QB 367 (CA), the claimant had occupied bombed land in the East End of London for about seven years and then offered to buy it from the owner. No sale followed and, after a further ten years, he claimed adverse possession. It was held that the offer to buy was an acknowledgement of the owner's title and that therefore the squatter's possession was interrupted.

Under section 32 of the Limitation Act, the adverse possessor must prove that she did not deliberately conceal her activities or keep her possession through fraud. If there is any deception, time starts to run from the date when the paper owner 'could with reasonable diligence have discovered it'. In *Beaulane Properties Ltd v Palmer* [2006] Ch 79 (Ch), Palmer had originally occupied the disputed land under the terms of a licence granted by Beaulane's predecessor in title, but continued in occupation when this was terminated in 1986. In 1991, Palmer told a representative of the then paper owner of the land that he had an arrangement to use the land without making it clear that it had been terminated in 1986. Nicholas Strauss QC, sitting as a deputy judge in the Chancery Division, held that this informal and unexpected conversation was sufficient to amount to concealment, and that the period of adverse possession only started to run in 1991.

13.5 Establishing title to registered land

Until the relevant provisions of the LRA 2002 came into force on 13 October 2003, the rules applying to claims of adverse possession over registered land were very similar to those that applied to unregistered land. In its 1998 Consultation Paper, the Law Commission recognised that many of the traditional justifications for adverse possession (see Section 13.2) hold no relevance in a regime where title to land is registered. The Commission went on to propose the fundamental changes to the operation of the principles of adverse possession which were enacted in the LRA 2002 (see (1998) Law Com No 254, Part X). Consequently, although the kind of conduct that will amount to adverse possession is the same whether title to the land is registered or unregistered (LRA 2002, Sched. 6, para 11(1)), the rules that determine the consequences of such possession are very different.

13.5.1 The old rules: the LRA 1925

Prior to 13 October 2003, where the title to the land was registered, the rules prevented the registered owner from bringing an action to evict the squatter after 12 years. Unlike the position in unregistered land, however, her title was not extinguished; instead, she held it on trust for the squatter (LRA 1925, s 75(1)). The squatter could also, if she wished, apply to the Land Registry to become the registered proprietor after 12 years (LRA 1925, s 75(2)).

13.5.2 The new rules: the LRA 2002

The rules in the LRA 2002 mean that since 13 October 2003, it has been much more difficult for a squatter to obtain title. The most significant changes are that:

- the rules set out in the Limitation Act 1980 do not apply to registered land after this date (LRA 2002, s 96): registered proprietors are no longer statute barred from pursuing claims against trespassers; and
- an adverse possessor must now claim the land by applying to the Registrar to be registered as the proprietor of the land, following the procedure set out in Schedule 6 to the LRA 2002.

An outline of the Schedule 6 process

Para 1   In most cases, a squatter may apply to the Land Registry to be registered as owner of the land after *ten* years' adverse possession (60 years in the case of the foreshore owned by the Crown: see para 13).

Para 2   The Registrar informs the following of the squatter's claim: the registered proprietor, the owner of any registered charge on the land (such as a mortgage lender) and, if the land is leasehold, the registered proprietor of the freehold.

Para 4   If the Registrar has received no response within three months, the adverse possessor becomes the new registered proprietor.

Para 5   If there is an objection within the three-month period, the squatter's application will automatically be rejected unless:

Para 5(2)   (a) *The paper owner has acted unconscionably and is estopped from denying title.* This would not include a situation where the applicant is on the land with the permission of the owner, since such occupation could not amount to adverse possession (see Section 13.3.3). However, it could arise where a person has developed land thinking it belonged to her, and the paper owner, aware of the true position, has allowed this to happen. It could also occur where a buyer of land has paid the purchase price but there has been no valid contract and thus no transfer of the equitable title.

Para 5(3)   (b) *The adverse possessor is entitled to be registered as the owner for some reason other than her adverse possession of the land.* This might arise, for example, where the possessor is entitled to a conveyance of the land under the terms of a will. It might also occur when, despite having purchased and paid for the land, the registered title has not yet been transferred to the buyer (see Section 12.5), although in this case, it might be simpler for the possessor to seek specific performance of the contract.

Para 5(4)   (c) *The disputed land is next to land already owned by the adverse possessor, the boundary between the two plots is unclear and she has occupied the land for ten years, reasonably believing that it belonged to her.*

Para 6   If the squatter's application is rejected and none of the conditions in para 5 applies, she may make a further application to have title to the land transferred into her name provided that the registered proprietor has not taken steps through the courts to evict her. Following this second application, the registered proprietor cannot prevent the claimant being registered as the new proprietor of the land with the same class of title as that of the paper owner she has dispossessed.

These reforms in respect of registered land mean that the paper owner does not automatically lose her right to evict a trespasser after 12 years' adverse possession, as formerly, but will be warned by the Registry that a squatter is attempting to gain title to her land. However, if she does nothing to regain possession of the land, she will lose it unless it subsequently becomes apparent that the squatter had not been in adverse possession (as defined at Section 13.3) for the relevant period at the date of the application to the Registrar (as was the case in *Baxter v Mannion* [2011] 1 WLR 1594 (CA); see Section 15.9.1).

Other important differences between the new rules and those that apply to unregistered land include:

- Neither written acknowledgement of title nor concealment nor fraud by the squatter has any specific consequences under Schedule 6 (compare ss 29–31 and 32 of the Limitation Act 1980; see Section 13.4.4). In many cases, however, such factors will be sufficient to demonstrate that the squatter did not meet the requirements for being in adverse possession (see Section 13.3.2). They are only likely to be relevant if the registered proprietor fails to object in time to the squatter's application to be registered as proprietor of the land.
- Paragraph 11 of Schedule 6 limits the circumstances in which occupation by a previous squatter can count towards the ten-year period to:
  - where the applicant is the successor in title of the first squatter, having bought the land from her or having inherited it, and then moved into possession; or
  - where the applicant was the original squatter, was dispossessed by another squatter but then was able to regain possession.

13.6 Leases and adverse possession

The rules about leases and adverse possession can be complex, and, again, the results may differ depending on whether title to the land is registered or unregistered.

If a squatter takes possession of land subject to a lease, the possession is adverse to the tenant; that is, it is the tenant who is liable to lose her interest in the land, not the lessor. This is because it is the tenant who is entitled to possession; the lessor is entitled only to the rent. The lessor has no right to possession until the lease ends, and it is also at that time that the squatter's period of adverse possession against the lessor begins.

An interesting situation arises if a tenant (of an unregistered 99-year lease, let us say) against whom a squatter has been in adverse possession for 12 years and who therefore could now look forward to many more years of possession surrenders her lease to her lessor (see Section 5.7). There is little point in the tenant continuing with the lease, since she now has no cause of action against the squatter. Rather surprisingly, perhaps, following the tenant's surrender of the lease, the lessor can bring an action for possession against the squatter (*Fairweather v St Marylebone Property Co Ltd* [1963] AC 510 (HL)). Having evicted the squatter, there is then nothing to prevent the lessor from granting a new lease to her former tenant.

Under the LRA 1925 rules for registered land, the position was different. In *Central London Commercial Estates Ltd v Kato Kagaku Ltd* [1998] 4 All ER 948 (Ch), a squatter had adversely possessed registered land against the tenant for more than 12 years. However, the squatter failed to make an application under section 75(2) of the LRA 1925 to be registered as proprietor (see Section 13.5) before the tenant surrendered the lease to the landlord. Applying section 75(1) of the LRA 1925, Sedley J held that the tenant was trustee for the squatter, who was now entitled to remain on the land for the remaining term of the lease. This decision effectively prevented a tenant of registered land from surrendering her lease once the 12-year period of adverse possession had been completed.

It is unlikely that this situation will arise under the new rules contained in Schedule 6 of the LRA 2002, as adverse possession now gives rise to a right to apply to become the registered proprietor of the estate, rather than to a trust. The tenant will have no need to surrender the lease to the landlord, since either she will object to the squatter's application and subsequently gain possession, or the squatter will succeed in her application, with the result that the squatter's name will be registered at the Land Registry with the title of the former tenant (see Section 13.5). This means that she will now be subject to the covenants in the lease, and failure to comply with them may result in forfeiture of the lease by the lessor (see Section 6.5).

13.7 Adverse possession and human rights

In *JA Pye (Oxford) Ltd v Graham* [2003] 1 AC 419 (HL) the question was raised as to whether the use of the Limitation Act to deny a landowner the right to bring an action to recover her land amounted to a breach of Article 1, Protocol 1 of the European Convention on Human Rights (depriving a person of her property without compensation). Although the action was between private individuals, the deprivation of the property resulted from statutory authority (LRA 1925, s 75), thus allowing the Convention to be invoked. By the time the case had reached the House of Lords, it had become clear that the Human Rights Act 1998 had no retrospective effect and so did not apply in *Pye v Graham*. However, Pye was able to refer the matter to the European Court of Human Rights at Strasbourg. The period between the decisions of the House of Lords and the Court of Human Rights provides the context for the first instance judgment in *Beaulane Properties Ltd v Palmer* [2006] Ch 79 (Ch) (see Sections 13.3.3 and 13.4.4). Like *Pye v Graham*, this case concerned section 75 of the LRA 1925, but unlike *Pye v Graham* the Human Rights Act 1998 applied. The judge held that section 75 of the LRA 1925 could only be interpreted as being consistent with the Human Rights Act 1998 if the doctrine of adverse possession were limited to those cases where the squatter's use was inconsistent with the paper owner's purpose for the land. He went on to hold that for that reason, he was not bound by the House of Lords' decision to the contrary in *Pye v Graham*.

The Grand Chamber of the European Court of Human Rights finally settled the *Pye* case in 2007 (see *JA Pye (Oxford) Ltd v UK* (2008) 46 EHRR 45). A majority of the court concluded that the pre-LRA 2002 law of adverse possession was compatible with the principles of the European Convention on Human Rights, since:

- it was already accepted that periods of limitation were compatible with the Convention;
- the period required in this case was not excessively short;
- the paper owner should have been aware of the limitation period; and
- relatively limited action was required by the paper owner to stop the period from running.

The decision in *Pye v UK* means that section 75 of the LRA 1925 is generally compliant with the Convention and that compliance does not need to be determined on a case-by-case basis (*Ofulue v Bossert* [2009] Ch 1 (CA), applying *Harrow LBC v Qazi* [2004] 1 AC 983 (HL)). It also means that the decision in *Beaulane Properties Ltd* (see Section 13.4.4) is wrong.

There is little doubt that the provisions in Schedule 6 to the LRA 2002 are compliant with the Human Rights Act; indeed, this was expressly recognised by the dissenting minority of the Grand Chamber in *Pye v UK*.

13.8 Adverse possession in the twenty-first century

The traditional justifications for retaining adverse possession in a private system of unregistered title to land remain as convincing as ever. In unregistered land, titles to land are relative and an English court will assist the party with the better claim to possession, even if the final outcome in a particular case seems disproportionate or unjust. In a public system of registered land, where most titles are absolute and guaranteed by the State, some of the traditional justifications are not so persuasive. However, adverse possession is retained within the LRA 2002 scheme as it helps to ensure that land remains marketable and can prevent injustice.

It is evident that the LRA 2002 scheme in registered land will make it much more difficult for a squatter to gain title to the land. Indeed, this is a deliberate policy which the framers of the Act (and the Land Registry) hope will provide a strong incentive for the owners of unregistered titles to apply for voluntary registration. Much of the land that remains unregistered is made up of large estates, and the owners of such land (often public authorities or large corporations) must remain vigilant in order to protect themselves from being dispossessed by a squatter.

The first decade of the twenty-first century saw a number of significant cases concerning adverse possession, including those that explored the interface between land law and human rights. It seems likely that the doctrine will attract less attention from the courts as the rules of the LRA 2002 become increasingly dominant. However, while the role of the doctrine in high-value cases, such as *JA Pye (Oxford) Ltd v Graham* and *Ofulue v Bossert*, may be on the wane, it seems that it will continue to be highly significant to neighbours who find themselves in dispute, as the Williams and the Usherwoods did. Disputes relating to adverse possession now form a significant part of the business of the Land Registration Division of the Property Chamber of the First-tier Tribunal (and its predecessor, the Adjudicator to Her Majesty's Land Registry. (More details can be found by following the links Land Registry Division's website at www.justice.gov.uk/tribunals/land-registration.)

Summary

13.1 The doctrine of adverse possession allows a person who has been in possession of land for a significant period of time to claim title to (that is, ownership of) that land.

13.2 The main justifications for recognising title by adverse possession are based on the weaknesses of a deeds-based conveyancing system. The LRA 2002 significantly restricts the doctrine insofar as it applies to registered titles.

13.3 To be in adverse possession, a person must:

- act as owner of the land, showing an appropriate degree of physical control; and
- have sufficient intention to possess the land (known as *animus possidendi*).

13.4 The Limitation Act 1980 is central to the operation of adverse possession in *unregistered* land. Twelve years' unconcealed adverse possession, without interruptions, prevents the paper owner repossessing the land.

Summary cont'd

13.5 A person claiming title of registered land can now apply to be registered as proprietor after ten years' adverse possession. The registered proprietor is given warning of the threat to her land and, except in a number of specific circumstances, can prevent the squatter being registered as proprietor. However, if the registered proprietor then fails to evict the squatter within two years of the initial application, the squatter will automatically be entitled to be registered as proprietor of the title.

13.6 Care must be taken when dealing with adverse possession claims where the land is subject to a lease, especially if the land is unregistered or the rules of the LRA 1925 apply.

13.7 After some controversy, it is now accepted by the courts that the various rules relating to adverse possession are generally compliant with the European Convention on Human Rights.

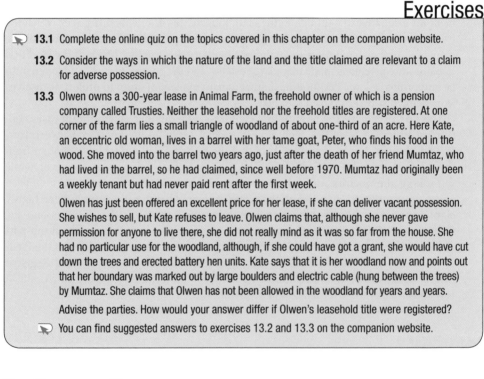

Exercises

13.1 Complete the online quiz on the topics covered in this chapter on the companion website.

13.2 Consider the ways in which the nature of the land and the title claimed are relevant to a claim for adverse possession.

13.3 Olwen owns a 300-year lease in Animal Farm, the freehold owner of which is a pension company called Trusties. Neither the leasehold nor the freehold titles are registered. At one corner of the farm lies a small triangle of woodland of about one-third of an acre. Here Kate, an eccentric old woman, lives in a barrel with her tame goat, Peter, who finds his food in the wood. She moved into the barrel two years ago, just after the death of her friend Mumtaz, who had lived in the barrel, so he had claimed, since well before 1970. Mumtaz had originally been a weekly tenant but had never paid rent after the first week.

Olwen has just been offered an excellent price for her lease, if she can deliver vacant possession. She wishes to sell, but Kate refuses to leave. Olwen claims that, although she never gave permission for anyone to live there, she did not really mind as it was so far from the house. She had no particular use for the woodland, although, if she could have got a grant, she would have cut down the trees and erected battery hen units. Kate says that it is her woodland now and points out that her boundary was marked out by large boulders and electric cable (hung between the trees) by Mumtaz. She claims that Olwen has not been allowed in the woodland for years and years.

Advise the parties. How would your answer differ if Olwen's leasehold title were registered?

You can find suggested answers to exercises 13.2 and 13.3 on the companion website.

Further reading

Davis, 'Informal Acquisition and Loss of Rights in Land: What Justifies the Doctrines?' (2000) 20 LS 198

Dixon, 'Adverse Possession and the Land Registration Act 2002' [2009] 73 Conv 169

Dixon, 'Human Rights and Adverse Possession: The Final Word' [2008] 72 Conv 160

Dockray, 'Why Do We Need Adverse Possession?' [1985] Conv 272

McCormick, 'Adverse Possession and Future Enjoyment' [1986] Conv 434

Tee, 'A Harsh Twilight' [2003] CLJ 36

Wallace, 'Limitation, Prescription and Unsolicited Permission' [1994] Conv 196

Chapter 14 follows overleaf.

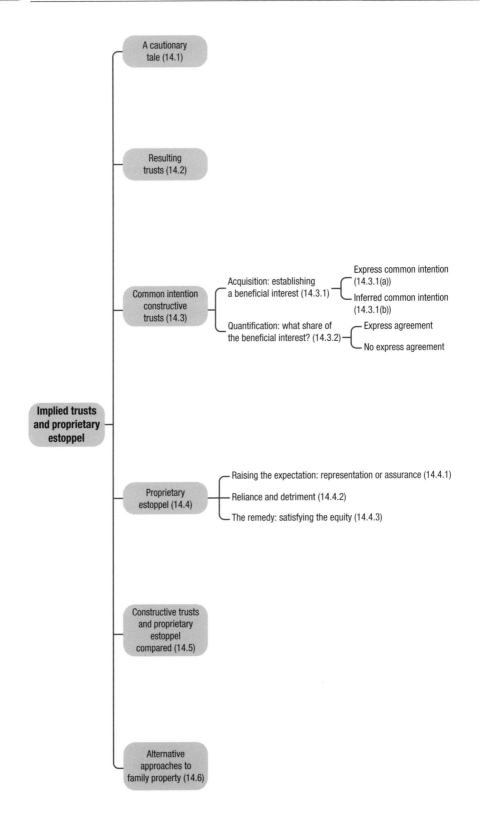

Key concepts

- **Common intention constructive trust** – a trust arising out of an express or implied agreement to share the ownership of property.
- **Implied trust** – a trust created by operation of law rather than by express words or statutory provision.
- **Proprietary estoppel** – a right in equity arising out of the claimant's detrimental reliance on representations or assurances given by the defendant as to the claimant's interest in certain property.
- **Resulting trust** – a trust arising by operation of law in which the beneficial interest is vested in the person who financed the acquisition of that property or in the person who transferred the property to the legal owner without also transferring the entire beneficial interest.

14.1 A cautionary tale

This is a cautionary tale, which all unmarried couples who are contemplating the purchase of residential property as their home, and all solicitors who advise them, should study. The facts are not in dispute and are unusual only in the sense that a great deal of time has elapsed since the parties separated.

Thus begins the judgment of Wall LJ in *Jones v Kernott* [2010] 1 WLR 2401 (CA). The relationship between the parties had lasted from 1984 to 1993. They never married, but they had two children and in 1984 they purchased a house in joint names. Ms Jones conceded that had the house been sold when the relationship first broke down, she and Mr Kernott would have been entitled to equal shares in the proceeds. However, this was not what happened. Instead, Ms Jones continued to live in the family home with the children, paying the mortgage and all the other outgoings. She did not ask for, and did not receive, any financial assistance from Mr Kernott, who purchased another house in his sole name in 1996. It was not until ten years later that Mr Kernott sought to recover his share in the family home. The question was whether he was still entitled to half of the value of the house or whether the proportion of his share had changed after he left the house and ceased to contribute to the mortgage. The Supreme Court gave its judgment in the case in November 2011. How it finally answered the question is considered at Section 14.3.2.

When a marriage or civil partnership comes to an end, the courts have considerable powers to make the best provision in the circumstances under the Matrimonial Causes Act 1973 and the Civil Partnership Act 2004. However, these powers are not available in other circumstances. Consequently, disputes between partners who are neither married nor civil partners, or between siblings and between friends who have bought a house together, fall to be decided under the general principles of property law. These principles were developed in the context of the nineteenth and early twentieth centuries, when property law was concerned more with enabling people to realise their investment than with sharing (or distributing) a family home. Despite a broad consensus of opinion that some relationships need to be given special treatment, there seems to be insufficient political will to provide a statutory solution. For example, a new statutory scheme to apply to cohabitants proposed by the Law Commission in 2007 (Law Com No 307, *Cohabitation: The Financial Consequences of Relationship Breakdown*) was broadly welcomed, but not implemented.

Of course,

> In an ideal world, those who intend to own property or a share in it would do three things: they would agree what they intended to do; they would then record their intentions; and they would take legal advice to ensure that what they wanted had been achieved in a manner which the law recognises. However … life is not like that (Clarke, 1992).

In fact, this is often what is done in the case of a business venture. It is relatively rare for commercial cases concerning implied trusts in land to come before the courts. Unfortunately, the situation tends to be very different when the land is the family home. However sensible it might be for two people to sort out their property and financial arrangements before they buy a house (or before a person moves in to live with someone who already owns a house), to open these kinds of negotiations might be thought to be somewhat calculating and might risk undermining the relationship between the parties. Equally, such thoughts might never have crossed the parties' minds at such an emotional stage in their relationship. Alternatively, there may have been some informal, but unexpressed, understanding between the parties. Even where this was the case, the circumstances may have changed beyond what was ever envisaged by the parties when the house was acquired: the relationship may break down, or a mortgage lender might seek possession of the land because of mortgage arrears.

The simplest form of solution in such circumstances is the doctrine of resulting trusts (see Section 14.2). However, this doctrine (based on equating beneficial interest to financial contribution) is now almost redundant in cases concerning the family land. In most domestic cases, the court will seek to discern from the wider circumstances of the case what the parties intended (hence the term 'common intention' constructive trust). If a claimant is unable to establish either a resulting trust or a common intention constructive trust, he may still be able to establish some right to the land through the doctrine of proprietary estoppel (see Section 14.4).

14.2 Resulting trusts

A resulting trust can arise when a person contributes towards the purchase price of land, but the legal title is transferred into the name of someone else. In such circumstances, the *presumption* is that the parties intended that the legal owner hold the land on trust for the benefit of the contributors in the same proportions as their contributions. Thus, when Mrs Boland (see *Williams & Glyn's Bank Ltd v Boland* [1981] AC 487 (HL), considered in detail in Section 15.8.2) contributed to the purchase price of the house, Mr Boland, as the sole registered proprietor, was deemed to be holding the land on trust for himself and his wife through a resulting trust. However, in the more recent case of *Stack v Dowden* [2007] 2 AC 432 (HL), the House of Lords indicated that where family land is held in joint names, it should normally be treated as a common intention constructive trust (see Section 14.3) rather than a resulting trust. The reason for this is that constructive trusts are much more flexible. When determining the terms of the trust and the extent of the various beneficial shares, 'a resulting trust "crystallises" on the date that the property is acquired' (per Peter Gibson LJ *Curley v Parkes* [2004] EWCA Civ 1515 at [18]), whereas the common intention trust allows the court to take a much wider variety of factors into account in order to determine the terms of that trust (see Section 14.3.2). However, the fact that all of the parties to a transaction are related does not necessarily mean that the arrangement is not a business enterprise to which the resulting trust analysis will be more appropriate. In *Laskar v Laskar* [2008] 1 WLR 2695 (CA), a mother and daughter joined together to purchase the mother's council house, with the purpose of renting it out to tenants. Neuberger LJ (who dissented from the *ratio* in *Stack v Dowden*, but not its outcome) held that despite the familial appearance of the case, it gave rise to a resulting trust because:

> the primary purpose of the purchase of the property was as an investment, not as a home …
> To my mind it would not be right to apply the reasoning in *Stack v Dowden* to such a case as this, where the parties primarily purchased the property as an investment for rental income and capital appreciation, even where their relationship is a familial one (at [17]).

When the land that is subject to a resulting trust is sold, the proceeds of sale are divided between the co-owners in direct proportion to their contributions to the purchase price. If the contribution is by way of a gift or a loan to the legal owner, the presumption of a resulting trust will be rebutted, and the contributor will not gain a beneficial interest (see, for example, *Fowkes v Pascoe* (1874–75) 10 Ch App 343 (CACh)). There is also an old doctrine called the 'presumption of advancement'. The courts used to presume that money given by a husband to his wife, or by a father to his child, for the purchase of land was a gift, and that it was not intended that the parent should acquire any interest in the land. In *McGrath v Wallis* [1995] 2 FLR 114 (CA) the Court of Appeal followed the modern line that this presumption is now a 'judicial instrument of the last resort' and is rebuttable by even the slightest evidence. Here, where a father had provided money to help his son buy a house for them to live in together, there was evidence (from an incomplete deed) of an intention that the land was to be held on trust for them both as tenants in common. Therefore, the presumption of advancement did not operate, and when the father died intestate, the son's sister was entitled on the intestacy to a share in her father's interest in the land. The presumption of advancement will finally be abolished if and when section 199 of the Equality Act 2010 is brought into force.

Since nowadays people tend to depend on mortgage loans to finance the purchase of their homes, it is common for people who do not hold legal title to attempt to establish a beneficial interest in the land through their contributions to the mortgage repayments. Accepting liability for a mortgage at the time the property is purchased may be sufficient to give rise to a resulting trust, as in the case of *Cowcher v Cowcher* [1972] 1 WLR 425 (Fam). However, merely contributing to the repayments of a mortgage granted by the legal owner is not sufficient (see *Curley v Parkes*).

14.3 Common intention constructive trusts

Constructive trusts are potentially much wider than resulting trusts. There are a number of types of constructive trust. This section focuses on constructive trusts that arise out of the *common intention* of the parties, and brief reference is made to *remedial* constructive trusts in Section 14.6. Other types of constructive trust tend to be covered as part of courses on equity and trusts rather than land law, and detailed accounts of them can be found in most of the standard textbooks on the law of trusts.

There are two main questions that need to be addressed in common intention constructive trust cases.

- *Acquisition*   Is the claimant entitled to a beneficial interest in the land?
- *Quantification* If so, what is the extent of that interest?

Where legal title to the land is vested in all the parties to the dispute, the beneficial interests will be acquired under the terms of any express trust or by virtue of a statutory trust imposed by sections 34–36 of the LPA 1925 (see Section 11.2). Unless there is clear evidence of intention to the contrary:

> it should be assumed that equity follows the law and that the beneficial interests reflect the legal interests in the property (per Baroness Hale, *Stack v Dowden* [2007] 2 AC 432 (HL) at [54]).

Consequently, if legal title to the family home is vested in both partners, the court will normally move directly to the question of quantification. *Jones v Kernott* [2012] 1 AC 776 (SC) falls into this category. The main issue before the court was Ms Jones' argument that Mr Kernott's entitlement to the land had been reduced by the change of circumstances after their relationship broke down. However, in cases where there is no express or statutory trust (because, for example, the legal title is vested in only one partner, rather than in both partners), the court must consider whether a beneficial interest exists at all, before turning to the question of quantification.

14.3.1 Acquisition: establishing a beneficial interest

In *Lloyds Bank plc v Rosset* [1991] 1 AC 107 (HL), Mr and Mrs Rosset wished to buy a semi-derelict farmhouse using money from a Swiss trust fund, but the trustees of the fund insisted that legal title was transferred to Mr Rosset alone. For six months, Mrs Rosset supervised the renovation and decoration of the house. Mr Rosset subsequently mortgaged the house to the bank without his wife's knowledge. When the bank brought possession proceedings, she claimed that she had an equitable interest under an informal trust. This, she argued, would enable her to claim an overriding interest under section 70(1)(g) of the LRA 1925 (see Section 15.8.2) and thus defeat the mortgage. The House of Lords held that she had not shown that she had gained an interest, and therefore the bank was able to defeat her claim.

Since the land was held in the sole name of Mr Rosset, and since there had been no express declaration of trust, Lord Bridge said that an equitable interest would only arise if Mrs Rosset could demonstrate that there had been a *common intention* that she should own a share in the land. Lord Bridge said that this could only be shown by either:

1. an *express agreement* that the land should be co-owned, together with some act by the claimant to her detriment or some significant alteration of her position in reliance on the agreement; or
2. in the absence of an express agreement, *an act by the claimant from which the court may infer a common intention*, giving rise to an interest under a constructive trust. Lord Bridge thought that the only act which would be sufficient to justify inferring an agreement would be the direct contribution of money (such as the repayment of a mortgage) towards the purchase of the property.

Mrs Rosset failed under the first category because there had been no express agreement that she should have a beneficial interest. She failed under the second category because her work on the house did not amount to a sufficient act from which to infer such an agreement.

14.3.1(a) Express common intention

In *Rosset*, Lord Bridge approved the earlier Court of Appeal decision in *Grant v Edwards* [1986] Ch 638 (CA) in which a man and a woman lived together for about ten years and had two children. He had told her that her name should not go on the legal title of the house that they shared because this might prejudice her divorce proceedings. Although clearly he never intended that she should have a beneficial share in the house, the Court of Appeal was prepared to find that his excuse for not putting her name on the title amounted to evidence of a common intention, since otherwise no excuse would have been needed. In addition, the couple had shared equally some money left over from an insurance claim when the house had partly burnt down. The woman had acted to her detriment in reliance on the common intention by paying all the household bills:

> In a case such as the present, where there has been no written declaration or agreement, nor any direct provision by the plaintiff of part of the purchase price so as to give rise to a resulting trust in her favour, she must establish a common intention between her and the defendant, acted on by her, that she should have a beneficial interest in the property ... In my judgment [she must prove] conduct on which [she] could not reasonably be expected to embark unless she was to have an interest in the house (per Nourse LJ at 646).

As the claimant had established that there had been a common intention that the house should be co-owned and that she had relied on this to her detriment, the Court imposed a constructive trust on the man and awarded her a share of the beneficial interest.

In *Hammond v Mitchell* [1991] 1 WLR 1127 (Fam), a man and woman lived together for 12 years in a bungalow registered in his name. He had promised her that she was equally the owner of the property but said that he could not put her name on the Register for tax reasons. There were also several businesses and a house in Spain, and she claimed a half-share in all of these. Waite J, in some despair at the detailed and conflicting evidence and the 19 days of the trial, finally awarded her a half-share in the bungalow. The full flavour of the dispute can only be gained from reading the report. There was evidence of a promise that the land was half hers, of her involvement in the businesses and their sharing of whatever money they had, and of her agreement to risk any interest she might have in the bungalow as security for a bank loan for business purposes. All these taken together showed a common agreement plus an act to her detriment. She therefore satisfied what is now known as the first *Rosset* category. However, the judge commented:

> The primary emphasis accorded by the law in cases of this kind to express discussions between the parties ... means that the tenderest exchanges of a common law courtship may assume an unforeseen significance many years later when they are brought under equity's microscope and subjected to an analysis under which many thousands of pounds of value may be liable to turn on fine questions as to whether the relevant words were spoken in earnest or in dalliance and with or without representational intent (at 1139).

To establish a common intention constructive trust under this heading, the claimant must establish an express agreement relating to the ownership of the land and detrimental reliance on that agreement. The claimant does not, however, have to show that the acts of reliance formed part of the bargain, or that they were specifically envisaged by the defendant:

> once a finding of an express arrangement or agreement has been made, all that the claimant to a beneficial share under a constructive trust needs to show is that he or she has 'acted to his or her detriment or significantly altered his or her position in reliance on the agreement' (per Rimmer LJ, *Parris v Williams* [2009] 1 P & CR 9 (CA) at [42]).

An express agreement that falls short of granting co-ownership (such as a loan between the parties) is not a sufficient foundation for a trust under this heading. Neither can the claimant rely upon an agreement that is unenforceable. For example, in *Smith v Cooper* [2010] EWCA Civ 722 the claimant was ultimately unable to establish a constructive trust because he had used undue influence to obtain his agreement with the defendant.

14.3.1(b) Inferred common intention

Under this second category, the claimant must establish that there are sufficient grounds to enable the court to infer the presence of an agreement to share ownership of the land. This is not the same as saying that the court can impose a trust or impute an agreement wherever it would be fair to do so (see Section 14.6). In *Rosset*, Lord Bridge indicated that he considered that nothing short of a monetary contribution to the purchase would be sufficient to justify inferring such an agreement.

There is support for this view from the earlier case of *Burns v Burns* [1984] Ch 317 (CA), where an unmarried couple lived together for 19 years in a house, legal title to which was held by the man. The woman brought up their children, kept house and, when the children were older, took a job which allowed her to contribute to the housekeeping and buy various household items such as a washing machine. She also decorated inside the house. When their relationship ended, her claim to a beneficial interest failed:

> What is needed, I think, is evidence of a payment or payments by the plaintiff which it can be inferred was referable to the acquisition of the house ... the mere fact that the parties live together and do the ordinary domestic tasks is, in my view, no indication at all that they thereby intended to alter the existing property rights of either of them (per Fox LJ at 328, 331).

The level of the hurdle set by Lord Bridge for establishing inferred intention is lower than what is required for a resulting trust. The payment of mortgage instalments and a discount given to a sitting tenant by the landlord selling a flat are sufficient to found an inferred common intention, but not a resulting trust (see *Curley v Parkes* [2004] EWCA Civ 1515 at [16]). However:

> Lord Bridge's extreme doubt 'whether anything less will do' was certainly consistent with many first-instance and Court of Appeal decisions, but I respectfully doubt whether it took full account of the views (conflicting though they were) expressed in *Gissing v Gissing* [1971] AC 886 [HL] ... It has attracted some trenchant criticism from scholars as potentially productive of injustice ... Whether or not Lord Bridge's observation was justified in 1990, in my opinion the law has moved on, and your Lordships should move it a little more in the same direction (per Lord Walker *Stack v Dowden* at [26]).

Even before *Stack v Dowden*, there was some evidence that the strict approach taken by Lord Bridge in *Rosset* was being relaxed. Indeed, as Lord Walker observed, the House of Lords itself had pointed towards a more liberal approach in case of *Gissing v Gissing* [1971] AC 886 (HL), some 20 years before *Rosset*. In *Gissing;* Lord Diplock was of the opinion that indirect financial contributions to the household expenses might be sufficient to enable a claimant to gain a beneficial interest, but only if they enabled the legal owner to make the mortgage repayments. Ten years after *Rosset*, Nicholas Mostyn QC, sitting as a deputy judge in the Family Division, reflected on the arbitrary level of the hurdle when giving judgment in *Le Foe v Le Foe* [2001] 2 FLR 970 (Fam), a case in which a mortgagee was seeking possession:

> I have no doubt that the family economy depended for its function on [the wife's] earnings. It was an arbitrary allocation of responsibility that [the husband] paid the mortgage ... whereas [the wife] paid for day-to-day domestic expenditure (at [10]).

More recently, the hurdle set by Lord Bridge has been criticised by the House of Lords in *Stack v Dowden* and by the Privy Council in *Abbott v Abbott* [2008] 1 FLR 1451 (PC). In *Stack v Dowden*, Baroness Hale questioned whether it was binding on lower courts:

> There is undoubtedly an argument for saying, as did the Law Commission in *Sharing Homes, A Discussion Paper* [(2002) Law Com No 278], para. 4.23 that the observations, which were

strictly obiter dicta, of Lord Bridge of Harwich in *Lloyds Bank Plc v Rosset* [1991] 1 AC 107 have set that hurdle rather too high in certain respects (at [63]).

Baroness Hale believed that the court should look at the whole of the parties' relationship in order to discern the nature of their agreement:

> Many more factors than financial contributions may be relevant to divining the parties' true intentions (at [69]; see also Section 14.3.2).

Baroness Hale's comments on *Rosset* are themselves *obiter*: the only issue in *Stack v Dowden* was quantifying the beneficial interests of the two parties. *Abbott* is an acquisition case, but as it is an opinion of the Privy Council it is not binding on the English courts. However, in the recent case of *Hapeshi v Allnatt* [2010] EWHC 392 (Ch), Judge Hodge QC, sitting as a judge of the High Court, felt able to apply what he referred to as 'the holistic approach commended by the Law Commission and accepted in both *Stack* and *Abbott*' to the question of the acquisition of a beneficial interest as well as its quantification. It has yet to be seen whether the Court of Appeal feels able to accept this approach without clearer authority from the Supreme Court that the law has 'moved on' from *Rosset*.

14.3.2   Quantification: what share of the beneficial interest?

Once a court has found that there is a trust, it must then go on to quantify the share of the equity to which the successful claimant is entitled. This is unlikely to be a problem where the parties have expressly agreed the size of their respective shares. As Baroness Hale explained in *Stack v Dowden* at [49]:

> No one now doubts that such an express declaration of trust is conclusive unless varied by subsequent agreement or affected by proprietary estoppel: see *Goodman v Gallant* [1986] Fam 106 (CA).

The law has been much less clear about how to quantify the beneficial interest where there is no express agreement. Two approaches can be identified. In the first, based on resulting trust principles, the parties are entitled to a share of the beneficial interest in proportion to their contribution to the purchase price. This approach, however, now seems to have been superseded by the second approach, described by the Law Commission in *Sharing Homes, A Discussion Paper* ((2002) Law Com No 278) as:

> a 'holistic approach' to quantification, undertaking a survey of the whole course of dealing between the parties and taking account of all conduct which throws light on the question what shares were intended (at para 4.27).

In *Oxley v Hiscock* [2005] Fam 211 (CA), Mrs Oxley and Mr Hiscock had both contributed to the purchase of the house that they shared. Despite being advised to the contrary by her solicitor, Mrs Oxley agreed that the house be registered in the sole name of Mr Hiscock. Since the purchase of the house in 1991, both parties had contributed towards the maintenance and improvement of the property from pooled resources. When the relationship between the parties broke down, the court was asked to determine their beneficial shares in the proceeds of sale. The trial judge divided the proceeds of sale in equal shares. After a monumental review of the law, Chadwick LJ reached the following conclusion:

> in a case where there is no evidence of any discussion between them as to the amount of the share which each was to have – and even in a case where the evidence is that there was no discussion on that point … [it] must now be accepted that (at least in this court and below) the answer is that each is entitled to that share which the court considers fair having regard

to the whole course of dealing between them in relation to the property. And, in that context, 'the whole course of dealing between them in relation to the property' includes the arrangements which they make from time to time in order to meet the outgoings (at [69]).

After considering the history of the parties' relationship, and their respective contributions, the Court of Appeal concluded that a fair division of the proceeds of sale of the property would be 60 per cent to Mr Hiscock and 40 per cent to Mrs Oxley.

In the earlier case of *Midland Bank plc v Cooke* [1995] 4 All ER 562 (CA) a wife contributed £550 (her share of a wedding present) to the original purchase of the matrimonial home. The trial judge applied a resulting trust analysis and held that she was entitled to some 7 per cent of the value of the house. However, the Court of Appeal held that once there was evidence of the common intention to share the property, then the judge has to:

> undertake a survey of the whole course of dealing between the parties relevant to their ownership and occupation of the property and their sharing of its burdens and advantages … [The court] will take into consideration all conduct which throws light on the question what shares were intended. Only if that search proves inconclusive does the court fall back on the maxim that 'equality is equity' (per Waite LJ at 574).

Here, the Court felt that it was very clear from the wife's involvement in their complex financial arrangements that the parties had intended to share the property equally. The wife was therefore awarded a half-share in the equitable ownership.

In *Stack v Dowden*, both Mr Stack and Ms Dowden were registered proprietors of the land concerned (and, therefore, joint tenants at law). Unfortunately, when they completed the Land Registry transfer form, they failed to indicate (by ticking the relevant box on the form) whether they held the beneficial interest as joint tenants or tenants in common. Normally in these circumstances, it is presumed that the parties hold the beneficial interest as joint tenants, since 'equity follows the law.' However, a majority of the House of Lords accepted that there were exceptional cases where the unexpressed intentions of the parties could displace this assumption: the court should use the same approach as in single legal owner cases (see *Oxley v Hiscock* and *Midland Bank plc v Cooke* above). Baroness Hale provided a substantial list of the factors that might be relevant at paragraph [69] of her speech. Unfortunately, *Stack v Dowden* fails to give any guidance as to when the circumstances would be sufficiently exceptional to allow the presumption of joint tenancy to be rebutted.

Of more serious concern to both academics and the Court of Appeal was the question of whether the reasoning used in *Stack v Dowden* allowed the court to impose the result it considered fair, or whether the court was limited to inferring some actual intention of the parties. *Jones v Kernott* [2012] 1 AC 776 (SC) offered the Supreme Court 'an opportunity for some clarification' of the principles in *Stack v Dowden*. In paragraph 51 of their joint judgment, Lord Walker and Baroness Hale JJSC summarise the principles that apply where a family home is bought in the joint names of a cohabiting couple, where both are responsible for the mortgage, but without any express declaration as to their beneficial interests (subject to minor reformatting):

1. The starting point is that equity follows the law and they are joint tenants both in law and in equity.
2. That presumption can be displaced by showing
   (a) that the parties had a different common intention at the time when they acquired the home, or

(b) that they later formed the common intention that their respective shares would change.

3. Their common intention is to be deduced objectively from their conduct ...

4. In those cases where it is clear either

   (a) that the parties did not intend joint tenancy at the outset, or

   (b) had changed their original intention,

   but it is not possible to ascertain by direct evidence or by inference what their actual intention was as to the shares in which they would own the property, 'the answer is that each is entitled to that share which the court considers fair having regard to the whole course of dealing between them in relation to the property': Chadwick LJ in *Oxley v Hiscock* ...

5. Each case will turn on its own facts. Financial contributions are relevant but there are many other factors which may enable the court to decide what shares were either intended (as in case (3)) or fair (as in case (4)).

Case 4 as propounded by Lord Walker and Baroness Hale is significant because it recognises that there are circumstances in which the court can *impute* intentions to the parties where it is not possible to *infer* their actual intentions from the facts.

On the facts in *Jones v Kernott*, all five members of the court agreed that there was sufficient evidence from which to infer that the parties had changed their intentions as to the ownership of the property after the relationship broke down (case 2(b) of [51]). However, they did not agree whether case 4(b) had been engaged; that is, whether it was possible to infer in what proportions the property was to be shared between Mr Kernott and Ms Jones. Lord Walker and Baroness Hale, with whom Lord Collins agreed, felt that the proportions in which the property was to be owned could be objectively deduced as 90:10 (case 3). Lord Wilson and Lord Kerr disagreed, but felt able to impute a 90:10 ratio as reasonable in all the circumstances. As all five judges reached the same conclusion (despite their different lines of reasoning), the decision of the Court of Appeal (that the property was held in equal shares) was reversed, and the order of the trial judge (that Ms Jones held a 90% share in the property) was restored. (For a sample of three different academic perspectives on *Jones v Kernott*, see the series of case notes in [2012] Conv 149–180.)

14.4 Proprietary estoppel

A successful argument of estoppel can prevent a person enforcing his strict legal rights if to do so would be unfair on a claimant who has acted to his detriment as a result of that person's actions or representations. In contract law, the doctrine is known as promissory estoppel and is thought to provide a defence only. In land law, the doctrine of proprietary estoppel has a greater scope and can found an action; in other words, it can be a 'sword' as well as a 'shield'. The relevance of proprietary estoppel to cases where an agreement to buy land does not comply with section 2 of the Law of Property (Miscellaneous Provisions) Act 1989 has already been considered in Section 12.4.5. However, the doctrine is relevant in a wide range of circumstances where one person is attempting to establish a right in another person's land.

Over the years, the doctrine of proprietary estoppel has developed from a fairly strict set of requirements (summarised in the so-called five *probanda* (criteria) of *Willmott v*

Barber (1880) LR 15 Ch D 96 (Ch); (1881) LR 17 Ch D 772) to the broader, more flexible modern approach of Oliver J in *Taylors Fashions Ltd v Liverpool Victoria Trustees Co Ltd* [1982] 1 QB 133n (Ch), which:

> is directed rather at ascertaining whether, in particular individual circumstances, it would be unconscionable for a party to be permitted to deny that which, knowingly, or unknowingly, he has allowed or encouraged another to assume to his detriment (at 151–52; approved by the Privy Council in *Lim Teng Huan v Ang Swee Chuan* [1992] 1 WLR 113 (PC)).

In what is now the leading case of *Thorner v Major* [2009] 1 WLR 776 (HL), Lord Walker acknowledged that while there is no single comprehensive definition of proprietary estoppel:

> most scholars agree that the doctrine is based on three main elements … a representation or assurance made to the claimant; reliance on it by the claimant; and detriment to the claimant in consequence of his (reasonable) reliance (at [29]).

In his more cautious opinion in the same case, Lord Scott accepted this threefold classification, adding:

> These [three] elements would, I think, always be necessary but might, in a particular case, not be sufficient. Thus, for example, the representation or assurance would need to have been sufficiently clear and unequivocal; the reliance by the claimant would need to have been reasonable in all the circumstances; and the detriment would need to have been sufficiently substantial to justify the intervention of equity (at [15]).

In some ways, the doctrine of proprietary estoppel is similar to that of the common intention constructive trust (see Section 14.3). For example, in *Lloyds Bank plc v Rosset* [1991] 1 AC 107 (HL), Lord Bridge discussed rights acquired 'under a constructive trust or proprietary estoppel'. However, it is best to treat constructive trusts and proprietary estoppel as two separate, although not unrelated, doctrines. Common intention constructive trusts provide a successful claimant with a beneficial interest in the land as equitable co-owner. Proprietary estoppel is a much more flexible creature, offering the courts considerable discretion as to the nature of the remedy that they can award. The distinctions between the two doctrines are considered in more detail in Section 14.5.

In what follows, it is convenient to address reliance and detriment under a single heading. In fact, as Robert Walker LJ (as he then was) warned in *Gillett v Holt* [2001] Ch 210 (CA):

> it is important to note at the outset that the doctrine of proprietary estoppel cannot be treated as subdivided into three or four watertight compartments … [It is] apparent that the quality of the relevant assurances may influence the issue of reliance, that reliance and detriment are often intertwined … Moreover the fundamental principle that equity is concerned to prevent unconscionable conduct permeates all the elements of the doctrine. In the end the court must look at the matter in the round (at 225).

This section must also address a further question: what remedy should the court give to the claimant if the estoppel is established?

The main elements of proprietary estoppel

- representation or assurance;
- reliance;
- detriment; and
- relief.

14.4.1   Raising the expectation: representation or assurance

The expectation in the claimant can be raised either by an express representation as to her present or future rights in the land or by 'wilful silence' (that is, acquiescence). In the latter case, an estoppel may be established if a landowner, knowing the true position, stands by while the claimant does something on the landowner's land in the mistaken belief that the land belongs to her. As Lord Wensleydale stated in *Ramsden v Dyson* (1866) LR 1 HL 129 (HL):

> If a stranger build upon my land, supposing it to be his own, and I knowing it to be mine, do not interfere but leave him to go on, equity considers it to be dishonest in me to remain passive and afterwards to interfere and take profit (at 168).

The courts have given a great deal of attention to the characteristics required of a representation or assurance for it to be a sufficient foundation for establishing an estoppel. In many cases, the character of the representation will be relatively clear. For example, in *Yaxley v Gotts* [2000] Ch 162 (CA), Mr Yaxley had agreed orally with Mr Gotts senior that he would take the ground floor of a house that Mr Gotts was about to buy, in return for renovating and rebuilding the house as a number of flats. After Mr Yaxley carried out the work as he had promised, Mr Gotts' son (who actually purchased the building) was estopped from denying Mr Yaxley use of the ground floor (and the estoppel gave rise to a constructive trust; see Section 12.4.5). It is now accepted that a promise that a person will inherit under another's will can be the basis of an estoppel claim, even though a will can be revoked at any time up to the death of the person who made it. In *Gillett v Holt*, Mr Gillett had worked for a farmer for some 40 years, giving up opportunities to develop his career. During this time, the farmer gave him and Mr Gillett's family repeated express assurances that Mr Gillett would inherit the farm and the farm business. Eventually, however, the farmer transferred his attentions to someone else, dismissed Mr Gillett from his employment and excluded him from his will. The Court of Appeal found that the express promises that Mr Gillett would inherit the farm under the farmer's will were sufficiently certain to establish an estoppel in his favour. Detrimental reliance on the promise of inheriting under the will made the promise binding.

However, detrimental reliance cannot operate upon a representation that neither party expected to be binding on them. Consequently, an agreement labelled 'subject to contract' (see Section 12.4.2(a)) will not ordinarily be capable of giving rise to a proprietary estoppel (*Haq v Island Homes Housing Association* [2011] 2 P & CR 17 (CA)). In *Cobbe v Yeoman's Row Management Ltd* [2008] 1 WLR 1752 (HL), Mr Cobbe, an experienced property developer, informally agreed to purchase a property comprising a number of flats from Yeoman's Row Management Ltd for £12 million. The sale was to take effect once planning permission had been obtained for the development of the flats. Mr Cobbe put a great deal of time and money into obtaining the necessary planning consents, only for the directors of Yeoman's Row Management Ltd to demand a higher price for the flats.

The House of Lords held that Mr Cobbe's claim failed, because, as Lord Walker explained:

> as persons experienced in the property world, both parties knew that there was no legally binding contract, and that either was therefore free to discontinue the negotiations without legal liability – that is, liability in equity as well as at law … Mr Cobbe was therefore running a risk … Whatever his reasons for doing so, the fact is that he ran a commercial risk, with his eyes open, and the outcome has proved unfortunate for him (at [91]).

Lord Scott, who gave the main opinion in *Cobbe*, made a strong defence of the need for sufficient certainty in the representation or assurance:

> Proprietary estoppel requires, in my opinion, clarity as to what it is that the object of the estoppel is to be estopped from denying, or asserting, and clarity as to the interest in the property in question that that denial, or assertion, would otherwise defeat. If these requirements are not recognised, proprietary estoppel will lose contact with its roots and risk becoming unprincipled and therefore unpredictable, if it has not already become so (at [28]).

Lord Scott emphasised the need for the representation to be clear and unequivocal, suggesting that a claimant needed to prove that the landowner intended or expected the representation or assurance to be relied upon in precisely the way that the claimant subsequently did for an estoppel to arise. Several judicial and academic commentators were very alarmed by the decision in *Cobbe* and suggested that it 'severely curtailed, or even virtually extinguished, the doctrine of proprietary estoppel', as Lord Walker observed in *Thorner v Major* [2009] 1 WLR 776 (HL) at [31]. Fortunately, *Thorner v Major* gave the House of Lords the opportunity to set the record straight.

David Thorner had worked for nearly 30 years without pay on Steart Farm, in Somerset, which belonged to his father's cousin, Peter Thorner. During this time, David came to hope, and then to expect, that he would inherit Peter's farm. Nothing was ever said directly (distinguishing the case from the otherwise similar facts of *Gillett v Holt*). However, in 1990 Peter gave David the bonus notice on two assurance policies on his own life and said, 'That's for my death duties'. David interpreted this as Peter's way of saying that he would inherit Steart Farm on Peter's death. Indeed, Peter's remark in 1990 was a major factor in David's decision not to pursue other opportunities that became available to him. Unfortunately, when Peter died in 2005, he did not leave a valid will, and under the intestacy rules, Steart Farm passed to Peter's heirs rather than to David. At first instance, Mr John Randall QC, sitting as a deputy judge of the Chancery Division, ordered that David should receive the land and other assets of the farm. However, the Court of Appeal reversed this decision on the ground that the statement made implicitly in 1990 did not amount to a clear and unequivocal representation upon which David could reasonably have been intended to rely (see *Thorner v Major* at [74]).

The House of Lords unanimously reversed the decision of the Court of Appeal and awarded the farm to David. The majority line of reasoning in *Thorner* makes it clear that what is required for an estoppel is that the representation or assurance conveys an understanding that it is to be treated seriously. This, and the closely related question of whether it was reasonable for the claimant to rely on the representation, are questions of fact and will be dependent upon the wider circumstances of the case.

> The promise must be unambiguous and must appear to have been intended to be taken seriously. Taken in its context, it must have been a promise which one might reasonably expect to be relied upon by the person to whom it was made (*Thorner v Major* at [56] per Lord Walker, quoting Hoffmann LJ (as he then was) in the unreported case of *Walton v Walton* [1994] CA Transcript No 479).

Consequently, much greater clarity of expression will be required in a business context (such as *Cobbe*) than in a case where both parties are unusually 'taciturn and undemonstrative' (as in *Thorner v Major*).

In *Thorner v Major*, the House of Lords also had to consider the related question of whether David could know with sufficient certainty what he was expecting to inherit. The boundaries of farms tend to change from time to time, and Steart Farm had been no exception during the years that David worked there. It was decided that this did not cause a problem on the facts. Both David and Peter had known that the extent of the farm was likely to vary from time to time, and on the facts it was sufficiently clear that the assurances given by Peter related to Steart Farm as it would exist at the time of Peter's death.

14.4.2 Reliance and detriment

Once the claimant has shown that he was encouraged to act in a certain way, the courts will presume that his actions were in reliance on that encouragement, unless the legal owner is able to rebut this presumption (*Greasley v Cooke* [1980] 1 WLR 1306 (CA)). The question is one of whether the claimant would have acted to his detriment in any case as part of the relationship between the parties, or whether the actions were undertaken in reliance on the promise.

The Privy Council surveyed the leading authorities concerning the relationship between detriment and reliance in the case of *Henry v Henry* [2010] 1 All ER 988 (PC). Sir Jonathan Parker concluded that:

> just as the inquiry as to reliance falls to be made in the context of the nature and quality of the particular assurances which are said to form the basis of the estoppel, so the inquiry as to detriment falls to be made in the context of the nature and quality of the particular conduct or course of conduct adopted by the claimant in reliance on those assurances. Thus, notwithstanding that reliance and detriment may, in the abstract, be regarded as different concepts, in applying the principles of proprietary estoppel they are often intertwined (at [55]).

Consequently, one of the tasks of the court is to determine the correct balance between any disadvantages suffered by the claimant due to his reliance and any advantages he received because of that reliance. On the facts of *Henry v Henry*, Mr Henry had opted for a hard life, in which he had to struggle to make ends meet and to provide for his family, because of the promises made to him, despite more attractive prospects elsewhere. The Privy Council found that this detriment was not outweighed by the fact that Mr Henry had lived rent-free on a plot of land, living off its produce and the sale of any surplus.

The expenditure of money is usually sufficiently clear an act to show reliance on a promise. For example, in *Pascoe v Turner* [1979] 1 WLR 431 (CA), a woman who had been promised that the house in which she was living 'was hers' spent 'a quarter of her modest capital' (a few hundred pounds) on maintaining and improving the property. The true owner, her former partner, was estopped from denying her interest in the house. However:

> The detriment need not consist of the expenditure of money or other quantifiable financial detriment, so long as it is something substantial. The requirement must be approached as part of a broad inquiry as to whether repudiation of an assurance is or is not unconscionable in all the circumstances (per Sir Jonathan Parker, *Henry v Henry* at [38]).

In *Greasley v Cooke*, a young woman went to work as a maid in a household. After some time, she formed a relationship with one of the sons and lived with him as if she were his wife. Although she was no longer paid for her work, she continued to look after the family, including a daughter who was ill, and was assured that she could live in the house for the rest of her life. Her partner, who had inherited the house, died, and the heirs attempted to evict her. Lord Denning MR held that her unpaid work in caring for the family, especially the daughter, amounted to acts in reliance on the assurances that had been made to her. Mr Henry, Mr Gillett and David Thorner clearly fall within this latter category: they would hardly have acted as they did had it not been for assurances they had received (see discussions of *Henry v Henry*, *Gillett v Holt* and *Thorner v Major* above).

14.4.3 The remedy: satisfying the equity

A successful estoppel claim has the effect of raising an equity in the property. The courts must then find a means of 'satisfying the equity', and they have considerable discretion, within equitable principles, as to what remedy (often referred to as *relief* in estoppel cases) to award to the claimant.

It might be thought that the obvious relief would be to require the defendant to fulfil the promise. However, an 'expectation-based' approach potentially impinges on the law of contract and the doctrine of consideration, as well as on the rules of formality in land law. There are also practical problems with such an approach. Not only does it assume that the claimant's expectations are clearly focused upon a specific interest in the land, but it could lead to injustice where the consequences of honouring the expectation are disproportionate to the detriment the claimant will suffer if the promise is not kept. As Robert Walker LJ observed in *Jennings v Rice* [2003] 1 P & CR 8 (CA):

> The essence of the doctrine of proprietary estoppel is to do what is necessary to avoid an unconscionable result, and a disproportionate remedy cannot be the right way of going about that (at [56]).

The approach generally now taken by the courts was summarised by Mason CJ in the Australian case of *Commonwealth of Australia v Verwayen* (1990) 170 CLR 394:

> A central element of that doctrine is that there must be a proportionality between the remedy and the detriment which [it] is its purpose to avoid (at 414).

However,

> that does not mean that the court should ... abandon expectations completely, and look to the detriment suffered by the claimant as defining the appropriate measure of relief (per Robert Walker LJ, *Jennings v Rice* at [51]).

Instead,

> The court's aim is ... to form a view as to what is the minimum required to satisfy [the equity] and do justice between the parties. The court must look at all the circumstances, including the need to achieve a 'clean break' so far as possible and avoid or minimise future friction (per Robert Walker LJ, *Gillett v Holt* at 237).

The minimum necessary to satisfy the equity of estoppel will vary according to the circumstances of each individual case. In *Pascoe v Turner*, the court ordered the legal owner of a house to convey the fee simple to the claimant, who had spent a few hundred pounds on maintaining and improving it (see Section 14.4.2). Without more, this appears to be a windfall for the claimant and unjust on her former partner. In fact, the man was prosperous and, according to Cumming-Bruce LJ:

> determined to pursue his purpose of evicting her from the house by any legal means at his disposal with a ruthless disregard of the obligations binding on conscience (at 438).

The court felt that the woman could only be protected from the man's harassing behaviour by requiring him to perfect his gift and convey the land to her. The award of some lesser right in the land, such as a licence to remain there during her lifetime, would not have been enough to achieve this. Similarly, in *Re Basham (decd)* [1986] 1 WLR 1498 (Ch), the stepdaughter was awarded the house that had been promised to her; in *Yaxley v Gotts*, Mr Yaxley received a long lease of one of the flats in the building he had been renovating; and in *Thorner v Major* the claimant received the land, buildings, live and dead stock and other assets of the farm on which he had laboured for so many years.

In *Campbell v Griffin* [2001] EWCA Civ 990, Mr Campbell had initially been a lodger in a house owned by a retired couple. He gradually took on responsibilities as their carer, and they came to rely on him completely and treated him as their son. They assured him that he had a home for life, and the husband changed his will in order to leave Mr Campbell a life interest in the house. The husband died before the wife, who took the property by right of survivorship as the sole surviving joint tenant. She, however, was unable to make a will in the man's favour because she was suffering from senile dementia. Mr Campbell established that he had an equity in the property through estoppel. However, the Court of Appeal felt unable to give effect to the promise of a life interest, since this would have been disproportionate to the detriment Mr Campbell had suffered, and unfair on others who were to benefit from the estate. Mr Campbell was awarded £35,000, charged on the property.

Similarly, in *Gillett v Holt*, the court did not require the farmer to fulfil all his promises to Mr Gillett, who instead was awarded the freehold of the farmhouse and some land, along with £100,000 to compensate him for his exclusion from the farm business. In *Jennings v Rice*, an old woman's part-time gardener became, over the course of a number of years, her unpaid full-time carer, even sleeping on the sofa in her sitting room during the last three years of her life. Despite promising him that the house would be his one day, the woman never made a will. After her death, the man made a claim on her estate for the house. Although his argument of estoppel was successful, the Court again emphasised the need for proportionality between the expectation and the detriment. Instead of fulfilling his expectation by ordering the transfer of the house, the Court awarded him £200,000, less than half its value.

On occasion, this approach, essentially based on restitution, may result in no award at all being made, even though the claimant is successful in her estoppel claim. In *Sledmore v Dalby* (1996) 72 P & CR 196 (CA), Mrs Sledmore sought possession of a house she owned against Mr Dalby, her son-in-law, who had lived there for many years. Mr Dalby had undertaken some work on the property initially in reliance on an assurance that his wife would be left the property after her parents' death, and subsequently (his wife having died) on the assumption that he would be able to live there for the rest of his life. However, Mrs Sledmore had little money, was in danger of losing her home and had a greater need for the house than her son-in-law. He could afford to pay for his own accommodation and was actually only spending a few nights each week at the house. The Court of Appeal granted possession to Mrs Sledmore, and nothing to Mr Dalby, on the basis that this was the 'the minimum equity to do justice to the respondent on the facts of this case' (per Roch LJ at 205):

> The effect of any equity … has long since been exhausted and no injustice has been done to the defendant (per Hobhouse LJ at 209).

14.5 Constructive trusts and proprietary estoppel compared

There is a considerable degree of overlap between constructive trusts and proprietary estoppel. In *Yaxley v Gotts* [2001] Ch 162 (CA), Robert Walker LJ stated:

> At a high level of generality, there is much common ground between the doctrines of proprietary estoppel and the constructive trust … [a]ll are concerned with equity's intervention to provide relief against unconscionable conduct, whether as between neighbouring landowners, or vendor and purchaser, or relatives who make informal arrangements for sharing a home, or a fiduciary and the beneficiary or client to whom he owes a fiduciary obligation (at 176).

In *Jennings v Rice* [2003] 1 P & CR 8 (CA), he was of the view that:

> Sometimes the assurances, and the claimant's reliance on them, have a consensual character falling not far short of an enforceable contract … [and] the proprietary estoppel may become indistinguishable from a constructive trust (at [45]).

In both constructive trusts and proprietary estoppel there is detrimental reliance on an understanding that the claimant will gain an interest in the land. However, whereas a constructive trust is based on an agreement between the parties, an estoppel does not require there to be a meeting of minds. An estoppel arises because the courts will not permit a legal owner to stand back while the claimant acts in reliance on a mistaken belief as to her rights.

A further difference arises when considering the nature of the remedy a successful claimant might obtain. Under a constructive trust, he will have a beneficial interest in the land which is deemed to have arisen at the time of the acts of detrimental reliance. The only question will be the extent of the share to be awarded by the court. In proprietary estoppel, however, the nature of the right is not known until the court gives its decision. As discussed above, the relief granted to give effect to an estoppel can range from the award of the fee simple (as in *Pascoe v Turner*) to nothing at all (as in *Sledmore v Dalby*).

It is also necessary to consider whether rights arising under a constructive trust or a proprietary estoppel are binding on third parties, such as later mortgage lenders or purchasers of the land. The rules on the circumstances in which a beneficial interest under a trust is binding are now well established (see Section 11.6.1). Case law previously indicated that an equity arising from proprietary estoppel could bind a purchaser of registered land (see *Lloyd v Dugdale* [2002] 2 P & CR 13 (CA)), and this is now confirmed by section 116 of the LRA 2002. It seems that such an equity can now be protected by the entry of a notice on the Register, although this is unlikely to happen, since the person in whose favour the equity has arisen will probably not know that it should be formally protected. However, when coupled with actual occupation, the equity will be an interest overriding subsequent dispositions (see Section 15.8.2). A major difficulty remains, however: the precise nature of the right will not be known until the court has granted relief.

14.6 Alternative approaches to family property

Lord Justice Wall described his judgment in the case of *Jones v Kernott* [2010] 3 All ER 423 (CA) as 'a cautionary tale' for all unmarried couples (see Section 14.1). The same might be, and has been, said of many of the other judgments referred to in this chapter. Even where justice is thought to be done, the rules are, to adopt the words of the Law Commission in its 2002 discussion paper *Sharing Homes* (Law Com No 278), 'unfair, uncertain and illogical'. One of the reasons for this is that principles that belong to (and work relatively well within) the commercial context are being used to resolve disputes where the relationship between the parties is based on commitment and trust rather than contract and property. For example, the common intention constructive trust is based on discerning the terms of a fictitious agreement between the parties. The evidential difficulties in establishing either an express or an implied agreement (see Section 14.3.1) are hardly surprising, given that neither party may have given any thought to their common intention until the non-legal owner found his possession threatened, either by a mortgagee or by the end of his relationship with the legal owner.

It seems that the circumstances in which common intention can been inferred are now somewhat broader than envisaged by Lord Bridge in *Lloyds Bank plc v Rosset*

[1991] 1 AC 107 (HL) (see Section 14.3.1(b)). This may temper the indirect discrimination against claimants (most commonly female cohabitees) who, because of social expectations or personal circumstances, are not able to make a financial contribution towards the purchase of the home. However, it fails to address the fundamental problem: family disputes need to be addressed using principles that respect the character of the family relationship.

One alternative solution would be to use a different type of constructive trust, familiar to many other common law jurisdictions: the remedial constructive trust. Remedial constructive trusts are based on unconscionability and allow the court to impose a trust on a defendant who knowingly retains property of which the claimant has been unjustly deprived. Since the remedy can be tailored to the circumstances of the particular case, innocent third parties are not prejudiced, and restitutionary defences, such as change of position, are available (see Lord Browne-Wilkinson's comments in *Westdeutsche Landesbank Girozentrale v Islington LBC* [1996] AC 669 (HL) at 716). For example, the Australian case of *Rasmanis v Jurewitsch* (1969) 70 SR (NSW) 407 concerned three legal and beneficial joint tenants (A, B and C). A killed B, and the question arose as to how the beneficial entitlement was now shared. If the beneficial joint tenancy was automatically severed by the homicide (see Section 10.5.5), then A and C would hold the legal title on trust for themselves and B's estate in equal shares as tenants in common. The Court of Appeal of New South Wales felt that this would mean that A profited by his crime, and instead imposed a constructive trust with the beneficial interest being divided one-third to C and the remaining two-thirds to A and C as joint tenants. In England and Wales, during the late 1960s and 1970s, Lord Denning MR used remedial trusts as a means of achieving a fair solution to family disputes over land. However, this approach was firmly rejected by the House of Lords in the two seminal cases of *Pettitt v Pettitt* [1970] AC 777 (HL) and *Gissing v Gissing* [1971] AC 886 (HL). Despite some significant judicial support for the remedial constructive trust in subsequent years (see, for example, Lord Browne-Wilkinson in *Westdeutsche Landesbank Girozentrale* and even Lord Scott in the recent case of *Thorner v Major* [2009] 1 WLR 776 (HL) at [20]), they are not yet accepted as part of English law (see, for example, the remarks of Patten LJ in the recent case of *De Bruyne v De Bruyne* [2010] EWCA Civ 519 (CA) at [48]).

A second alternative is for Parliament to provide a 'fairer' solution through legislation, as it has already done for those cases where a marriage or civil partnership is dissolved (see the Matrimonial Causes Act 1973 and the Civil Partnership Act 2004). It seems that a majority of people do not appreciate that English law does not extend similar protection to common law spouses (see Appendix A of Law Commission, *Cohabitation: The Financial Consequences of Relationship Breakdown* ((2007) Law Com No 307)). After a wide consultation, in 2007 the Law Commission suggested such a scheme that would apply specifically to eligible cohabiting couples who separate ((2007) Law Com No 307). However, as Baroness Hale observed in *Stack v Dowden* [2007] 2 AC 432 (HL), a few months before the report was published:

> unlike most Law Commission reports, this one will not contain a draft Bill. Implementation will therefore depend, not only upon whether its proposals find favour with Government, but also on whether the resources can be found to translate them into workable legislative form (at [47]).

It seems that Baroness Hale's concerns were justified. Neither the political nor legislative will has been found to put the recommendations into statutory form.

Summary

14.1 There are three main ways in which a person may informally acquire a beneficial interest in land: resulting trusts, common intention constructive trusts and the doctrine of proprietary estoppel.

14.2 A resulting trust requires a direct contribution to the initial purchase price of the property or to the mortgage. The beneficiary will gain a share in the property proportionate to his contribution to the purchase price.

14.3 A common intention constructive trust will be imposed on the legal owner when there has been an agreement that the claimant should have a beneficial share in the property, and the claimant has detrimentally altered his position in reliance upon that agreement. The agreement can be demonstrated by evidence of an express agreement between the parties, or it may be inferred where there are sufficient grounds for the court to do so. The courts now tend to adopt a 'broad brush' approach to the quantification of the beneficiary's interest, seeking, through an examination of their whole relationship, to establish how the parties intended the property to be shared.

14.4 Proprietary estoppel has many similarities to a constructive trust. A successful claimant will establish an equity in the property through detrimental reliance on an expectation, encouraged by the legal owner, that he will get an interest in the land. In order to satisfy the equity raised by a successful estoppel claim, the courts aim to achieve proportionality between the remedy and the detriment suffered and will award the minimum remedy necessary.

14.5 The precise relationship between common intention constructive trusts and the doctrine of estoppel is unclear. They are best treated as separate doctrines.

14.6 The recognition of an informal trust or an interest by way of proprietary estoppel is a property-based remedy. It is not primarily concerned with achieving the fairest distribution of the property in the light of all the circumstances of the parties.

Exercises

14.1 Complete the online quiz on the topics covered in this chapter on the companion website.

14.2 To what extent have the decisions in *Lloyds Bank plc v Rosset* [1991] 1 AC 107 (HL), *Stack v Dowden* [2007] 2 AC 432 (HL) and *Jones v Kernott* [2012] 1 AC 776 (SC) produced a coherent approach to the law of equitable ownership of the family home?

14.3 Jerome, who used to be a prosperous businessman, was the sole registered proprietor of a house which he bought 12 years ago for £200,000, paying for it with £20,000 from his savings and the rest by means of a mortgage. Two years later, he asked his student girlfriend, Lena, to move in with him, telling her that she would always have a home there. Lena looked after the house and garden, and carried out any maintenance on the property. Seven years ago, Jerome's business failed and he took paid employment, but did not earn enough to cover all the outgoings. Lena, therefore, gave up her studies and took a job, and her contributions to the household budget enabled Jerome to pay the mortgage. Last month, Jerome was killed in a road accident. In his will, he left everything to his mother, who has told Lena to leave the house, now worth £400,000, since she wants to sell it.

Advise Lena.

You can find suggested answers to exercises 14.2 and 14.3 on the companion website.

Further reading

Clarke, 'The Family Home: Intention and Agreement' (1992) 22 Fam Law 72

Davis, Hughes and Jacklin, '"Come Live with Me My Love": A Consideration of the 2007 Law Commission Proposals on Cohabitation Breakdown' [2008] 72 Conv 197

Dixon, 'Confining and Defining Proprietary Estoppel: The Role of Unconscionability' (2010) 30 LS 408

Etherton, 'Constructive Trusts and Proprietary Estoppel: the Search for Clarity and Principle' [2009] 73 Conv 104

Gardner, 'Family Property Today' (2008) 124 LQR 422

Hopkins, 'Regulating Trusts of the Home: Private Law and Social Policy' (2009) 125 LQR 310

McFarlane and Robertson, 'Apocalypse Averted: Proprietary Estoppel in the House of Lords' (2009) 125 LQR 535

Piška, 'Hopes, Expectations and Revocable Promises in Proprietary Estoppel' (2009) 72 MLR 998

Sparkes, 'Non-Declarations of Beneficial Co-Ownership' [2012] 76 Conv 207

Thompson, 'Constructive Trusts, Estoppel and the Family Home' [2004] 68 Conv 496

Part V

Priorities

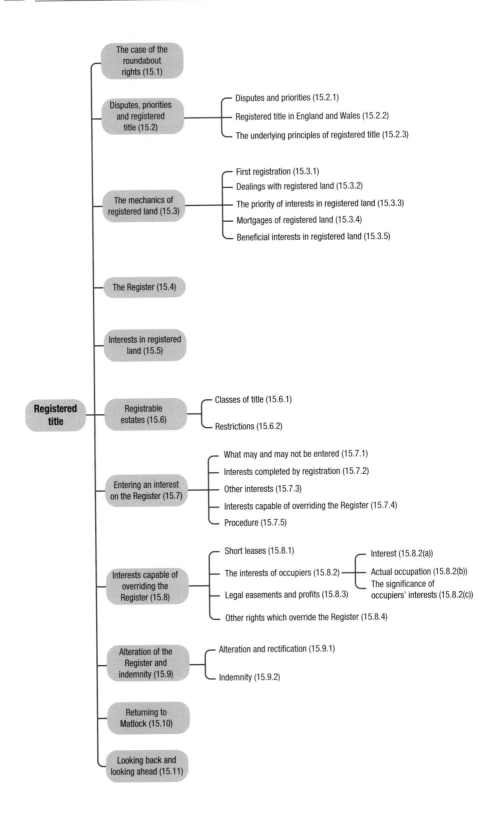

Chapter 15

Registered title

Key concepts

▶ **Overriding interests** – interests that are capable of binding a person with an interest in registered land, even though they do not appear in the register of the title concerned.
▶ **Registered interests** – subordinate interests in land entered in the Charges Register of a registered estate.
▶ **Registrable estates** – interests capable of being substantively registered with their own title number.
▶ **Title by registration** – a system in which proof of title to estates in land is based on entries in a register controlled by the State.

15.1 The case of the roundabout rights

In August 1998, British Gas sold some land at Matlock in Derbyshire to Mr Hughes. At the date of the sale, title to the land was unregistered. However, the transfer of the land to Mr Hughes triggered its compulsory first registration. Unfortunately, Mr Hughes' application to register his title to the land was subsequently cancelled by the Land Registry because of his failure to respond to a number of requisitions raised by the Registrar. In the meantime, Mr Hughes had entered into an agreement with Sainsbury's Supermarkets Ltd to convey or make available to them such part or parts of the land as might be required for the construction of a roundabout. This roundabout would be needed to enable access to a significant development that Sainsbury's had planned for Matlock. Sainsbury's sought to protect their interest (and estate contract) by lodging various documents at the Land Registry. They did not, however, take any steps to register it as a Class C (iv) Land Charge (which is necessary to protect an estate contract in unregistered land; see Section 16.3.2). In February 2000, Westpac Banking Corporation obtained a charging order over Mr Hughes' interest in the land. Four years later, with the appropriate authorisation of the court, Westpac sold the land to Olympia Homes Ltd. Olympia were then registered as the freehold proprietors of the land and free from Sainsbury's interest. During the process of registration the Land Registry had asked Sainsbury's to justify their claim to an interest in the land, but Sainsbury's had failed to respond within the stipulated time limit. Initially, Olympia had been happy for Sainsbury's to build its roundabout, but gradually Olympia's attitude hardened, and ultimately it refused to release the land to Sainsbury's. It was not obliged to do so, it argued, since there was no direct contract between Olympia and Sainsbury's. Further, any interest that Sainsbury's might have in the land was not binding on Olympia as it was not protected by registration.

Eventually, the matter reached the Chancery Division of the High Court of Justice. The outcome would depend on what the judge decided about the precise nature of Sainsbury's rights: were they interests in the land or purely personal rights? It would also depend on the provisions of the Land Registration Act (LRA) 2002, which came into force on 13 October 2003, some four months before Olympia acquired the land.

Mr Justice Mann's judgment in *Sainsbury's Supermarkets Ltd v Olympia Homes Ltd* [2006] 1 P & CR 17 (Ch) will be considered in Section 15.10, after the rules relating to registered title have been examined in some detail.

15.2 Disputes, priorities and registered title

15.2.1 Disputes and priorities

Part II of this book considered the main types of estate and interest that can exist in land. Any one estate may be subject to a wide range of interests. In the vast majority of cases such interests are enjoyed, created and transferred (see Part IV) without difficulty or controversy. At times, however, parties find themselves in dispute about the interests that they are claiming over the same legal estate in land. The rules for dealing with disputes between co-owners of land are explored in Chapter 11. This chapter and the chapter that follows are concerned with the rules that are used for determining other types of disputes about interests in land.

In many cases, such disputes will arise when the estate changes hands and there is a conflict between the new owner of the land and a person who owns another, pre-existing interest in the land, such as an easement (see Figure 15.1). However, not all disputes are triggered by a sale; for example, they can also arise because of a breakdown in the relationship between neighbours or when a mortgagee enforces its security. One of the tasks of lawyers handling the sale and purchase of land is to identify any potential conflicts and resolve them prior to the transfer of the land to the new owner.

> Resolving a dispute about conflicting interests in land involves deciding:
> ▶ what interests actually exist in the land (Parts II and IV); and
> ▶ the order of *priority* of these interests.

The law of England and Wales has two distinct sets of rules for resolving the order or priority between competing interests: those that apply to *unregistered land* (Chapter 16) and the rules of *registered title* (this chapter). It is important to recognise that the systems of unregistered and registered title are fundamentally separate and different. (See Section 2.5 for a comparison of the two systems.)

The rules of registered title are by far the more important of the two sets today. It is estimated that some 23.5 million titles in England and Wales had been registered by the middle of 2013, representing some 82 per cent of the total area of the land. The remaining titles must be registered the next time that they are transferred or made subject to a

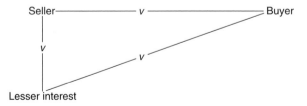

Lesser interest

Figure 15.1 The triangle of potential conflict

first legal mortgage. Landowners can also register their title voluntarily. The rules relating to adverse possession of registered land introduced by the LRA 2002 (see Chapter 13) make voluntary registration attractive to owners of large areas of land, and intense work is being done by the Land Registry to encourage local authorities, charities and fund managers to register title to their land.

15.2.2 Registered title in England and Wales

The idea of a register of land ownership was promoted in the nineteenth century by a non-lawyer, Robert Torrens, who worked in a deeds registry in South Australia. He was dismayed by the complexity of traditional unregistered conveyancing based on proving title by reference to a number of private documents (the title deeds) usually in the possession of the landowner or a mortgagee. Not only might it be necessary to find and refer to many such deeds each time there was any dealing with the land, but they could easily be lost or misplaced. Torrens devised a system in which the titles to individual estates in land are recorded and ownership depends not upon deeds but upon the entries in the centrally held register. His scheme, which worked efficiently in Australia, gradually spread through the common law world, although title registration was never widely accepted in the United States.

After two earlier attempts in the nineteenth century to introduce a system of voluntary land registration in England, some success was achieved when the Land Transfer Act 1897 made registration compulsory in London. A more effective scheme (although not the Torrens system) was introduced by the LRA 1925. The system of registration was to be gradually extended across England and Wales, district by district. All districts of England and Wales became areas of compulsory land registration in 1990. Freehold land and leases over 21 years were required to be registered on sale (and, in the case of such leases, on creation). Since then, the triggers for first registration of title have been extended on a number of occasions (see Section 15.3.1 for the present list), and a significant majority of titles in England and Wales are now registered. The Land Registry is continuing to take positive steps to persuade owners of unregistered titles, predominantly the Crown Estate, public bodies and the owners of large private estates, of the advantages of land registration. A further 4.5 million hectares of land were added in 2009 and 2010 alone.

Although the Land Registry and the courts worked hard to make the 1925 scheme work, the LRA 1925 had serious shortcomings. A number of amendments to the 1925 Act were introduced, but by the 1990s it was clear that wholesale revision was needed, especially if there was to be any prospect of moving from a paper-based system to an electronic system of conveyancing. *Land Registration for the Twenty-First Century* (Law Com No 254), published by the Law Commission and Land Registry together in 1998, contained a summary and criticism of the existing law along with initial proposals for its radical reform. A draft Bill was published in Law Com No 271 in 2001, which was enacted as the Land Registration Act 2002. Most of the LRA 2002 came into force on 13 October 2003, replacing the LRA 1925. The new scheme introduced by the 2002 Act is supported by the regulatory framework contained in the Land Registration Rules 2003.

The 2002 Act has brought about major changes to the system of title registration. It was anticipated that the most important of these would be the progressive introduction of electronic conveyancing allowing instantaneous creation and transfer of estates and interests in land. It is now possible to create and discharge mortgages electronically, but at the end of June 2011, the Land Registry announced that it had no immediate plans to extend electronic completion to any other types of transaction.

15.2.3 The underlying principles of registered title

Traditionally, there are three essential elements of title registration.

The mirror principle	The Register should *mirror* the actual structure of title and third-party rights in the land. A potential buyer (or anyone else, for that matter) should be able to discover who owns the land and who else has an interest in it simply by reading the Register. The uncertainties of deeds-based conveyancing, and especially the doctrine of notice (see Section 16.2.2), should have no place in a system of registered title.
The curtain principle	The *curtain* principle refers to overreaching, the mechanism by which land subject to beneficial trust interests can safely be bought (see Section 11.6.1).
The guarantee principle	To ensure that everyone has confidence in the system, the State must *guarantee* the accuracy of the titles on the Register and indemnify anyone who suffers loss as a result of any mistake on it.

The three principles provide a useful benchmark against which the scheme of the LRA 2002 can be assessed. However, it should be remembered that no system of land registration has been able completely to achieve these ideals in practice. Any system that did so would uncritically favour certainty over justice, whatever the circumstances and fairness of a particular case. The appropriate question is not whether the 2002 Act completely embodies the three principles of land registration but whether it properly balances the need for certainty, transparency and security against the need for justice to be done.

The distinction between legal and equitable estates is preserved in registered land. However, the LRA 2002 contains its own rules for determining the impact of land interests upon third parties. In particular:

▶ A deed alone is not normally sufficient to create a legal interest in registered land. The interest must be completed by entry on the Register if it is to have effect at law.
▶ Most equitable interests will only bind a purchaser of a legal estate if they have been protected by registration (although there are a limited number of interests that enjoy what is known as 'overriding' status; see Section 15.8).

It is very important to remember that:

▶ land registration is based on the registration of title to (*ownership* of) an estate in land: lesser rights are registered against the relevant registered estate and not in their own right or against the name of one the original parties (as in the Land Charges Register); and
▶ the Land Charges Register has no connection with registered title: it is a register of some types of rights held over unregistered land (see Section 16.3).

15.3   The mechanics of registered land

Before we examine some of the technicalities of the rules of registered title in England and Wales, it may be helpful to consider how the scheme operates in practice.

15.3.1   First registration

Section 3 of the LRA 2002 allows a landowner to apply voluntarily for the registration of her title at any time. However, certain events (set out in LRA 2002, s 4) result in the title holder being obliged to register her estate. Freehold land and legal leases over seven years must now be registered on:

- creation (in the case of a lease);
- transfer (whether or not the transfer is for value);
- the grant of a first legal mortgage;
- partition; and
- the appointment of new trustees to a land holding.

The application to register the title must be made within two months of the relevant transaction (LRA 2002, s 6); otherwise it becomes void. Section 7 of the LRA sets out some of the consequences in more detail:

The transfer of the legal freehold or legal lease exceeding seven years	The legal title (which has already vested in the new owner under the traditional unregistered procedure) reverts to the former owner who holds it on a bare trust for the new owner (s 7(2)(a)).
The creation of a new lease or the grant of a first legal mortgage	The transaction takes effect as if it were a contract for valuable consideration (s 7(2)(b)). The grantee will have the benefit of an equitable estate contract (see Section 12.3) and not a legal lease.
The transfer of the estate to new trustees	The estate reverts to the person or persons in whom it was vested immediately before the transfer (s 7(2)(aa)).

Consequently, the title deeds, together with the appropriate form and fee, should be sent to the relevant office of the Land Registry immediately after the event giving rise to first registration has occurred. Interests which are capable of substantive registration (legal freeholds and legal leases over seven years) are each given their own unique title number. On first registration, the Registrar checks the title as if he was buying the estate and decides whether the title is good enough for 'absolute title' (see Section 15.6.1) or only something less. Any benefits he discovers will be entered on the Register, as will any burdens, such as restrictive covenants found in the Land Charges Register. Once the land has been registered, however, anything in the Land Charges Register becomes irrelevant. Any other details, such as the title number of the freehold reversion of a lease, will also be noted in order to ensure that the Register really does mirror the title to the land. If Registry staff make a mistake, there are provisions for compensation: the State indemnity (see Section 15.9.2).

Under the 1925 scheme, the new proprietor of the land was issued with a Land Certificate containing a copy of the Register, unless the land was subject to a mortgage, in which case the mortgagee would be sent a Charge Certificate. The relevant certificate would have to be produced when subsequently registering a notice or a restriction or disposing of the land. The Law Commission and the Land Registry considered these certificates unnecessary, and incompatible with electronic convey-ancing. However, after consultation, and in order to reassure those who are not con-vinced by this policy, the Registry now issues 'title information documents' to the registered proprietor on completion of first registration and whenever the Register is changed.

15.3.2 Dealings with registered land

Subsequent dealings with the registered estate (for example, a transfer of the whole estate, a mortgage or the grant of a lease exceeding seven years) must be reported to the Land Registry using the appropriate form, together with the necessary fee. The trans-action will have no effect at law until it has been registered (LRA 2002, s 27). Until that time, all the purchaser will own is the equitable title. There is no two-month period of grace, as on first registration. The period between completion of the transaction and its registration is referred to as the 'registration gap'. One of the main benefits of electronic transfers of land (see Sections 15.2.2 and 15.11) would be the simultaneous completion of the transaction and registration via a computer link with the Land Registry, thus abolishing the registration gap.

15.3.3 The priority of interests in registered land

The basic rule is that third-party interests are ranked in order of their creation, not in order of registration (LRA 2002, s 28). However, this rule is significantly modified by the LRA 2002:

Event	Proprietor bound only by:	LRA 2002
First registered proprietor	▷ interests protected by entry on the Register; ▷ interests that are capable of overriding registration; ▷ the interests of anyone in adverse possession (see Chapter 13) of whom the registered proprietor has notice; and ▷ the covenants and obligations contained in the lease (if the estate is leasehold).	Section 11 (freehold), s 12 (leasehold) and Sched. 1
Sale or mortgage **for valuable consideration** of a registered estate or charge	▷ interests protected by entry on the Register; and ▷ interests which override registration.	Sections 29–31 and Sched. 3

Note: Valuable consideration does not include marriage or merely nominal money consideration (LRA 2002, s 132(1))

In all other circumstances (including gifts of registered estates), third-party interests are ranked in order of their creation, not in order of registration. Therefore, an unpro-tected third-party interest will have priority over one which, even though created later, has been protected on the Register.

15.3.4 Mortgages of registered land

Mortgages are entered as registered charges against the title number of the legal estate or estates to which they relate. Where there is more than one registered charge, priority between them is determined according to the date of registration, unless the chargees agree otherwise (which they may do without the chargor's consent). Mortgages of registered land can no longer be created by lease and sublease, but must be created by a charge by deed (LRA 2002, s 23(1)(a); see Section 7.3.1).

15.3.5 Beneficial interests in registered land

One of the three principles which underlie registered land is the drawing of a 'curtain' over any beneficial interests held under a trust of land (see Section 15.2.3). This, in turn, reflects the wider policy objective of trying to ensure that dealings with title can be completed as simply and conveniently as possible. Consequently, beneficial interests under a trust are one of the few classes of interest that cannot be protected by entering a notice of that interest in the register of title (LRA 2002, s 33(a); see Section 15.7.1). The only way to 'protect' a beneficial interest is by entering a restriction that prevents any disposition of the title being registered unless the proceeds of sale are paid to two or more trustees (Land Registration Rules 2003, r 94; see Section 15.6.2). However, this form of restriction will not result in the new registered proprietor being bound by the beneficial interest. Instead, it ensures that the beneficial interest is overreached by any disposition of the land

The conditions that need to be satisfied for overreaching to occur are set out in sections 2 and 27 of the LPA 1925 (see Section 11.6.1). Provided the buyer of any interest in land pays the purchase price to at least two trustees or a trust corporation, the rights of the beneficiaries are automatically detached from the land and attached to the purchase price, which is now in the hands of the trustees. The beneficial interests under the trust are thereby kept behind the 'curtain' of overreaching. If, however, the buyer pays the purchase price to a single trustee only, any beneficial interests will not be overreached. If the beneficiary is in actual occupation of the land concerned, her 'non-overreached' interest may be capable of overriding the disposition of the land, and may, therefore, be binding on the purchaser (see Section 15.8.2).

15.4 The Register

The Register, the mirror of the title to the land, is held on computerised record at one of a number of District Land Registries. It is now an open record and, for a small fee, anyone can easily get a copy of an individual Register, either by completing a form and sending it to the appropriate District Land Registry or instantaneously online through the Land Registry website. Each individual Register is divided into three sections: the *Property Register*, the *Proprietorship Register* and the *Charges Register*.

The three registers comprising a title

The Property Register
This part of the Register describes:

- ▶ the title to the land (freehold or leasehold); and
- ▶ any benefits attached to it (such as the benefit of an easement).

The address is given, and reference is made to a plan on which the plot of land is outlined in red.

The Land Register is a register of title. It is not a 'name-based' register (unlike the Land Charges Register; see Section 16.3). Neither is it a 'plot-based' register. One plot of land may have several registered titles – for example, the freehold and one or more long leases. Each registrable estate in the land has its own title number and entry in the Register.

The Proprietorship Register
The Proprietorship Register states:

- the nature (or status) of the title under the registration system (the various kinds of title are considered at Section 15.6.1);
- the name and address of the owner, who is called 'the registered proprietor'; and
- any restrictions which limit the power of the registered proprietor to deal with the land (see Section 15.6.2).

The Charges Register
This part of the Register contains details of burdens on the land such as mortgages and restrictive covenants (see Section 15.7).

15.5 Interests in registered land

The normal range of interests (e.g. freeholds, leases, easements) still exist in registered land. However, the LRA 2002 superimposes a new set of categories onto the traditional structure:

Registrable estates (see Section 15.6)	These are the most important interests. They must be substantively registered. Each registered estate is given its own title number.
Interests which are completed by registration (see Section 15.7.2)	The interests listed in section 27 of the LRA 2002 can only operate at law if they are completed by being entered on the Register. The most important of these are expressly created legal easements (s 27(2)(d)) and legal charges (s 27(2)(f)). At present, failure to register such interests means that they are unprotected equitable interests.
Other interests which are subject to an entry on the Register (see Section 15.7.3)	Almost all property interests in land can be protected by entering them on the Register. The only exceptions are those listed in section 33 of the LRA 2002. The most important of these are: - trusts of land; - leases for a term of three years or less; and - restrictive covenants made between a lessor and a lessee. Unless an interest is capable of overriding the Register, it will normally only be binding upon a transferee for value of the registered estate if it is noted on the Register (LRA 2002, s 29).
Interests capable of overriding registration (see Section 15.8)	These interests are binding on everyone who gains a later interest in the land even if they are not protected by entry on the Register. The rules for determining whether a particular category of interest is capable of overriding the first registered proprietor (LRA 2002, Sched. 1) differ from the rules that apply after any subsequent dealing with the registered title (LRA 2002, Sched. 3).

In the 1925 scheme, the interests that needed to be protected by an entry on the Register were known collectively as 'minor interests'. This term is not found in the LRA 2002, but is still used in textbooks and judgments.

15.6 Registrable estates

These are the interests which, on sale, transfer or first legal mortgage (and also, in the case of leases, on creation), must be substantively registered with independent title and their own title number. Essentially, this means freeholds and leases granted for more than seven years (although, by section 118 of the LRA 2002, this period of seven years can be, and probably will be, reduced in the future by the Lord Chancellor). In addition, certain other short leases must be registered, the most important of which are reversionary leases (see Section 5.5.2(a)) granted for less than seven years which take effect in possession after three months from the date of the grant. (An example might be student tenancies granted in May or June but not taking effect until the new academic year in September or October.)

15.6.1 Classes of title

In unregistered land, some titles, such as a title obtained by adverse possession, are in practice not as secure as others, since there are no title deeds to prove them. In registered land, the Register reflects the actual state of the title to the land, so it is necessary to classify the titles to show how strong they are. There is provision for weaker titles to be upgraded (LRA 2002, s 62). The classes of title available, which differ slightly between leasehold and freehold (LRA 2002, ss 9 and 10), are as follows:

Absolute title	Absolute freehold or leasehold title is the strongest class of title available. The registered proprietor with absolute title has a better right than anyone else to the land (although there are still circumstances where the title might be open to alteration by the courts or the Registrar; see Section 15.9). A registered proprietor with title absolute is subject only to: ▶ third-party interests protected on the Register; ▶ interests which have overriding status (Section 15.8); ▶ the terms of any trust upon which she holds the title; and ▶ the covenants in the lease if the title is leasehold.
Good leasehold title	Good leasehold title is given to a leasehold estate when the Registrar is unable to guarantee that the freeholder had the right to grant the lease because the freehold has not yet been registered.
Possessory title	Possessory titles are granted by the Registrar when the alleged owner's title is based only on possession, not on title deeds. The Registrar guarantees the title only as far as dealings after first registration are concerned. No promises are made concerning the right of the first registered proprietor to the land. Such titles are very rare.
Qualified title	Qualified titles are granted only if the Registrar has some specific reservation about the title. They are almost unheard of.

15.6.2 Restrictions

A restriction may be entered in the Proprietorship Register by the registered proprietor or the Registrar that prevents the registered proprietor dealing with the title unless certain conditions are met (LRA 2002, s 40). The most commonly encountered restriction is that used to protect beneficiaries under a trust by requiring payment to two trustees before a sale or other disposition will be registered (Land Registration Rules 2003, r 94).

This restriction, combined with the rule that beneficial interests are not referred to on the Register, gives effect to the 'curtain' principle in registered land (see Section 15.2.3).

15.7 Entering an interest on the Register

The LRA 2002 provides two main ways to protect interests on the Register: directly by use of a notice and indirectly by use of a restriction (see Section 15.6.2). In the 1925 scheme, there were four such methods: restriction, notice, caution and inhibition. Students will need to be aware of the earlier methods as they will still be encountered in cases decided under the 1925 provisions. A summary of the four methods and how they differ from those in the 2002 scheme is available on the companion website.

Entering a notice merely protects the priority of that interest if it proves to be valid (see Section 15.3.3). The fact that a notice of an interest has been entered on the Register does not necessarily mean that the interest itself is valid. The validity of the interest will depend upon the rules relating to that type of interest. (See Part II of this book.)

15.7.1 What may and may not be entered

Mortgages of registered estates are entered in the Charges Register against the relevant title number as *registered charges* (see Part 5 of the LRA 2002). It is possible to protect almost all types of interest in land by entering a *notice* in the Charges Register (LRA 2002, s 32). There are only five types of interest that cannot be protected by entering a notice. These are listed in section 33 of the LRA 2002, and the most important are:

- trusts of land;
- leasehold estates for a term of three years or less (unless they are required to be registered by another section of the LRA 2002); and
- restrictive covenants between a lessor and lessee that relate to the premises demised by the lease.

Several of the excluded interests are capable of overriding the Register, at least in certain circumstances (see Section 15.8).

15.7.2 Interests completed by registration

The interests listed in section 27(2)(d–f) of the LRA 2002 will only operate at law once they have been entered on the Register. The most important of these are expressly created legal easements (s 27(2)(d)) and legal charges (s 27(2)(f)). Failure to register such interests means that they do not operate at law, but as unprotected equitable interests (some of which may be capable of overriding the Register; see Section 15.8).

15.7.3 Other interests

All interests that are not capable of overriding the Register (see Section 15.8) must be entered on the Register if they are to be binding on purchasers of the registered title.

15.7.4 Interests capable of overriding the Register

Many interests capable of overriding the Register can be protected by entering a notice on the Register (a lease with a term of between three and seven years, for example).

The Land Registration Rules 2003 impose a duty on anyone applying for registration to disclose any unregistered interests which they are aware of that override registered dispositions (see rr 28 and 57). However, failure to disclose such an interest does not appear to prevent it continuing to be capable of overriding the Register. Once an interest capable of overriding has been entered on the Register, it will cease to be overriding, even if the notice is subsequently deleted from the Charges Register (see LRA 2002, s 29(3)).

15.7.5 Procedure

Under the 2002 regime, notices can be entered with the agreement of the registered proprietor or unilaterally by the person claiming the interest to be protected (LRA 2002, s 34(2)). The Land Registrar must inform the registered proprietor of the relevant estate of any unilateral notices registered against it (LRA 2002, s 35(1)). The registered proprietor may apply to have a unilateral notice cancelled. If the person who registered the notice does not agree to this, the matter is determined by the Registrar, with an appeal (since 1st July 2013) to the Land Registration division of the Property Chamber, First-tier Tribunal.

15.8 Interests capable of overriding the Register

There are certain third-party interests which do not need to be protected by entry on the Register. These interests override the buyer's interests, whether or not she knew, ought to have known, or even could have known, about them. Since they do not appear on the Register, the greater the number of interests which are given overriding status, the less the Register acts as an accurate reflection of the title. Overriding interests are, therefore, potentially a considerable crack in the 'mirror' (see Section 15.2.3). The traditional explanation given for the existence of overriding interests is that people who have the benefit of these particular rights cannot reasonably be expected to protect them through registration. By their very nature, some interests do not lend themselves to protection by entry on the Register, including, for example, easements created through prescription or by implication and the rights of people in actual occupation of the land. The 1925 scheme also gave overriding status to a number of other types of interests that could be expected to be reasonably apparent to any purchaser, including expressly created legal easements and legal leases for 21 years or less. This helped to reduce the amount of information held at the Land Registry to practicable proportions in a pre-computer age. By the end of the twentieth century, the Law Commission and the Land Registry were agreed that the list of potential overriding interests should be rationalised ((2001) Law Com No 271, para 2.25), and the 2002 Act reduced the number and scope of these interests.

The main overriding interests are now short leases, the rights of people in actual occupation and legal easements and profits. The 2002 Act makes certain distinctions between those interests which will override first registration (listed in Schedule 1; see Table 15.1) and those which will override subsequent, registered dispositions of the land (listed in Schedule 3; see Table 15.2).

At first sight, the rules in Schedule 1 seem to encompass a much wider range of interests than those in Schedule 3, where a number of significant provisos apply (compare, in particular, the respective paragraphs 2 and 3). However, in practice, the difference will be much less significant than might appear. This is because the first registered

Table 15.1 The main unregistered interests which override first registration (Land Registration Act 2002, Sched. 1)

Para 1	*Legal leases for a term not exceeding seven years.*
	Note that:
	▶ leases falling within the categories set out in LRA 2002, s 4(1)(d–f) are not capable of overriding and must be registered (the most important example is a reversionary lease taking effect more than three months after the date of the grant); and
	▶ legal leases with a term of between three and seven years may be protected by entering a notice (see LRA 2002, s 33(b)).
Para 2	*Interests of persons in actual occupation of the land concerned*
	The meanings of the words 'interest' and 'actual occupation' are considered in more detail in Section 15.8.2.
Para 3	*Legal easements and* profits à prendre
	Only legal easements are now capable of overriding the Register. The LRA 2002 effectively reversed the controversial case of *Celsteel Ltd v Alton House Holdings Ltd (No 1)* [1986] 1 WLR 512 (CA), which held that both legal and equitable easements were overriding interests within the 1925 scheme.
	Squatters' rights (ss 11, 12)
	Any rights of a squatter under the Limitation Act 1980 of which the first registered proprietor has notice will override first registration (LRA 2002, ss 11(4)(c) and 12(4)(d)). In other words, a squatter who has successfully adversely possessed the (unregistered) land for 12 years, even though no longer in possession, will be able to have the Register altered in his favour, provided that the new owner had notice of the adverse possession. The doctrine of adverse possession is considered in Chapter 13.

proprietor can only be bound by interests that were valid under the rules of unregistered conveyancing (see Chapter 16). These rules still applied to the land at the date of the transfer (and, indeed, until an application for registration has been made). For example, whether the interests of persons in occupation survive the transfer (that is, are capable of binding the newly registered title) will depend upon whether the interests were properly protected at the time of the transfer by registration as a Land Charge or under the doctrine of notice (see Sections 16.3 and 16.5).

15.8.1 Short leases

Leases granted for more than seven years are substantively registrable (see Section 15.6). Most legal leases granted for seven years or less override on first and subsequent registration, and a purchaser will be bound by them. However, there are certain special types of lease of seven years or less that do not have overriding status and must, therefore, be substantively registered (s 4(1)(d–f)). The most important example is a reversionary lease taking effect more than three months after the date of the grant.

15.8.2 The interests of occupiers

The LRA 2002 recognises the need to protect the third-party interests of people who are in actual occupation of land but who have not protected their rights in the land by registration. This may be because the right arose informally or because they thought that the mere fact of their occupation was enough protection against a purchaser (see (2001)

Table 15.2   The main unregistered interests which override dispositions of registered land (Land Registration Act 2002, Sched. 3)

Para 1	*Legal leases for a term not exceeding seven years, except for:*
	▶ a lease falling within the categories set out in LRA 2002, s 4(1)(d–f) (the most important example is a reversionary lease taking effect more than three months after the date of the grant); and
	▶ a lease which is a registrable disposition for some other reason (see LRA 2002, s 27(2)(b)).
	Legal leases with a term of between three and seven years may be protected by entering a notice (see LRA 2002, s 33(b)).
Para 2	*Interests of persons in actual occupation of the land concerned, unless:*
	▶ the occupier did not disclose her right when asked about it, when she could reasonably have been expected to do so (para 2(b)); or
	▶ the occupation was not obvious on a reasonably careful inspection of the land, and the purchaser did not have actual knowledge of the interest (para 2(c)); or
	▶ the interest being claimed is a reversionary leasehold estate which takes effect in possession after three months from the date of the grant and which had not taken effect at the date of the disposition (para 2(d)). It is unlikely that this third exception will occur very often.
Para 3	*Legal easements or profits à prendre, unless:*
	▶ the new proprietor did not actually know about it (para 3(1)(a)); and
	▶ its existence was not apparent on a reasonably careful inspection of the land (para 3(1)(b)). *However*, even if these conditions are not satisfied, an informally created easement or profit can still override the disposition if the person entitled to it can prove that it had been exercised in the year before the disposition was made (para 3(2)).

Law Com No 254, para 5.61). The provisions in the LRA 2002 replace section 70(1)(g) of the LRA 1925, which was, perhaps, the most contentious and certainly the most litigated of the overriding interests under the 1925 Act. Much of the case law concerning section 70(1)(g) remains relevant. However, care must be taken when using this case law as the provisions of the 2002 Act modify the old law in several important ways. For this reason, a brief comparison of the provisions is set out in Table 15.3.

In order to override, both Schedules provide that the interest must be an 'interest belonging to a person in actual occupation, so far as relating to the land of which he is in actual occupation'. As has been noted above, Schedule 3 contains certain exceptions which prevent the interest of an occupier from overriding *subsequent registered dispositions* of the land. The meanings of 'interest' and 'actual occupation' will now be examined in turn.

15.8.2(a) Interest

The interest must be a proprietary interest in the land, such as possessory rights arising out of a period of adverse possession, or an estate contract (a contract to buy land). A beneficial interest under a trust of land is sufficient (see *Williams & Glyn's Bank Ltd v Boland* [1981] AC 487 (HL)), as is a right arising out of an estoppel (LRA 2002, s 116). Most licences to occupy land are not property interests (see Section 3.7). However, if such a licence affected the conscience of the buyer, then a constructive trust might be imposed (see Section 14.3). The beneficial interest under such a trust would almost certainly be sufficient to potentially override. Some rights are expressly excluded by statute, including rights of occupation under the Family Law Act 1996, rights under the Access to Neighbouring Land Act 1992 and an original tenant's right to an overriding lease under the Landlord and Tenant (Covenants) Act 1995.

Table 15.3 Comparison of Land Registration Act 1925, s 70(1)(g) with Land Registration Act 2002, Sched. 1, para 2 and Sched. 3, para 2

	LRA 1925	LRA 2002	
	s 70(1)(g)	Sched. 1, para 2	Sched. 3, para 2
Who is protected?	A person: (i) in actual occupation; or (ii) in receipt of rents and profits.	Only a person in actual occupation.	
What land is affected?	All land over which the interest is claimed, provided the claimant is in occupation of part of that land.	Only the land actually occupied by the claimant.	
Main exceptions	Enquiry was made of the person in occupation, and the rights were not disclosed.	Rights which are not binding on the purchaser because of the rules of unregistered land (for example, failure to register a land contract as a Land Charge). In such cases, there is no interest in the land for the occupation to protect.	(i) Enquiry was made of the person in occupation, and he failed to disclose the right when he could reasonably have been expected to disclose it; or (ii) the purchaser did not actually know about the interest, and the interest would not have been obvious on a reasonably careful inspection of the land.

It must be stressed that occupation, of itself, is insufficient to override the interests of a purchaser, as the case of *Southern Pacific Mortgages Ltd v Scott* [2014] 3 WLR 1163 illustrates. This case concerned one of nearly a hundred claims arising out of the activities of a nebulous entity called North East Property Buyers (NEPB) in the north of England. Each of the claimants had sold their homes to a nominee of NEPB in return for a cash sum (less than the market value, although this was not apparent on the face of the transfer) and a promise that they could continue to live in their homes for as long as they wished. In recent years many people with financial difficulties have taken advantage of such arrangements to enable them to pay off their debts. Unfortunately, this particular equity release scheme was a scam. NEPB financed each individual purchase with an acquisition mortgage which was registered at the same time as the transfer of the freehold title. None of the lenders was aware of the promises made to the sellers and the terms of the mortgages prohibited the properties concerned being occupied in this way. The scam came to light when NEPB defaulted on the mortgages and the various lenders began to try to realise their security. Lady Hale JSC (giving the majority judgment) concluded that whatever the precise legal status of the nominee purchaser between exchange of contracts and completion of the transaction, the purchaser 'could not create an interest which was capable of being a protected interest for the purpose of the 2002 Act' ([112]). Further, accepting the reasoning promulgated in the House of Lords case of *Abbey National Building Society v Cann* [1991] 1 AC 56 that a transfer and the mortgage financing it are effectively a single transaction, Lady Hale held that there was no *scintilla temporis* during which the nominee held the legal estate unaffected by the lender's charge over it. Consequently, although there was no question that the sellers had been in occupation of the properties at all the material times, there was no proprietary interest which their occupation could protect.

Similarly, a beneficial interest in land can only be protected by occupation if that interest is not overreached by the sale or mortgage. At first sight the facts of *City of London Building Society v Flegg* [1988] AC 54 (HL) seem similar to those of *Williams & Glyn's Bank Ltd v Boland*. Like Mrs Boland, Mr and Mrs Flegg had an unprotected beneficial interest under a trust in a house. However, in their case, the property was vested in two registered proprietors (Mr and Mrs Flegg's daughter and son-in-law), who were both parties to the mortgage. Despite the fact that the Fleggs were in actual occupation, and no enquiry had been made of them, the building society was able to defeat their interest. The House of Lords held that, from the moment that the lender overreached the beneficial interests by paying the mortgage money to two trustees, the beneficiaries no longer had a right to occupy the land but merely a right to share in the proceeds of sale. (For the rules of overreaching, see Section 11.6.1.) Lord Templeman said:

> The right of the [beneficiaries] to be and remain in actual occupation of Bleak House ceased when [their] interests were overreached by the legal charge … There must be a combination of an interest which justifies continuing occupation plus actual occupation to constitute an overriding interest. Actual occupation is not an interest in itself (at 73, 74).

City of London Building Society v Flegg was applied in *State Bank of India v Sood* [1997] Ch 276 (CA), where the interests of the five beneficiaries were overreached on execution of the charge to the bank, even though no capital money was payable.

The moral for beneficiaries is that they must protect themselves by applying for a restriction to be entered on the Register: a beneficial interest cannot be protected by a notice (see LRA 2002, s 33). However, if there is only one legal owner (as in *Williams & Glyn's Bank Ltd v Boland*), the beneficiary is safe for as long as she remains in actual occupation (unless, of course, a second trustee is appointed). Conversely, a buyer of registered land paying two trustees is safe from any beneficial owners provided that the moneys are paid to both trustees. Buyers of land from a single registered proprietor remain subject to what Lord Templeman referred to in *City of London Building Society v Flegg* as 'the waywardness of actual occupation', although for a prudent buyer of an already registered title this is significantly mitigated by the provisos in Schedule 3, paragraph 2.

15.8.2(b) Actual occupation

Since *Williams & Glyn's Bank Ltd v Boland*, whether a person is 'in actual occupation' is a question of fact, not of law. One of the arguments used by the bank in that case was that Mrs Boland could not occupy the house in her own right because, despite her beneficial interest, her occupation was 'nothing but a shadow of her husband's'. Lord Wilberforce declared this doctrine, based on the perceived unity of husband and wife, obsolete. What constitutes 'actual occupation' in any given case will depend on the nature of the land concerned. However:

> Occupation must be, or be referable to, personal physical activity by some one or more individuals: see Lord Wilberforce in *Williams & Glyn's Bank v Boland* [1981] AC 487 at 505B-C – 'physical presence, not some entitlement in law' (per Lloyd LJ, *Chaudhary v Yavuz* [2013] Ch 249 (CA) at [32]).

In *Chaudhary*, the court held that the passage to and fro of tenants and their visitors on a shared staircase did not amount to occupation for the purposes of paragraph 2 of Schedule 3. In *Link Lending Ltd v Bustard* [2010] EWCA Civ 424, Mummery LJ referred, with approval, to the judgment of Lewison J in *Thompson v Foy* [2010] 1 P & CR 16 (Ch), which contains the following five-point summary of the principles of 'actual occupation'.

Actual occupation

Thompson v Foy [2010] 1 P & CR 16 (Ch) at [127]:

(i)   The words 'actual occupation' are ordinary words of plain English and should be interpreted as such. The word 'actual' emphasises that physical presence is required: *Williams & Glyn's Bank v Boland* [1981] AC 487 per Lord Wilberforce at 504;

(ii)   It does not necessarily involve the personal presence of the person claiming to occupy. A caretaker or the representative of a company can occupy on behalf of his employer: *Abbey National BS v Cann* [1991] 1 AC 56 per Lord Oliver at 93;

(iii)   However, actual occupation by a licensee (who is not a representative occupier) does not count as actual occupation by the licensor: *Strand Securities Ltd v Caswell* [1965] Ch 958 per Lord Denning MR at 981;

(iv)   The mere presence of some of the claimant's furniture will not usually count as actual occupation: *Strand Securities Ltd v Caswell* [1965] Ch 958 per Russell LJ at 984;

(v)   If the person said to be in actual occupation at any particular time is not physically present on the land at that time, it will usually be necessary to show that his occupation was manifested and accompanied by a continuing intention to occupy: compare *Hoggett v Hoggett* (1980) 39 P & CR 121, per Sir David Cairns at 127.

Although this summary is helpful, it must be used with care. As Mummery LJ explained during his judgment in *Link Lending v Bustard*:

> The trend of the cases shows that the courts are reluctant to lay down, or even suggest, a single legal test for determining whether a person is in actual occupation. The decisions on statutory construction identify the factors that have to be weighed by the judge on this issue. The degree of permanence and continuity of presence of the person concerned, the intentions and wishes of that person, the length of absence from the property and the reason for it and the nature of the property and personal circumstances of the person are among the relevant factors (at [27]).

The House of Lords had expressed similar caution in the earlier case of *Abbey National Building Society v Cann* [1991] 1 AC 56 (HL). Lord Oliver explained that:

> 'occupation' is a concept which may have different connotations according to the nature and purpose of the property which is claimed to be occupied. It does not necessarily, I think, involve the personal presence of the person claiming to occupy. A caretaker or the representative of a company can occupy, I should have thought, on behalf of his employer. On the other hand, it does, in my judgment, involve some degree of permanence and continuity which would rule out mere fleeting presence. A prospective tenant or purchaser who is allowed, as a matter of indulgence, to go into property in order to plan decorations or measure for furnishings would not, in ordinary parlance, be said to be occupying it, even though he might be there for hours at a time (at 93).

In *Abbey National Building Society v Cann*, the House of Lords held that a mother whose belongings were moved into her new house some 35 minutes before completion of the purchase was not sufficiently in occupation at the time as her occupation lacked the necessary degree of 'permanence and continuity'.

A person may be deemed to be in actual occupation even though she is elsewhere, provided that there is sufficient physical presence 'to put the purchaser on notice that there is someone in occupation' (*Malory Enterprises Ltd v Cheshire Homes (UK) Ltd* [2002] Ch 216 (CA) at [81] (Arden LJ)). Schedule 3, paragraph 2(c) of the LRA 2002 provides that if such physical presence is lacking, the interest will not be overriding unless the purchaser had actual knowledge of it.

A tenant who has sublet all or part of her land is not in actual occupation of the land for the purposes of Schedule 1 and Schedule 3 of the LRA 2002. Intermediate lessors must, therefore, protect their leasehold interest by registration against the freehold title, unless the lease has overriding status in its own right as a legal lease for seven years or less (see Section 15.8.1). This is a change from the situation under the 1925 scheme, which gave overriding status to the interests of a landowner who was 'in receipt of rents and profits'. The 2002 Act removed this protection except where the landowner's interest existed and was protected under section 70(1)(g) before 13 October 2003.

Another important question is the stage at which the person must be in actual occupation. It was established in *Abbey National Building Society v Cann* that for section 70(1)(g), both the right and the occupation must have existed at the moment the transfer was executed, rather than at the time of registration, as the statute seemed to indicate. Further, if the transfer was financed by a contemporaneous mortgage, the transfer and mortgage should be treated as a single, indivisible transaction with no *scintilla* of time between them in which occupation can take place. The Supreme Court has now confirmed in *Southern Pacific Mortgages Ltd v Scott* that the principle in *Cann* applies to cases falling within paragraph 2 of Schedule 3 of the 2002 Act and that the relevant time is the time of the completion of the transaction. As Baroness Hale JSC explained in *Southern Pacific Mortgages Ltd v Scott* [2014] 3 WLR 1163 (SC) at [113]:

> Until registration, the purchaser (and indeed the mortgagee) have only equitable interests ... However, this is machinery, not substance. Assuming that all relevant registration requirements are met, the purchaser has now acquired an absolute right to the legal estate (and the mortgagee an absolute right to the charge).

Where a person has a right over land but is only occupying part of the land concerned, only the land actually occupied will be subject to the overriding interest. The express provisions to this effect in Schedule 1, paragraph 2 and Schedule 3, paragraph 2 reverse the decision in *Ferrishurst v Wallcite* [1999] Ch 355 (CA).

15.8.2(c) The significance of occupiers' interests

Paragraph 2 protects those occupiers who have an otherwise unprotected interest in the land. *Williams & Glyn's Bank Ltd v Boland* represented the high point of protection for beneficial owner-occupiers in registered land. The effect of *Williams & Glyn's Bank Ltd v Boland* was that institutional lenders began, properly, to ensure that there were no resident beneficiaries with rights. Anyone who was going to live in the house was required to agree that the mortgage would take priority over his or her interest, if any. As a result, occupying beneficiaries were less likely to be caught out by a secret mortgage or sale by their trustee. Beneficiaries who were aware of their rights in the land also began to insist on their names being placed on the legal title so that their co-owners could not mortgage the land without their agreement and, as in the case of *City of London Building Society v Flegg*, destroy their property rights. This, in turn, has almost certainly contributed to the considerable increase in the number of cases of undue influence in recent years, which itself has led the courts to develop principles which must be followed by mortgage lenders in order to prevent their commercial interests being defeated (see *Royal Bank of Scotland plc v Etridge* (No 2) [2002] 2 AC 773 (HL) and Section 7.4.4).

15.8.3 Legal easements and profits

The first registered proprietor of a title holds the land subject to any legal easements and *profits à prendre* that affected the registered estate at the date of registration (LRA 2002, ss 11, 12; Sched. 1, para 3). The situation following subsequent dealings with the registered title is, however, more complicated. This is because of the underlying objective of trying to balance the competing demands of preserving important third-party rights in land and not burdening land with rights that a new owner could not have discovered. The consequences of paragraph 3 of Schedule 3 are as follows.

1. Any easements and profits which existed as overriding interests under section 70(1)(a) of the LRA 1925 before 13 October 2003 will continue to have overriding status by virtue of paragraph 9 of Schedule 12 of the LRA 2002. (The LRA 1925 gave overriding status to a much wider class of easements and profits than the LRA 2002, including equitable easements. Paragraph 9 of Schedule 12 ensures that the benefit of these pre-existing rights is not lost.)
2. No easement or profit expressly created out of a registered title after the LRA 2002 came into force on 13 October 2003 is capable of overriding a registered disposition of the land. This is because:
   a. Paragraph 3 protects only legal easements and profits; and
   b. an express easement or profit will not operate at law unless it has been entered on the Register (LRA 2002, ss 27(1) and 27(2)(d)).
3. Any legal easements or profits registered under Part 1 of the Commons Act 2006 will be protected by the scheme contained in that Act.
4. Since 13 October 2006 (see Sched. 12, para 10) legal easements and profits (except those protected by Part 1 of the Commons Act 2006) will override a registered disposition of the land unless (at the time of the disposition):
   a. the disponee (purchaser) had no actual knowledge of the easement or profit (para 3(1)(a)); and
   b. the easement or profit would not have been obvious on a reasonably careful inspection of the land (para 3(1)(b)); and
   c. the easement or profit had not be exercised within the previous year (para 3(2)).

The important exception contained in paragraph 3(2) is designed to protect what Law Com No 271 terms 'invisible' easements, such as rights of drainage (see para 8.70), which could otherwise be easily defeated. The overall policy of the 2002 scheme, however, is to encourage owners of easements which are used only intermittently to protect them by registration rather than rely on them being disclosed to the prospective purchaser during pre-contract enquiries (which provides actual knowledge of the interest).

15.8.4 Other rights which override the Register

For the sake of completeness, it is necessary to consider other rights which override. Perhaps the most important of these is the local land charge. Although they do not appear on the Register, anyone contemplating the purchase of land should check at the local authority's Local Land Charges Registry for any local land charges affecting the property. Other rights which will bind a purchaser on first registration and subsequent transfers of the land are customary rights, public rights, an interest in coal or a coal mine, and certain rights to other mines and minerals.

There is a further category of old section 70(1) of the LRA 1925 overriding interests which had their origin in feudal tenure only temporarily preserved by the LRA 2002. These interests, such as manorial rights, have been described as 'relics from past times' ((2001) Law Com 271, para 8.88). They ceased to be capable of overriding the Register on 13 October 2013 (ten years after the introduction of the 2002 Act). They have not necessarily disappeared altogether, since if they had, the State would, perhaps, be in breach of Article 1, Protocol 1 of the European Convention on Human Rights. Instead, their owners must now protect them by registration or, if the land is not yet registered, by a caution against first registration.

In exceptional circumstances, an otherwise unprotected interest may give rise to a constructive trust that will override the Register. This occurred in the case of *Lyus v Prowsa Developments Ltd* [1982] 1 WLR 1044 (Ch). Mr and Mrs Lyus had acquired an option to purchase a plot of land in a housing development. The developer went bankrupt, and the mortgagee sold the land to Prowsa. This first sale was expressly subject to the option, although it did not have to be, as the option was not an overriding interest (Mr and Mr Lyus were not 'in actual occupation') and there was no way in which the option could have been protected against either the mortgagee or their purchaser (Prowsa) by an entry on the Register. When Prowsa sold the land on, the question arose as to whether the option was enforceable. Dillon J imposed a constructive trust on the buyer because it would be a fraud if Prowsa were allowed to renege on its express undertaking to the mortgagee in favour of Mr and Mrs Lyus. It is important to note that the constructive trust that arises in these circumstances is based not upon the doctrine of notice (see Section 16.5) but upon whether 'the conscience of the estate owner is affected so that it would be inequitable to allow him to deny the claimant an interest in the property' (per Sir Christopher Slade, *Lloyd v Dugdale* [2002] 2 P & CR 13 (CA) at [52]). *Lyus v Prowsa* was considered at length by Lloyd LJ in *Chaudhary v Yavuz* [2013] Ch 249 (CA). He concluded that the LRA 2002:

> does not exclude the possibility that the court may find an obligation binding on the registered proprietor personally, by way of, for example, a constructive trust, as a result of which an obligation which is not protected on the register is nevertheless effective. *Lyus v Prowsa Developments Ltd* is an example of that, and a rare one (at [68]).

It is interesting to compare *Lyus v Prowsa* with decisions in unregistered land such as *Midland Bank Trust Co Ltd (No 1) v Green* [1981] AC 513 (HL) (see Section 16.3.5). Although many people would say that justice was done in *Lyus v Prowsa*, the case created another blank spot on the mirror of the Register.

15.9 Alteration of the Register and indemnity

The Land Registry is concerned to ensure that the Register accurately reflects the title interests and third-party interests in the land, since prospective new owners have no choice but to rely on it. Even so, however careful the Registrar may have been at first registration, and however carefully a buyer may have checked the Register, a registered proprietor might find he has in fact bought nothing, since, under certain circumstances, the Register can be altered.

15.9.1 Alteration and rectification

The provisions on alteration of the Register are found in Schedule 4 of the 2002 Act. This Schedule provides that the court may order alteration (para 2), and the Registrar may alter the Register (para 5) to:

- correct a mistake on the Register; or
- bring the Register up to date; or
- give effect to any estate, right or interest excepted from the effect of registration.

The Registrar is also able to remove superfluous entries.

The most significant type of alteration permitted by the 2002 Act is 'rectification'. This is defined in Schedule 4, paragraph 1 of the Act as:

- the correction of a *mistake*
- that will *prejudicially affect the title of the registered proprietor.*

No rectification may take place against the title of a registered proprietor in possession without his consent unless the conditions in paras 3(2) and 6(2) are satisfied; that is, unless:

- the registered proprietor has substantially contributed to the mistake through fraud or carelessness, or
- it would be unjust for any other reason not to correct the Register (paras 3(2) and 6(2)).

If the interests in Schedules 1 and 3 of the 2002 Act constitute cracks in the mirror, rectification is an exclusion clause in the guarantee of title. The extent of this exclusion depends upon the meaning of the word 'mistake' and the circumstances in which it will be deemed 'unjust' not to alter the Register.

What constitutes a 'mistake' was considered by the Court of Appeal in *Baxter v Mannion* [2011] 1 WLR 1594. Mr Baxter had been registered as proprietor of land owned by Mr Mannion on the basis of Mr Baxter's claim to ten years' adverse possession of the land (see Section 13.5.2). Mr Mannion had not opposed Mr Baxter's original application for registration. However, it was subsequently discovered that Mr Baxter had not actually been in adverse possession for the requisite period. Jacob LJ, who gave the main judgment, concluded that this amounted to a mistake for the purposes of Schedule 4 of the LRA 2002, there being 'no reason for limiting "correction of a mistake" to a mistake through some official error in the course of examination of the application' (at [25]).

In *Fitzwilliam v Richall Holdings Services Ltd* [2013] 1 P & CR 19 (Ch), the defendant was registered as the proprietor of the land by virtue of a fraudulent transfer. In *Malory Enterprises Ltd v Cheshire Homes (UK) Ltd* [2002] Ch 216 (CA) the Court of Appeal had held that a fraudulent transfer was not a 'disposition' of land for the purposes of the LRA 1925. Newey J concluded that the relevant provisions in the 2002 Act were sufficiently similar to those considered in *Malory Enterprises Ltd* for him to be bound by that decision and he ordered that the Register be altered to restore Mr Fitzwilliam as the registered proprietor. *Fitzwilliam*, like *Malory Enterprises Ltd* before it, has been criticised for undermining the philosophy behind the 2002 Act (and section 58 of that Act in particular). Whether these concerns are shared by the senior judiciary is, for the present, unknown: Mr Fitzwilliam and Richall Holdings settled their case before it was heard by the Court of Appeal. However, it is worth comparing Mr Fitzwilliam's circumstances with those of Mr Guy in the earlier case of *Barclays Bank plc v Guy* [2008] EWCA Civ 452. This case concerned a 48-acre site in Manchester originally belonging to Mr Guy, but to which Ten Acre Ltd became the registered proprietor as the result of a fraudulent transfer document. Ten Acre Ltd then granted a legal charge to Barclays Bank, before becoming insolvent. Mr Guy claimed that the original transfer document was void, and sought to set aside both the original transfer and Barclay's legal charge. Had Mr Guy taken action before the bank's legal charge had been entered on the Register, there seems little doubt that the court could have ordered rectification (as Newey J did in *Fitzwilliam*). However, the Court of Appeal concluded that section 58 of the LRA 2002 means that the Proprietorship Register is conclusive, even when the registered proprietor was not actually entitled to be registered as such. Consequently, so far as the registration of the charge was concerned, there was no mistake to be corrected.

> I simply cannot see how it could be argued that if the purchaser or chargee knows nothing of the problem underlying the intermediate owner's title, that the registration of the charge or sale to the ultimate purchaser or chargee can be said to be a mistake. That seems to me inconsistent with the structure and terms of the 2002 Act (per Lloyd LJ at [23]).

The question of when it is 'for any other reason unjust for the alteration not to be made' for the purpose of paras 3(2) and 6(2) has, however, been considered by the Court of Appeal. In *Baxter v Mannion* (the facts of which are set out above) it was held that it would be unjust not to order rectification, as the loss of the title would be disproportionate to Mr Mannion's '[M]ere failure to operate bureaucratic machinery' (at [42]). On this reasoning, it is difficult to see many circumstances in which rectification will not be ordered once a mistake has been proved, unless there has been some dealing with the registered title since the mistake occurred. *Walker v Burton* [2014] 1 P & CR 9 (CA) concerned manorial rights in Ireby, a small village near the highest point in Lancashire. The Burtons had, erroneously as it turned out, been recognised as the lords of the manor and, as a result, been registered as proprietors of 362 acres of moorland known as Ireby Fell. The question before the Court of Appeal was whether the register should be rectified by the cancellation of the registration of title to the freehold of the Fell. Mummery LJ, who gave the only substantial judgment, held at that:

> Whether or not there would be an injustice is an assessment to be made by the fact-finding tribunal in the light of all the relevant data. An appellate court should not interfere with that assessment, unless there has been a self-misdirection of law, or an error of principle, or the assessment is one which no reasonable Adjudicator, properly directing himself, would have made ([at 100]).

In particular, the fact that just because the mistake was consequential on a mistake that had been corrected (the erroneous registration of title to the Lordship of the Manor), did not automatically mean that it would be unjust not to alter the registered title to the fell.

In *Sainsbury's Supermarkets Ltd v Olympia Homes Ltd* (see Section 15.1 and 15.10), Mann J held that it would be unjust not to order rectification against the registered proprietor because it had been aware of the right being claimed when it acquired the land and had, until relatively late in the day, believed itself to be bound by that right. Not to order rectification would give the registered proprietor an unexpected windfall. This solution also saved the State from having to bear the cost of such a windfall, as presumably the claimant would have applied for indemnity under Schedule 8 to the LRA 2002 if rectification had not been ordered.

15.9.2 Indemnity

Schedule 8 provides for State compensation to be paid for loss caused by rectification or failure to rectify. Anyone hoping for an indemnity must take care, since paragraph 5 provides that there will be no compensation if the loser caused the loss by fraud or lack of proper care, and his compensation will be reduced if his negligence contributed to his loss. No compensation is payable to a proprietor affected by a pre-existing interest which overrides registration.

15.10 Returning to Matlock

Sainsbury's Supermarkets Ltd v Olympia Homes Ltd [2006] 1 P & CR 17 (Ch), the facts of which are summarised in Section 15.1, illustrates why it is still important to clearly distinguish between legal and beneficial ownership of land. It is also an illustration of how wider aspects of land law often need to be combined with a systematic use of the relevant rules from the LRA 2002 in order to resolve land disputes. It will be helpful to consider the chain of reasoning which led Mann J to order that the Register be rectified in Sainsbury's favour.

1. On the facts, the agreement between Mr Hughes and Sainsbury's had given Sainsbury's an equitable interest in the land (an estate contract).
2. Under the rules of the LRA 1925, which applied at the time, the cancellation of Mr Hughes' application for first registration meant that the legal estate reverted to British Gas holding it on trust for Mr Hughes ([69]–[71]). The same result is now achieved by LRA 2002, s 7(2).
3. Consequently, at the date of the charging order in favour of Westpac, Mr Hughes had only an equitable interest in the land. Since the charging order could not charge a greater interest in the land than that enjoyed by Mr Hughes, it was an equitable charge over an equitable interest in the land ([72]).
4. Westpac could not, therefore, sell a legal estate in the land to Olympia. Olympia had acquired only the beneficial interest in the land ([79]). In such circumstances, usual rules of priority apply, and the earlier equity (the interest belonging to Sainsbury's) would prevail.
5. The Land Registry should not have registered Olympia with freehold title absolute as Olympia had no legal title to the land ([84]). However, as Olympia was a registered proprietor in possession for the purposes of paragraph 3(2) of Schedule 4 to the LRA 2002, rectification could only be ordered if one or more of the conditions in paragraph 3(2) were satisfied.
6. It would be unjust under paragraph 3(2)(b) of Schedule 4 to the LRA 2002 not to order rectification of the Register to protect Sainsbury's rights. Olympia had believed at all material times, both before and after completion of its acquisition of the land, that it would have to make land available for the roundabout without payment from Sainsbury's ([95]). To hold otherwise would mean that Olympia might be able to negotiate a significant payment from Sainsbury's in return for enabling the roundabout to be constructed.

7. Although Olympia was not entitled to be registered as proprietor of the estate, little point would be served by cancelling the registration ([97]). This pragmatic approach saved the various parties from the expense and inconvenience of the considerable legal formalities that would have been required to cancel the existing title number, formally transfer legal title to Olympia and register that title under a new number.

15.11 Looking back and looking ahead

The 2002 Act has had fundamental consequences for the way lawyers think about and deal with land. One of the main objectives of the scheme of registration was to do away with the difficulties caused by the doctrine of notice (discussed in more detail in Section 16.2.2 and 16.5). Law Com No 271 stated that the doctrine 'as a general principle … has no application whatever in determining the priority of interests in registered land' (para 5.16). The report recognised, however, that on first registration, the new proprietor should take the land subject to any rights under the Limitation Act 1980 of which he had notice. It also recognised that something similar to notice is relevant in two further categories of interests that have overriding status: the interests of those in actual occupation and certain legal easements. However, the report was at pains to point out that 'knowledge' in these circumstances is not the same as the old doctrine of notice in unregistered land, but comes from a conveyancing rule which requires a seller to disclose to the buyer any burdens on the land which would not be obvious on a reasonable inspection and which the buyer does not know about.

Another major shift in legal thinking, reflected in the 2002 Act, is the acceptance by the Law Commission and the judiciary that registered and unregistered title are two distinct systems:

> it is now highly desirable that land registration in England and Wales should develop according to principles that reflect both the nature and the potential of land registration … there seems little point in inhibiting the rational development of the principles of property law by reference to a system that is rapidly disappearing, and in relationship to which there is a diminishing expertise amongst the legal profession … both the computerisation of the register and the move to electronic conveyancing make possible many improvements in the law that cannot be achieved with an unregistered system ((1998) Law Com No 254, para 1.6).

This is quite a change from the approach taken by the judge in *Kingsnorth Finance Co Ltd v Tizard* [1986] 1 WLR 783 (Ch), some 12 years before Law Com No 254. In that case, considered in more detail in Section 16.5, Judge Finlay QC seems to have assumed that the outcome (and the underlying rules) should be the same regardless of ... the title to the land is registered or unregistered.

The LRA 2002 did much to pave the way for the tronic conveyancing, where, except in the case of interests, the creation or transfer of interests is only a istration. Such a scheme would eliminate the 'registra between disposition and registration and remove the mentation (including contracts and deeds). More recen electronic conveyancing has declined. There are variou technical challenges and concerns about the security o 2011, the Land Registry suspended its programme to de transactions beyond the creation and discharge of legal

The Land Registry's aim of completing the Register means that it must continue to find ways of encouraging landowners to register unregistered titles. Much progress has been made, but some landowners remain reluctant to have their titles open to public inspection, and others will not wish to pay the fees associated with registration. The Act itself encourages landowners to register their titles, including offering significant protection against adverse possessors (see Section 13.5.2). In addition, section 79 of the LRA 2002 makes specific provision for the Queen to grant herself freehold title out of her demesne land, which she must then register. Demesne land is land which the Crown holds for itself as the 'ultimate feudal overlord' and which is not therefore held on a fee simple or term of years – the only estates which can be registered. The Law Commission believes that this could lead to the disappearance of feudal tenure in England and Wales (see (2001) Law Com No 271, para 2.37).

Although some may regret the passing of unregistered conveyancing, registration of title to land is generally considered 'A Good Thing'. Nonetheless, it is valuable to consider its failings and limitations. Only then is it possible to decide whether, as is usually assumed, registration of title really is of benefit to all buyers and sellers of land. For example, it is clear that title registration does not, of itself, solve the conflicts of interests that arise between people with interests in the same parcel of land. Land can be enjoyed in different ways, and people have different needs in relation to it.

The Land Register was originally introduced to simplify conveyancing by removing the need for repetitive examinations of title deeds. One of the main driving forces behind the 2002 Act was the need to simplify the process further, and to make the Register as far as possible a perfect mirror of title, in readiness for the electronic revolution to come. Should simplification of the conveyancing process be the dominant rationale behind all land law? What is the place of other important principles, such as security of occupation? Are equitable doctrines such as estoppel robust enough to protect the person who, through no fault of her own, fails to comply with the formalities prescribed by the LRA 2002?

Summary

15.1 Registration of title to land is designed to offer a simple and efficient form of conveyancing, by providing a guaranteed mirror of most rights in the land and promising State compensation for loss.

15.2 The rules needed to determine when an owner of registered land (the registered proprietor) will be bound by other people's interests in her land are contained in the LRA 2002.

15.3 Almost all dealings with legal estates (except for leases not exceeding seven years) trigger first registration of the relevant title. Subsequent dealings with a title that has been registered must be reported to the Land Registry using the appropriate form.

15.4 The Register is divided into three sections: property, proprietorship and charges. Each part of the Register contains specific information about the land, the title and the burdens on the land.

15.5 Interests in registered land are divided into four main groups:

▸ registrable estates;

▸ legal interests listed in LRA 2002, s 27(2) that must be completed at law by entry on the Register;

Summary cont'd

- interests capable of protection on the Register; and
- interests which override registration.

15.6 Legal freeholds and leases over seven years are substantively registrable; title to them may be absolute, possessory or qualified, or good leasehold.

15.7 Legal charges are protected by entering a registered charge on the Register. Most other interests in land are capable of being protected by entering a notice. The exceptions are listed in LRA 2002, s 33.

15.8 The interests capable of overriding the Register are listed in Schedules 1 and 3 LRA 2002 (depending on whether it is a first registration or a subsequent registered disposition) and include easements, leases and the interests of people in actual occupation of land. Overriding interests override any buyer of an interest in registered land.

15.9 The Register may be altered, even against a registered proprietor in possession (rectification). The State may provide compensation where anyone suffers loss by reason of rectification.

Exercises

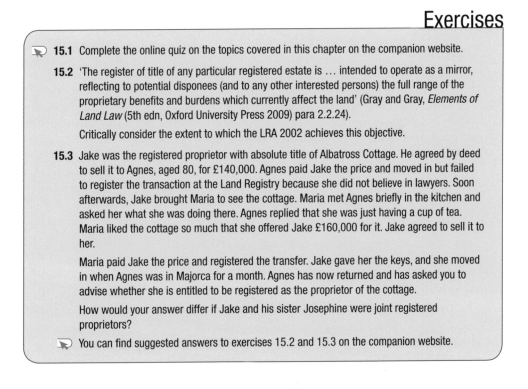

15.1 Complete the online quiz on the topics covered in this chapter on the companion website.

15.2 'The register of title of any particular registered estate is … intended to operate as a mirror, reflecting to potential disponees (and to any other interested persons) the full range of the proprietary benefits and burdens which currently affect the land' (Gray and Gray, *Elements of Land Law* (5th edn, Oxford University Press 2009) para 2.2.24).

Critically consider the extent to which the LRA 2002 achieves this objective.

15.3 Jake was the registered proprietor with absolute title of Albatross Cottage. He agreed by deed to sell it to Agnes, aged 80, for £140,000. Agnes paid Jake the price and moved in but failed to register the transaction at the Land Registry because she did not believe in lawyers. Soon afterwards, Jake brought Maria to see the cottage. Maria met Agnes briefly in the kitchen and asked her what she was doing there. Agnes replied that she was just having a cup of tea. Maria liked the cottage so much that she offered Jake £160,000 for it. Jake agreed to sell it to her.

Maria paid Jake the price and registered the transfer. Jake gave her the keys, and she moved in when Agnes was in Majorca for a month. Agnes has now returned and has asked you to advise whether she is entitled to be registered as the proprietor of the cottage.

How would your answer differ if Jake and his sister Josephine were joint registered proprietors?

You can find suggested answers to exercises 15.2 and 15.3 on the companion website.

Further reading

Battersby, 'More Thoughts on Easements under the Land Registration Act 2002' [2005] 69
   Conv 195
Bogusz, 'Defining the Scope of Actual Occupation under the Land Registration Act 2002:
   Some Recent Judicial Clarification' [2011] 75 Conv 268

Further reading cont'd

Cooke, 'The Register's Guarantee of Title' [2013] 77 Conv 345

Dixon, 'Proprietary Rights and Rectifying the Effect of Non-registration' [2005] 69 Conv 447

Dixon, 'Protecting Third-Party Interests under the Land Registration Act 2002: To Worry or Not to Worry, That Is the Question' in Dixon and Griffith (eds), *Contemporary Perspectives on Property, Equity and Trusts Law* (Oxford University Press 2007) 19

Gardner, 'Alteration of the Register: An Alternative View' [2013] 77 Conv 531

Gravells, 'Getting Your Priorities Right' [2010] 74 Conv 169

Law Commission, *Land Registration for the Twenty-First Century* (Law Com No 254, 1998)

Law Commission, *Land Registration for the Twenty-First Century: A Conveyancing Revolution* (Law Com No 271, 2001)

Chapter 16 follows overleaf.

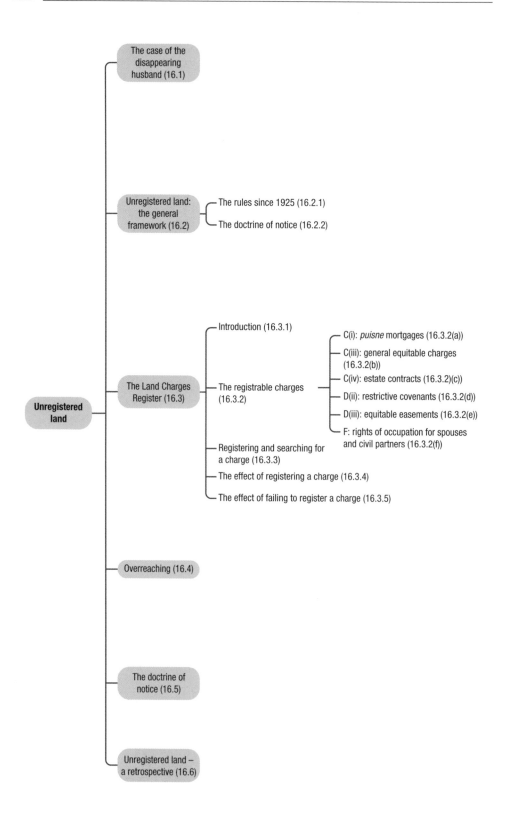

Unregistered land

Key concepts

- ▶ **Land charges** – interests in unregistered land capable of protection through registration in the Land Charges Register.
- ▶ **Notice** – the rule, now of limited application, which governed whether a purchaser of an unregistered legal estate for value took the title subject to any equitable interests in the land.
- ▶ **Overreaching** – transferring the beneficial interest from the land that was subject to the trust to the proceeds of sale (or mortgage) of the land.

The significance of the rules of unregistered title

A significant majority of titles to land in England and Wales are already registered. In most cases, therefore, the priority of any interests in land will fall to be determined using the rules considered in Chapter 15. However, there are a number of reasons why some understanding of the rules of unregistered land can be helpful.

- ▶ The rules are of practical importance because they:
  - – apply to any dispute concerning land to which the title is still unregistered; and
  - – are relevant to determining what interests were capable of binding the title at the date of first registration (see Sections 15.3.1 and 15.8).

- ▶ The rules equip the land lawyer to better understand and evaluate important doctrines and concepts because:
  - – they are the legal context in which most of the basic doctrines of land law first developed; and
  - – they provide an alternative against which, through comparison, to illuminate and test the rules of registered title.

16.1 The case of the disappearing husband

In 1978, Mr and Mrs Tizard purchased a plot of land at Lechlade. Although they effectively contributed to the purchase in equal shares, legal title to the land was in Mr Tizard's name alone. There they built Willowdown, to be home to them and their two children. Unfortunately, their relationship became strained, and sometime in 1982 Mrs Tizard moved into the spare bedroom. Eventually, she began to spend some nights away from the house, staying at her sister's house or the cottage of a friend. However, early each morning she would drive to Willowdown to give the children breakfast, and she returned there each evening so that she and the children could eat their evening meal together. On the frequent occasions when Mr Tizard did not spend the night at the house, Mrs Tizard would stay at Willowdown overnight. Most of her clothes, toiletries and nightwear were there. In April 1983, Mr Tizard obtained a three-month loan of £66,000 secured by way of mortgage on Willowdown. Two months later, Mrs Tizard arrived at the house to find a note from Mr Tizard saying that he was going on holiday abroad with one of the children. Neither returned. The loan was not repaid, and the lender sought possession of the house.

Kingsnorth Finance Co Ltd v Tizard [1986] 1 WLR 783 (Ch) is one of a number of significant cases from the 1980s in which the court had to balance the interests of an institutional lender against those of an innocent person claiming a beneficial interest in mortgaged land. Most of these cases, the most important of which is *Williams & Glyn's Bank Ltd v Boland* [1981] AC 487 (HL), concerned registered land and turned on whether the beneficiary's interest was capable of overriding the mortgage (see Section 15.8.2(a)). However, in 1983 the title to Willowdown was still unregistered. Consequently, it fell to Judge John Finlay QC, sitting as a judge of the High Court, to determine whether the finance company could enforce its charge against Mrs Tizard's share of the land. Would the rules of unregistered land produce a similar result to that in *Williams & Glyn's Bank Ltd v Boland*?

16.2 Unregistered land: the general framework

The main differences between registered and unregistered title are summarised in Section 2.5 and in Table 2.3). Fundamentally, in unregistered land, title is established by producing the title deeds, whereas in registered land it is the registration of ownership at the Land Registry that counts.

16.2.1 The rules since 1925

The basic rules of unregistered land

A buyer in good faith and for money or money's worth of a legal interest is bound by:

▷ any pre-existing legal interest (except an unregistered *puisne* mortgage; see Section 16.3.2(a)); and
▷ any interest which must be registered under the Land Charges Act 1972, and is properly registered; and
▷ any other interest:
   – which could not have been registered under the Land Charges Act 1972; and
   – which has not been overreached within the statutory limits imposed in 1925; and
   – of which the buyer has actual, imputed or constructive notice.

A buyer of an equitable interest is bound by almost all pre-existing legal and equitable interests.

Legal interests are normally discovered during the enquiries made before purchase. However, even if they are not discovered until later, the buyer is still bound by them, although the seller would be liable in damages if he has failed to deliver the unburdened land he promised.

When the land is unregistered, four sets of rules must be applied in turn:

---

1. *Legal estates and interests*	All prior legal estates and interests, except for *puisne* mortgages, automatically bind the owner of the land.
2. *Land charges*	The Land Charges Act 1972 contains a list of burdens on unregistered land that must be protected by entry in the Land Charges Register. (The relevant rules are summarised in Section 16.3.)
3. *Overreaching*	Beneficial interests in the land will be overreached if the conditions in sections 2 and 27 of the LPA 1925 are satisfied (see Section 11.6.1).
4. *The doctrine of notice*	The status of any interests not falling within rules 1–3 is determined using the equitable doctrine of notice (see Sections 16.2.2 and 16.5).

16.2.2   The doctrine of notice

It can be seen from the summary of the four sets of rules above that the doctrine of notice now plays only a residuary role in determining disputes concerning unregistered land. The doctrine is used only when none of the other sets of rules apply. However, until the reforms introduced by the 1925 legislation, the doctrine of notice was of much greater importance. Prior to 1926, the buyer of a legal interest in land was bound by any equitable interests of which he had, or was deemed to have, notice. One of the objectives behind the 1925 legislation was the desire to protect both the buyer of the land and the holders of equitable interests by releasing them from the uncertainties of the doctrine of notice. It is helpful, therefore, to summarise the equitable doctrine of notice before considering the post-1925 rules in more detail.

Under the doctrine of notice, an equitable interest will not bind the *bona fide* purchaser of a legal estate for value without notice (actual, imputed or constructive) of the interest. Such a person is known as 'Equity's Darling'.

Equity's Darling:

Bona fide	in good faith (the meaning of this term is discussed in a slightly different context in *Midland Bank Trust Co Ltd v Green (No 1)* [1981] AC 513 (HL))
purchaser	▸ includes: ▸ a sale and purchase; ▸ a gift; ▸ the grant of a lease; and ▸ a mortgage; ▸ but not intestacy or bankruptcy (see LPA 1925, s 205(1)(xxi))
for value	money, money's worth, or a future marriage
of a legal estate	not an equitable estate
without notice	actual, constructive or implied (see below)

The three types of notice:

Actual notice	Has the mind of the purchaser 'been brought to an intelligent apprehension of the nature of the incumbrance which has come upon the property so that a reasonable man, or an ordinary man of business, would act upon the information and would regulate his conduct by it' (per Lord Cairns LC, *Lloyd v Banks* (1867–68) LR 3 Ch App 488 (ChApp) at 490)?
Constructive notice	'Constructive notice is the knowledge which the courts impute to a person ... either from his knowing something which ought to have put him to further inquiry or from his wilfully abstaining from inquiry, to avoid notice' (per Farwell J, *Hunt v Luck* [1901] 1 Ch 45 (Ch) at 52). Constructive notice will only extend to the facts which would have been discovered had the necessary further enquiries been made.
Imputed notice	A purchaser is deemed to have the same actual or constructive notice as his professional advisors (LPA 1925, s 199(1)(ii)(b)).

The difficulty with the doctrine of notice is that someone with an equitable interest in land cannot be sure that it will survive the sale of a legal estate in that land. Nor can a buyer ever be completely sure that he has done enough to be free from constructive notice of all the equitable rights that might exist over the land he is purchasing. For example, in one nineteenth-century case, the defendant had bought a house with 12 flues in it, but 14 chimneys in the wall. Sir John Romilly MR concluded:

> The question is, was he not bound to see that he alone had twelve out of the fourteen, and does it not follow that two must have been used by the adjoining neighbour? He might not have thought fit to count them, or look at them, but I think he was put on inquiry, and that he cannot now say that he had no notice of the agreement by which [the neighbouring house used the other two chimneys] (*Hervey v Smith* (1856) 22 Beav 299 at 302, 52 ER 1123 (Ch) at 1125).

16.3 The Land Charges Register

16.3.1 Introduction

The introduction by the 1925 legislation of the need to register certain interests in land was intended to release both the buyer of the land and the holder of the interest in it from the uncertainties of the doctrine of notice. Registering an interest in the appropriate regis-ter is now deemed to be 'actual notice' of the charge, and so it binds the buyer (LPA 1925, s 198). The Land Charges Department is responsible for five separate registers under the Land Charges Act (LCA) 1972 (which replaced the Land Charges Act 1925). The most important of these is the Land Charges Register. Failure to register a land charge usually means that the interest does not bind the buyer (LCA 1972, s 4; see Section 16.3.5).

Land charges are burdens on land; there are 11 altogether, divided into 'classes' A to F. The interests which can be registered there are, in theory, those which are otherwise difficult for the buyer of land to discover. The registrable interests are mostly equita-ble and are often described as 'commercial' rather than 'family' interests (trusts). Since 1925, family interests are dealt with by overreaching (see Section 11.6.1).

Many students find the presence of a register within a system called 'unregistered land' confusing and counter-intuitive. It is important to remember, however, that the question of whether land is registered or unregistered refers to the status of the title to the land (that is, how ownership is proved), rather than how particular interests in the land are protected. The Land Charges Register must not be confused with the registers of title to registered land (see Chapter 15). Neither should it be confused with the reg-ister of local land charges held by each local authority under the Local Land Charges Act 1975. The register of local land charges records other types of burdens on land fall-ing within the jurisdiction of the relevant local authority, including financial matters (resulting, for example, from non-payment of council tax) and planning matters such as planning consents and tree preservation orders.

16.3.2 The registrable charges

Interests registrable in the Land Charges Register under LCA 1972, s 2

The most important interests are shown in **bold**.

Class	Interest
A	Charges created by a person making an application for them under a statute (for example, the costs of certain works carried out by a public authority, but payable by the landowner)

B	Charges created automatically by a statute (for example, a charge on land in respect of unpaid contributions towards legal aid relating to the recovery of that land)
C(i)	**A legal mortgage where the borrower did not deposit the title deeds with the lender (a *puisne* mortgage)**
C(ii)	A limited owner's charge; this arises where an owner's interest is limited by a trust: if he pays a tax bill himself instead of mortgaging the land to pay it, he owns this equitable interest
C(iii)	**A general equitable charge; this seems to cover, for example, an equitable mortgage of a legal estate without deposit of title deeds, and certain annuities**
C(iv)	**An estate contract: a contract to transfer a legal interest in land**
D(i)	An Inland Revenue charge: a charge on land arises automatically if the tax due on an estate at death is not paid
D(ii)	**A restrictive covenant *created since 1925*, excluding leasehold covenants**
D(iii)	**An equitable easement *created since 1925***
E	Annuities; now obsolete
F	**A right of occupation in the family home due to civil partnership or marriage**

16.3.2(a) C(i): puisne mortgages

Puisne mortgages are legal mortgages that have not been protected by requiring the borrower to deposit the title deeds of the property with the lender. This will usually occur when the mortgage is not the first loan secured on the land: the title deeds will remain in the hands of the first mortgagee. If *puisne* mortgages are automatically binding on a purchaser (as is normally the case with legal interests), there is a significant risk that a purchaser may not discover the existence of such a charge until too late. Consequently, since 1925, buyers have been protected from undisclosed *puisne* mortgages by the requirement that the lender register them as a Class C(i) land charge.

16.3.2(b) C(iii): general equitable charges

This residuary category of equitable land charge is actually more limited than its title suggests. Section 2(4) of the LCA 1972 provides that it does not extend to interests arising under a trust. Neither does it appear to include interests arising by way of proprietary estoppel. According to *ER Ives Investment Ltd v High* [1967] 2 QB 379 (CA) the doctrine of estoppel was of too recent development to have been within the contemplation of Parliament during the passage of the original Land Charges Act in 1925 (see Section 16.3.2(e)).

16.3.2(c) C(iv): estate contracts

[An] estate contract is a contract by an estate owner ... to convey or create a legal estate, including a contract conferring ... a valid option of purchase, a right of pre-emption or any other like right (LCA, s 2(4)(iv)).

As shown in Section 12.3, a buyer of land (whether of a fee simple or a lease or some other interest) is normally recognised as having some equitable interest in the land as soon as there is a contract. This right is an estate contract. Most solicitors do not bother to register such estate contracts because the contracts are nearly always successfully completed. If, however, completion is likely to be delayed, or if the buyer is suspicious of the seller, then the charge should be registered. Some types of contract should always be registered, including:

- *Options to purchase.* An option to purchase will bind a purchaser only if protected by registration in the Land Charges Register.
- *Rights of pre-emption.* A right of pre-emption is the right to be given first refusal if the landowner decides to sell the land. In the case of *Pritchard v Briggs* [1980] Ch 338 (CA) it was held that no interest in land can arise until the decision to sell is made. Consequently, such rights can only be registered after the landowner has decided to sell. The decision in *Pritchard* has been heavily criticised and was distinguished in *Dear v Reeves* [2002] Ch 1 (CA) (although that case was not about the LCA 1972).
- *Equitable leases* that are also estate contracts must be registered. In *Hollington Brothers Ltd v Rhodes* [1951] 2 All ER 578n (Ch), the owner of the equitable lease failed to protect it by registration. It was therefore held void against the buyer of the freehold reversion, even though the buyer of the freehold had known about the equitable lease from the outset and had paid less for the land because of it.
- *A tenant's option to renew a lease or to buy the freehold.* These options are registrable interests within this class. This is so even if the option is contained within a legal lease and was known about by all parties (*Phillips v Mobil Oil Co Ltd* [1989] 1 WLR 888 (CA)).

16.3.2(d) D(ii): restrictive covenants

The registration requirement only applies to restrictive covenants created after 1925.

16.3.2(e) D(iii): equitable easements

This is:

> an easement, right or privilege over or affecting land created on or after 1st January 1926 being merely an equitable interest (LCA, s 2(5)(iii)).

Unfortunately, this definition is not as simple as it appears. An equitable easement often arises out of an informal arrangement which no one would think of seeing a solicitor about, in which case it is unlikely to be protected by registration. In *ER Ives Investments Ltd v High*, a block of flats was being built on a bomb-site, and it was discovered that the foundations trespassed on the neighbouring plot. Mr High, the owner of that plot, agreed (unfortunately not by deed) that he would allow the foundations to remain there if he could use a drive over the developer's land. He then built a garage on his own land at the end of the drive. This arrangement was clearly an equitable easement. However, it was never protected by registration as a Class D(iii) land charge. Both plots of land changed hands, and the new owners of the flats decided they wanted to stop their neighbour's use of their drive. They argued that the equitable easement was void for non-registration. The Court of Appeal decided that the LCA 1925 (the case preceded the 1972 Act) 'was not the end of the matter' since there were rights arising from the mutuality principle and from estoppel (see Section 14.4) which were not affected by the failure to register. Mutuality is an ancient principle: a person cannot reject a burden, the neighbour using the drive, so long as she wants to enjoy a related benefit, the trespass of the foundations (see also Section 9.6.2). The estoppel arose because the landowner had allowed Mr High to spend a considerable amount on building the garage, knowing that Mr High believed himself to have a legal right to use the drive. Mr High was, therefore, allowed to continue to use the drive so long as the foundations of the flats remained on his land.

ER Ives Investments Ltd v High represents one of the very few examples of courts finding a way around the LCA in order to arrive at a just result.

16.3.2(f) F: rights of occupation for spouses and civil partners

Section 30 of the Family Law Act (FLA) 1996 (as amended by the Civil Partnership Act 2004) gives a spouse or civil partner who is not already a co-owner a statutory right to occupy the dwelling house owned by the other spouse. This right of occupation, available to either party to the marriage or civil partnership, was originally created under the Matrimonial Homes Act 1967 in an attempt to solve some of the problems which can arise when one party to the relationship (historically, usually the husband) is the sole legal owner of the home. Under the pre-1967 law, he could sell it and run off whenever he liked, and the deserted partner could not protect herself and their children in advance (see *National Provincial Bank Ltd v Ainsworth* [1965] AC 1175 (HL)). In theory, the Class F charge is a simple, cheap and efficient solution. In *Wroth v Tyler* [1974] Ch 30 (Ch), the contracts were exchanged for the sale of the family home, which was in Mr Tyler's sole name. A day later, Mrs Tyler registered a Class F land charge. This prevented Mr Tyler from being able to transfer the house to the buyers with vacant possession. In the circumstances, however, the court refused to grant the claimants the equitable remedy of specific performance because this would force Mr Tyler to begin proceedings against his wife. Instead, the court awarded the claimants damages calculated to place them in the same financial position that they would have been in had the sale been completed.

Wroth v Tyler is somewhat unusual. Many non-owning partners do not discover the possibility of registering a Class F charge until it is too late, and it is of no use to people living together who are not married or in a civil partnership. Although the right of occupation is binding on a purchaser if it has been protected by registration, the court has discretion to terminate the rights against a purchaser where it is just and reasonable to do so. (See FLA 1996, section 34(2) which places the decision in *Kaur v Gill* [1988] Fam 110 (CA) on a statutory footing.)

16.3.3 Registering and searching for a charge

Registering an interest is a simple matter. Its owner fills in a short form giving his own details, the nature of the charge and the name of the owner of the land which is subject to the charge (the estate owner). All charges are registered against the name of the landowner and not against the land itself. Such a name-based register causes all kinds of problems, not least because people who fill in forms make typing errors. Apparently, the Register contains charges registered against people with first names like Nacny, Brain and Farnk. If the wrong name is given on the charge registration form, and the purchaser searches against the correct name, the purchaser will normally take free from the charge. In an extraordinary case where both the registration and the search were against (different) incorrect names, the attempt at registration was held to be valid against a mortgagee who had taken two years from his discovery of the mistake to take action (*Oak Cooperative Building Society v Blackburn* [1968] Ch 730 (CA)).

Registration protects an interest that is valid, but cannot perfect an invalid interest. Although it is possible to register ineffective charges on the Register, registration alone does not make the charge valid. For example, a prospective purchaser will need to ensure that the benefit and burden of any registered restrictive covenants have run with the land. The Registrar has the power to 'vacate the Register' (that is, to remove invalid charges). In fact, many charges in the Register are a waste of space (including the many estate contracts which have been completed and the many *puisne* mortgages which have been redeemed). The Register thus tends to increase, rather than reduce, the apparent burdens on title.

Anyone can search the Register, but it is usual – and safer – to have an official search carried out by the staff at the Registry. To search for a charge is also a simple matter, requiring a form giving the names of the people who have owned the land, and the appropriate fee. Legal professionals can also make searches electronically and by telephone. The staff at the Registry search against the estate owners' names as requested and send back a form giving details of any charges they discover. In practice, these are often already known to the buyer from the investigations before exchange of contracts (see Section 12.1).

The official certificate of search is conclusive (LCA 1972, s 10). If it fails to give details of a charge, the charge is void, despite the fact that the charge appears on the Register (the owner of the charge will receive compensation for the negligence of the Registry). The official certificate also gives the person who requested the search 15 working days' protection from having any further charges registered (LCA 1972, s 11). Thus, once the official search has been made, the buyer is safe, provided the sale is completed within the 15 days.

One of the problems with using the Land Charges Register is that it is possible that a charge was registered against the name of the correct estate owner, but that today's buyer of the land is unable to discover the name of that owner because it is hidden behind the root of the title. A seller of unregistered land must provide a deed (the 'root of title') proving that she has a good legal title going back only at least 15 years (LPA 1969, s 23). The buyer cannot insist that the seller produce any documents earlier than the root of title. However, the buyer is deemed to have notice of, and to be bound by, any charge that was registered before the date of the root of title, even though no amount of prudence could have uncovered it. In these circumstances, the buyer can claim compensation (LPA 1969, s 25). As time passes, more and more charges lie behind the root of title. Wade (1956) described this problem as a 'Frankenstein's monster' which grows more dangerous and harder to kill as the years pass, although his fears have yet to be realised.

16.3.4 The effect of registering a charge

Section 198 of the LPA 1925 (as amended) states that:

> The registration of any instrument or matter in any register kept under the Land Charges Act 1972 ... shall be deemed to constitute actual notice ... to all persons and for all purposes connected with the land affected.

The land charges system is, therefore, a statutory way of giving notice of an interest to a buyer of land. Registration of a charge binds everyone because registration is 'actual notice'. The pre-1926 rules of actual, constructive and imputed notice (see Section 16.2.2) are, therefore, not relevant to interests that are caught by the LCA 1972. A prudent buyer cannot now protect himself through diligent enquiries, because he has actual notice of any properly registered charge, whether or not he could ever have found it in the Register. The only exception to the rule that registration is actual notice is where the official search certificate fails to mention a charge that has been properly registered (see Section 16.3.3). It is therefore effectively the official certificate of search which counts as notice, not the Register.

16.3.5 The effect of failing to register a charge

As shown in *Hollington Brothers Ltd v Rhodes* [1951] 2 All ER 578n (Ch), an unregistered estate contract does not bind the buyer: it is void. However, the rules of voidness are more nuanced:

Unregistered land charges	Void against:
Classes A, B, C(i), C(ii), C(iii), F	anyone who gives 'value' for *any* interest in land (legal or equitable; LCA 1972, s 4(2), (5) and (8))
Classes C(iv), D(i), D(ii), D(iii)	anyone who gives 'money or money's worth' for a *legal* estate (LCA 1972, s 4(6))

Value means money, money's worth or an agreement to convey land in consideration of marriage. In *registered* land, marriage has ceased to be valuable consideration. The Law Commission ((1998) Law Com No 254) was of the view that:

> marriage consideration is an anachronism and should cease to be regarded as valuable consideration in relation to dealings with registered land. A transfer of land in consideration of marriage is in substance in most cases a wedding gift (para 3.43).

Money's worth means anything that is worth money, such as other land or company shares. An unregistered charge within Classes C(iv), D(i), D(ii) or D(iii) is, therefore, not void against someone who is buying only an equitable interest in the land or who is getting married as consideration (that is, not paying money or money's worth). Whether such a person is bound by the unregistered interest will still depend upon the doctrine of notice (see Section 16.2.2 and Section 16.5).

It is only when the burdened land changes hands that a charge becomes void for non-registration. Between the original parties, the charge is, of course, enforceable, and damages for breach of contract may still be available even if a charge is void against a later buyer of the land. Anyone who gains land through adverse possession or as a gift will also be bound by all interests in the land, whether or not protected by registration, because she is not a buyer.

Section 4 of the LCA 1972 is given even more force by section 199 of the LPA 1925, which provides that an unregistered charge is void even if the buyer actually knew about it:

> A purchaser shall not be prejudicially affected by notice of ... any instrument or matter capable of registration under the provisions of the [LCA 1972] ... which is void or not enforceable against him under that Act ... by reason of the non-registration thereof.

This section has been ruthlessly interpreted by some judges, as in *Hollington Bros v Rhodes*, where express notice in writing of an unregistered estate contract (an option to renew a lease) was held to be irrelevant. This was taken even further in *Midland Bank Trust Co Ltd v Green (No 1)* [1981] AC 513 (HL). A father granted his son a ten-year option to purchase his farm, which the son was managing and occupying with his family. This was an estate contract, registrable as a Class C(iv) land charge, but the son never registered it. Later the father changed his mind about the option and discovered that, if he were to sell the legal estate in the land to 'a purchaser for money or money's worth', the son's estate contract would be void. He did just that. The purchaser was his wife – the mother of the owner of the unregistered charge. She knew about the father's scheme and paid far less than the market value of the land. One after another, those concerned in the conflict died, and the executors had to sort out who had owned what, and who was now entitled to it. The House of Lords (reversing the Court of Appeal) held that the unregistered charge was void against the mother. She was the purchaser of the legal estate for money, and that was all that was needed:

> The case is plain: the Act is clear and definite. Intended as it was to provide a simple and understandable system for the protection of title to land, it should not be read down or glossed; to do so would destroy the usefulness of the Act (per Lord Wilberforce at 528).

Unlike the position in registered land (see Section 15.8.2), the LCA 1972 makes no special allowance for a person in occupation of the land. It seems that the 1925 legislation was intended to give occupants some degree of protection. Section 14 of the LPA 1925 expressly provides that:

> This part of this Act shall not prejudicially affect the interest of any person in possession or in actual occupation of land to which he may be entitled in right of such possession or occupation.

Unfortunately, however, section 14 is in Part I of the LPA 1925, which means that it cannot affect either section 199 of the LPA 1925 or the LCA 1972 (neither of which are in Part 1 of the LPA 1925).

In *Lloyds Bank plc v Carrick* [1996] 4 All ER 630 (CA), an estate contract to buy a long lease of a maisonette was void for non-registration against a later mortgagee. Although the terms of the contract were not recorded in writing, Mrs Carrick had paid the full price to the seller, her brother-in-law, and had moved in. As the contract, made in 1982, pre-dated the Law of Property (Miscellaneous Provisions) Act 1989 (see Section 12.4.1), these acts were sufficient to make the contract enforceable. However, the title to the lease was never actually transferred to Mrs Carrick. The brother-in-law subsequently secretly mortgaged the property to Lloyds Bank, which, when he defaulted on the repayments, sought possession. Mrs Carrick argued that her brother-in-law held the property either on a bare trust for her (as any seller does between exchange of contracts and completion) or under a constructive trust (see Section 14.3) or through estoppel (see Section 14.4). If the trust arguments had found favour with the Court of Appeal, then Mrs Carrick's rights against the bank would have depended on the doctrine of notice: since she was in occupation, the bank would have had constructive notice of her interest. However, the Court held that her rights arose as a consequence of the contract, and her failure to protect it by registration as a land charge meant that it was void against the bank.

The harsh simplicity of these cases, where the buyer either knew or could easily have discovered the interest of the occupier of land, is the sort of thing that makes people cynical about lawyers and their justice. Just as in *Midland Bank Trust Co Ltd v Green (No 1)* [1981] AC 513 (HL), the opposite result would have been reached in *Carrick*, as Morritt LJ pointed out, if the rules of registered land (which offer protection to occupiers who have rights in the land; see Section 15.8.2) had applied: the farmer's son would have been able to exercise his option, and Mrs Carrick would have kept her home.

16.4   Overreaching

In order to simplify the process of buying and selling land subject to a trust, it was intended by the framers of the 1925 scheme that trust interests should all be capable of being overreached (LPA 1925, ss 2 and 27). The doctrine of overreaching operates when the purchase price is paid to two or more trustees or a trust corporation. In such circumstances, the beneficiaries' interests are transferred from the land into the proceeds of sale (now in the hands of the trustees). Overreaching is considered in detail in Section 11.6.1.

None of the LCA 1972 interests, such as equitable charges, restrictive covenants and estate contracts, can be overreached. As Robert Walker LJ pointed out in *Birmingham Midshires Mortgage Services Ltd v Sabherwal* (2000) 80 P & CR 256 (CA):

> The essential distinction is ... between commercial and family interests. [A commercial interest] cannot sensibly shift from the land affected by it to the proceeds of sale. [A family interest] can do so ... since the proceeds of sale can be used to acquire another home (at 263).

16.5   The doctrine of notice

If an interest cannot be registered because it does not fit into the categories set out in the LCA 1972, the next step is to decide whether the interest can be overreached. If it cannot be overreached (or if it has not been, because, for example, there was only one trustee), then any conflict between the buyers and the owners of pre-existing interests must be resolved by the pre-1925 rules of notice.

Table 16.1 shows the main interests to which the doctrine of notice is still relevant.

It must be stressed that this is a residual, open-ended category that will catch any interest in unregistered land that is not governed by the rules of the LCA 1972.

In *Kingsnorth Finance Co Ltd v Tizard* [1986] 1 WLR 783 (Ch) (the facts of which are set out in Section 16.1) Mrs Tizard's equitable interest in the house had not been overreached because the mortgage advance had only been paid to one trustee (her husband; see LPA 1925, s 2). Judge Finlay QC held that the finance company had constructive or imputed notice of Mrs Tizard's equitable rights because she was, on the facts, 'in occupation'. The bank's agent should have made more enquiries about the wife because

Table 16.1   The doctrine of notice in unregistered land

Type of interest	Section/case
Restrictive covenants created before 1926	Section 2(5)(ii) LCA 1972
Equitable easements created before 1926	Section 2(5)(iii) LCA 1972
Estate contracts, and Class D charges against purchasers other than of a legal estate for money or money's worth	Section 4(6) LCA 1972
Equitable easement arising out of mutual rights, estoppel	*ER Ives Investments Ltd v High* [1967] 2 QB 379 (CA)
Contractual licence	*Binions v Evans* [1972] Ch 359 (CA)
Equitable lessor's right of re-entry	*Shiloh Spinners Ltd v Harding* [1973] AC 691 (HL)
An equitable interest behind a trust that has not been overreached	*Kingsnorth Finance Co Ltd v Tizard* [1986] 1 WLR 783 (Ch)

the agent knew that Mr Tizard was married, even though he had described himself as 'single' on the mortgage application form:

> the plaintiffs had, or are to be taken to have had [through their agent], information which should have alerted them to the fact that the full facts were not in their possession and that they should make further inspections or inquiries; they did not do so and in these circumstances I find that they are fixed with notice of the equitable interest of Mrs Tizard (at 794).

What a prudent buyer ought to do depends on the facts of each case. There is no need to open drawers and wardrobes to see what clothes are there, but in suspicious circumstances an unannounced visit should probably be made. In this case, there should have been further enquiries, and Mrs Tizard should have been interviewed.

One of the interesting features of the judgment in *Tizard* is that Judge Finlay QC assumed that the outcome should have been the same as in the registered land case of *Williams & Glyn's Bank Ltd v Boland* [1981] AC 487 (HL). This illustrates the once common, but now widely abandoned, view that the two types of title were merely two different ways of administering the same rules. The result in *Tizard* is that the registered land concept of 'occupation' (see Land Registration Act (LRA) 1925, s 70(1) (g), now LRA 2002, Sched. 3, para 2) is imported into the unregistered land doctrine of notice. The generous view taken of occupation in this case applies to all cases of constructive notice. In the *Tizard* case, it was probably the right decision, although the wife's occupation was borderline. Of course, if the finance company had paid two trustees, Mrs Tizard's interest would have been overreached, and she would have had to leave the house.

16.6 Unregistered land – a retrospective

The 1925 modifications to the rules that applied to unregistered land, and the Land Charges Register in particular, were a temporary measure to facilitate the gradual introduction of title registration across the whole of England and Wales. Universal registration has taken much longer to introduce than was expected in 1925, so it is hardly surprising that the assortment of rules that govern unregistered land have shown signs of considerable strain. This is particularly true of the Land Charges Register, whose complexity usually absorbs more time than its importance deserves. One major problem is the way in which, contrary to the aim of the 1925 drafters, buyers can destroy the unregistered interests of occupiers even though they knew, or ought to have known, about them before buying the land. This is unjust, especially as there is no reason to believe that protecting the interests of occupiers would lead to an unacceptable degree of uncertainty. Not only does it appear that such protection was originally intended to be part of the 1925 scheme, but just such protection is given to occupiers of registered land, and even, in certain circumstances, to the owners of beneficial interests in unregistered land (such as Mrs Tizard).

Other problems with the Land Charges Register are the narrow definitions of the registrable interests, the illogical difference between the consequences of non-registration of interests falling within different classes, the nature of the name-based register and the way in which the system has tended to clog titles rather than to clear them. Various reforms have been suggested over the years, but the final answer seems to be that of the 1956 Report on Land Charges (Cmnd 9825). The Committee confessed that 'to rectify the machinery is a task beyond the wit of man' (Wade, 1956). However, the importance of the actual custom and practice of conveyancers is shown by the fact that 'fortunately, none of these deficiencies seem to matter in real life' (Wade, 1956, 234).

The final burial of the Land Charges Register is still some years away, but with universal registration of title in sight, the difficulties of unregistered land are of declining concern to landowners and their lawyers. However, it would be over-optimistic to expect that universal registration of title will solve all the problems encountered by buyers and sellers of land. The story of the tensions between the rights of people with interests in land and those of the buyers of that land (often a bank or building society lending money on the security of a mortgage) will continue, as the previous chapter shows only too clearly.

Summary

16.1 The rules for determining whether the owner of a legal estate in land is bound by another person's interest in that land depend upon whether title to the land is registered or unregistered.

16.2 Nearly all legal interests are automatically binding on the purchaser of an interest in unregistered land. The status of other types of interest depends upon the rules of the Land Charges Act 1972, the doctrine of overreaching and the doctrine of notice.

16.3 The interests listed in the Land Charges Act 1972 should be registered at the Land Charges Registry; failure to do so (or to do so correctly) will almost always result in them failing to bind any buyer of unregistered land.

16.4 'Family' (trust) interests are not registrable but can be overreached by a buyer who pays two trustees.

16.5 If an equitable interest is not registrable and has not been overreached, the rights of a buyer of a legal interest in unregistered land depend on the doctrine of notice; the buyer of an equitable interest is probably bound by any existing equitable interests.

Exercises

16.1 Complete the online quiz on the topics covered in this chapter on the companion website.

16.2 Hilary is the sole legal owner of a four-storey house, title to which is unregistered, and which is subject to a restrictive covenant that it should be used as a private dwelling house only. She lives on the first floor, and her aged mother, Lucy (who contributed a quarter of the cost of the house when it was bought), occupies the ground floor.

Hilary is a compulsive gambler on the Stock Exchange and recently lost a good deal of money. She met Emma at the hairdresser's, and in the course of a chat they agreed that Emma should rent the basement of Hilary's house for three years. Emma moved in and has paid rent regularly. Hilary then accepted £2,000 from Clive, a colleague, as a deposit on a ten-year lease of the top floor of her house. Nothing was put in writing for tax reasons.

Six weeks later, Hilary decided to emigrate. Clive has discovered that she has made an agreement in writing to sell the whole house to Dee.

Clive, Lucy and Emma seek your advice.

You can find suggested answers to exercise 16.2 on the companion website.

Further reading

Harpum, 'Purchasers with Notice of Unregistered Land Charges' (1981) 40 CLJ 213

Thompson, 'The Purchaser as Private Detective' [1986] Conv 283

Wade, 'Land Charge Registration Reviewed' [1956] CLJ 216

Yates, 'The Protection of Equitable Interests under the 1925 legislation' (1974) 37 MLR 87

Index